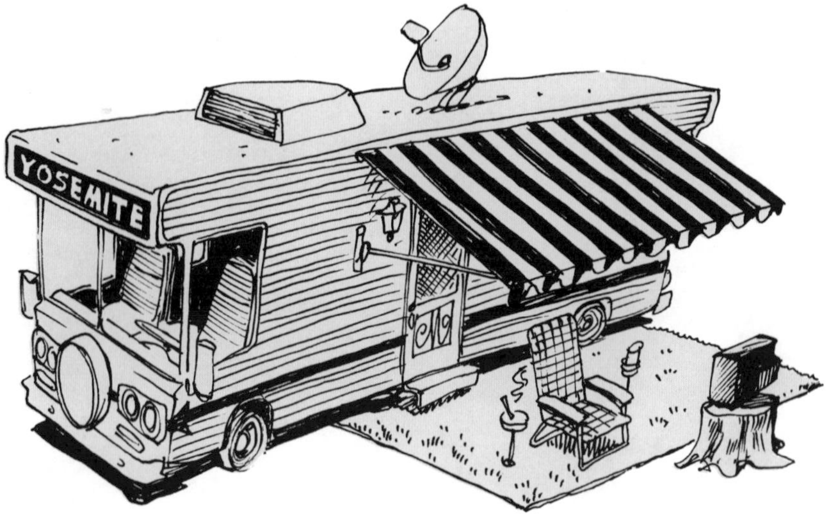
YOSEMITE

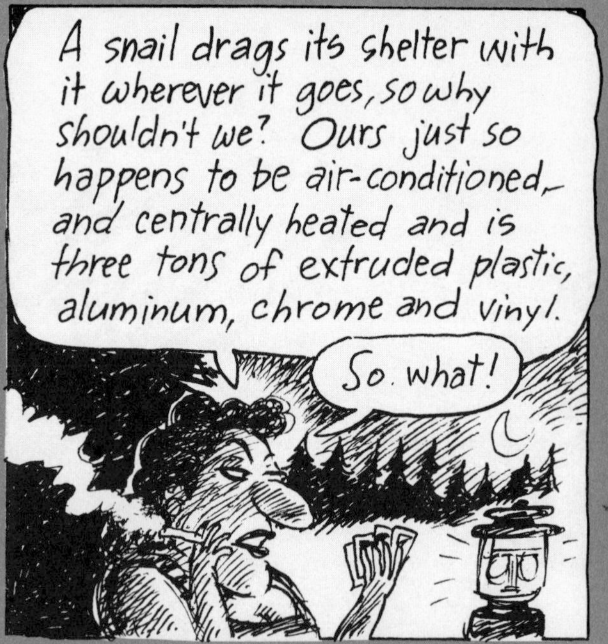
A snail drags its shelter with it wherever it goes, so why shouldn't we? Ours just so happens to be air-conditioned, and centrally heated and is three tons of extruded plastic, aluminum, chrome and vinyl.
So. what!

FUR AND LOAFING IN YOSEMITE

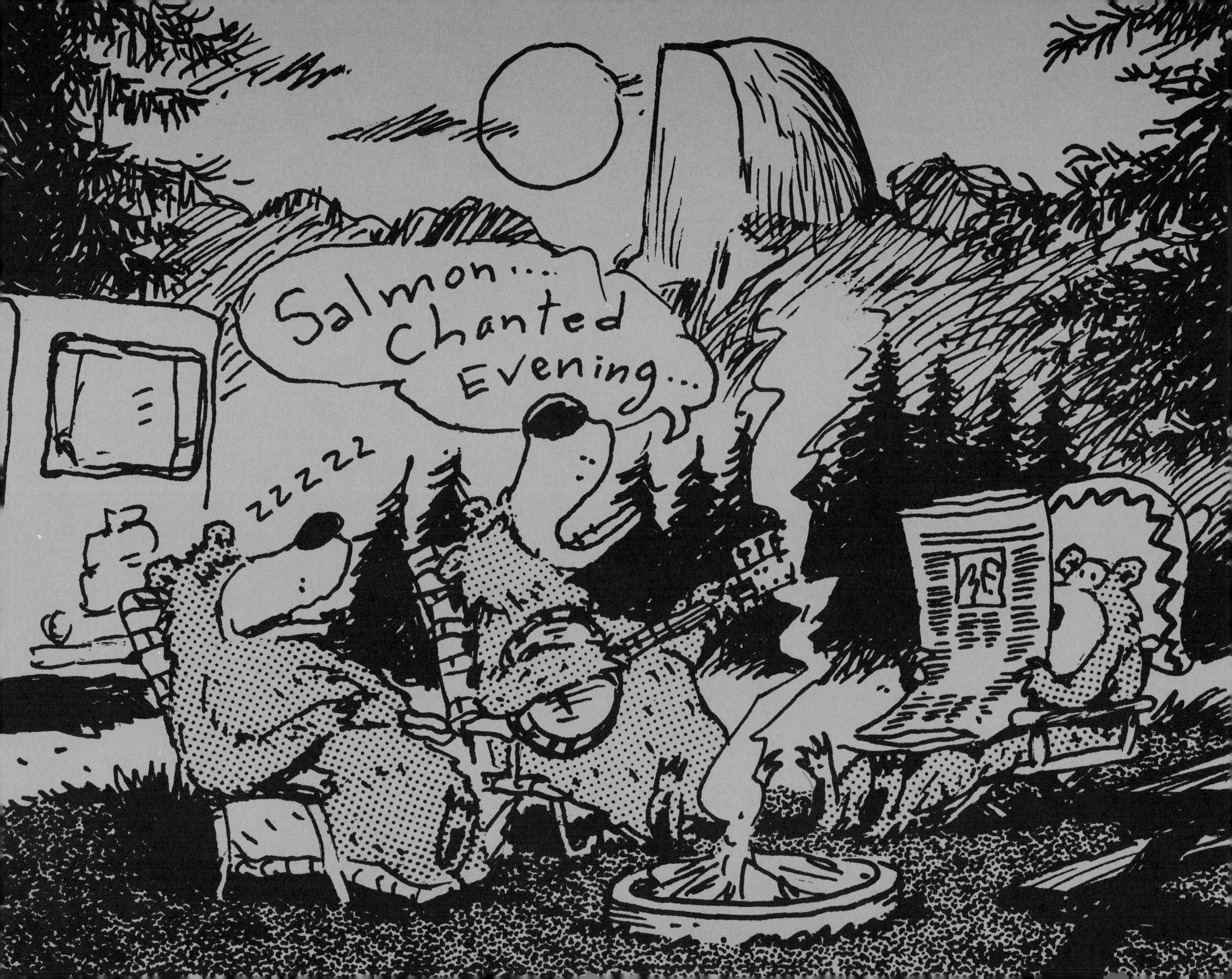
Salmon...
Chanted
Evening...
ZZZZZ

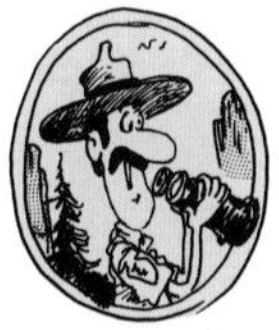

FUR AND LOAFING IN YOSEMITE

A COLLECTION OF "FARLEY" CARTOONS SET IN YOSEMITE NATIONAL PARK

PHIL FRANK

YOSEMITE ASSOCIATION
YOSEMITE NATIONAL PARK, CALIFORNIA

About the Cartoonist:

Phil Frank is the creator of the "Farley" cartoon strip, which now runs daily in the *San Francisco Chronicle*. For years it was nationally syndicated, but Phil chose to localize the cartoon so that he could better respond to current events in the greater Bay Area. He lives in Sausalito with his wife Susan, and maintains studios on a houseboat and in the San Franciso Chronicle clock tower. Yosemite is his favorite national park.

Printed in Singapore

Copyright © 1999 by the Yosemite Association

Cartoons copyright © 1999 Phil Frank

ISBN 0-939666-94-4

Design by:

Aufuldish & Warinner, San Anselmo, California

Yosemite Association

P.O. Box 230, El Portal, CA 95318

The Yosemite Association

is a non-profit, membership organization dedicated to the support of Yosemite National Park. Our publishing program is designed to provide an educational service and to increase the public's understanding of Yosemite's special qualities and needs. To learn more about our activities and publications, or for information about membership, please write to the address above, or call (209) 379-2646.

Visit the Yosemite Association web site at http://yosemite.org

Our Cast

THE REGULAR CHARACTERS IN THESE **YOSEMITE** ADVENTURES ARE FEW BUT THEIR HISTORY TOGETHER IS RATHER LONG. THEY ALL MET IN THE SYNDICATED COMIC STRIP **"TRAVELS WITH FARLEY"** WHICH RAN NATIONALLY FROM 1976-1986. THE SETTING FOR THEIR INTRODUCTIONS WAS A PLACE CALLED **ASPHALT STATE PARK**, WHERE MAN AND NATURE COLLIDED HEAD-ON. THE COMIC STRIP WAS LOCALIZED TO THE **SAN FRANCISCO CHRONICLE** IN 1986. SINCE THEN, FARLEY AND HIS COMPATRIOTS HAVE MOVED THEIR BASE OF OPERATIONS TO **YOSEMITE NATIONAL PARK**.

FARLEY...a former syndicated cartoon character who has evolved from a seasonal ranger to a reporter and an occasional camper.

BRUINHILDA...matriarch of the four-member bear clan. Met Farley in mid-70s when both were stationed at Asphalt State Park.

THE OTHER THREE... Alphonse, Franklin and Floyd. Presently staff of the Fog City Dumpster eatery in San Francisco. All are afraid of the woods.

HORACE MALONE... a near-sighted, self-serving bureaucrat. Prefers his oaks as office paneling.

RANGER STERN GROVE a bear management officer with a chip on his shoulder. Thinks the bears are lazy bums. He is right.

OLAF... the oldest bear in Yosemite Valley. He carries with him all the wisdom of the ages. Wears glasses.

VELMA MELMAC keeps the cleanest campsite in the Valley. Vacuums nature trails. Sports a tattoo: "Death to Dirt".

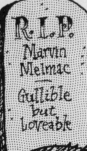

R.I.P. Marvin Melmac — Gullible but Loveable

MARVIN MELMAC... former husband of Velma. Died after consuming Velma's famous "Wild Mushroom Surprise."

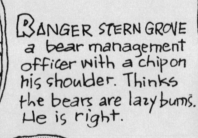

MAX, THE WONDER DOG — a hairless Chihuahua who is Velma Melmac's traveling companion, confidante and bartender.

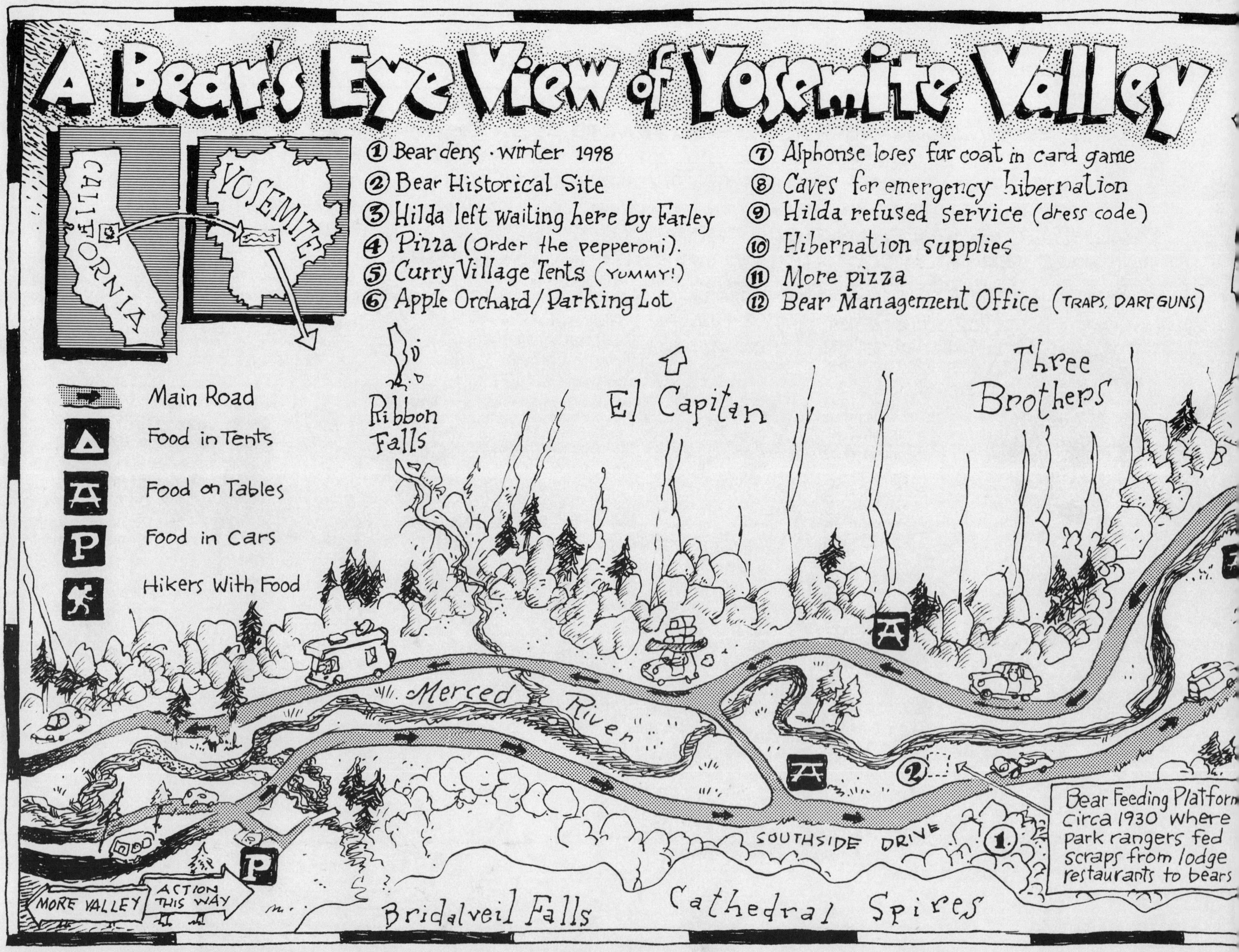
A Bear's Eye View of Yosemite Valley
CALIFORNIA
YOSEMITE
① Bear dens · winter 1998
② Bear Historical Site
③ Hilda left waiting here by Farley
④ Pizza (Order the pepperoni).
⑤ Curry Village Tents (YUMMY!)
⑥ Apple Orchard / Parking Lot
⑦ Alphonse loses fur coat in card game
⑧ Caves for emergency hibernation
⑨ Hilda refused service (dress code)
⑩ Hibernation supplies
⑪ More pizza
⑫ Bear Management Office (TRAPS, DART GUNS)
Main Road
Food in Tents
Food on Tables
Food in Cars
Hikers With Food
Ribbon Falls
El Capitan
Three Brothers
Merced River
SOUTHSIDE DRIVE
Bear Feeding Platform circa 1930 where park rangers fed scraps from lodge restaurants to bears
MORE VALLEY
ACTION THIS WAY
Bridalveil Falls
Cathedral Spires

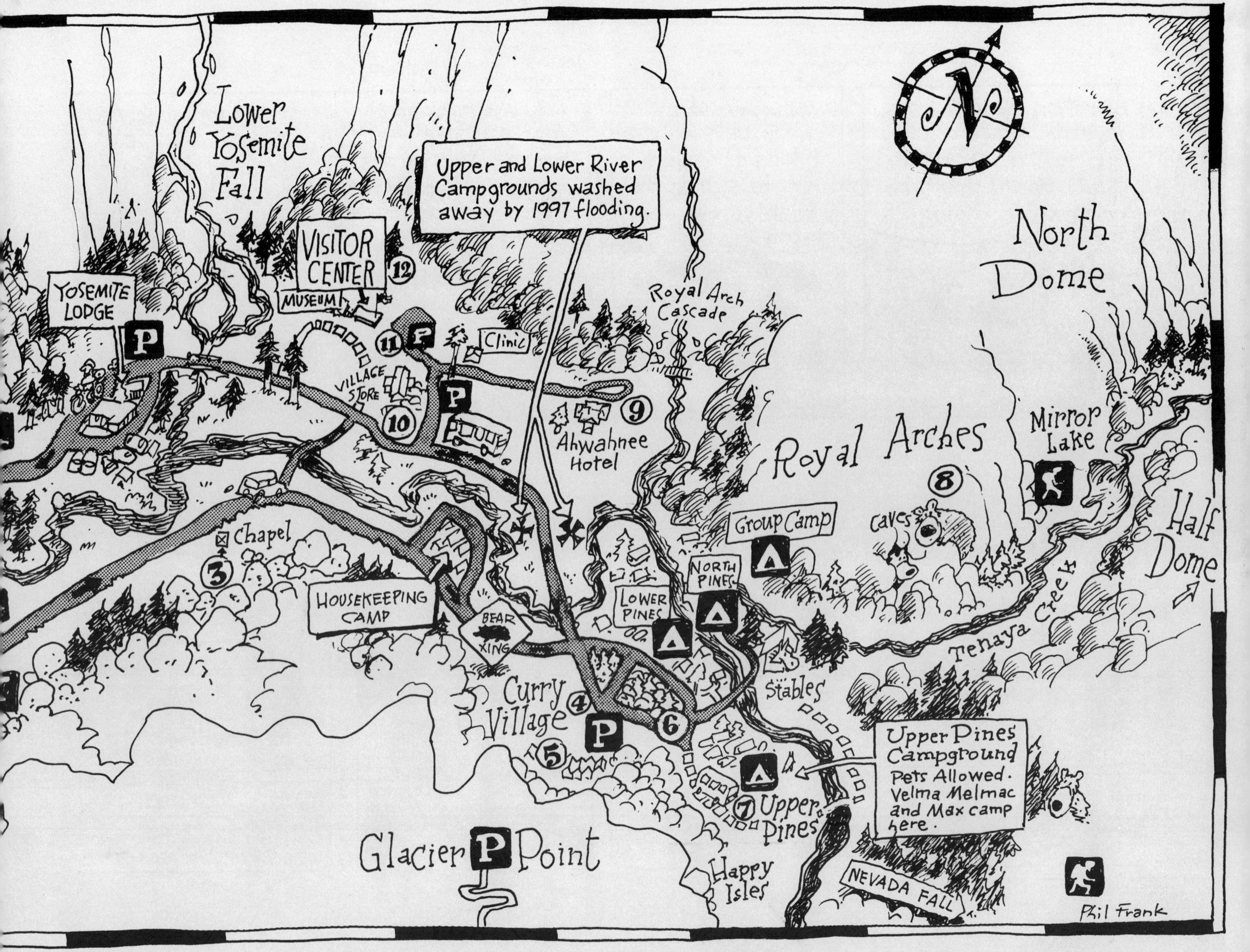
Lower Yosemite Fall
Upper and Lower River Campgrounds washed away by 1997 flooding.
North Dome
VISITOR CENTER
12
YOSEMITE LODGE
MUSEUM
Royal Arch Cascade
P
11
P
Clinic
VILLAGE STORE
P
10
9
Ahwahnee Hotel
Royal Arches
Mirror Lake
8
Half Dome
Caves
Group Camp
Chapel
3
NORTH PINES
LOWER PINES
HOUSEKEEPING CAMP
BEAR XING
Tenaya Creek
Curry Village
4
P
6
Stables
5
7
Upper Pines
Upper Pines Campground
Pets Allowed. Velma Melmac and Max camp here.
Glacier P Point
Happy Isles
NEVADA FALL
Phil Frank

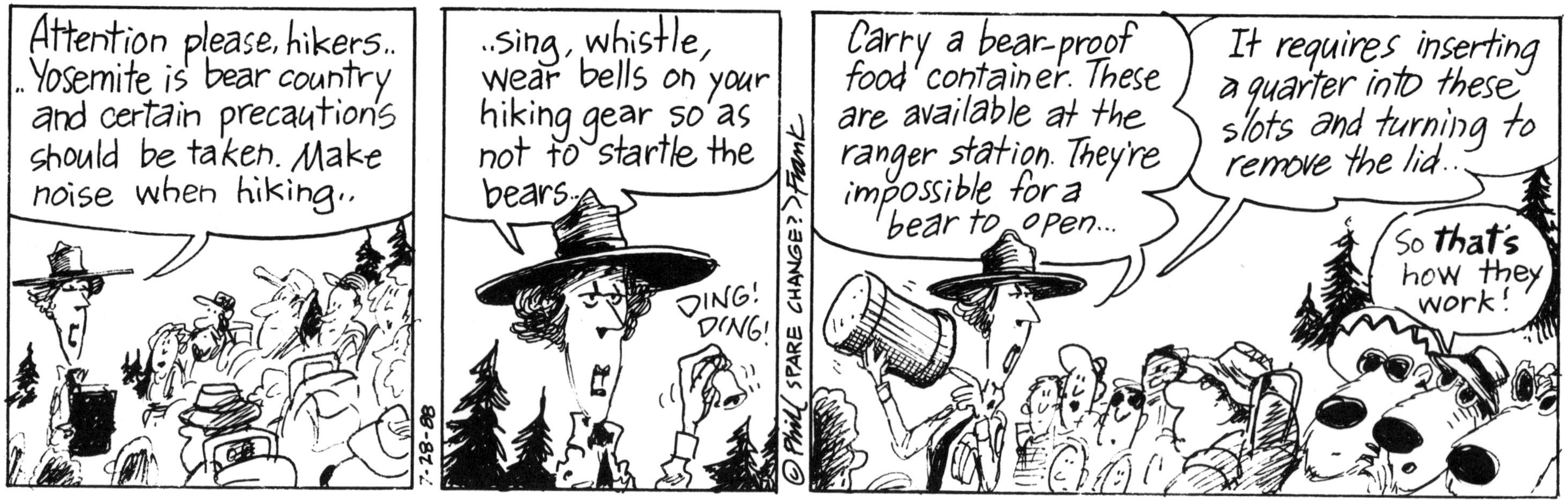
Attention please, hikers.. ..Yosemite is bear country and certain precautions should be taken. Make noise when hiking..
..sing, whistle, wear bells on your hiking gear so as not to startle the bears..
DING! DING!
7-28-88
© Phil Frank SPARE CHANGE?
Carry a bear-proof food container. These are available at the ranger station. They're impossible for a bear to open...
It requires inserting a quarter into these slots and turning to remove the lid..
So that's how they work!

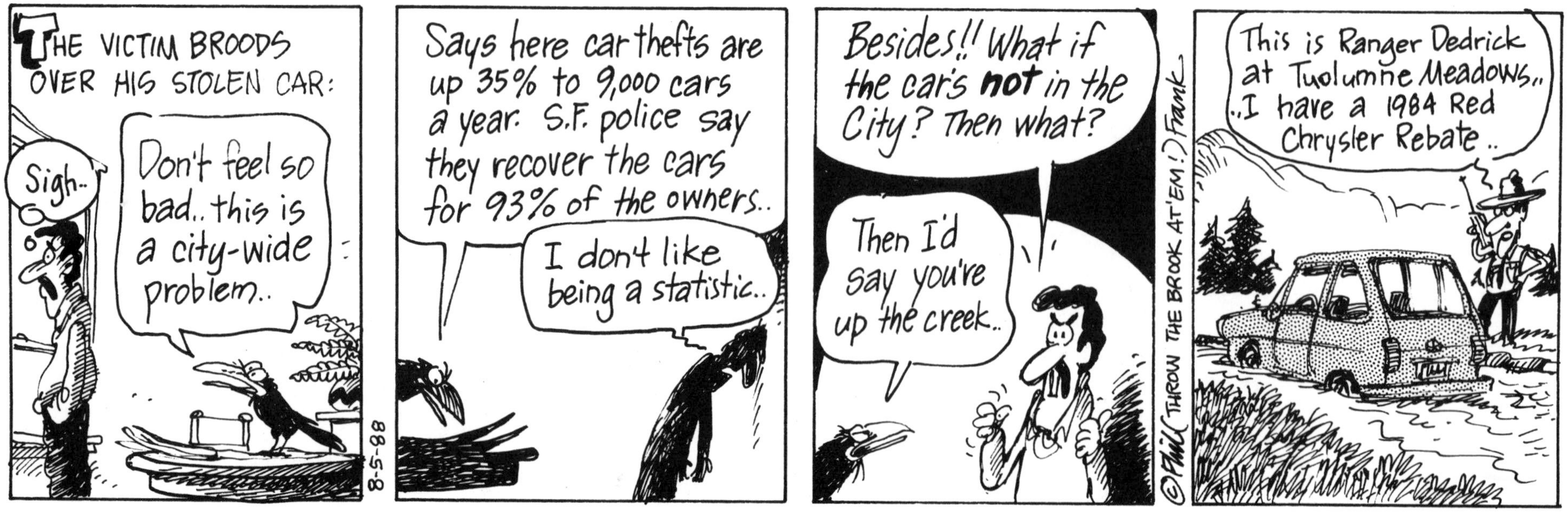
THE VICTIM BROODS OVER HIS STOLEN CAR:
Sigh..
Don't feel so bad.. this is a city-wide problem..
8-5-88
Says here car thefts are up 35% to 9,000 cars a year. S.F. police say they recover the cars for 93% of the owners..
I don't like being a statistic..
Besides!! What if the car's not in the City? Then what?
Then I'd say you're up the creek..
© Phil Frank (THROW THE BROOK AT 'EM!)
This is Ranger Dedrick at Tuolumne Meadows.. ..I have a 1984 Red Chrysler Rebate..

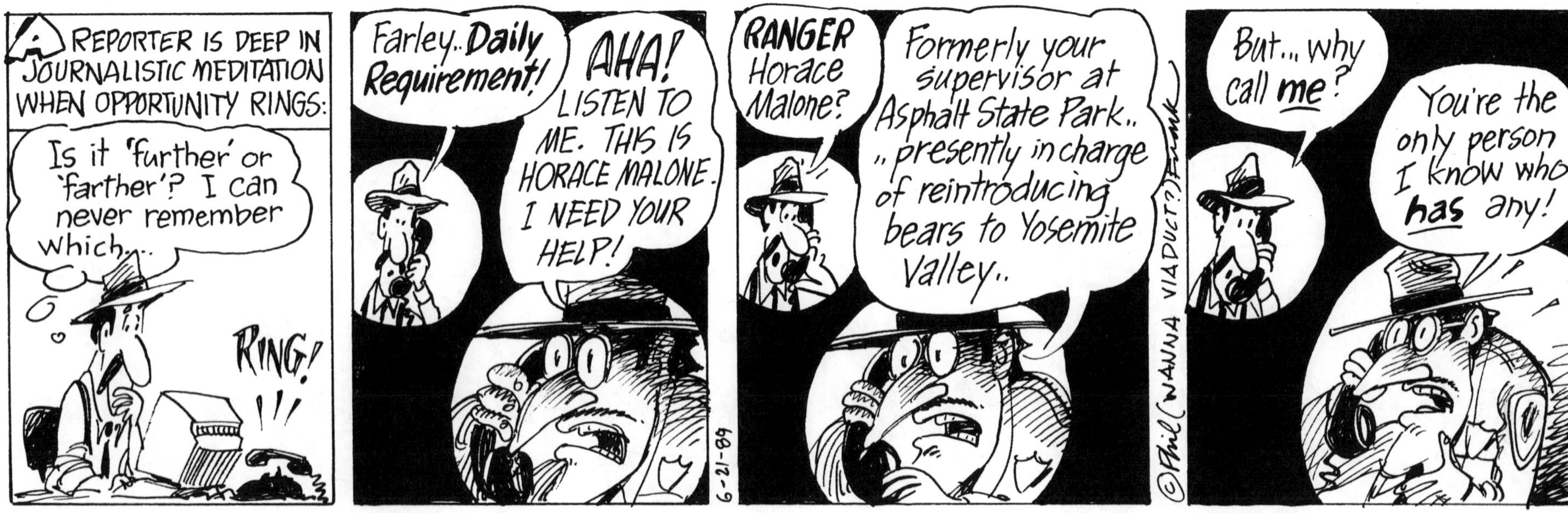
A REPORTER IS DEEP IN JOURNALISTIC MEDITATION WHEN OPPORTUNITY RINGS:
Is it 'further' or 'farther'? I can never remember which...
RING! !!!
Farley.. **Daily Requirement!**
AHA! LISTEN TO ME. THIS IS HORACE MALONE. I NEED YOUR HELP!
6-21-89
RANGER Horace Malone?
Formerly your supervisor at Asphalt State Park.. .. presently in charge of reintroducing bears to Yosemite Valley..
© Phil (WANNA VIADUCT?) Frank
But... why call **me**?
You're the only person I know who **has** any!

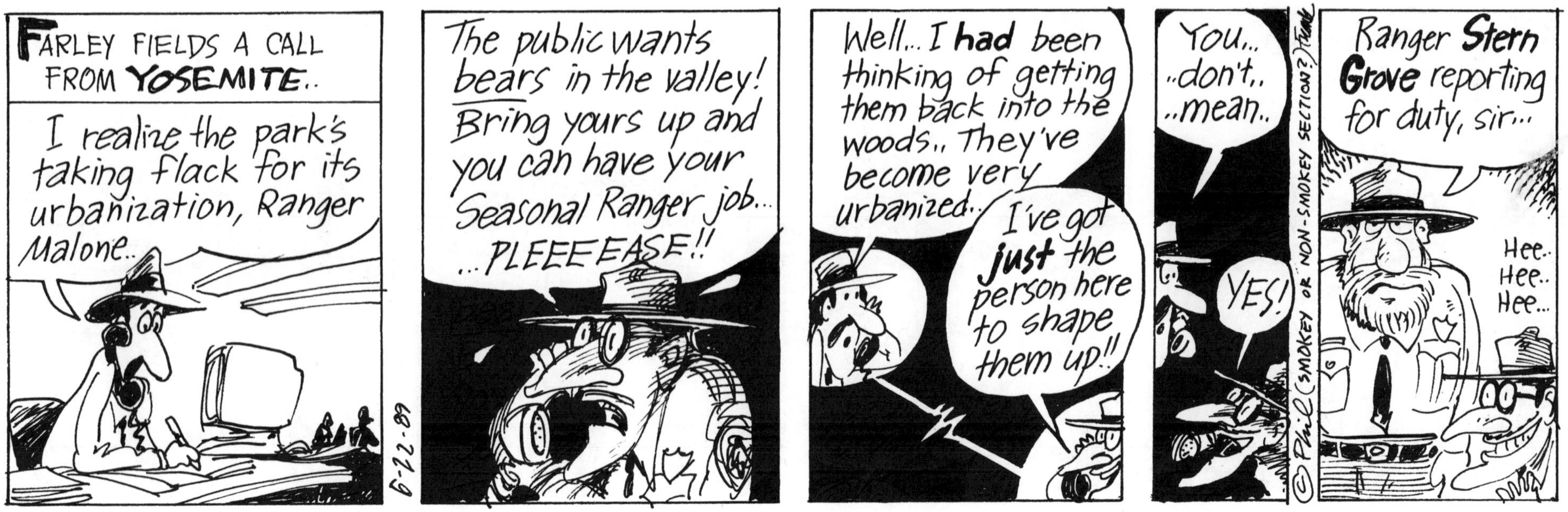
FARLEY FIELDS A CALL FROM **YOSEMITE**..
I realize the park's taking flack for its urbanization, Ranger Malone..
6-22-89
The public wants bears in the valley! Bring yours up and you can have your Seasonal Ranger job... ...PLEEEEASE!!
Well... I **had** been thinking of getting them back into the woods.. They've become very urbanized..
I've got **just** the person here to shape them up!!
You... ..don't.. ..mean..
YES!
© Phil (SMOKEY OR NON-SMOKEY SECTION?) Frank
Ranger **Stern Grove** reporting for duty, sir...
Hee.. Hee.. Hee...

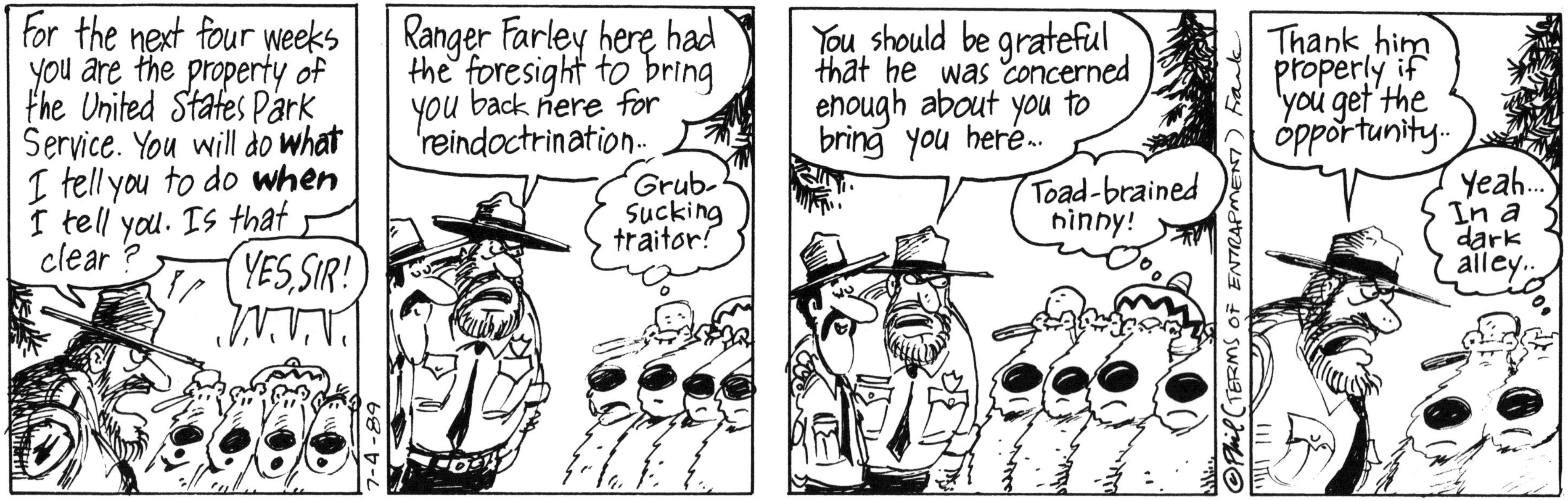

For the next four weeks you are the property of the United States Park Service. You will do **what** I tell you to do **when** I tell you. Is that clear ?
YES, SIR!
7-4-89
Ranger Farley here had the foresight to bring you back here for reindoctrination..
Grub-sucking traitor!
You should be grateful that he was concerned enough about you to bring you here..
Toad-brained ninny!
©Phil (TERMS OF ENTRAPMENT) Frank
Thank him properly if you get the opportunity..
Yeah... In a dark alley..

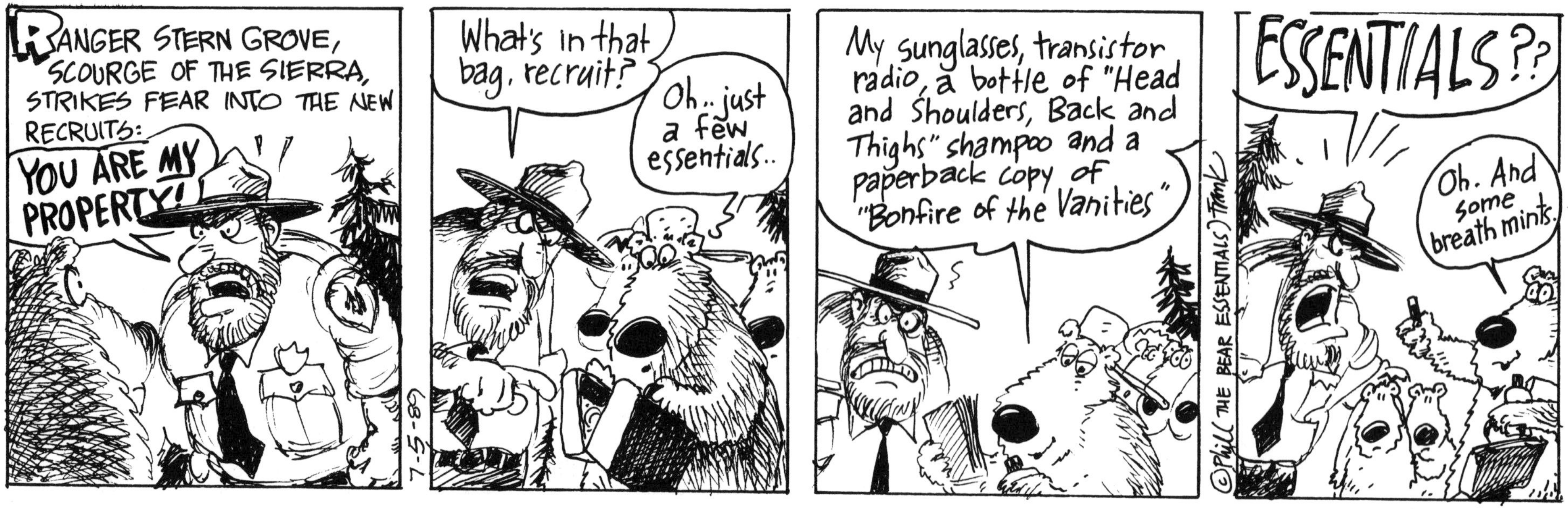

RANGER STERN GROVE, SCOURGE OF THE SIERRA, STRIKES FEAR INTO THE NEW RECRUITS:
YOU ARE MY PROPERTY!
7-5-89
What's in that bag, recruit?
Oh.. just a few essentials..
My sunglasses, transistor radio, a bottle of "Head and Shoulders, Back and Thighs" shampoo and a paperback copy of "Bonfire of the Vanities"
©Phil THE BEAR ESSENTIALS) Frank
ESSENTIALS??
Oh. And some breath mints.

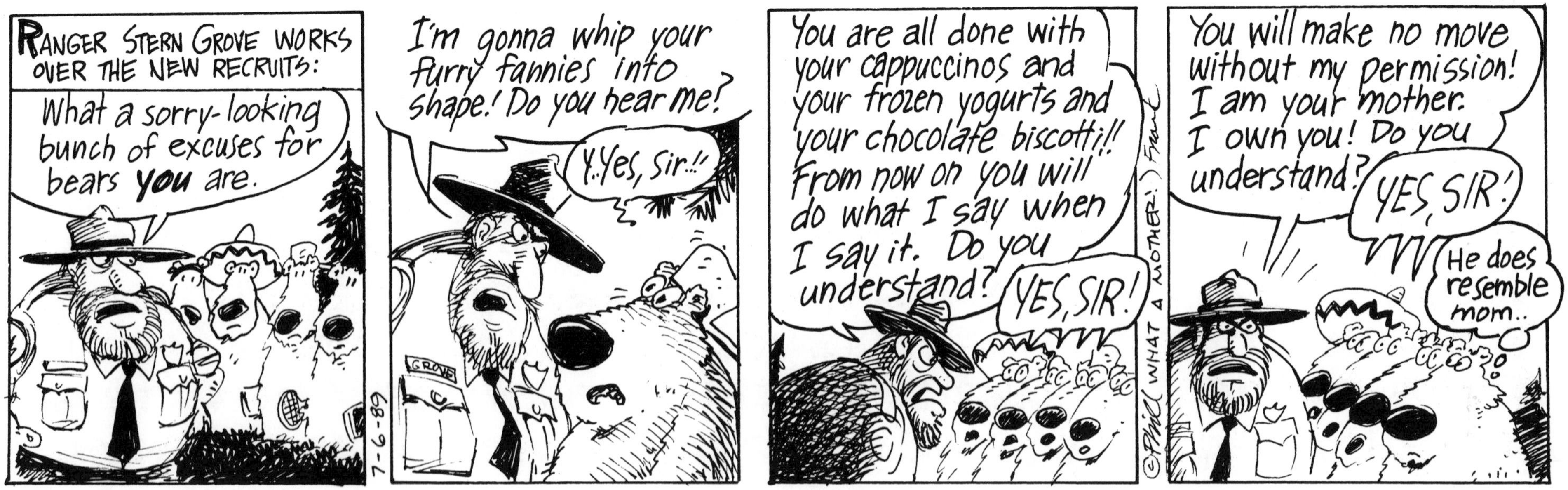
RANGER STERN GROVE WORKS OVER THE NEW RECRUITS:
What a sorry-looking bunch of excuses for bears **you** are.
I'm gonna whip your furry fannies into shape! Do you hear me?
Y..Yes, Sir.!!
GROVE
7-6-89
You are all done with your cappuccinos and your frozen yogurts and your chocolate biscotti!! From now on you will do what I say when I say it. Do you understand?
YES, SIR!
©Phil (WHAT A MOTHER!) Frank
You will make no move without my permission! I am your mother. I own you! Do you understand?
YES, SIR!
He does resemble mom..

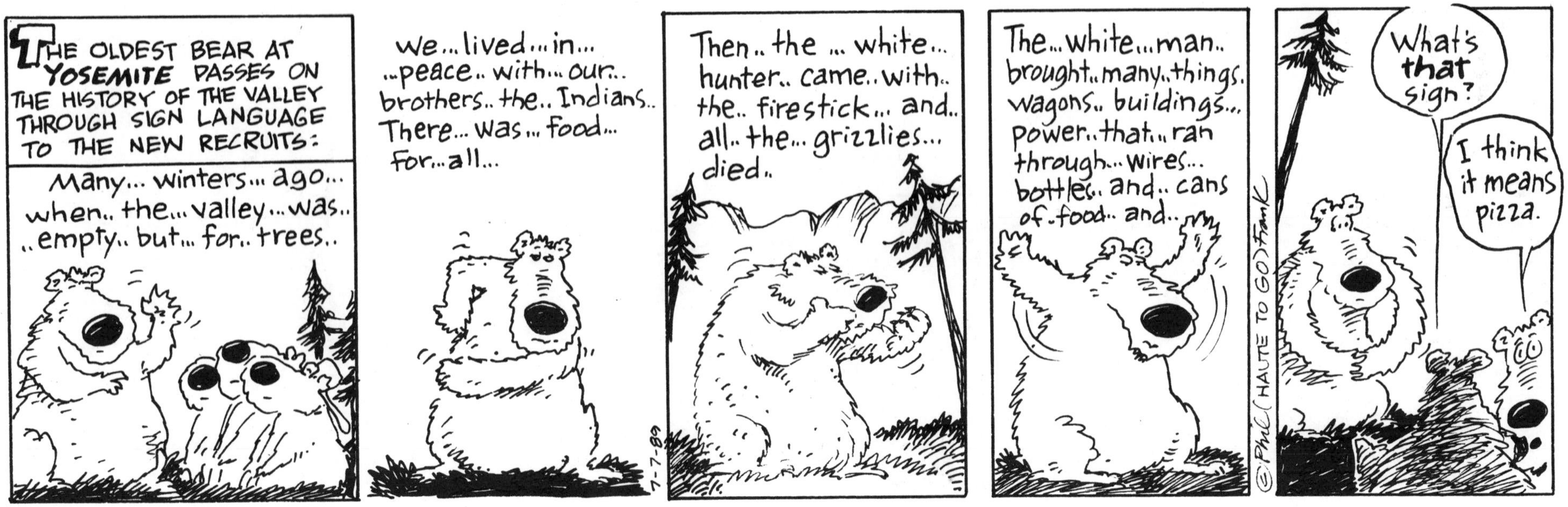
THE OLDEST BEAR AT **YOSEMITE** PASSES ON THE HISTORY OF THE VALLEY THROUGH SIGN LANGUAGE TO THE NEW RECRUITS:
Many... winters... ago... when.. the... valley... was.. ..empty.. but... for.. trees..
we... lived... in... ..peace.. with... our.. brothers.. the.. Indians.. There... was... food... for... all...
7-7-89
Then.. the ... white... hunter.. came.. with.. the.. firestick... and.. all.. the... grizzlies... died..
The... white... man.. brought.. many.. things. wagons.. buildings... power.. that.. ran through... wires... bottles.. and.. cans of..food.. and..
©Phil (HAUTE TO GO) Frank
What's **that** sign?
I think it means pizza.

The Bears: Urban Wildlife

BEARS ARE CONSIDERED AN ESSENTIAL PART OF THE AMERICAN WILDERNESS EXPERIENCE. THE PROBLEM, OF COURSE, IS THAT FAMILIARITY TAKES AWAY THE WILDNESS IN THE ANIMALS. THAT IS WHAT HAPPENED WITH THIS QUARTET. THE FIRST YEAR THAT FARLEY ENCOUNTERED THEM AT **ASPHALT STATE PARK** THEY WERE STEALING FOOD FROM CAMPERS. THE FOLLOWING SUMMER THEY WERE SWIPING RADIOS AND **TV**s. BY THE TENTH SUMMER THEY WERE OPERATING A 24-HOUR GROCERY SERVICE AND HAD FORMED A BEARS' UNION.

The quartet is led by Hilda (Bruinhilda on all official documents). She's the matriarch of the bear clan. It was she who decided to follow **Farley** to San Francisco when he moved there in 1986.

Finding a safe haven for four bears and a career path in San Francisco was quite a challenge.

One thing missing in the city's plethora of restaurants was an eatery for the animals of the city. A popular new place had just opened... the **Fog City Diner**.

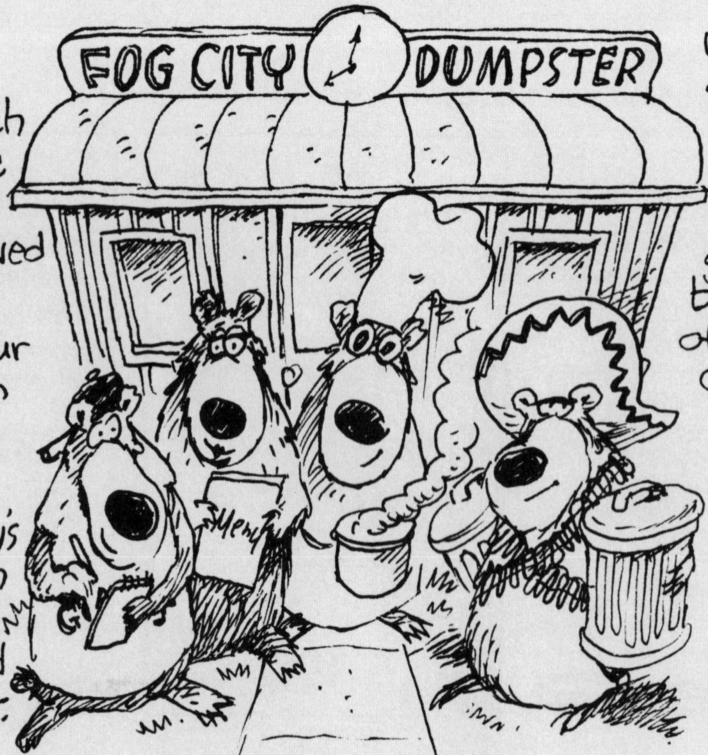
FOG CITY DUMPSTER
Menu

Why not open a place for the skunks, raccoons, possums, dogs, cats and deer? Hence, the **Fog City Dumpster** came into existence. The bears gather the scraps from the best restaurants and then offer them to their four-footed clientele at their eatery.

Hilda is the hostess. Floyd is the "chef", Alphonse, the Giants fan, is the waiter. Franklin, in the sombrero, is the busbear. Don't mess with Franklin. Their annual trips to Yosemite have become a highlight of the comic strip.

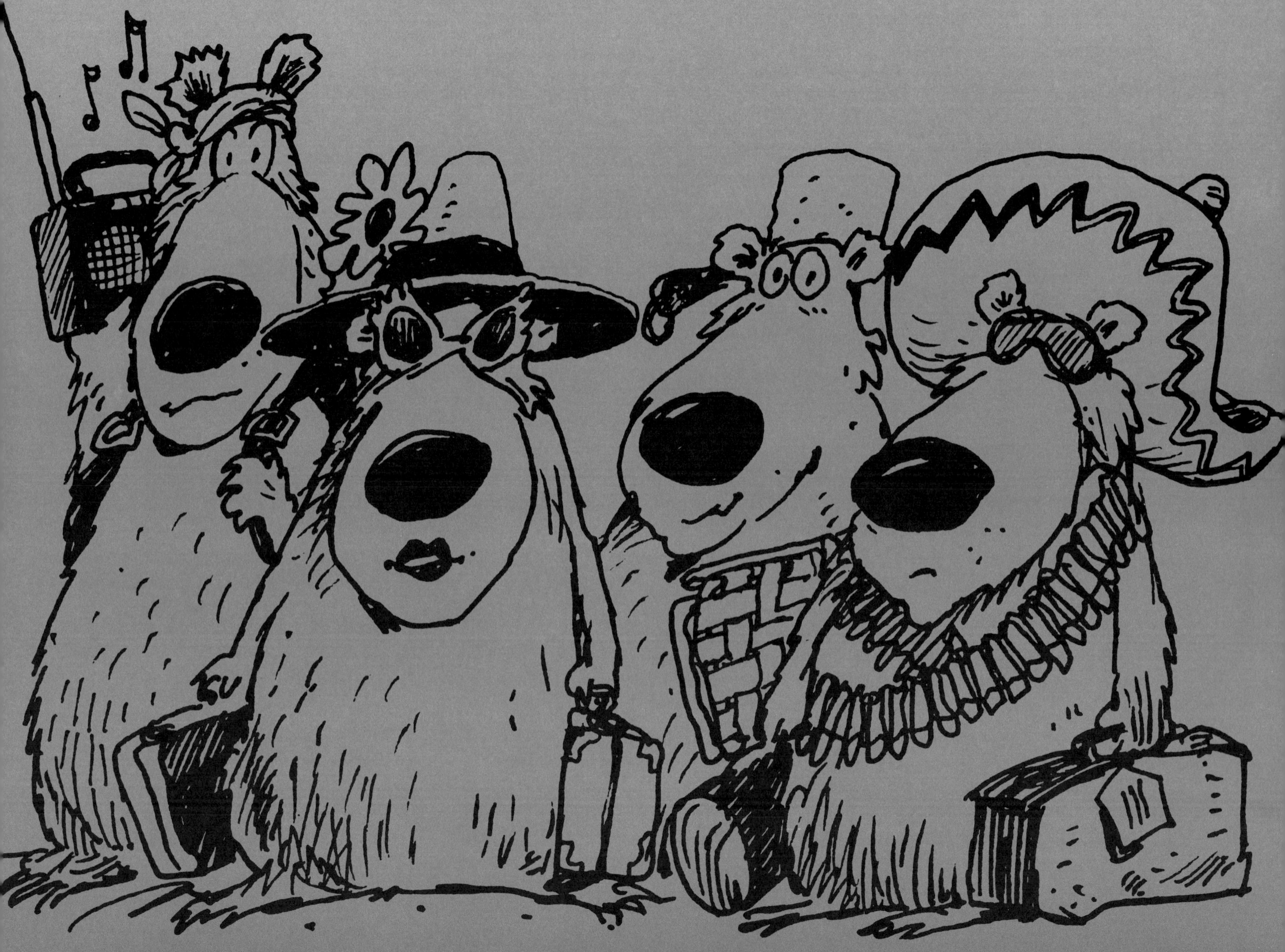

Yosemite plan just a memory

The National Park Service had completed an extensive - and expensive - plan in 1980 designed to alleviate some of the traffic pressure in the Valley and the resulting pollution. Unfortunately, the plan had lain dormant for nearly a decade when Farley, full-time reporter, part-time ranger, arrived at the park. Farley queried Chief Ranger Horace Malone about the plan's progress. At the time, a "Yosemite Master Plan Re-Examination Report" had been issued, proposing many changes to elements of the original document. The controversial report was later abandoned. Recently an "Implementation Plan" was released then retracted. The unimplemented "Master Plan" is now nearly twenty years old.

Farley!! I want to thank you for bringing your bears here to Yosemite Valley!

Well, I thought it'd help enhance the visitors' wilderness experience..

Speaking of which...
..What's happening with the General Plan for Yosemite.. the one that called for getting auto traffic out of the Valley?

7-11-89

Oh, yes...**that** plan.. ..an innovative concept to be certain. Where did I put it?

I was sure it was right here in my file..

Doesn't look good..

©PHIL (FILE AND FERMENT) FRANK

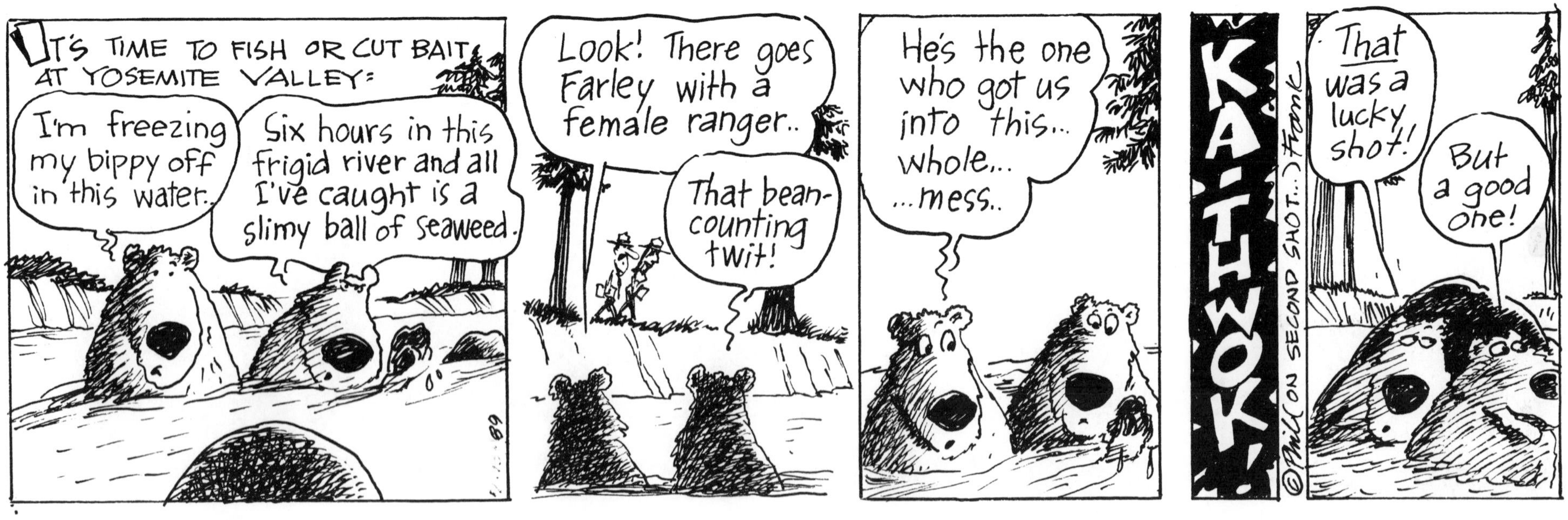
IT'S TIME TO FISH OR CUT BAIT AT YOSEMITE VALLEY:
I'm freezing my bippy off in this water..
Six hours in this frigid river and all I've caught is a slimy ball of seaweed.
Look! There goes Farley with a female ranger..
That bean-counting twit!
He's the one who got us into this... whole... ...mess..
KA-THWOK!
©Phill (ON SECOND SHOT...) Frank
That was a lucky shot!
But a good one!

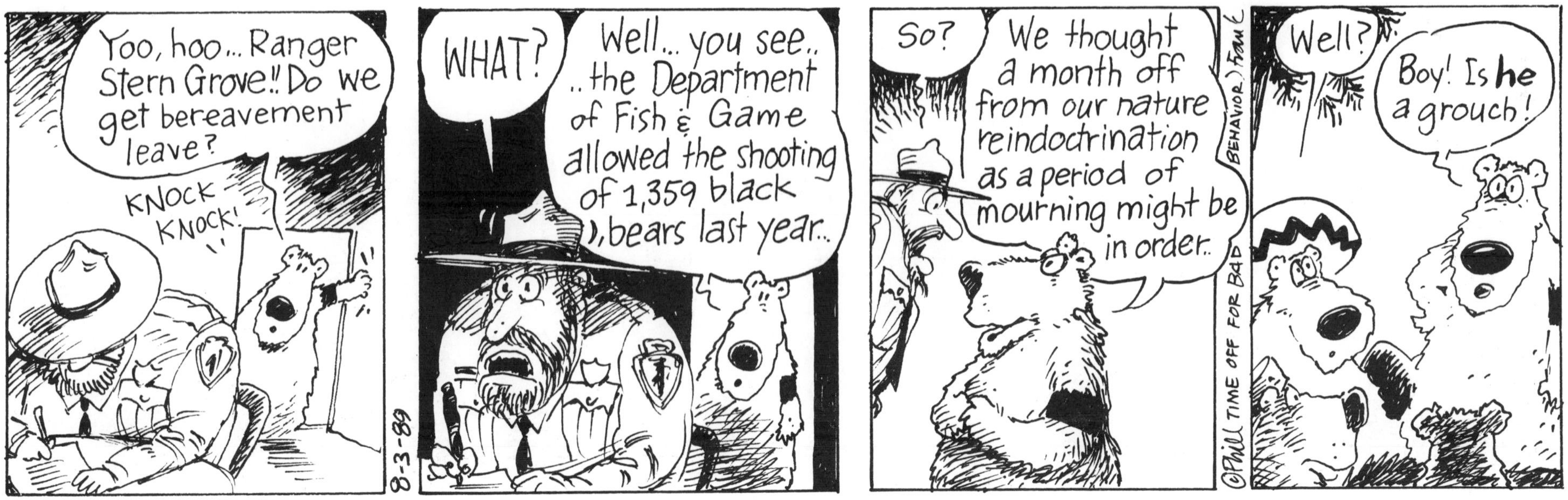
Yoo, hoo... Ranger Stern Grove!! Do we get bereavement leave?
KNOCK KNOCK!
8-3-89
WHAT?
Well... you see.. ..the Department of Fish & Game allowed the shooting of 1,359 black bears last year..
So?
We thought a month off from our nature reindoctrination as a period of mourning might be in order..
©Phill TIME OFF FOR BAD BEHAVIOR.) Frank
Well?
Boy! Is **he** a grouch!

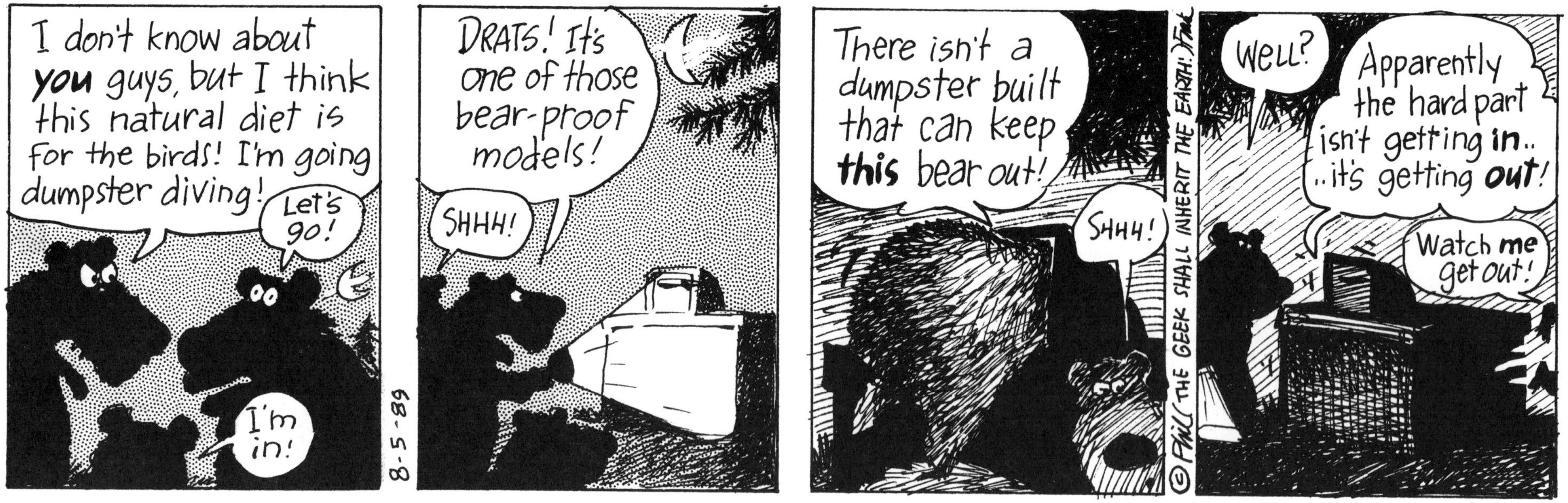
I don't know about you guys, but I think this natural diet is for the birds! I'm going dumpster diving!
Let's go!
I'm in!
8-5-89
DRATS! It's one of those bear-proof models!
SHHH!
There isn't a dumpster built that can keep this bear out!
SHHH!
© Phill THE GEEK SHALL INHERIT THE EARTH. Frank
WELL?
Apparently the hard part isn't getting in.. ..it's getting out!
Watch me get out!

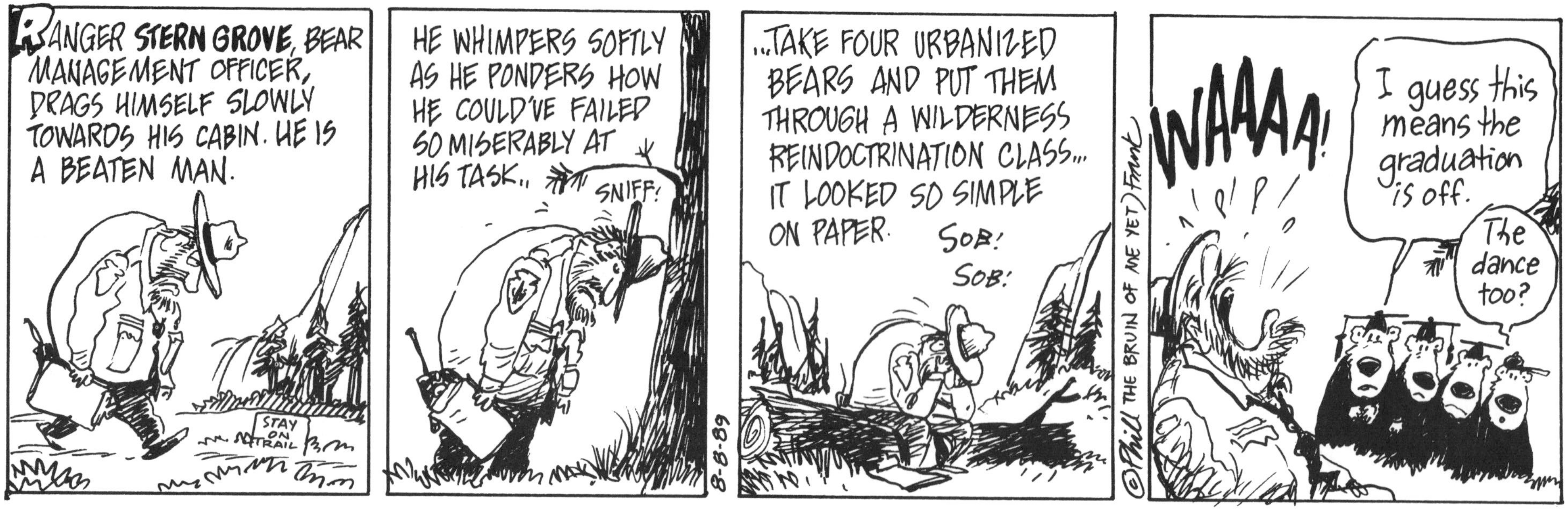
RANGER STERN GROVE, BEAR MANAGEMENT OFFICER, DRAGS HIMSELF SLOWLY TOWARDS HIS CABIN. HE IS A BEATEN MAN.
STAY ON TRAIL
HE WHIMPERS SOFTLY AS HE PONDERS HOW HE COULD'VE FAILED SO MISERABLY AT HIS TASK..
SNIFF!
8-8-89
...TAKE FOUR URBANIZED BEARS AND PUT THEM THROUGH A WILDERNESS REINDOCTRINATION CLASS... IT LOOKED SO SIMPLE ON PAPER.
SOB!
SOB!
© Phill THE BRUIN OF ME YET) Frank
WAAAA!
I guess this means the graduation is off.
The dance too?

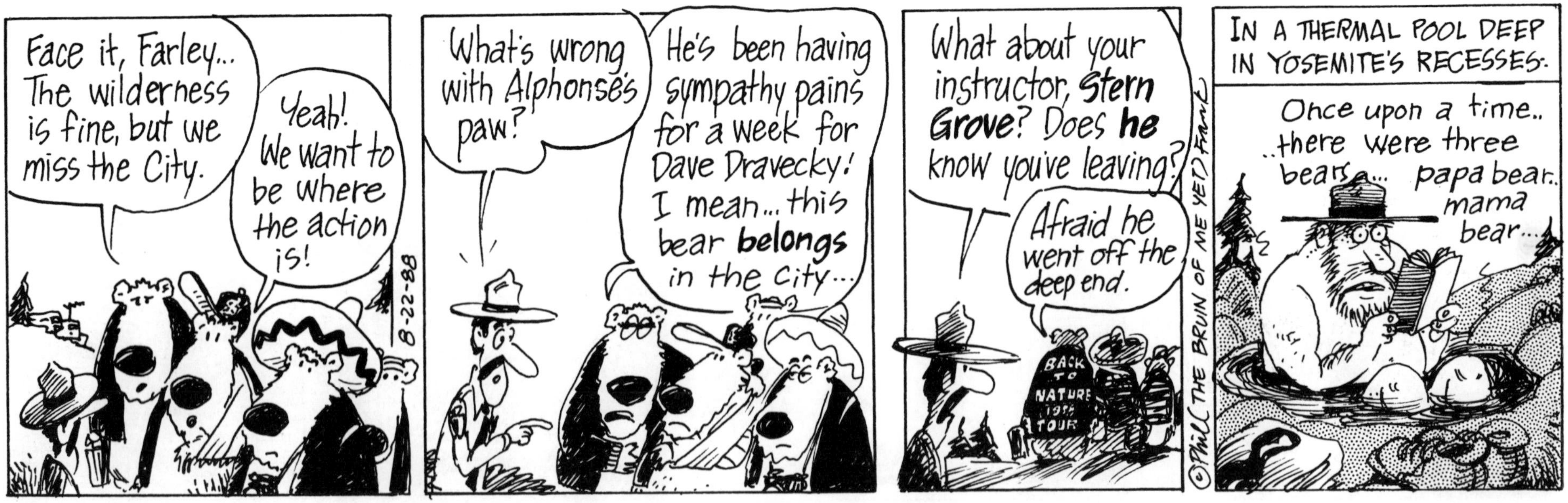

Face it, Farley... The wilderness is fine, but we miss the City.
Yeah! We want to be where the action is!
8-22-88
What's wrong with Alphonse's paw?
He's been having sympathy pains for a week for Dave Dravecky! I mean... this bear **belongs** in the city...
What about your instructor, **Stern Grove**? Does **he** know you've leaving?
Afraid he went off the deep end.
BACK TO NATURE 19th TOUR
©Phil (THE BRUIN OF ME YET) Frank
IN A THERMAL POOL DEEP IN YOSEMITE'S RECESSES.
Once upon a time.. ..there were three bears... papa bear.. mama bear...

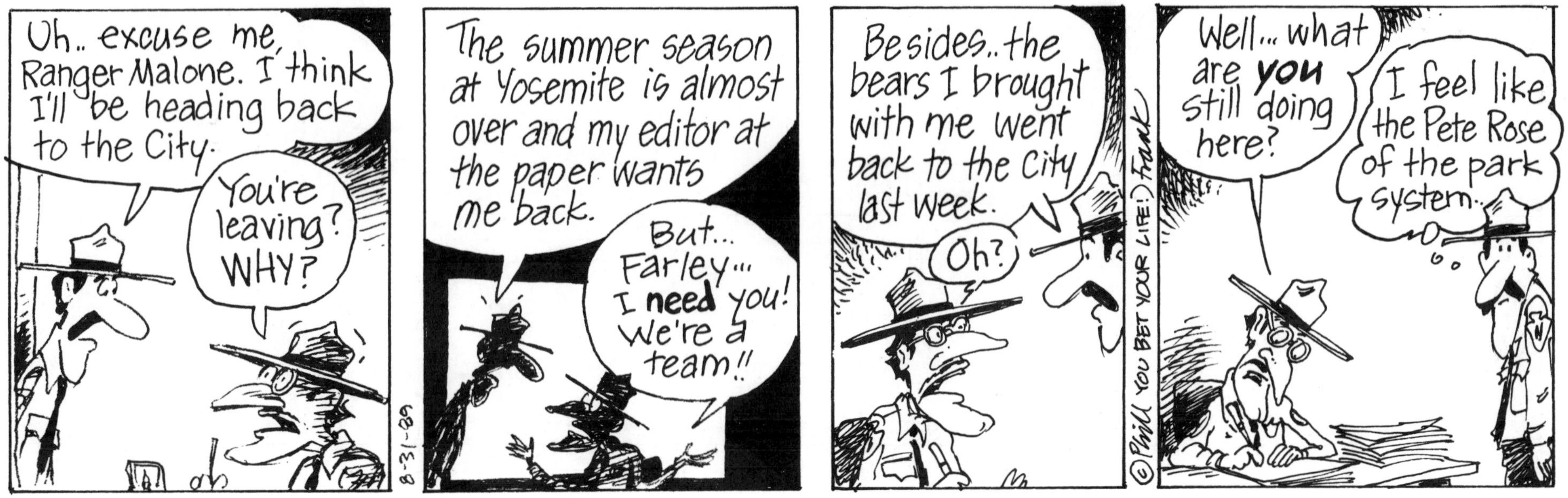

Uh.. excuse me, Ranger Malone. I think I'll be heading back to the City.
You're leaving? WHY?
8-31-89
The summer season at Yosemite is almost over and my editor at the paper wants me back.
But... Farley... I **need** you! We're a team!!
Besides.. the bears I brought with me went back to the City last week.
Oh?
©Phil (YOU BET YOUR LIFE!) Frank
Well... what are **you** still doing here?
I feel like the Pete Rose of the park system...

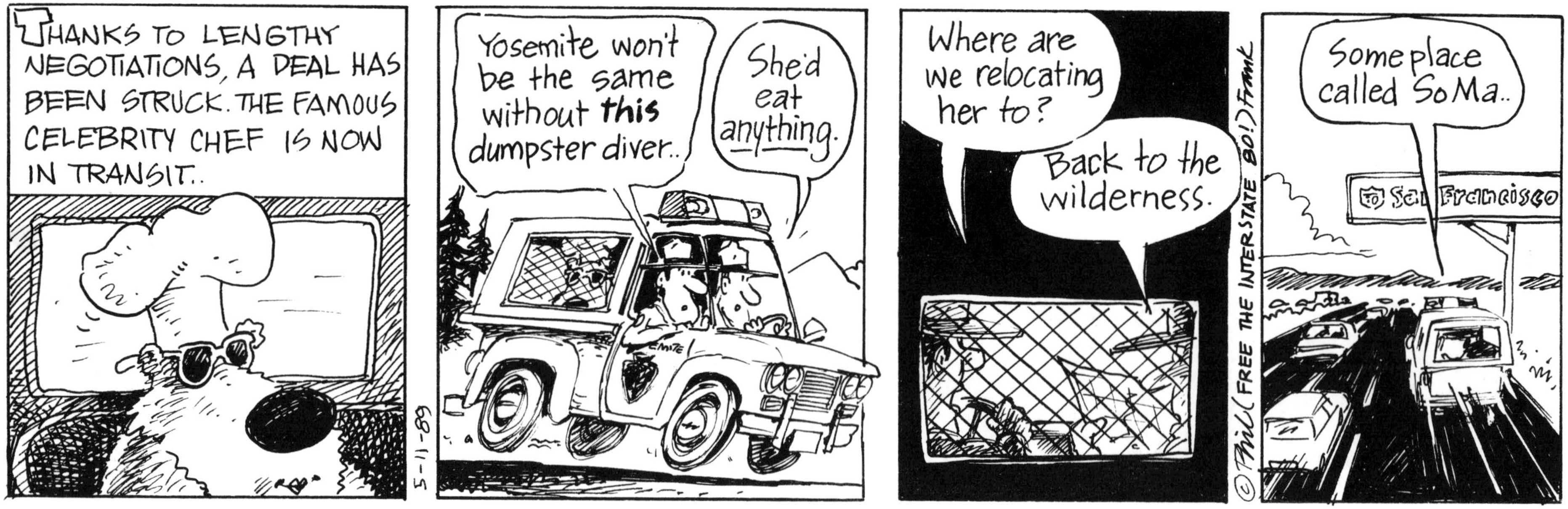
THANKS TO LENGTHY NEGOTIATIONS, A DEAL HAS BEEN STRUCK. THE FAMOUS CELEBRITY CHEF IS NOW IN TRANSIT..
5-11-89
Yosemite won't be the same without **this** dumpster diver..
She'd eat anything.
Where are we relocating her to?
Back to the wilderness.
© Phil (FREE THE INTERSTATE BO!) Frank
Some place called So Ma..

It's fall and the bears head again to Yosemite... by bus.

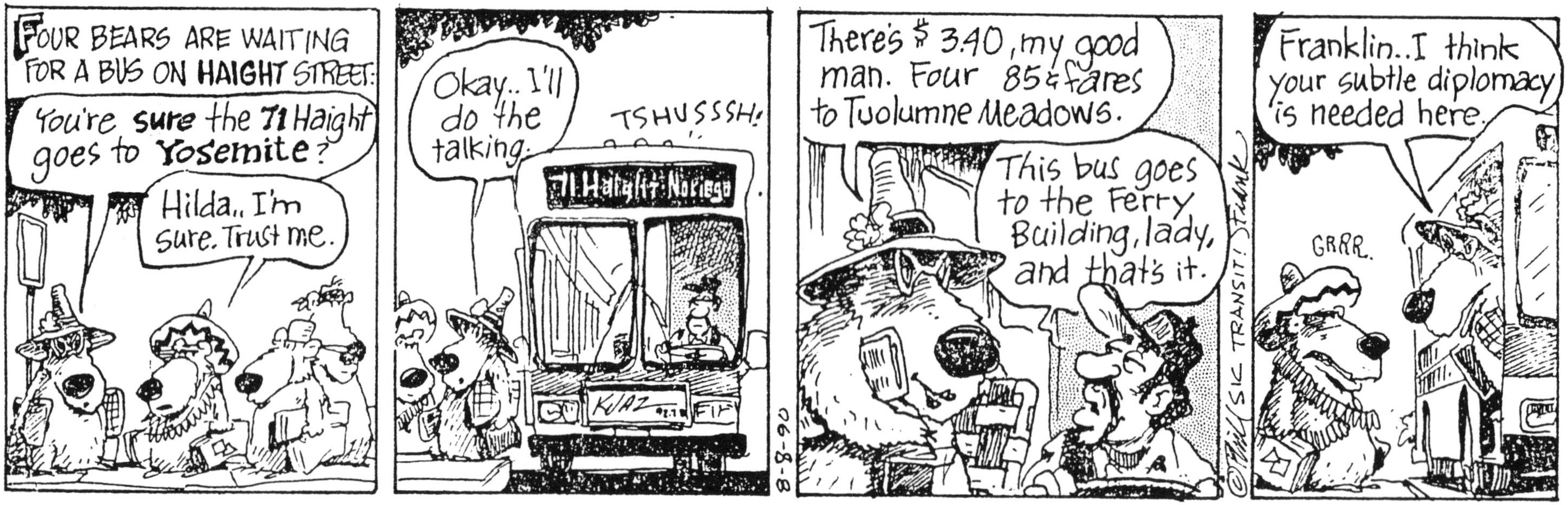
FOUR BEARS ARE WAITING FOR A BUS ON **HAIGHT** STREET:
You're **sure** the 71 Haight goes to **Yosemite**?
Hilda.. I'm sure. Trust me.
Okay.. I'll do the talking.
TSHUSSSH!
71 Haight Noriega
KJAZ
8-8-90
There's $3.40, my good man. Four 85¢ fares to Tuolumne Meadows.
This bus goes to the Ferry Building, lady, and that's it.
© Phil (SIC TRANSIT!) Frank
Franklin.. I think your subtle diplomacy is needed here.
GRRR.

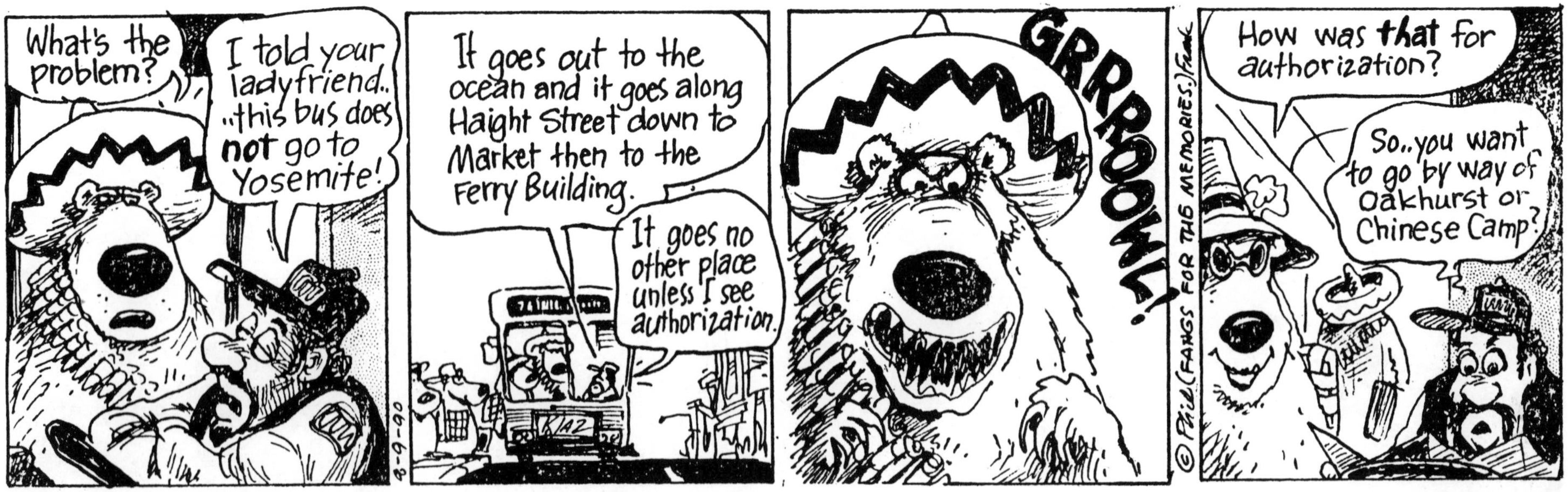
What's the problem?
I told your ladyfriend.. ..this bus does **not** go to Yosemite!
It goes out to the ocean and it goes along Haight Street down to Market then to the Ferry Building.
It goes no other place unless I see authorization.
8-9-90
GRRROOWL!
© Phil (Fangs for the memories!) Frank
How was **that** for authorization?
So..you want to go by way of Oakhurst or Chinese Camp?

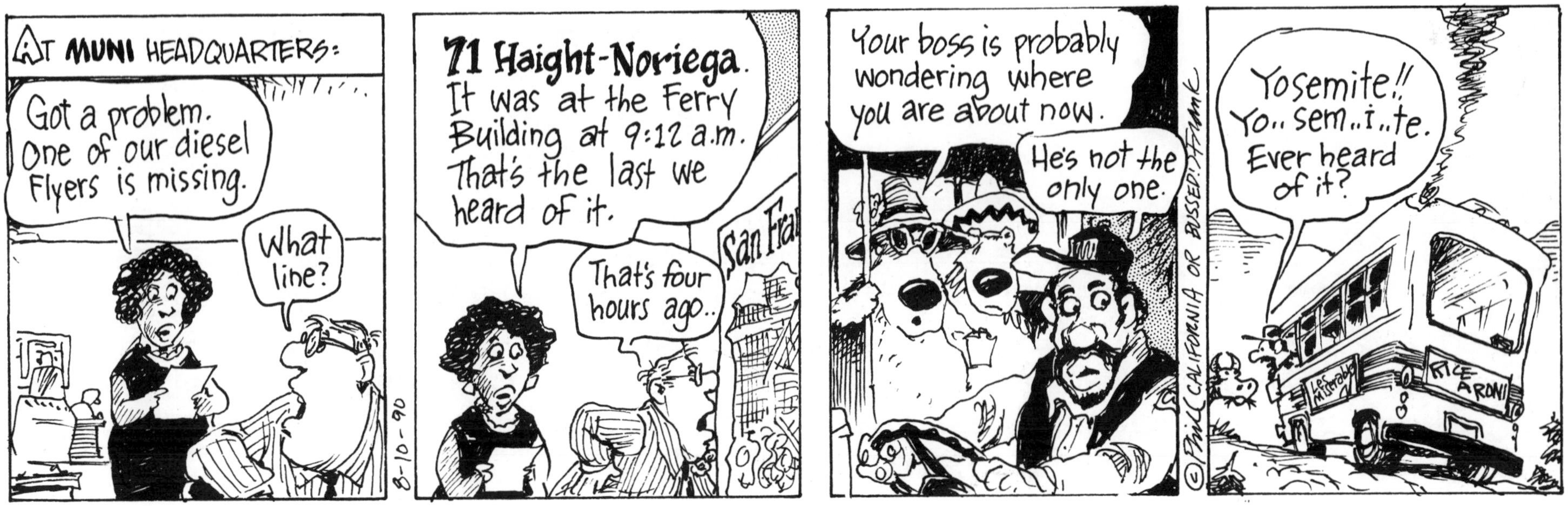
At **MUNI** HEADQUARTERS:
Got a problem. One of our diesel Flyers is missing.
What line?
8-10-90
71 Haight-Noriega. It was at the Ferry Building at 9:12 a.m. That's the last we heard of it.
That's four hours ago..
Your boss is probably wondering where you are about now.
He's not the only one.
© Phil (California or bussed!) Frank
Yosemite!! Yo.. sem..i..te. Ever heard of it?
Les Miserables
RICE A RONI

IN THE FOOTHILLS OF THE SIERRA TWO HIGHWAY PATROL CARS SIT SIDE BY SIDE:
Takin' the kids waterskiing at Lake Berryesa this weekend.
Sounds good..
HIGHWAY PATROL
8-11-90
COMING UP THE WINDING DIRT ROAD OUT OF CHINESE CAMP HEADED TOWARDS YOSEMITE IS A COMMANDEERED MUNI BUS.
..WITH FOUR VACATIONING CALIFORNIA BLACK BEARS ABOARD:
98 fillets of fish on the wall.. 98 fillets of fish.. if one..
35
©Phil Frank (GOLDEN STATE WORRIERS)
I didn't see that. Did you?
See what?

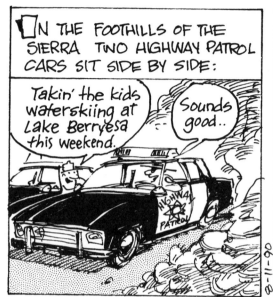

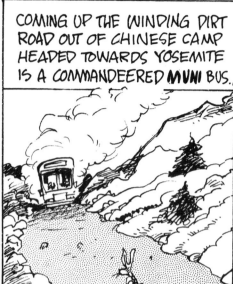

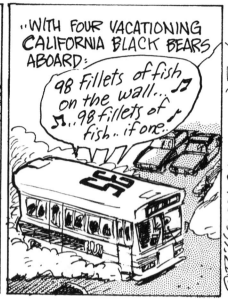

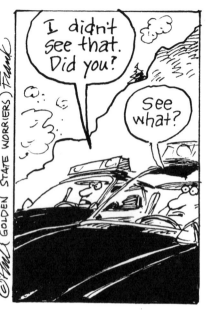

Wildfires Strand Thousands in Yosemite Park

While I work much closer to deadline than syndicated cartoonists, with only a few days between when I draw the cartoon and when it runs in the newspaper, I still get caught occasionally by the fickleness of news stories.

In this case I had my bears on their way to Yosemite in a San Francisco MUNI bus in 1990 when wildfires broke out, stranding thousands of park visitors. Readers called or faxed the San Francisco Chronicle with messages like this one: "FIRE! FIRE! STOP THE BUS! TURN AROUND!!" When the trapped visitors were evacuated, they abandoned their food coolers and meals on picnic tables. I did overnight changes in the script to include this bear bonanza in the storyline.

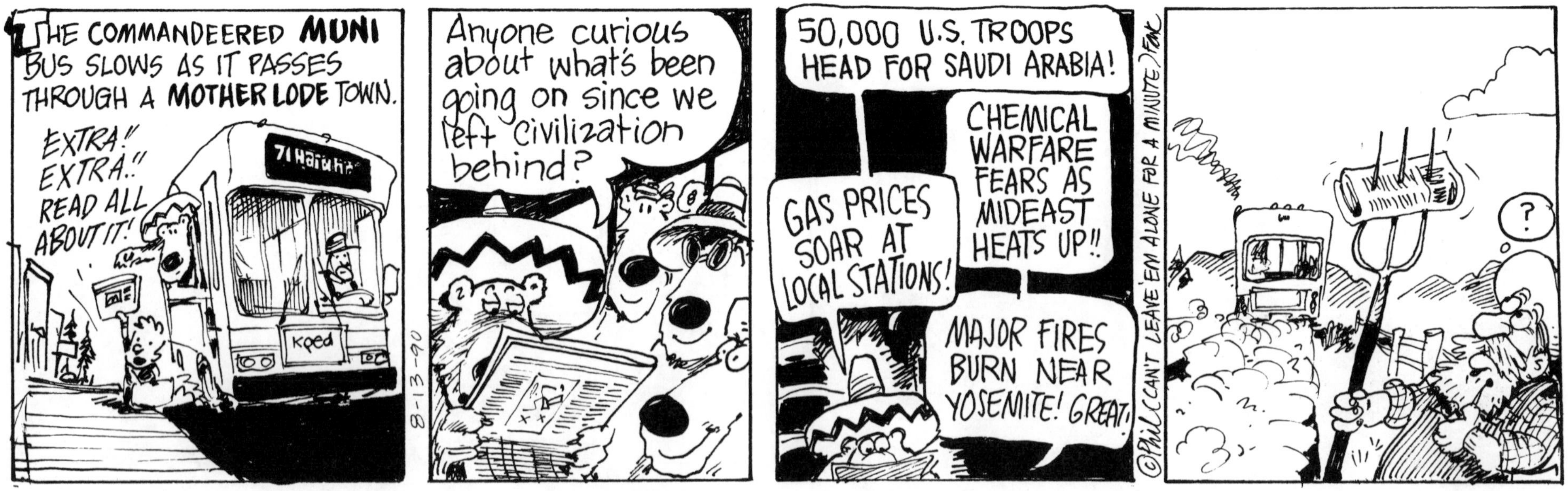
THE COMMANDEERED MUNI BUS SLOWS AS IT PASSES THROUGH A MOTHER LODE TOWN.
EXTRA! EXTRA! READ ALL ABOUT IT!
71 Haight
Kqed
8-13-90
Anyone curious about what's been going on since we left civilization behind?
50,000 U.S. TROOPS HEAD FOR SAUDI ARABIA!
GAS PRICES SOAR AT LOCAL STATIONS!
CHEMICAL WARFARE FEARS AS MIDEAST HEATS UP!!
MAJOR FIRES BURN NEAR YOSEMITE! GREAT!
©Phil (CAN'T LEAVE 'EM ALONE FOR A MINUTE) Frank
?

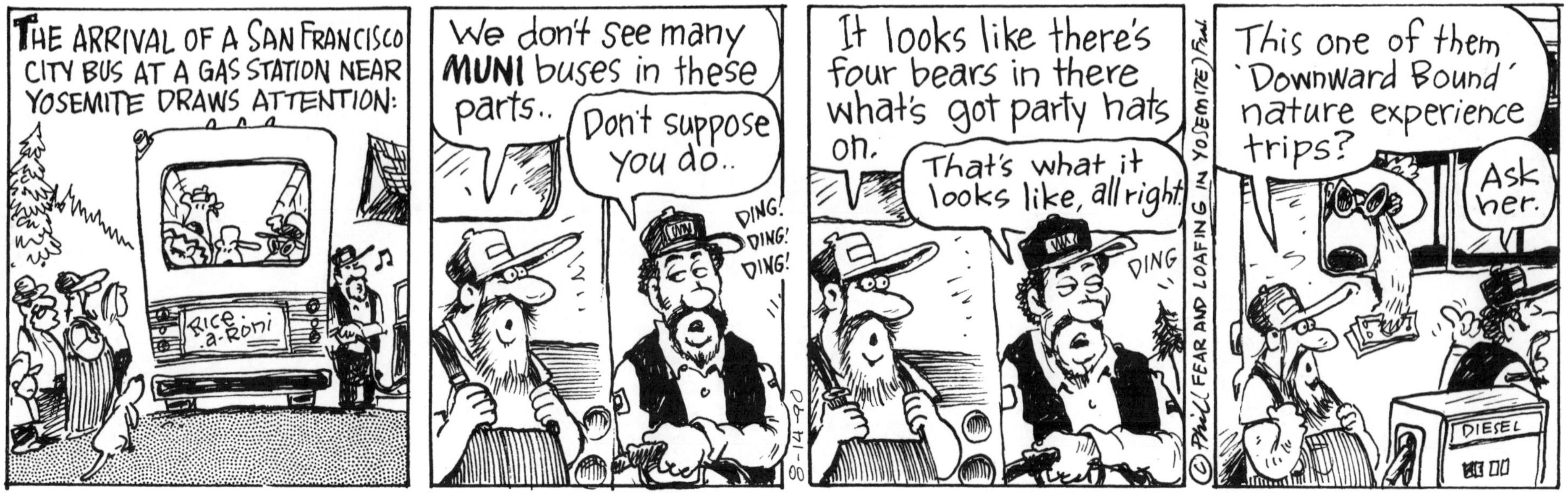
THE ARRIVAL OF A SAN FRANCISCO CITY BUS AT A GAS STATION NEAR YOSEMITE DRAWS ATTENTION:
Rice-a-Roni
We don't see many MUNI buses in these parts..
Don't suppose you do..
DING! DING! DING!
8-14-90
It looks like there's four bears in there what's got party hats on.
That's what it looks like, all right.
DING
© Phil FEAR AND LOAFING IN YOSEMITE Frank
This one of them 'Downward Bound' nature experience trips?
Ask her.
DIESEL

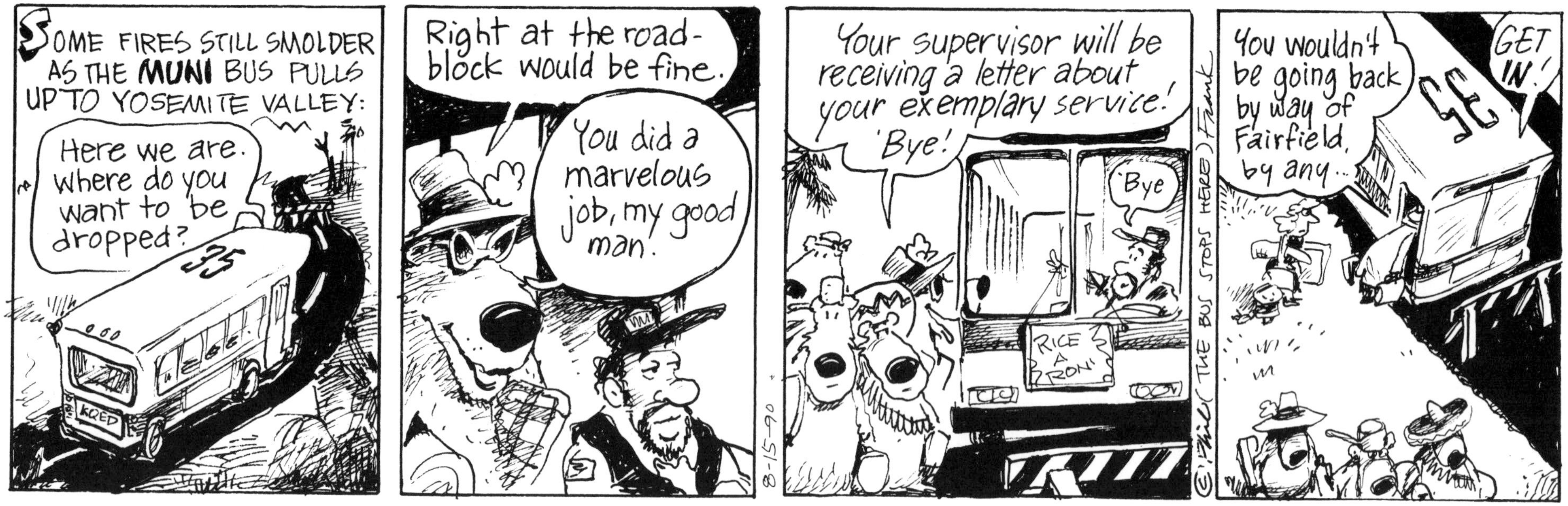
SOME FIRES STILL SMOLDER AS THE MUNI BUS PULLS UP TO YOSEMITE VALLEY:
Here we are. Where do you want to be dropped?
35
KQED
Right at the road-block would be fine.
You did a marvelous job, my good man.
8-15-90
Your supervisor will be receiving a letter about your exemplary service! 'Bye!
'Bye
RICE A RONI
© Phil (THE BUS STOPS HERE) Frank
You wouldn't be going back by way of Fairfield, by any...
GET IN!

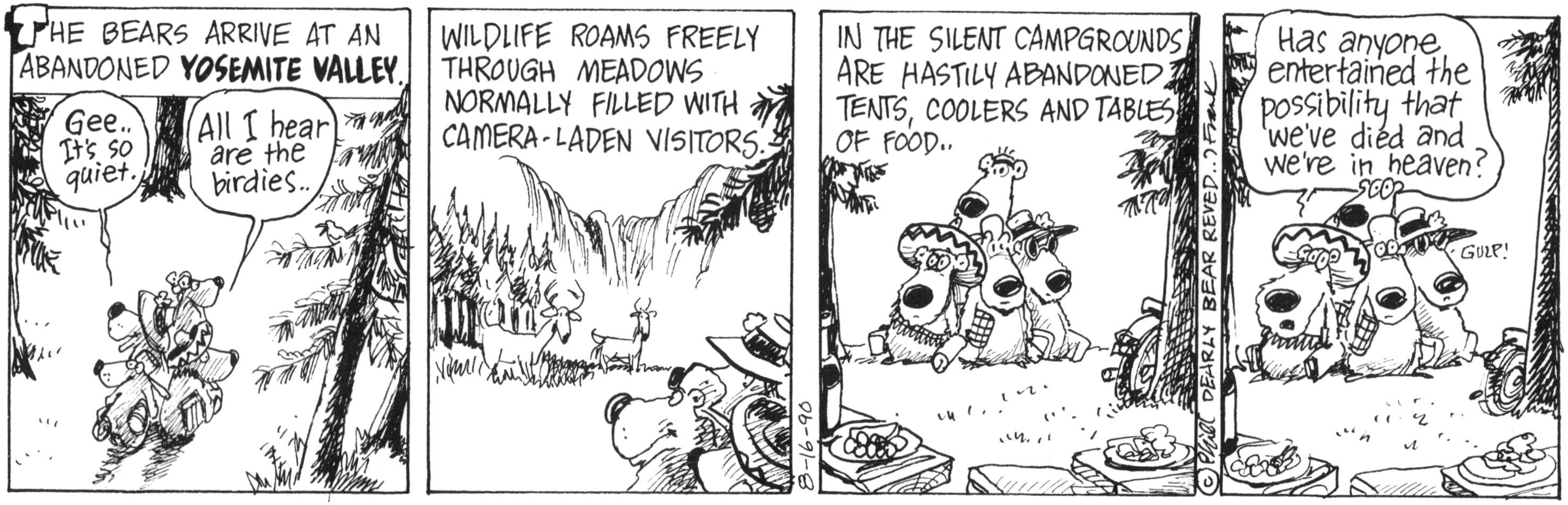
THE BEARS ARRIVE AT AN ABANDONED YOSEMITE VALLEY.
Gee.. It's so quiet.
All I hear are the birdies..
WILDLIFE ROAMS FREELY THROUGH MEADOWS NORMALLY FILLED WITH CAMERA-LADEN VISITORS.
8-16-90
IN THE SILENT CAMPGROUNDS ARE HASTILY ABANDONED TENTS, COOLERS AND TABLES OF FOOD..
© Phil (DEARLY BEAR REVED..?) Frank
Has anyone entertained the possibility that we've died and we're in heaven?
GULP!

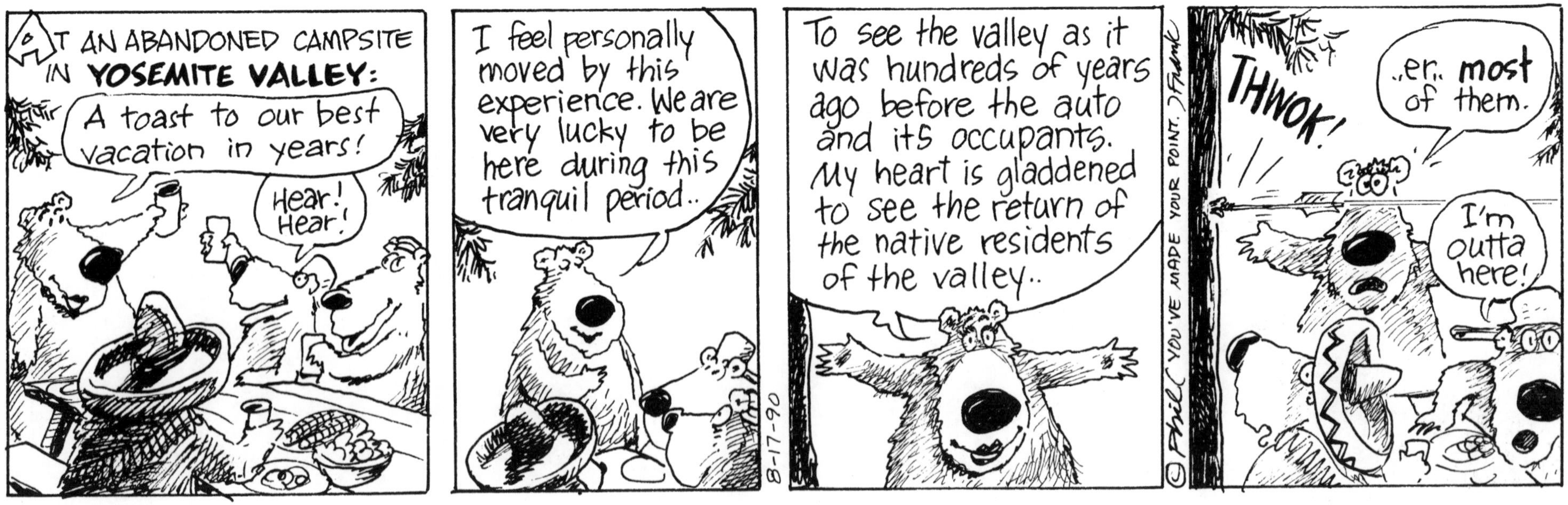
AT AN ABANDONED CAMPSITE IN **YOSEMITE VALLEY**:
A toast to our best vacation in years!
Hear! Hear!
I feel personally moved by this experience. We are very lucky to be here during this tranquil period..
8-17-90
To see the valley as it was hundreds of years ago before the auto and its occupants. My heart is gladdened to see the return of the native residents of the valley..
© Phil (YOU'VE MADE YOUR POINT.) Frank
THWOK!
..er.. **most** of them.
I'm outta here!

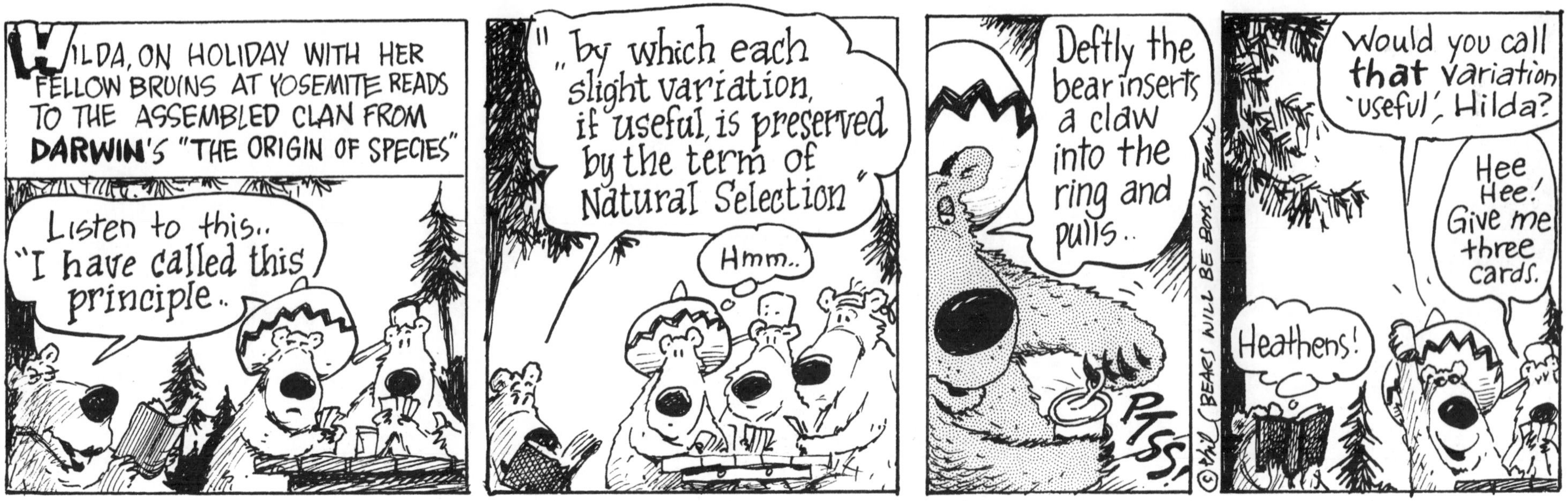
HILDA, ON HOLIDAY WITH HER FELLOW BRUINS AT YOSEMITE READS TO THE ASSEMBLED CLAN FROM **DARWIN**'S "THE ORIGIN OF SPECIES"
Listen to this.. "I have called this principle..
"..by which each slight variation, if useful, is preserved by the term of Natural Selection"
Hmm..
Deftly the bear inserts a claw into the ring and pulls..
PTSS!
© Phil (BEARS WILL BE BEARS.) Frank
Would you call **that** variation 'useful', Hilda?
Hee Hee! Give me three cards.
Heathens!

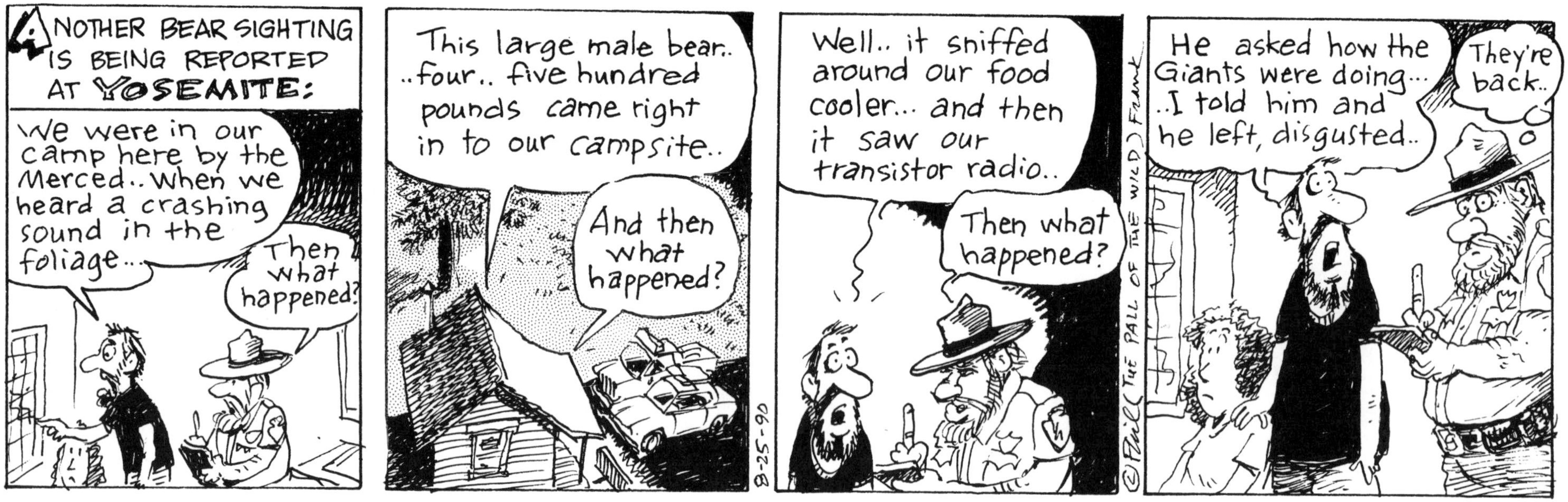

ANOTHER BEAR SIGHTING IS BEING REPORTED AT YOSEMITE:
We were in our camp here by the Merced.. When we heard a crashing sound in the foliage...
Then what happened?
This large male bear.. ..four.. five hundred pounds came right in to our campsite..
And then what happened?
8-25-90
Well.. it sniffed around our food cooler... and then it saw our transistor radio..
Then what happened?
© Phil (THE PALL OF THE WILD) Frank
He asked how the Giants were doing... ..I told him and he left, disgusted..
They're back..

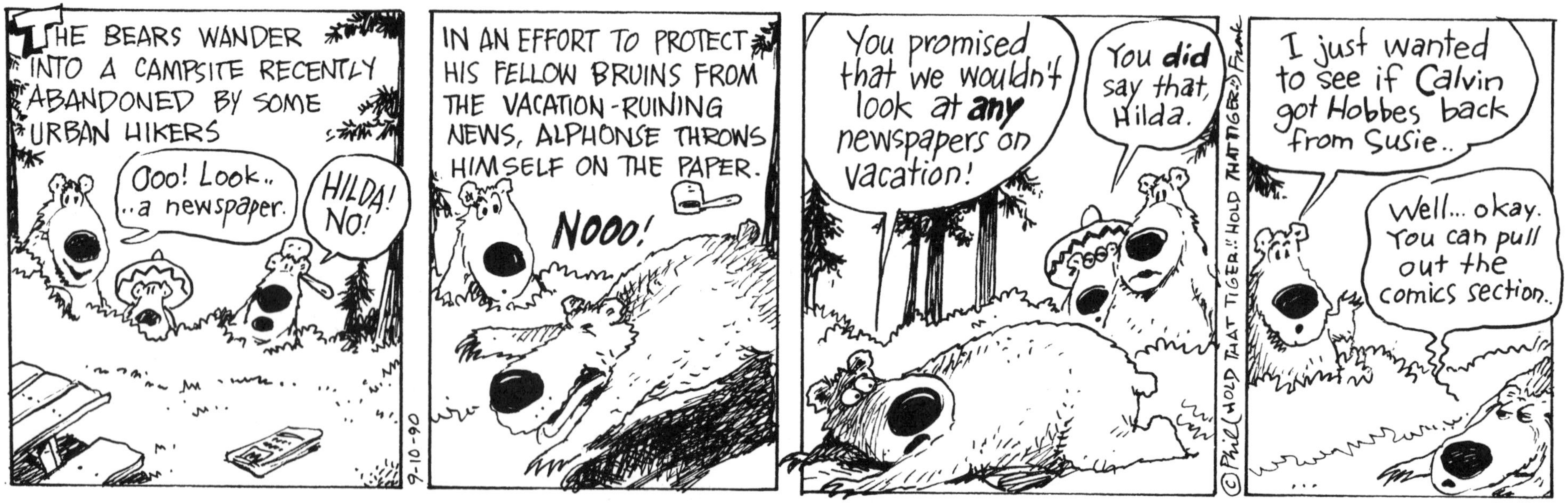

THE BEARS WANDER INTO A CAMPSITE RECENTLY ABANDONED BY SOME URBAN HIKERS
Ooo! Look.. ..a newspaper.
HILDA! NO!
9-10-90
IN AN EFFORT TO PROTECT HIS FELLOW BRUINS FROM THE VACATION-RUINING NEWS, ALPHONSE THROWS HIMSELF ON THE PAPER.
NOOO!
You promised that we wouldn't look at **any** newspapers on vacation!
You **did** say that, Hilda.
© Phil (HOLD THAT TIGER!! HOLD THAT TIGER!!) Frank
I just wanted to see if Calvin got Hobbes back from Susie..
Well... okay. You can pull out the comics section..

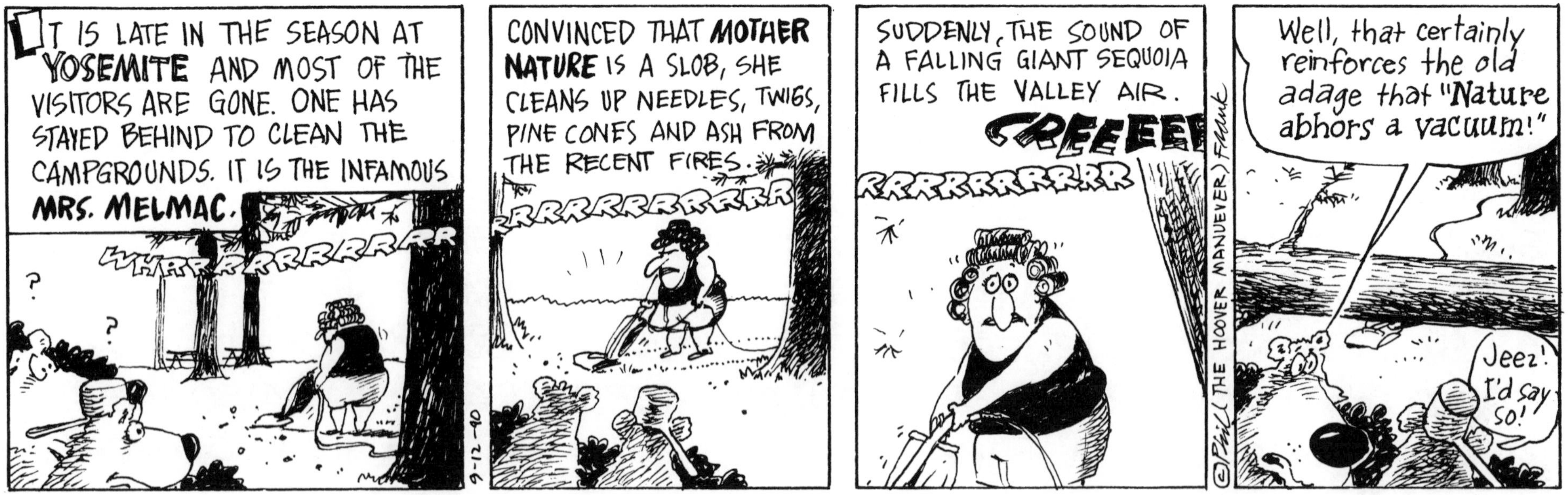
IT IS LATE IN THE SEASON AT YOSEMITE AND MOST OF THE VISITORS ARE GONE. ONE HAS STAYED BEHIND TO CLEAN THE CAMPGROUNDS. IT IS THE INFAMOUS MRS. MELMAC.
WHARRRRRRRRRR
?
?
9-12-90
CONVINCED THAT MOTHER NATURE IS A SLOB, SHE CLEANS UP NEEDLES, TWIGS, PINE CONES AND ASH FROM THE RECENT FIRES.
RRRRRRRRRRRR
SUDDENLY, THE SOUND OF A FALLING GIANT SEQUOIA FILLS THE VALLEY AIR.
CREEEEE
RRRRRRRRRRRR
© Phil (THE HOOVER MANUEVER) Frank
Well, that certainly reinforces the old adage that "Nature abhors a vacuum!"
Jeez! I'd say so!

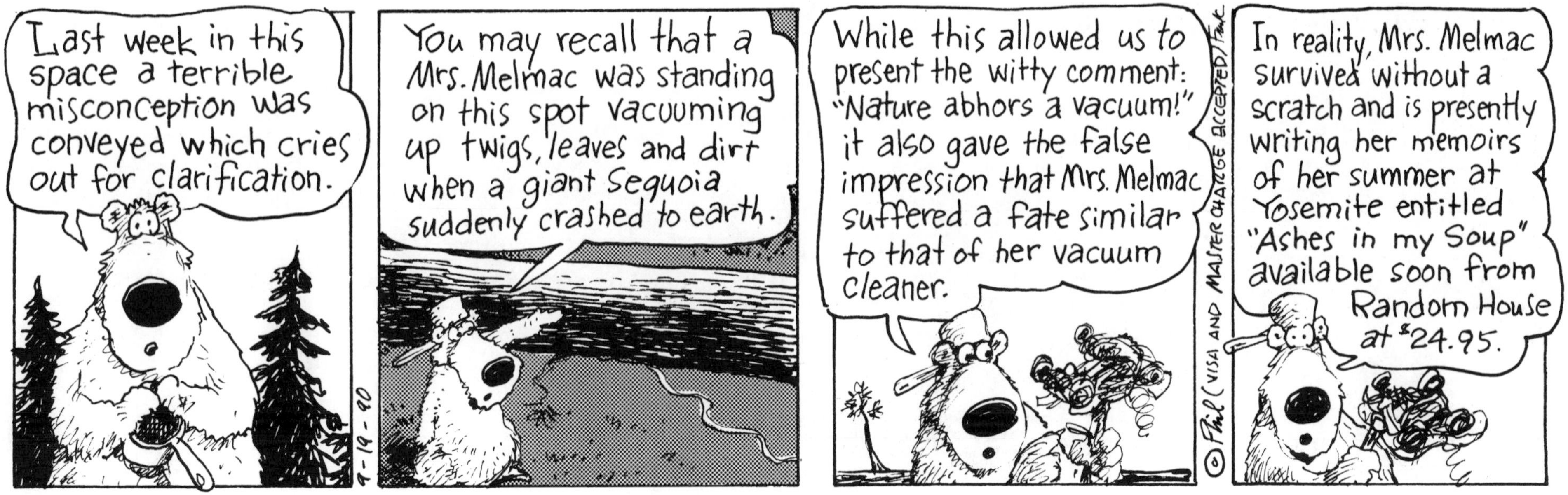
Last week in this space a terrible misconception was conveyed which cries out for clarification.
9-19-90
You may recall that a Mrs. Melmac was standing on this spot vacuuming up twigs, leaves and dirt when a giant Sequoia suddenly crashed to earth.
While this allowed us to present the witty comment: "Nature abhors a vacuum!" it also gave the false impression that Mrs. Melmac suffered a fate similar to that of her vacuum cleaner.
© Phil (VISA AND MASTER CHARGE ACCEPTED) Frank
In reality, Mrs. Melmac survived without a scratch and is presently writing her memoirs of her summer at Yosemite entitled "Ashes in my Soup" available soon from Random House at $24.95.

Stern Grove: Hardline Ranger

POLLS SHOW THAT THE PARK RANGER IS THE MOST RESPECTED PEACE OFFICER IN THE NATION. IT SEEMED ALMOST SACRILEGIOUS TO CREATE A PARK RANGER WITH AN ATTITUDE. BUT THERE ARE TIMES WHEN SUCH A CHARACTER IS NEEDED... WHEN A GOOD GUY JUST WON'T DO! ONE OF THE PROBLEMS WAS FINDING AN APPROPRIATE NAME FOR HIM. IN **SAN FRANCISCO** THERE IS A BEAUTIFUL OUTDOOR CONCERT AREA CALLED **STERN GROVE**. I REALIZED **STERN GROVE** WAS ALSO THE PERFECT NAME FOR A PARK RANGER WITH A CHIP ON HIS SHOULDER.

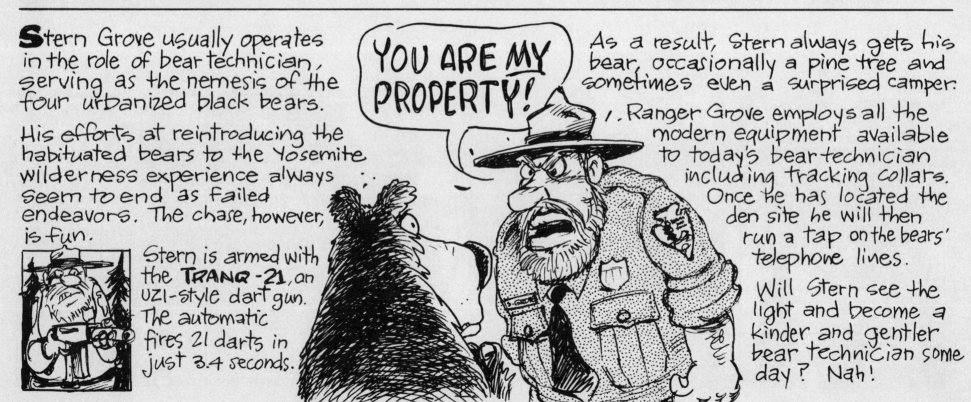

Stern Grove usually operates in the role of bear technician, serving as the nemesis of the four urbanized black bears.

His efforts at reintroducing the habituated bears to the Yosemite wilderness experience always seem to end as failed endeavors. The chase, however, is fun.

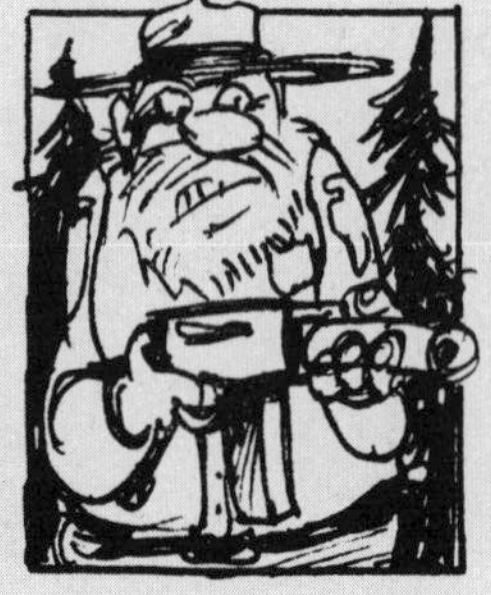

Stern is armed with the **TRANQ-21**, an UZI-style dart gun. The automatic fires 21 darts in just 3.4 seconds.

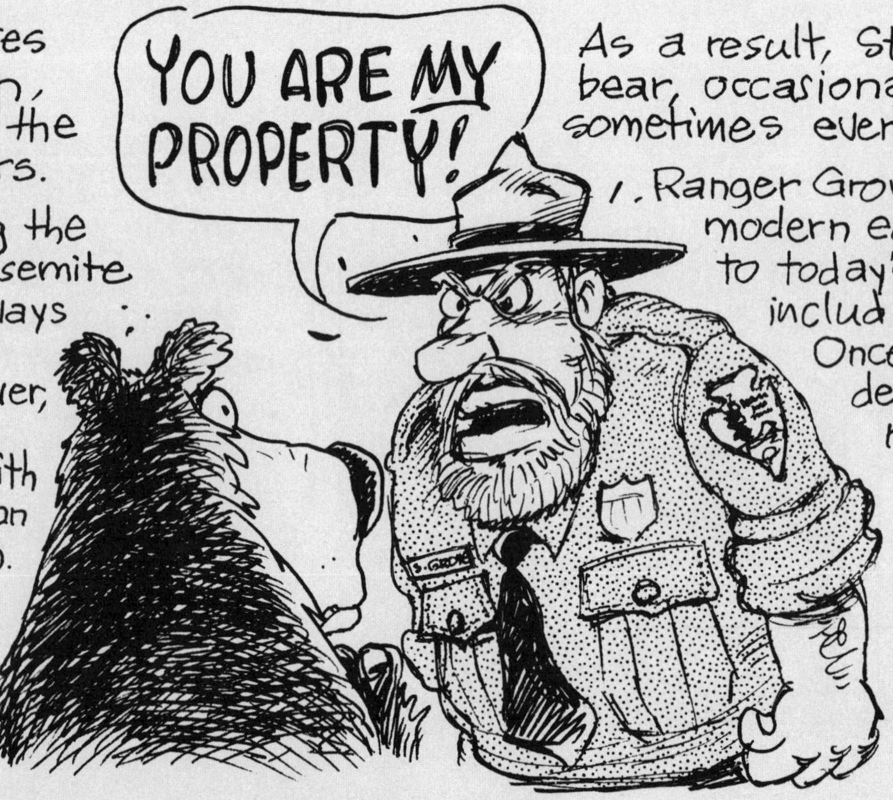
YOU ARE MY PROPERTY!

As a result, Stern always gets his bear, occasionally a pine tree and sometimes even a surprised camper.

.. Ranger Grove employs all the modern equipment available to today's bear technician including tracking collars. Once he has located the den site he will then run a tap on the bears' telephone lines.

Will Stern see the light and become a kinder and gentler bear technician some day? Nah!

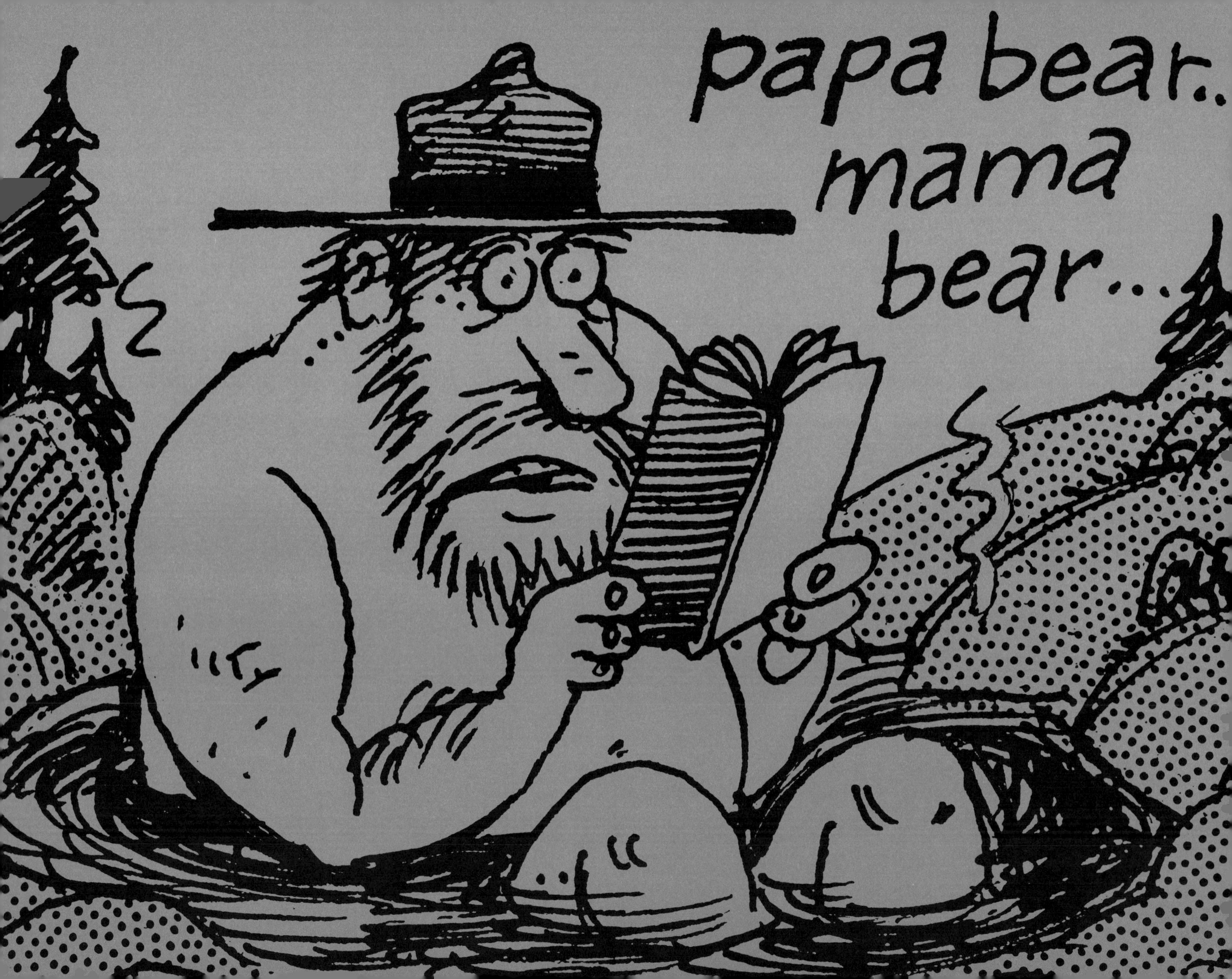
papa bear..
mama
bear...

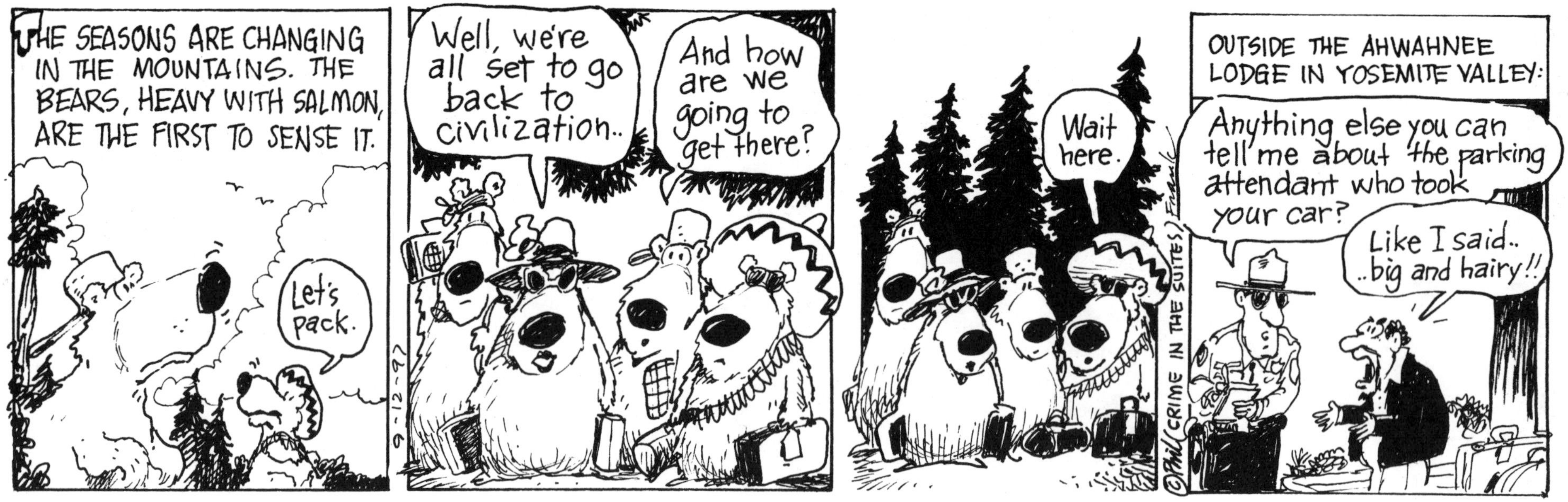
THE SEASONS ARE CHANGING IN THE MOUNTAINS. THE BEARS, HEAVY WITH SALMON, ARE THE FIRST TO SENSE IT.
Let's pack.
9-12-97
Well, we're all set to go back to civilization..
And how are we going to get there?
Wait here.
©Phil (CRIME IN THE SUITES) Frank
OUTSIDE THE AHWAHNEE LODGE IN YOSEMITE VALLEY:
Anything else you can tell me about the parking attendant who took your car?
Like I said.. ..big and hairy!!

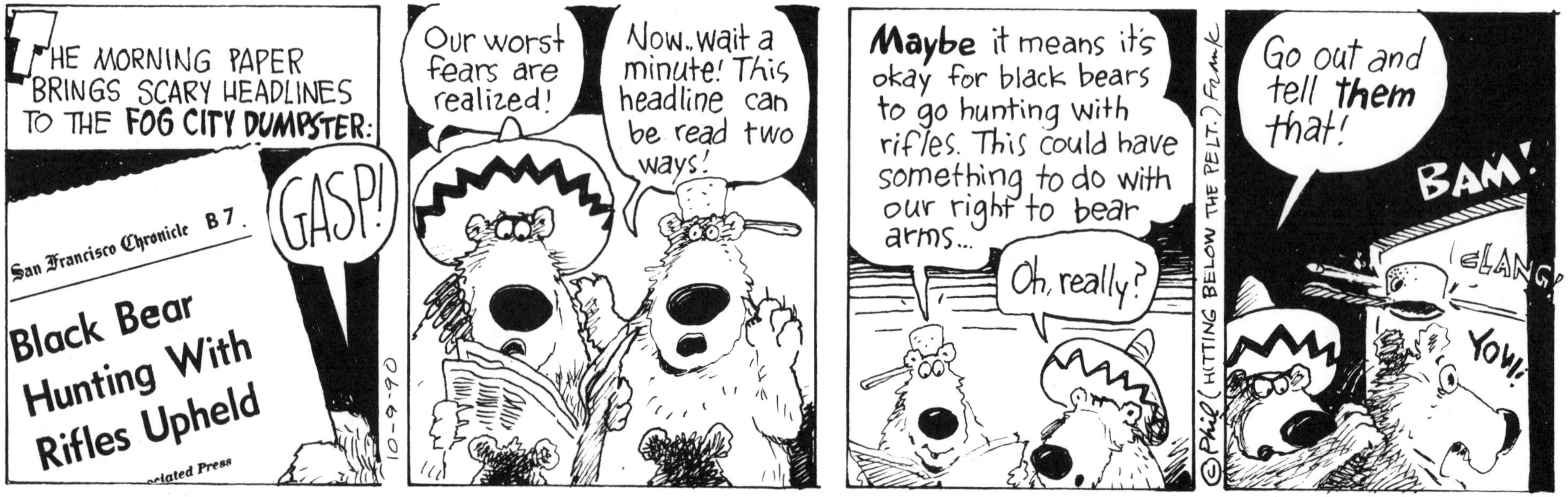
THE MORNING PAPER BRINGS SCARY HEADLINES TO THE FOG CITY DUMPSTER:
San Francisco Chronicle B7
Black Bear Hunting With Rifles Upheld
GASP!
10-9-90
Our worst fears are realized!
Now..wait a minute! This headline can be read two ways!
Maybe it means it's okay for black bears to go hunting with rifles. This could have something to do with our right to bear arms...
Oh, really?
©Phil (HITTING BELOW THE PELT.) Frank
Go out and tell them that!
BAM!
CLANG!
YOW!

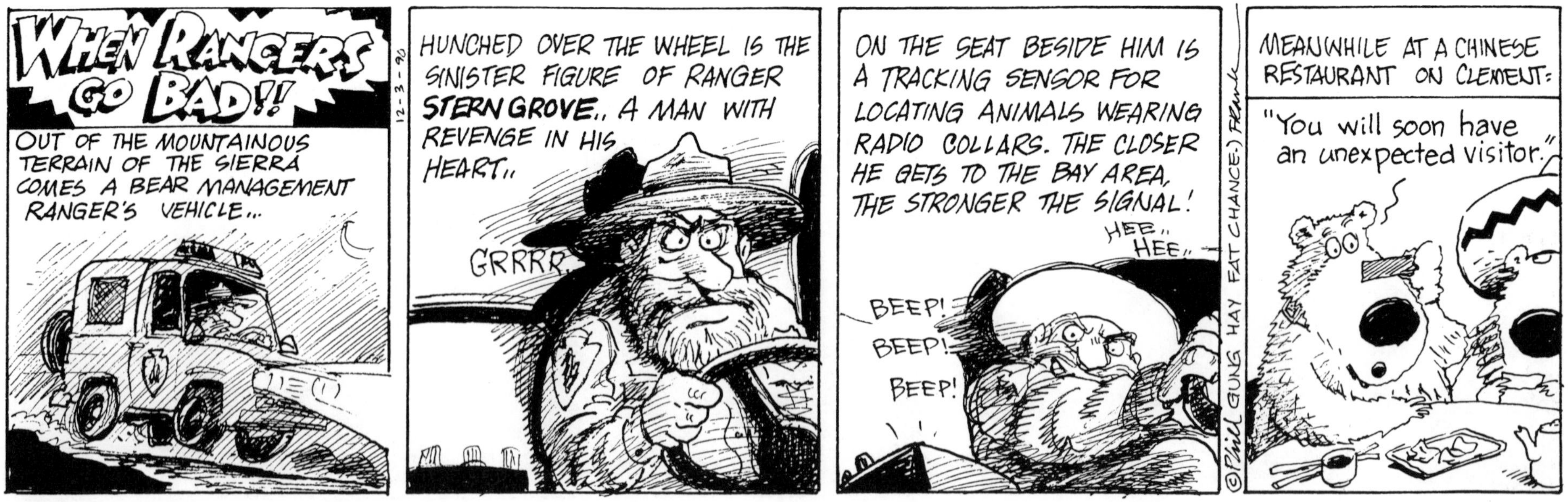
WHEN RANGERS GO BAD!!
OUT OF THE MOUNTAINOUS TERRAIN OF THE SIERRA COMES A BEAR MANAGEMENT RANGER'S VEHICLE...
12-3-90
HUNCHED OVER THE WHEEL IS THE SINISTER FIGURE OF RANGER **STERN GROVE**.. A MAN WITH REVENGE IN HIS HEART..
GRRRR
ON THE SEAT BESIDE HIM IS A TRACKING SENSOR FOR LOCATING ANIMALS WEARING RADIO COLLARS. THE CLOSER HE GETS TO THE BAY AREA, THE STRONGER THE SIGNAL!
HEE.. HEE..
BEEP!
BEEP!
BEEP!
©Phil GUNG HAY FAT CHANCE.) Frank
MEANWHILE AT A CHINESE RESTAURANT ON CLEMENT:
"You will soon have an unexpected visitor."

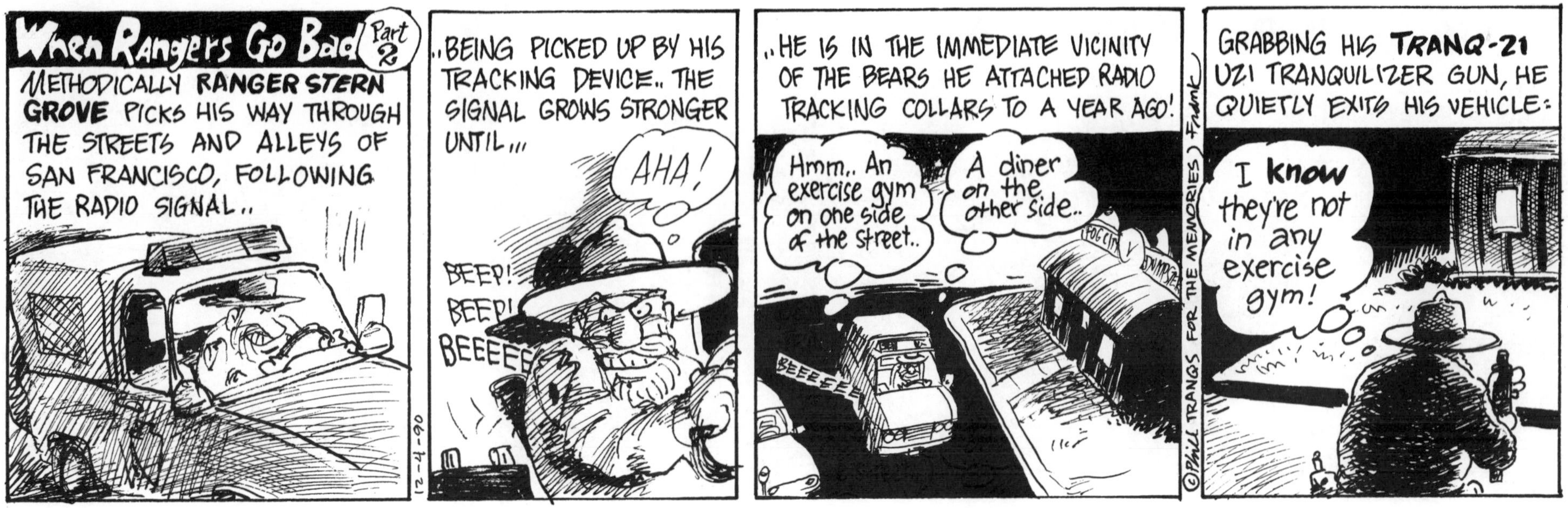
When Rangers Go Bad Part 2
METHODICALLY **RANGER STERN GROVE** PICKS HIS WAY THROUGH THE STREETS AND ALLEYS OF SAN FRANCISCO, FOLLOWING THE RADIO SIGNAL..
12-4-90
..BEING PICKED UP BY HIS TRACKING DEVICE.. THE SIGNAL GROWS STRONGER UNTIL...
AHA!
BEEP!
BEEP!
BEEEEE
..HE IS IN THE IMMEDIATE VICINITY OF THE BEARS HE ATTACHED RADIO TRACKING COLLARS TO A YEAR AGO!
Hmm.. An exercise gym on one side of the street..
A diner on the other side..
BEEEEEEE
©Phil TRANQS FOR THE MEMORIES.) Frank
GRABBING HIS **TRANQ-21** UZI TRANQUILIZER GUN, HE QUIETLY EXITS HIS VEHICLE:
I **know** they're not in any exercise gym!

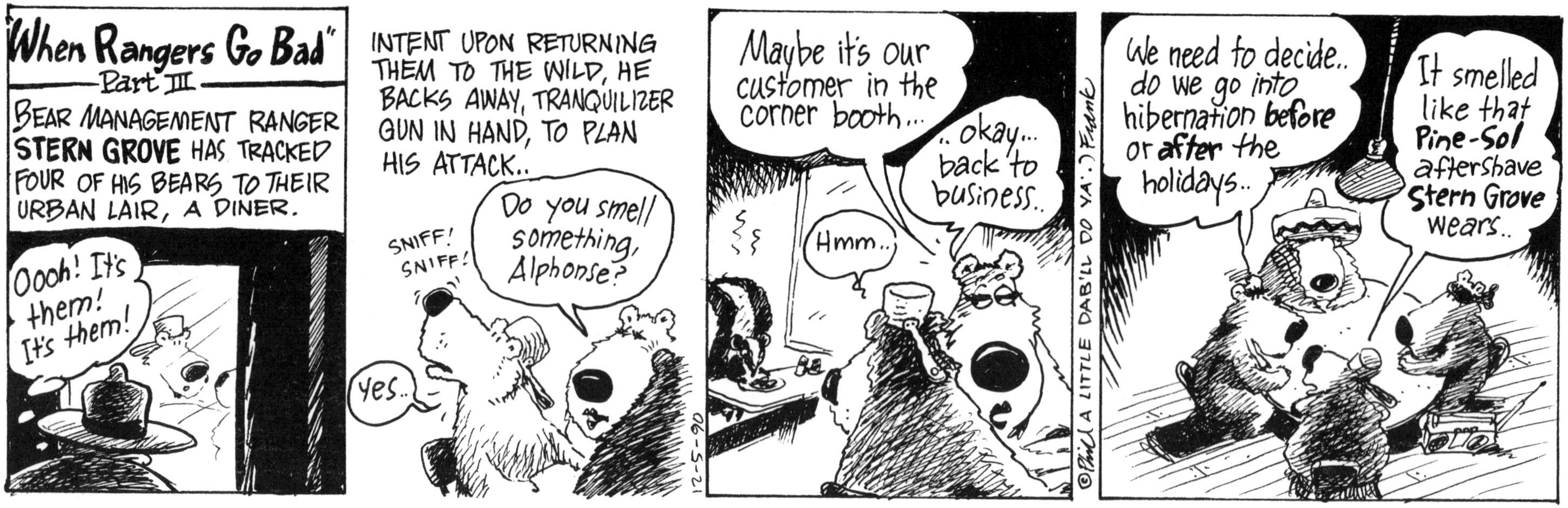
"When Rangers Go Bad"
Part III
BEAR MANAGEMENT RANGER STERN GROVE HAS TRACKED FOUR OF HIS BEARS TO THEIR URBAN LAIR, A DINER.
Oooh! It's them! It's them!
INTENT UPON RETURNING THEM TO THE WILD, HE BACKS AWAY, TRANQUILIZER GUN IN HAND, TO PLAN HIS ATTACK..
SNIFF! SNIFF!
Do you smell something, Alphonse?
Yes..
12-5-90
Maybe it's our customer in the corner booth...
Hmm..
.. okay... back to business..
©Phil (A LITTLE DAB'LL DO YA'.) Frank
We need to decide.. do we go into hibernation before or after the holidays..
It smelled like that Pine-Sol aftershave Stern Grove wears..

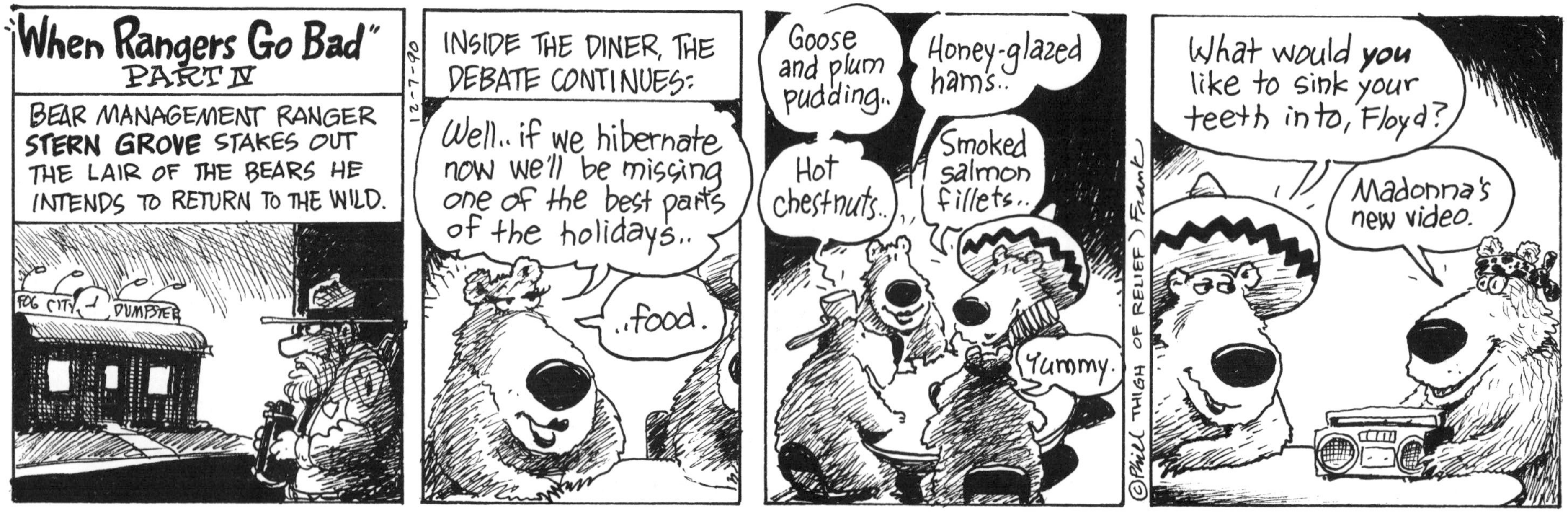
"When Rangers Go Bad"
PART IV
BEAR MANAGEMENT RANGER STERN GROVE STAKES OUT THE LAIR OF THE BEARS HE INTENDS TO RETURN TO THE WILD.
FOG CITY DUMPSTER
12-7-90
INSIDE THE DINER, THE DEBATE CONTINUES:
Well.. if we hibernate now we'll be missing one of the best parts of the holidays..
..food.
Goose and plum pudding..
Honey-glazed hams..
Hot chestnuts..
Smoked salmon fillets..
Yummy.
©Phil (THIGH OF RELIEF) Frank
What would you like to sink your teeth into, Floyd?
Madonna's new video.

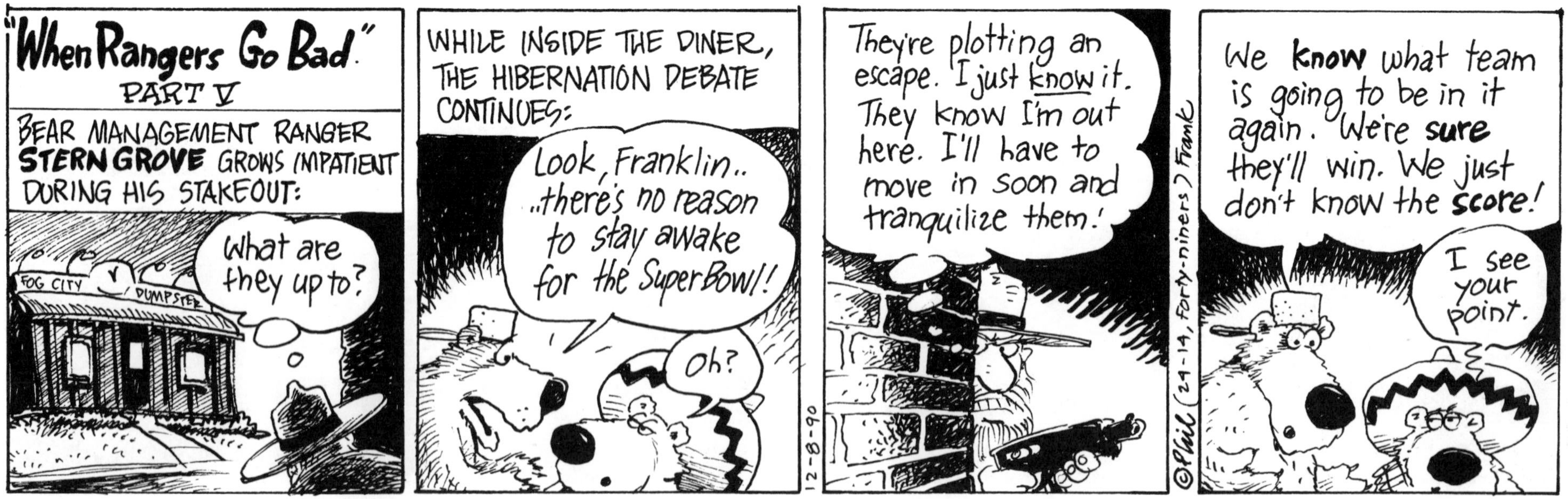
"When Rangers Go Bad"
PART V
BEAR MANAGEMENT RANGER STERN GROVE GROWS IMPATIENT DURING HIS STAKEOUT:
FOG CITY DUMPSTER
What are they up to?
WHILE INSIDE THE DINER, THE HIBERNATION DEBATE CONTINUES:
Look, Franklin.. ..there's no reason to stay awake for the SuperBowl!
Oh?
12-8-90
They're plotting an escape. I just know it. They know I'm out here. I'll have to move in soon and tranquilize them.
©Phil (24-14, Forty-niners) Frank
We know what team is going to be in it again. We're sure they'll win. We just don't know the score!
I see your point.

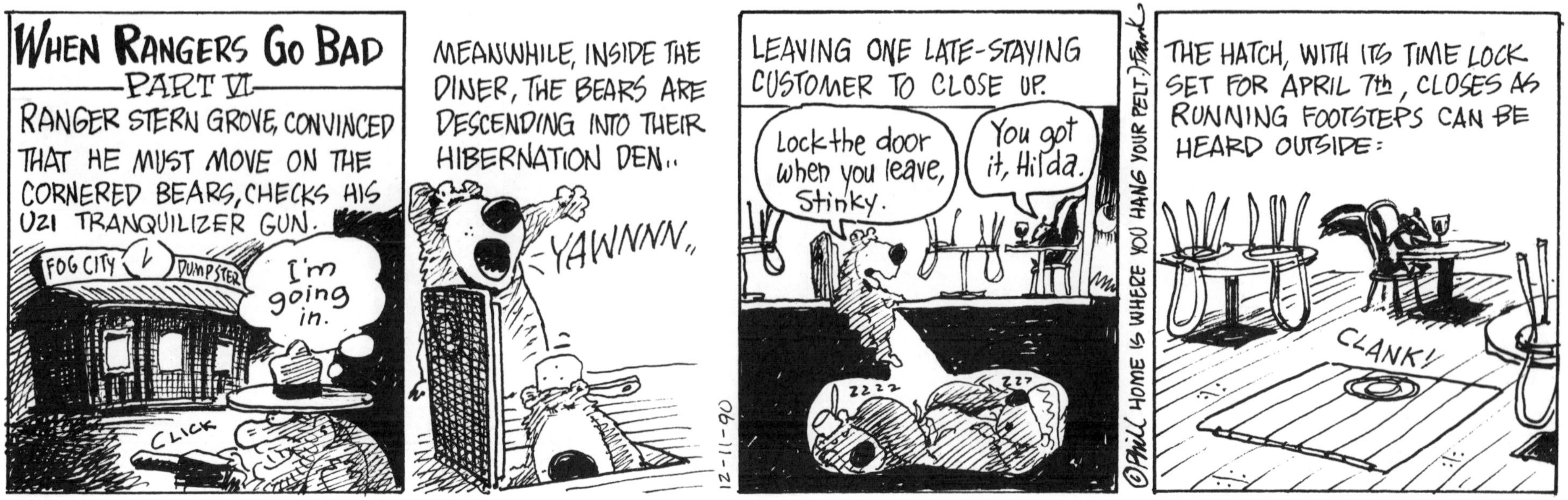
WHEN RANGERS GO BAD
PART VI
RANGER STERN GROVE, CONVINCED THAT HE MUST MOVE ON THE CORNERED BEARS, CHECKS HIS UZI TRANQUILIZER GUN.
FOG CITY DUMPSTER
I'm going in.
CLICK
MEANWHILE, INSIDE THE DINER, THE BEARS ARE DESCENDING INTO THEIR HIBERNATION DEN..
YAWNNN..
12-11-90
LEAVING ONE LATE-STAYING CUSTOMER TO CLOSE UP.
Lock the door when you leave, Stinky.
You got it, Hilda.
©Phil HOME IS WHERE YOU HANG YOUR PELT. Frank
THE HATCH, WITH ITS TIME LOCK SET FOR APRIL 7th, CLOSES AS RUNNING FOOTSTEPS CAN BE HEARD OUTSIDE:
CLANK!

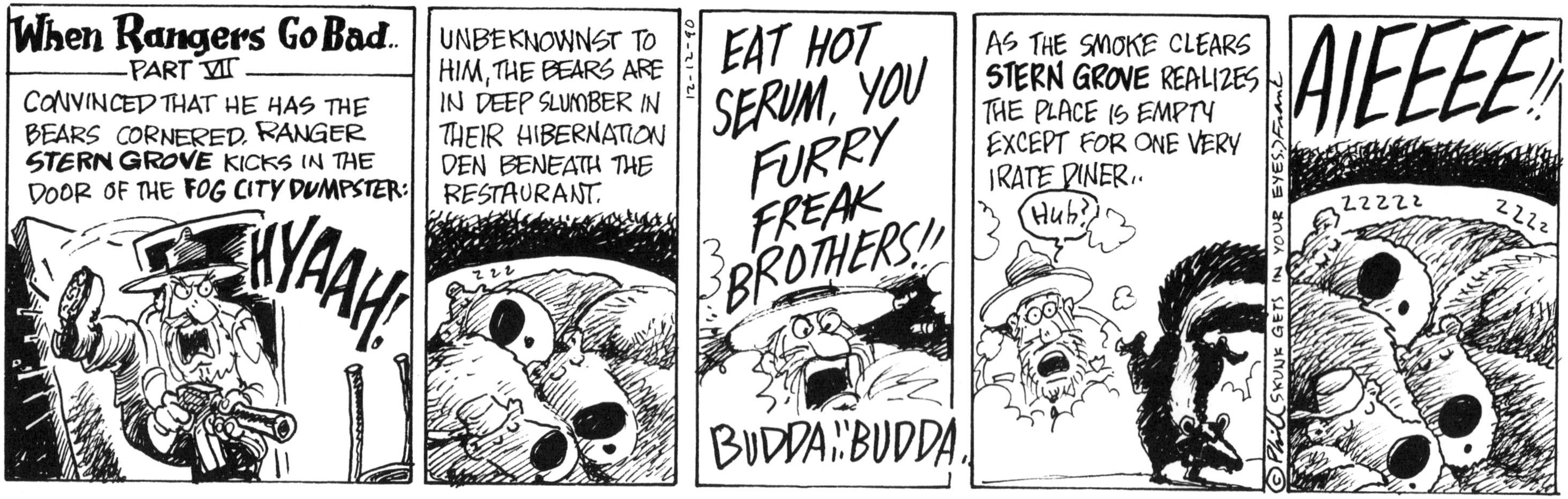
When Rangers Go Bad..
PART VII
CONVINCED THAT HE HAS THE BEARS CORNERED, RANGER STERN GROVE KICKS IN THE DOOR OF THE FOG CITY DUMPSTER:
HYAAAH!
UNBEKNOWNST TO HIM, THE BEARS ARE IN DEEP SLUMBER IN THEIR HIBERNATION DEN BENEATH THE RESTAURANT.
zzz
12-12-90
EAT HOT SERUM, YOU FURRY FREAK BROTHERS!!
BUDDA!! BUDDA..
AS THE SMOKE CLEARS STERN GROVE REALIZES THE PLACE IS EMPTY EXCEPT FOR ONE VERY IRATE DINER..
Huh?
© Phil SKUNK GETS IN YOUR EYES, Frank
AIEEEE!!
ZZZZZ
ZZZZ

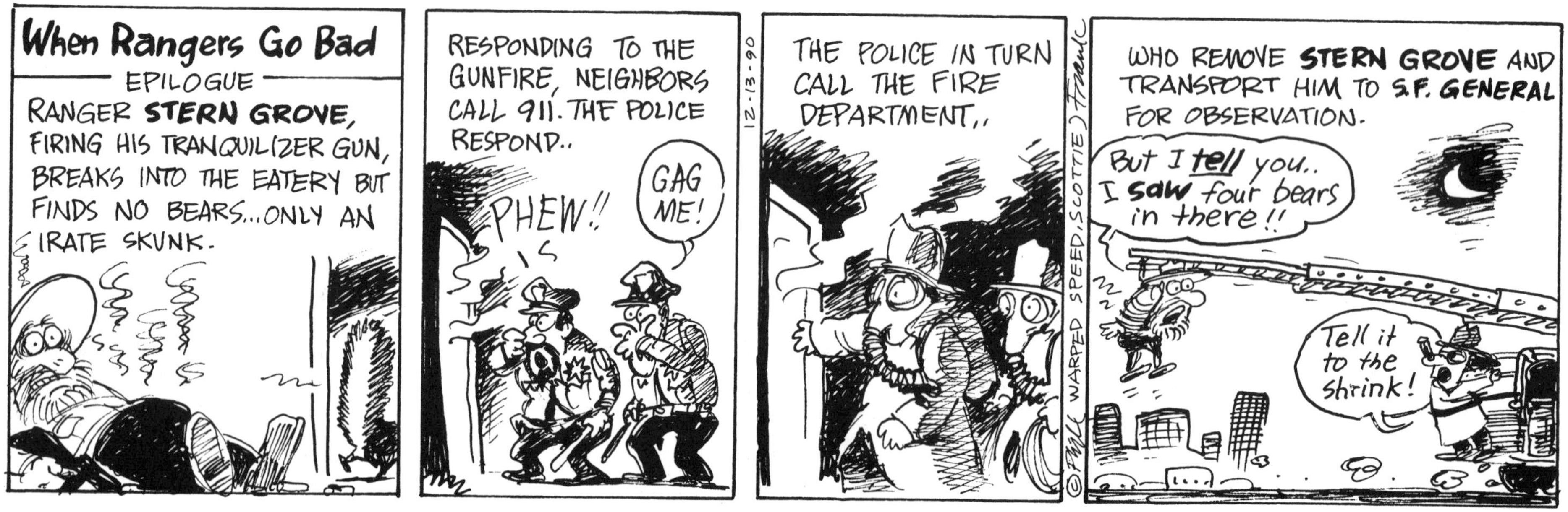
When Rangers Go Bad
EPILOGUE
RANGER STERN GROVE, FIRING HIS TRANQUILIZER GUN, BREAKS INTO THE EATERY BUT FINDS NO BEARS...ONLY AN IRATE SKUNK.
RESPONDING TO THE GUNFIRE, NEIGHBORS CALL 911. THE POLICE RESPOND..
PHEW!!
GAG ME!
12-13-90
THE POLICE IN TURN CALL THE FIRE DEPARTMENT,,
© Phil WARPED SPEED, SCOTTIE! Frank
WHO REMOVE STERN GROVE AND TRANSPORT HIM TO S.F. GENERAL FOR OBSERVATION.
But I tell you.. I saw four bears in there!!
Tell it to the shrink!

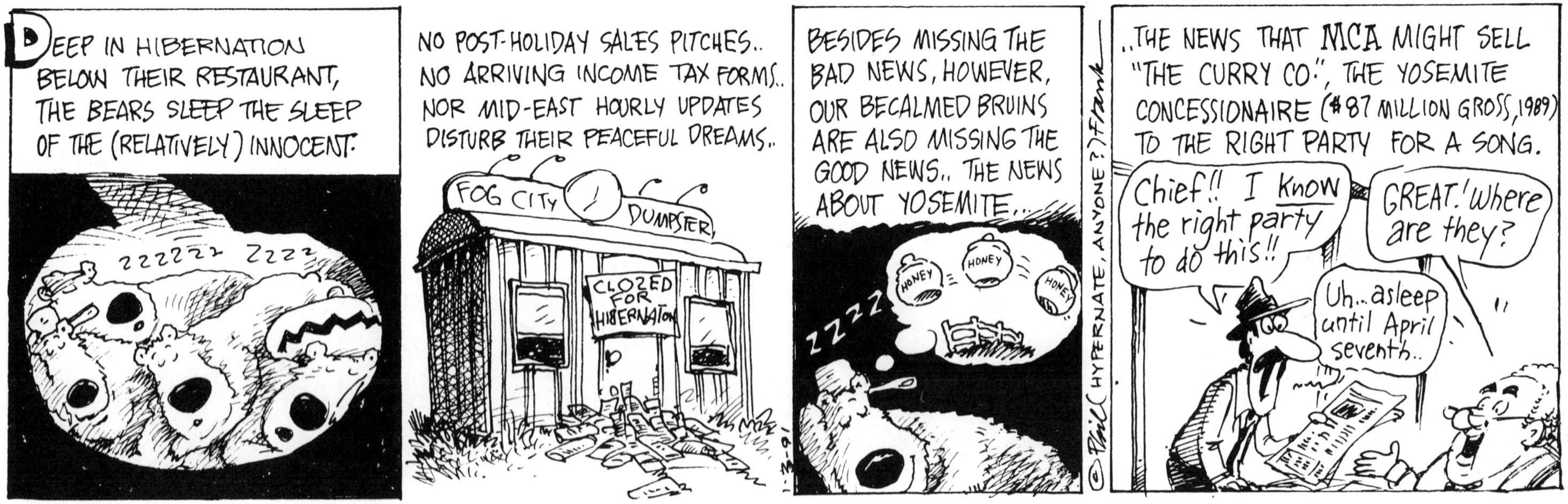
DEEP IN HIBERNATION BELOW THEIR RESTAURANT, THE BEARS SLEEP THE SLEEP OF THE (RELATIVELY) INNOCENT.
ZZZZZZ ZZZZ
NO POST-HOLIDAY SALES PITCHES.. NO ARRIVING INCOME TAX FORMS.. NOR MID-EAST HOURLY UPDATES DISTURB THEIR PEACEFUL DREAMS..
FOG CITY DUMPSTER
CLOZED FOR HIBERNATION
1-3-91
BESIDES MISSING THE BAD NEWS, HOWEVER, OUR BECALMED BRUINS ARE ALSO MISSING THE GOOD NEWS.. THE NEWS ABOUT YOSEMITE...
HONEY
HONEY
HONEY
ZZZZ
© Phil (HYPERNATE, ANYONE?) Frank
..THE NEWS THAT MCA MIGHT SELL "THE CURRY CO.", THE YOSEMITE CONCESSIONAIRE ($87 MILLION GROSS, 1989) TO THE RIGHT PARTY FOR A SONG.
Chief!! I know the right party to do this!!
GREAT! Where are they?
Uh.. asleep until April seventh..

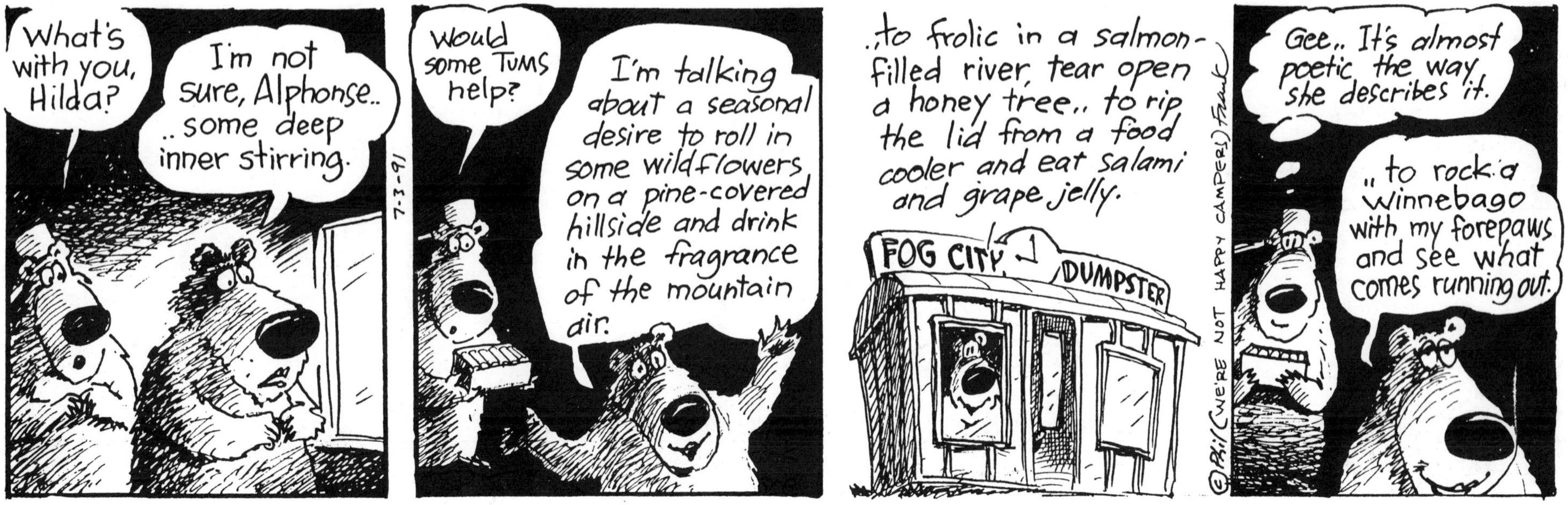
What's with you, Hilda?
I'm not sure, Alphonse.. ..some deep inner stirring.
7-3-91
Would some TUMS help?
I'm talking about a seasonal desire to roll in some wildflowers on a pine-covered hillside and drink in the fragrance of the mountain air.
..to frolic in a salmon-filled river, tear open a honey tree.. to rip the lid from a food cooler and eat salami and grape jelly.
FOG CITY DUMPSTER
© Phil (WE'RE NOT HAPPY CAMPERS) Frank
Gee.. It's almost poetic the way she describes it.
..to rock a Winnebago with my forepaws and see what comes running out.

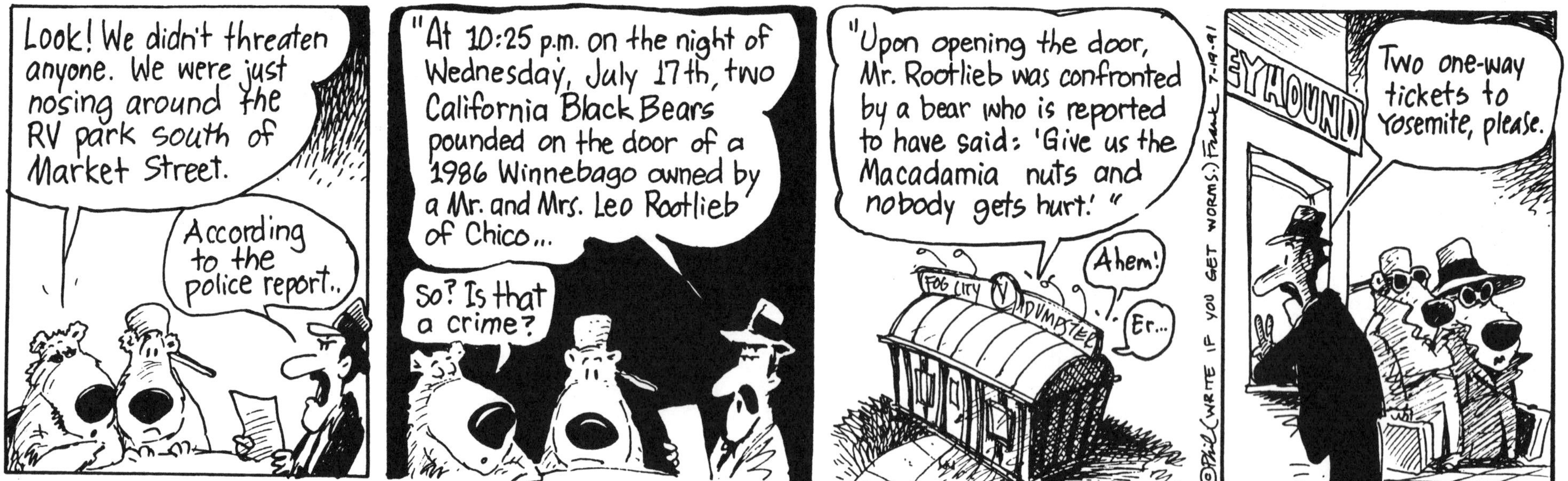
Look! We didn't threaten anyone. We were just nosing around the RV park south of Market Street.
According to the police report..
"At 10:25 p.m. on the night of Wednesday, July 17th, two California Black Bears pounded on the door of a 1986 Winnebago owned by a Mr. and Mrs. Leo Rootlieb of Chico...
So? Is that a crime?
"Upon opening the door, Mr. Rootlieb was confronted by a bear who is reported to have said: 'Give us the Macadamia nuts and nobody gets hurt.' "
FOG CITY
DUMPSTER
Ahem!
Er...
©Phil (WRITE IF YOU GET WORMS.) Frank 7-19-91
EYHOUND
Two one-way tickets to Yosemite, please.

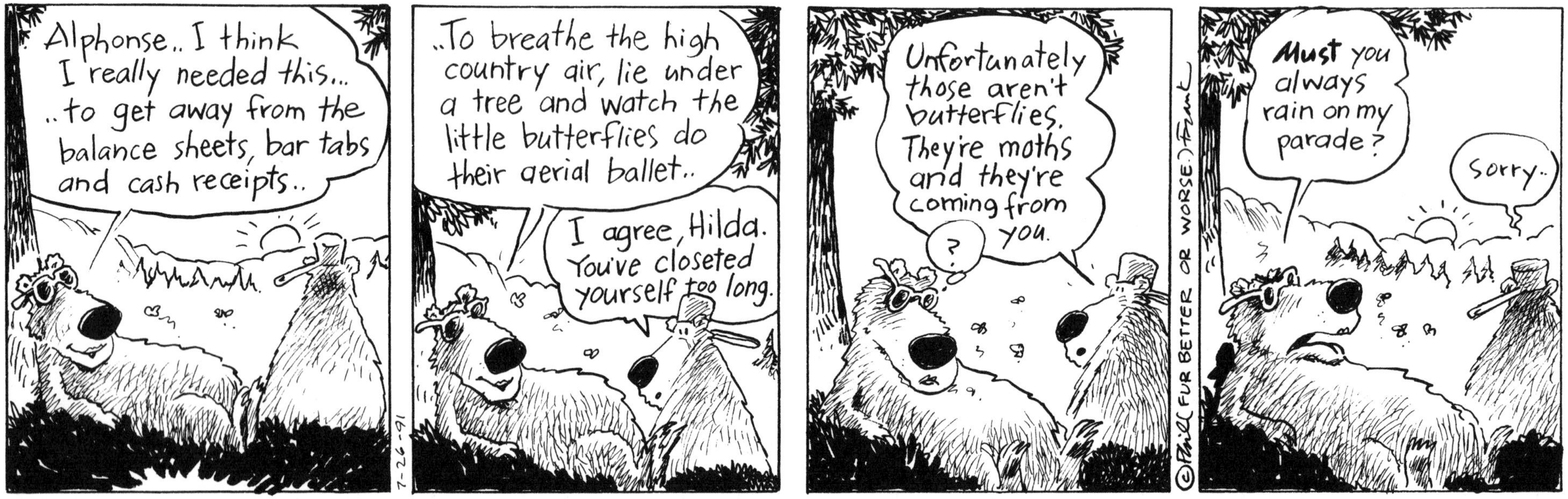
Alphonse.. I think I really needed this... ..to get away from the balance sheets, bar tabs and cash receipts..
7-26-91
..To breathe the high country air, lie under a tree and watch the little butterflies do their aerial ballet..
I agree, Hilda. You've closeted yourself too long.
Unfortunately those aren't butterflies. They're moths and they're coming from you.
?
©Phil (FUR BETTER OR WORSE.) Frank
Must you always rain on my parade?
Sorry..

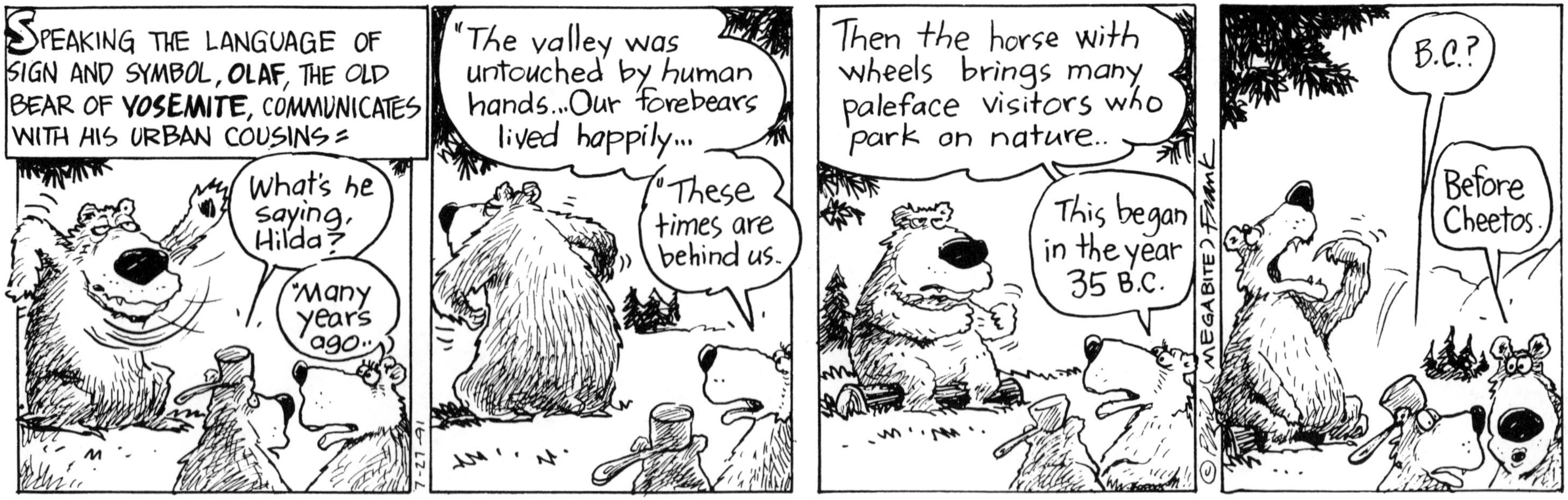
SPEAKING THE LANGUAGE OF SIGN AND SYMBOL, OLAF, THE OLD BEAR OF YOSEMITE, COMMUNICATES WITH HIS URBAN COUSINS=
What's he saying, Hilda?
"Many years ago..
7-27-91
"The valley was untouched by human hands...Our forebears lived happily...
"These times are behind us.
Then the horse with wheels brings many paleface visitors who park on nature..
This began in the year 35 B.C.
(MEGABITE)
B.C.?
Before Cheetos.

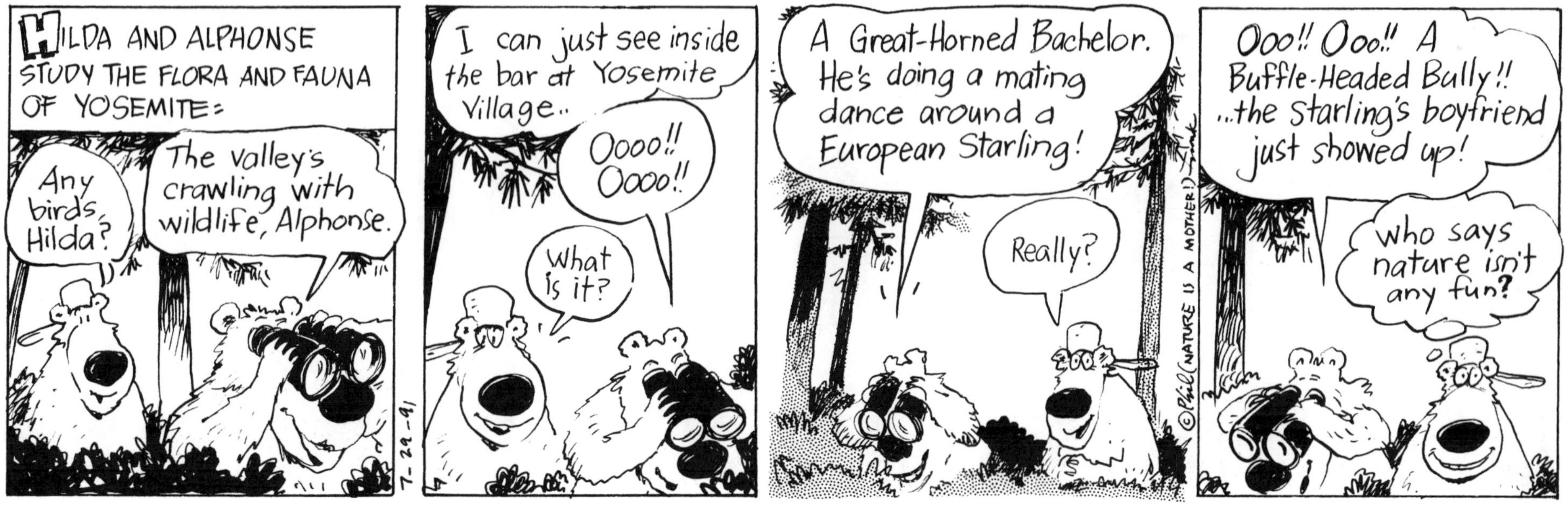
HILDA AND ALPHONSE STUDY THE FLORA AND FAUNA OF YOSEMITE=
Any birds, Hilda?
The valley's crawling with wildlife, Alphonse.
7-29-91
I can just see inside the bar at Yosemite Village..
Oooo!! Oooo!!
What is it?
A Great-Horned Bachelor. He's doing a mating dance around a European Starling!
Really?
(NATURE IS A MOTHER!)
Ooo!! Ooo!! A Buffle-Headed Bully!! ..the Starling's boyfriend just showed up!
Who says nature isn't any fun?

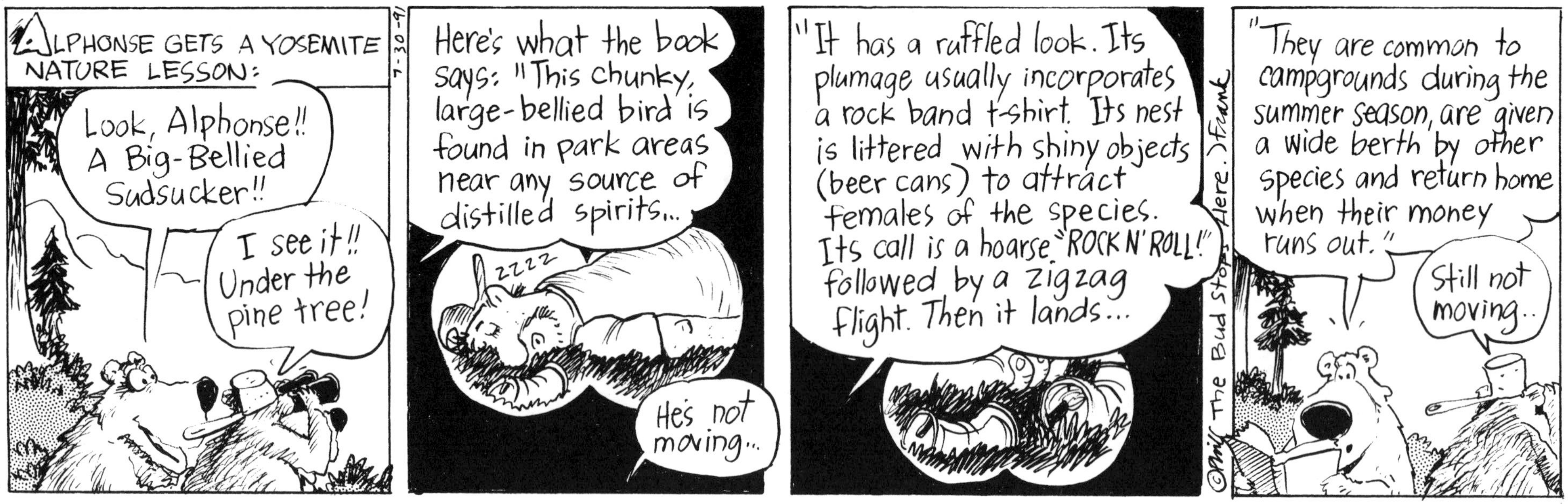
ALPHONSE GETS A YOSEMITE NATURE LESSON:
7-30-91
Look, Alphonse!! A Big-Bellied Sudsucker!!
I see it!! Under the pine tree!
Here's what the book says: "This chunky, large-bellied bird is found in park areas near any source of distilled spirits...
ZZZZ
He's not moving...
"It has a ruffled look. Its plumage usually incorporates a rock band t-shirt. Its nest is littered with shiny objects (beer cans) to attract females of the species. Its call is a hoarse "ROCK N' ROLL!" followed by a zigzag flight. Then it lands...
©Phil The Bud Stops Here. Frank
"They are common to campgrounds during the summer season, are given a wide berth by other species and return home when their money runs out."
Still not moving..

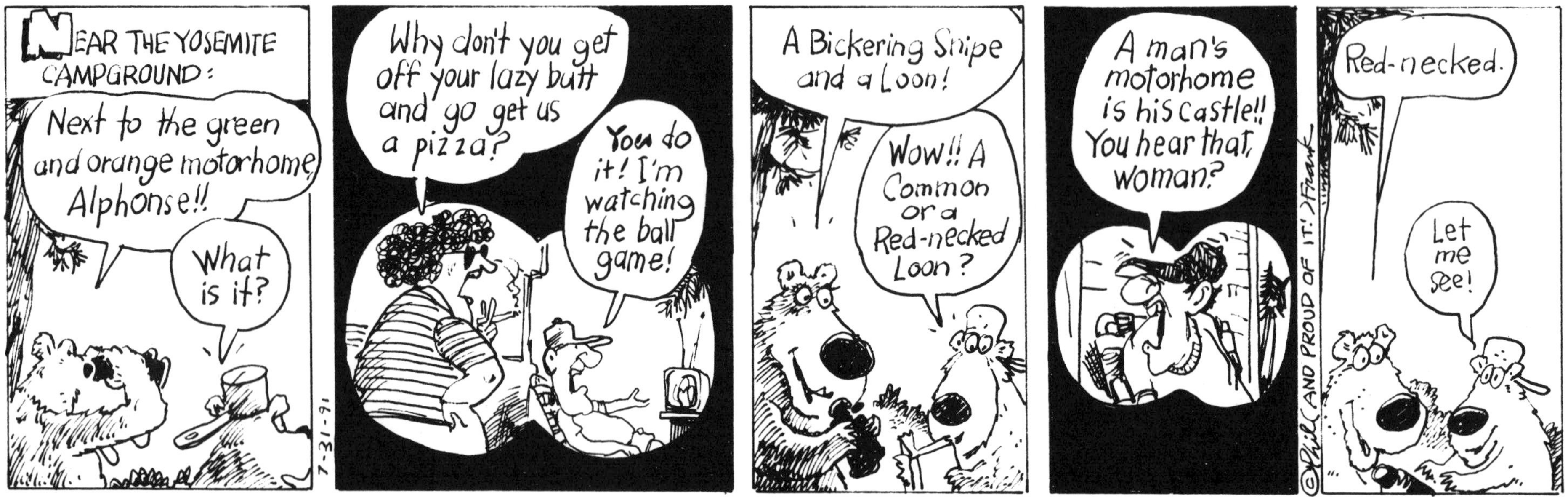
NEAR THE YOSEMITE CAMPGROUND:
Next to the green and orange motorhome, Alphonse!!
What is it?
7-31-91
Why don't you get off your lazy butt and go get us a pizza?
You do it! I'm watching the ball game!
A Bickering Snipe and a Loon!
Wow!! A Common or a Red-necked Loon?
A man's motorhome is his castle!! You hear that, woman?
©Phil (AND PROUD OF IT!) Frank
Red-necked.
Let me see!

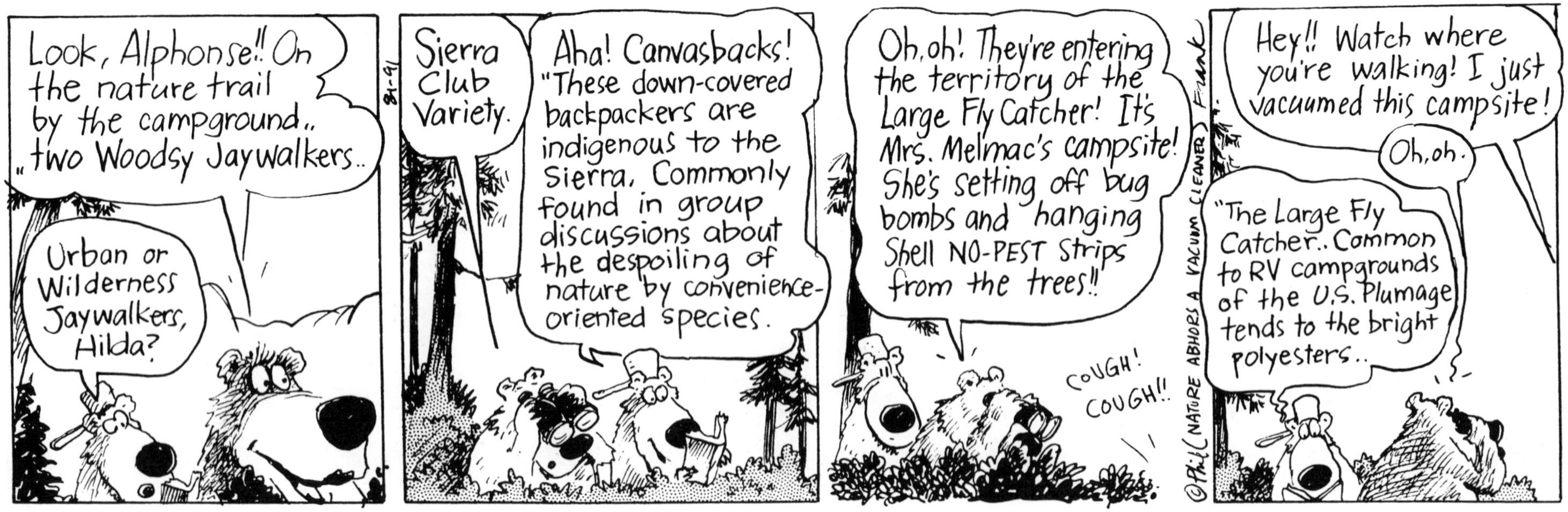
Look, Alphonse!! On the nature trail by the campground.. ..two Woodsy Jaywalkers..
Urban or Wilderness Jaywalkers, Hilda?
8-1-91
Sierra Club Variety.
Aha! Canvasbacks! "These down-covered backpackers are indigenous to the Sierra. Commonly found in group discussions about the despoiling of nature by convenience-oriented species.
Oh, oh! They're entering the territory of the Large Fly Catcher! It's Mrs. Melmac's campsite! She's setting off bug bombs and hanging Shell NO-PEST Strips from the trees!!
COUGH! COUGH!!
©Phil (NATURE ABHORS A VACUUM CLEANER) Frank
Hey!! Watch where you're walking! I just vacuumed this campsite!
Oh, oh.
"The Large Fly Catcher.. Common to RV campgrounds of the U.S. Plumage tends to the bright polyesters..

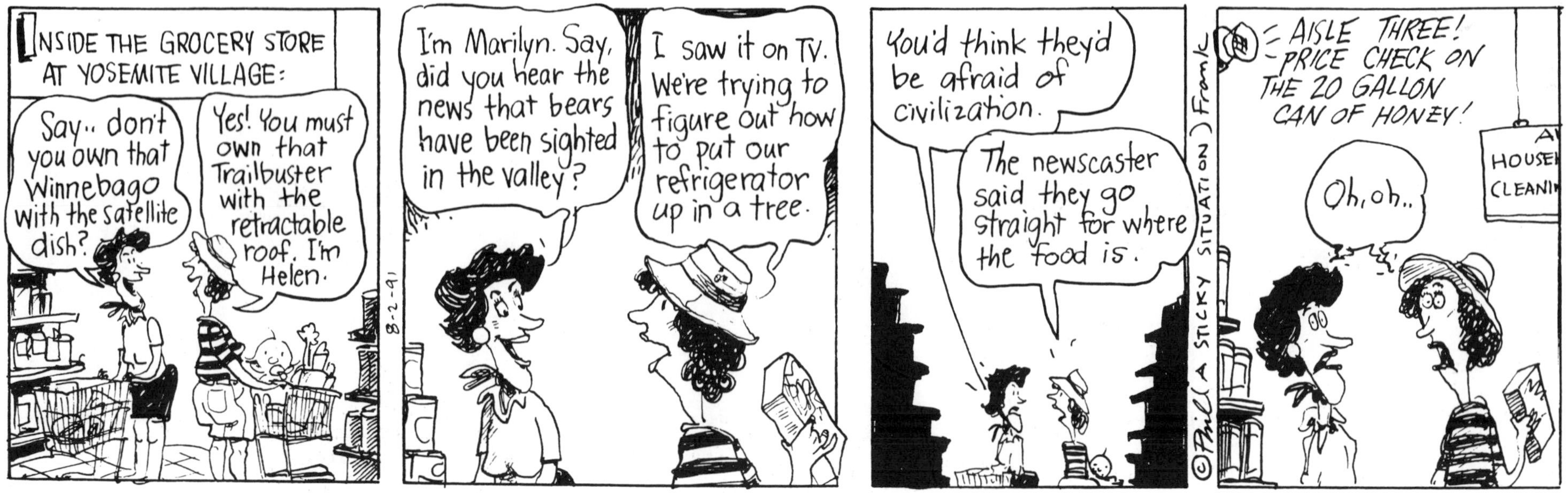
INSIDE THE GROCERY STORE AT YOSEMITE VILLAGE:
Say.. don't you own that Winnebago with the satellite dish?
Yes! You must own that Trailbuster with the retractable roof. I'm Helen.
8-2-91
I'm Marilyn. Say, did you hear the news that bears have been sighted in the valley?
I saw it on TV. We're trying to figure out how to put our refrigerator up in a tree.
You'd think they'd be afraid of civilization.
The newscaster said they go straight for where the food is.
©Phil (A STICKY SITUATION) Frank
AISLE THREE! PRICE CHECK ON THE 20 GALLON CAN OF HONEY!
Oh, oh..

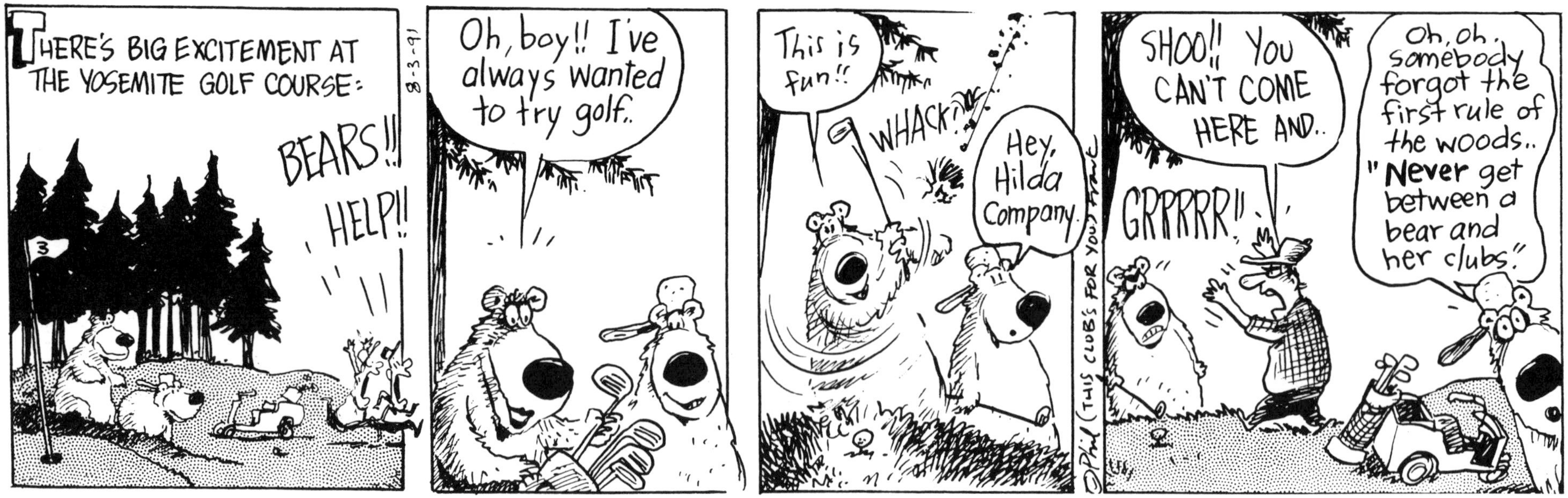
THERE'S BIG EXCITEMENT AT THE YOSEMITE GOLF COURSE:
BEARS!!
HELP!!
3
8-3-91
Oh, boy!! I've always wanted to try golf..
This is fun!!
WHACK!
Hey, Hilda Company.
(THIS CLUB'S FOR YOU) Frank
©Phil
SHOO!! YOU CAN'T COME HERE AND..
GRRRRR!!
Oh, oh. somebody forgot the first rule of the woods.. "**Never** get between a bear and her clubs."

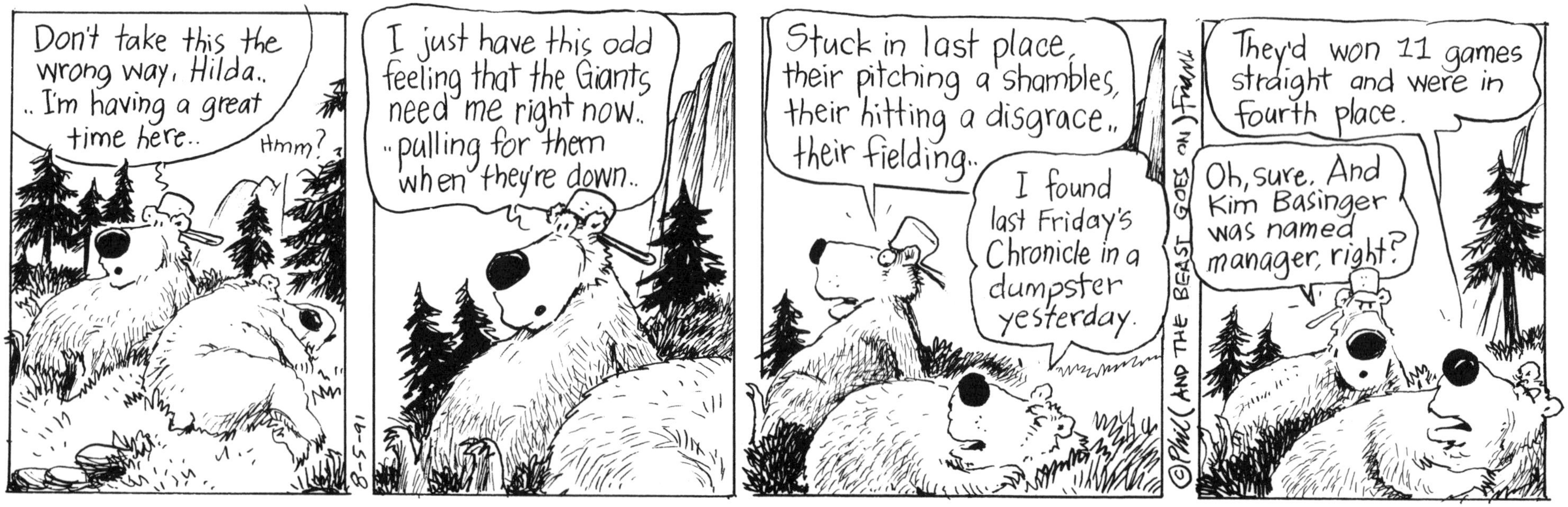
Don't take this the wrong way, Hilda.. .. I'm having a great time here..
Hmm?
8-5-91
I just have this odd feeling that the Giants need me right now.. ..pulling for them when they're down..
Stuck in last place, their pitching a shambles, their hitting a disgrace.. their fielding..
I found last Friday's Chronicle in a dumpster yesterday.
©Phil (AND THE BEAST GOES ON) Frank
They'd won 11 games straight and were in fourth place.
Oh, sure. And Kim Basinger was named manager, right?

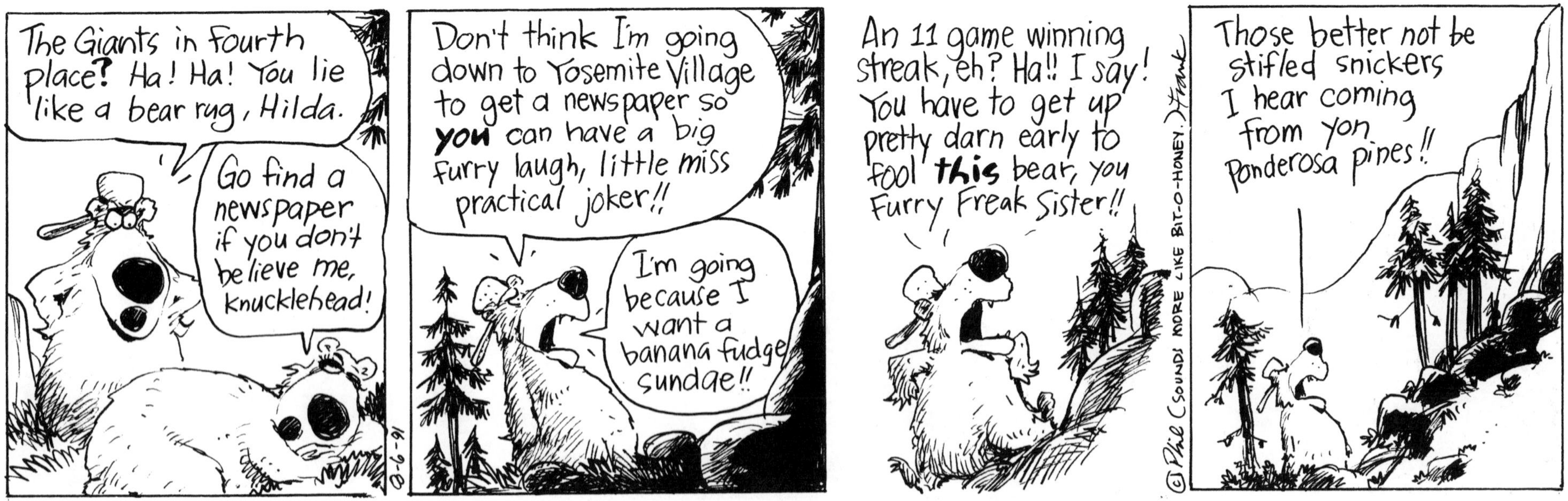
The Giants in Fourth place? Ha! Ha! You lie like a bear rug, Hilda.
Go find a newspaper if you don't believe me, knucklehead!
8-6-91
Don't think I'm going down to Yosemite Village to get a newspaper so **you** can have a big furry laugh, little miss practical joker!!
I'm going because I want a banana fudge sundae!!
An 11 game winning streak, eh? Ha!! I say! You have to get up pretty darn early to fool **this** bear, you Furry Freak Sister!!
© Phil (SOUNDS MORE LIKE BIT-O-HONEY) Frank
Those better not be stifled snickers I hear coming from yon Ponderosa pines!!

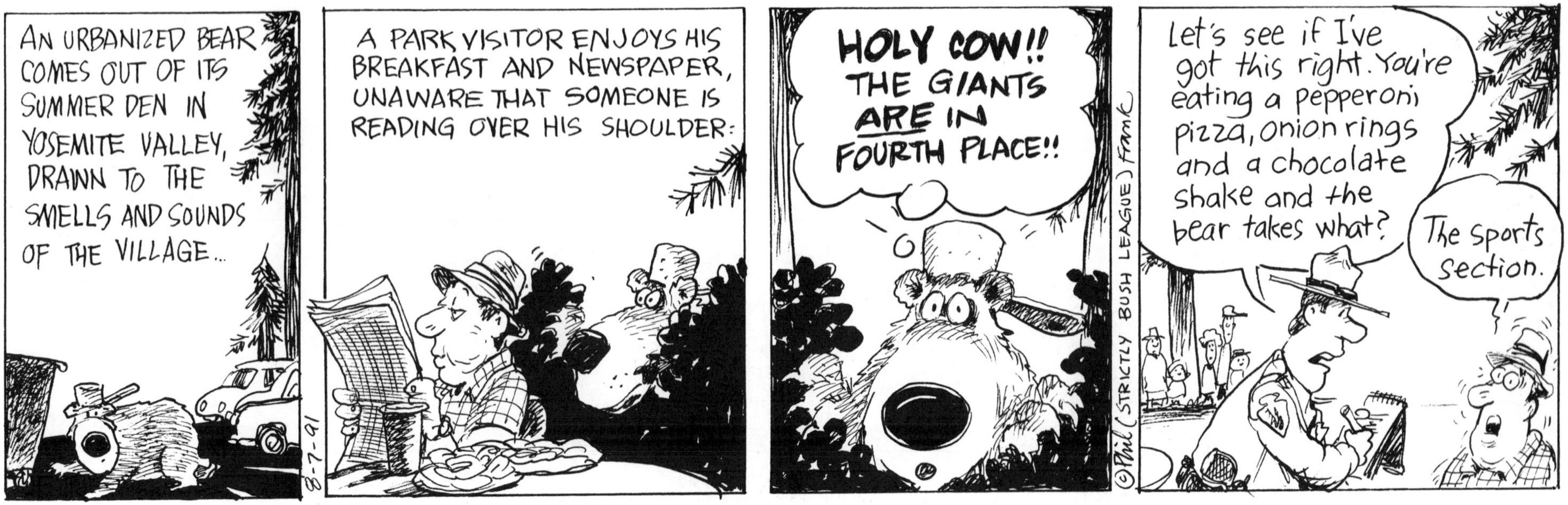
AN URBANIZED BEAR COMES OUT OF ITS SUMMER DEN IN YOSEMITE VALLEY, DRAWN TO THE SMELLS AND SOUNDS OF THE VILLAGE...
8-7-91
A PARK VISITOR ENJOYS HIS BREAKFAST AND NEWSPAPER, UNAWARE THAT SOMEONE IS READING OVER HIS SHOULDER:
HOLY COW!! THE GIANTS ARE IN FOURTH PLACE!!
© Phil (STRICTLY BUSH LEAGUE) Frank
Let's see if I've got this right. You're eating a pepperoni pizza, onion rings and a chocolate shake and the bear takes what?
The sports section.

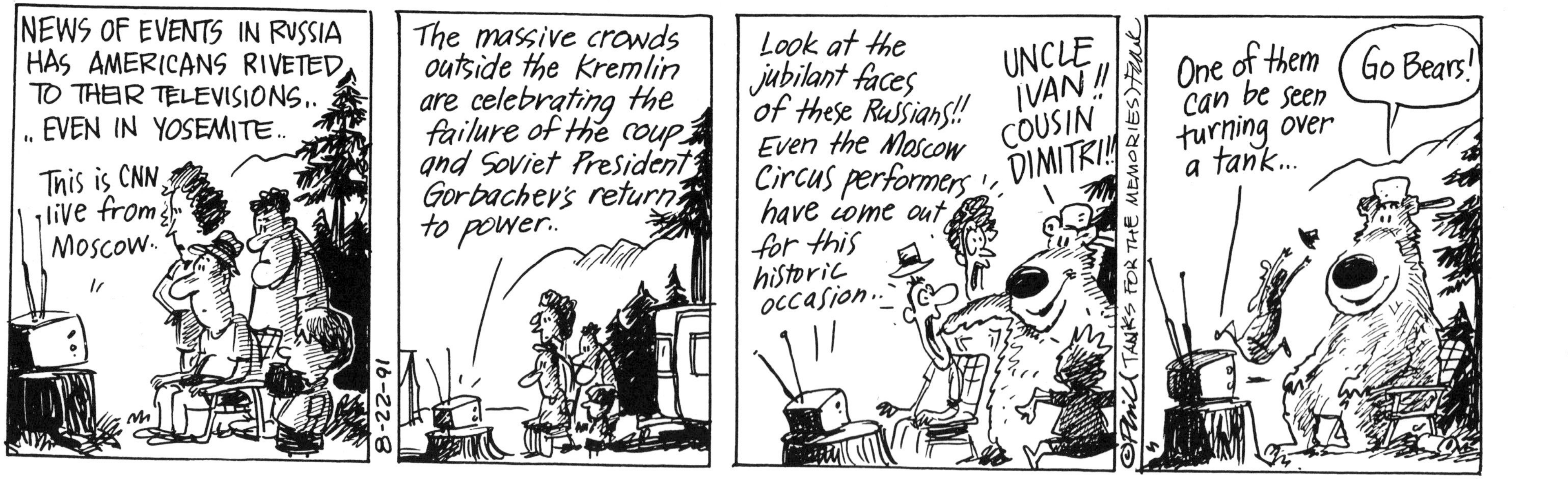
NEWS OF EVENTS IN RUSSIA HAS AMERICANS RIVETED TO THEIR TELEVISIONS.. .. EVEN IN YOSEMITE..
This is CNN live from Moscow..
8-22-91
The massive crowds outside the Kremlin are celebrating the failure of the coup and Soviet President Gorbachev's return to power..
Look at the jubilant faces of these Russians!! Even the Moscow Circus performers have come out for this historic occasion..
UNCLE IVAN!! COUSIN DIMITRI!!
©Phil (TANKS FOR THE MEMORIES) Frank
One of them can be seen turning over a tank...
Go Bears!

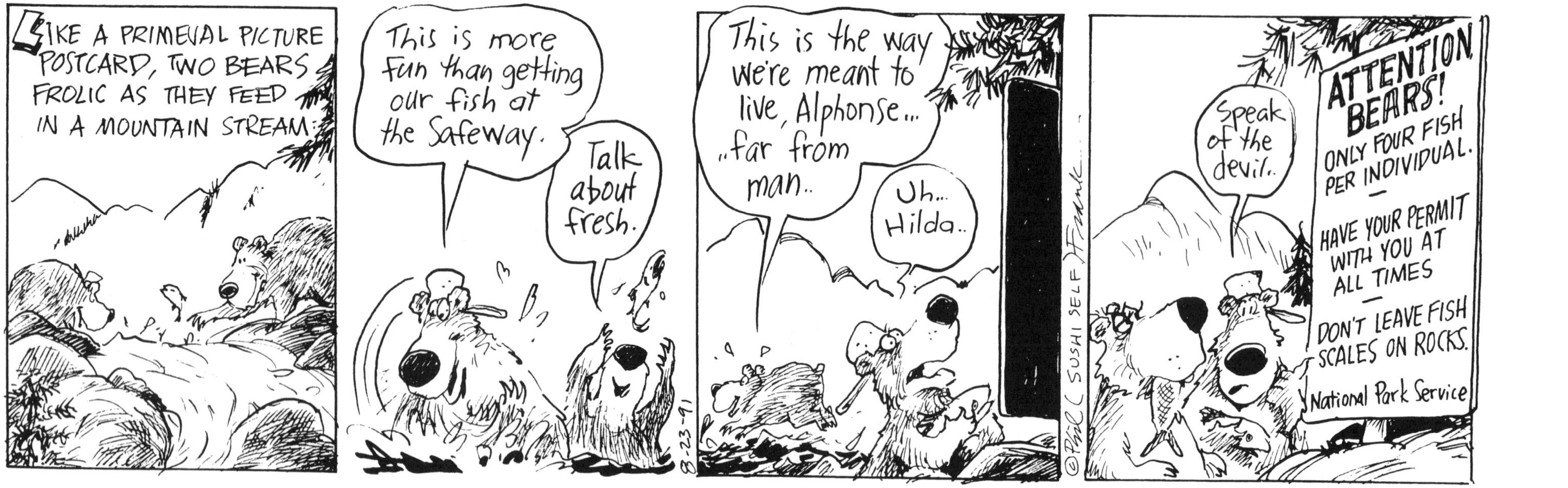
LIKE A PRIMEVAL PICTURE POSTCARD, TWO BEARS FROLIC AS THEY FEED IN A MOUNTAIN STREAM..
This is more fun than getting our fish at the Safeway.
Talk about fresh.
8-23-91
This is the way we're meant to live, Alphonse... ..far from man..
Uh... Hilda..
©Phil (SUSHI SELF) Frank
Speak of the devil..
ATTENTION BEARS!
ONLY FOUR FISH PER INDIVIDUAL.
HAVE YOUR PERMIT WITH YOU AT ALL TIMES
DON'T LEAVE FISH SCALES ON ROCKS.
National Park Service

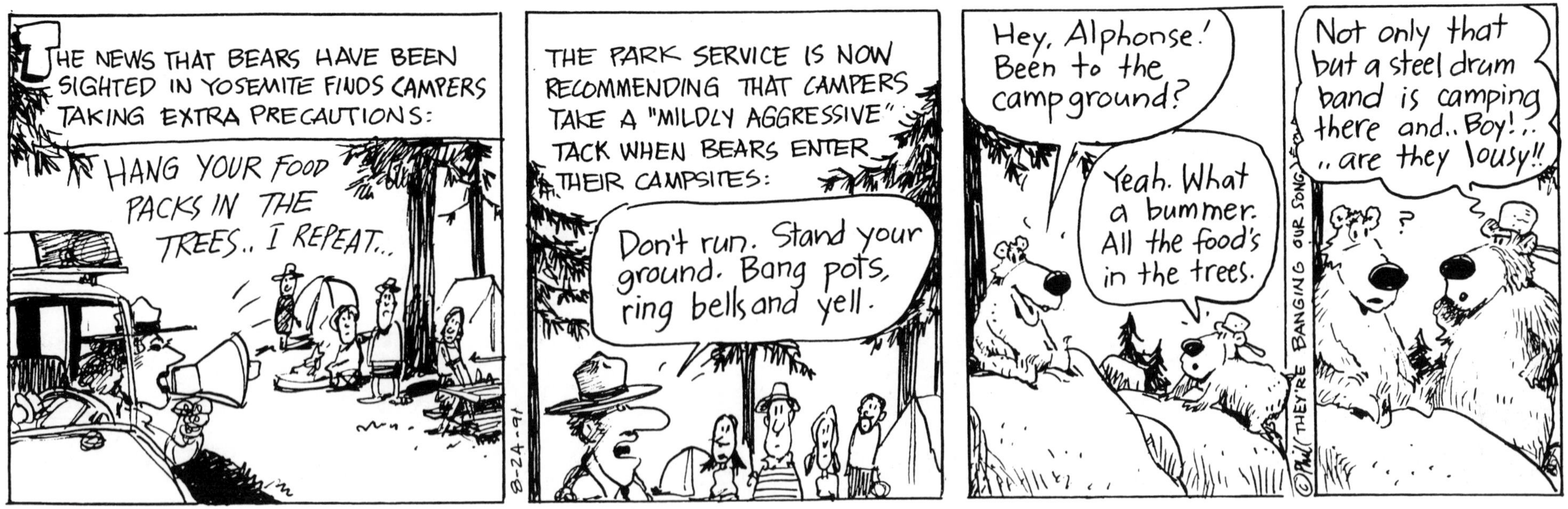
THE NEWS THAT BEARS HAVE BEEN SIGHTED IN YOSEMITE FINDS CAMPERS TAKING EXTRA PRECAUTIONS:
HANG YOUR FOOD PACKS IN THE TREES.. I REPEAT...
8-24-91
THE PARK SERVICE IS NOW RECOMMENDING THAT CAMPERS TAKE A "MILDLY AGGRESSIVE" TACK WHEN BEARS ENTER THEIR CAMPSITES:
Don't run. Stand your ground. Bang pots, ring bells and yell.
Hey, Alphonse! Been to the campground?
Yeah. What a bummer. All the food's in the trees.
©Phil THEY'RE BANGING OUR SONG Frank
Not only that but a steel drum band is camping there and.. Boy!.. ..are they lousy!!
?

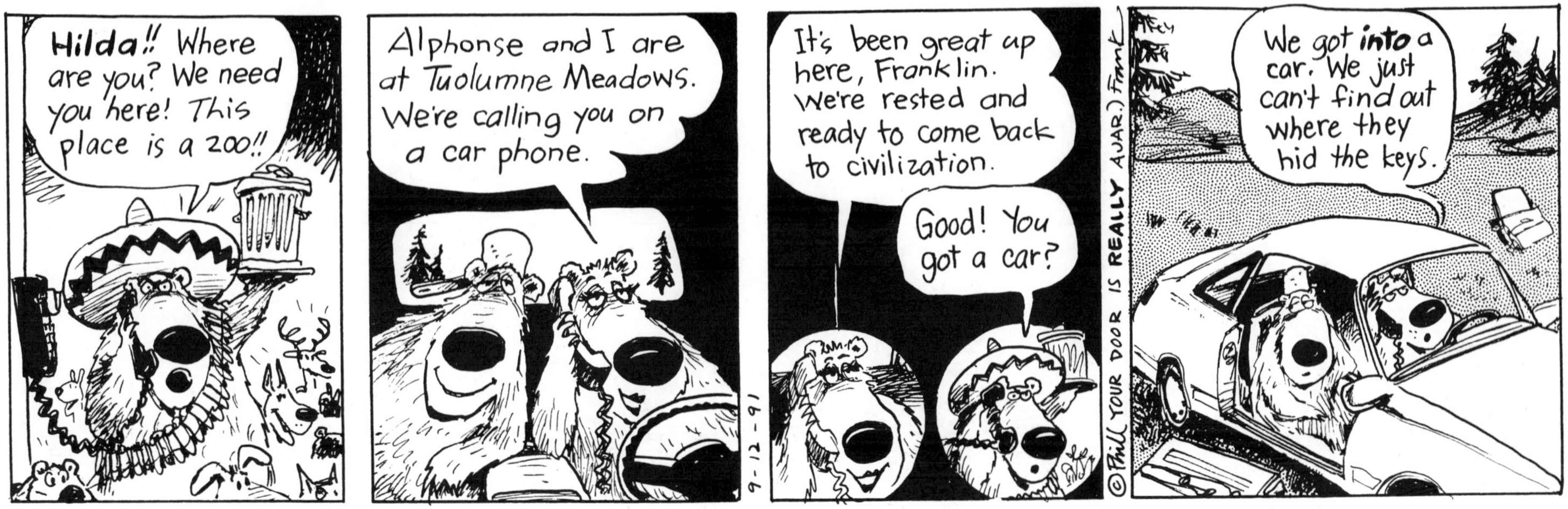
Hilda!! Where are you? We need you here! This place is a zoo!!
Alphonse and I are at Tuolumne Meadows. We're calling you on a car phone.
9-12-91
It's been great up here, Franklin. We're rested and ready to come back to civilization.
Good! You got a car?
©Phil YOUR DOOR IS REALLY AJAR.) Frank
We got into a car. We just can't find out where they hid the keys.

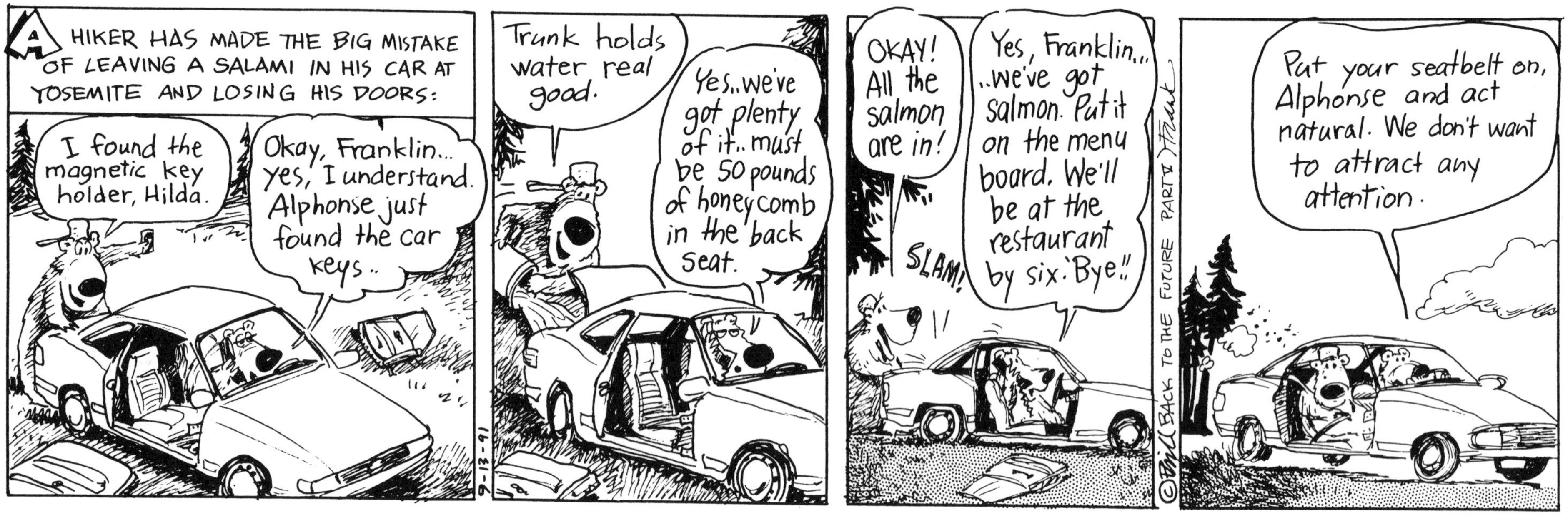
A HIKER HAS MADE THE BIG MISTAKE OF LEAVING A SALAMI IN HIS CAR AT YOSEMITE AND LOSING HIS DOORS:
I found the magnetic key holder, Hilda.
Okay, Franklin... yes, I understand. Alphonse just found the car keys..
Trunk holds water real good.
Yes.. we've got plenty of it.. must be 50 pounds of honeycomb in the back seat.
9-13-91
OKAY! All the salmon are in!
SLAM!
Yes, Franklin... ..we've got salmon. Put it on the menu board. We'll be at the restaurant by six. 'Bye.'
© Phil Frank (BACK TO THE FUTURE PART II)
Put your seatbelt on, Alphonse and act natural. We don't want to attract any attention.

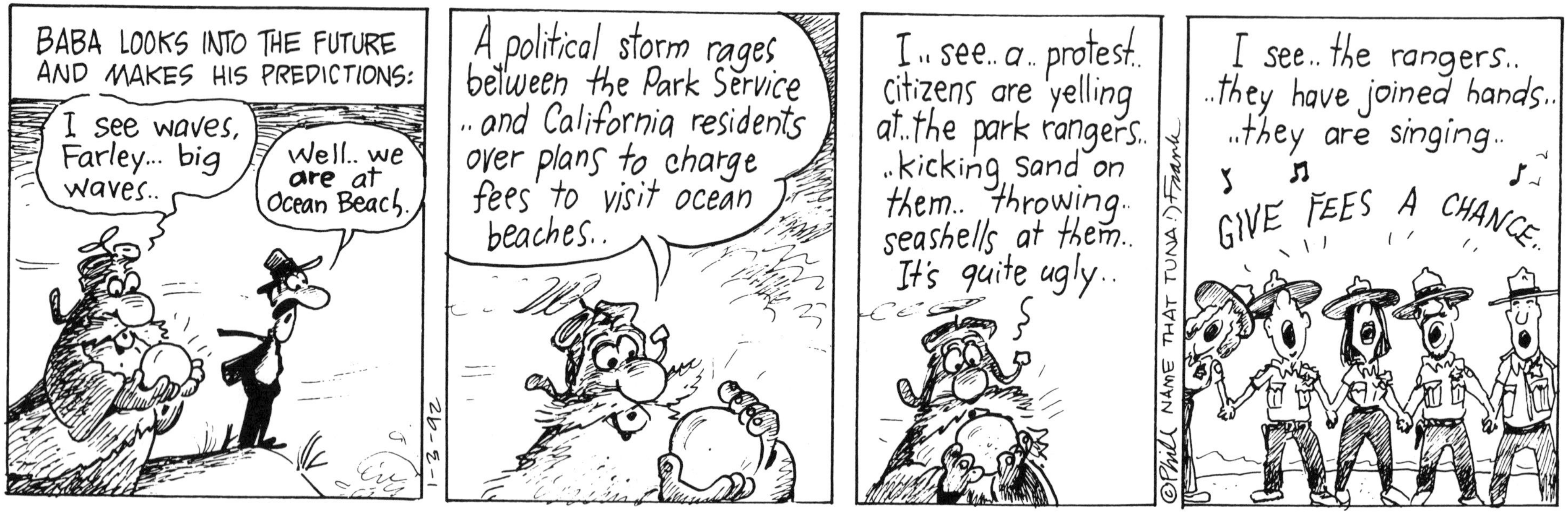
BABA LOOKS INTO THE FUTURE AND MAKES HIS PREDICTIONS:
I see waves, Farley... big waves..
Well.. we are at Ocean Beach.
1-3-92
A political storm rages between the Park Service ..and California residents over plans to charge fees to visit ocean beaches..
I.. see.. a.. protest.. citizens are yelling at.. the park rangers.. ..kicking sand on them.. throwing.. seashells at them.. It's quite ugly..
© Phil Frank (NAME THAT TUNA!)
I see.. the rangers.. ..they have joined hands.. ..they are singing..
GIVE FEES A CHANCE..

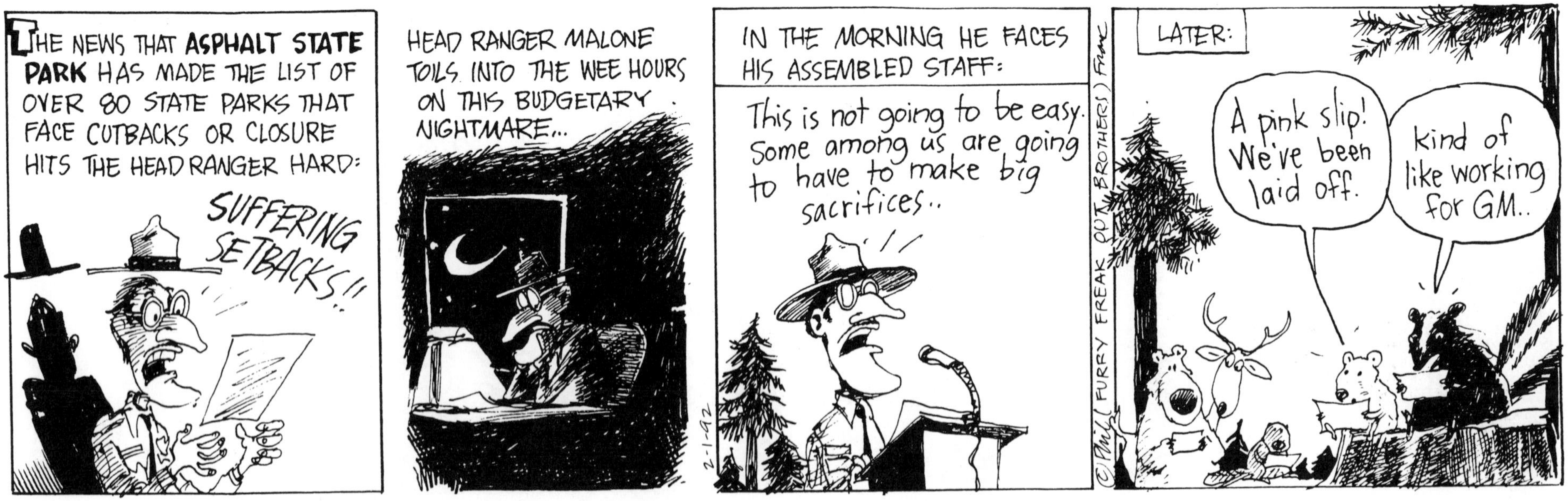
THE NEWS THAT ASPHALT STATE PARK HAS MADE THE LIST OF OVER 80 STATE PARKS THAT FACE CUTBACKS OR CLOSURE HITS THE HEAD RANGER HARD:
SUFFERING SETBACKS!!
HEAD RANGER MALONE TOILS INTO THE WEE HOURS ON THIS BUDGETARY NIGHTMARE...
2-1-92
IN THE MORNING HE FACES HIS ASSEMBLED STAFF:
This is not going to be easy. Some among us are going to have to make big sacrifices..
(FURRY FREAK OUT BROTHERS)
LATER:
A pink slip! We've been laid off.
kind of like working for GM..

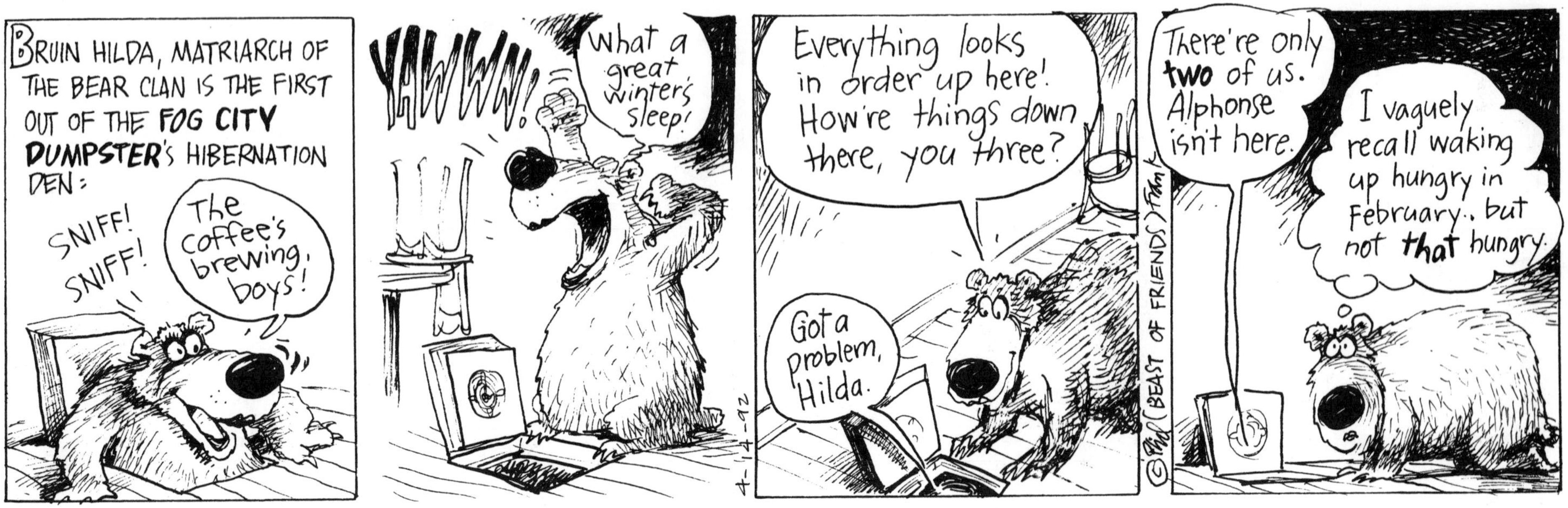
BRUIN HILDA, MATRIARCH OF THE BEAR CLAN IS THE FIRST OUT OF THE FOG CITY DUMPSTER'S HIBERNATION DEN:
SNIFF! SNIFF!
The coffee's brewing, boys!
YAWWN!
What a great winter's sleep!
4-14-92
Everything looks in order up here! How're things down there, you three?
Got a problem, Hilda.
(BEAST OF FRIENDS)
There're only two of us. Alphonse isn't here.
I vaguely recall waking up hungry in February.. but not that hungry.

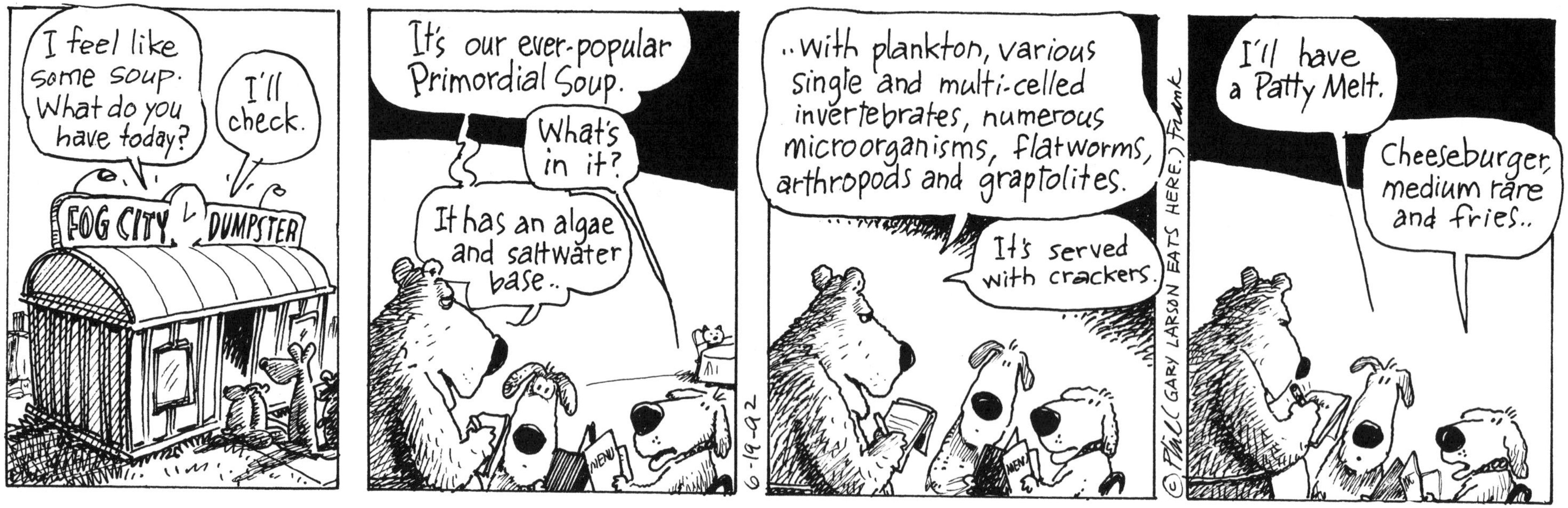

I feel like some soup. What do you have today?
I'll check.
FOG CITY DUMPSTER
It's our ever-popular Primordial Soup.
What's in it?
It has an algae and saltwater base..
MENU
6-19-92
..with plankton, various single and multi-celled invertebrates, numerous microorganisms, flatworms, arthropods and graptolites.
It's served with crackers.
MENU
© Phil (GARY LARSON EATS HERE.) Frank
I'll have a Patty Melt.
Cheeseburger, medium rare and fries..

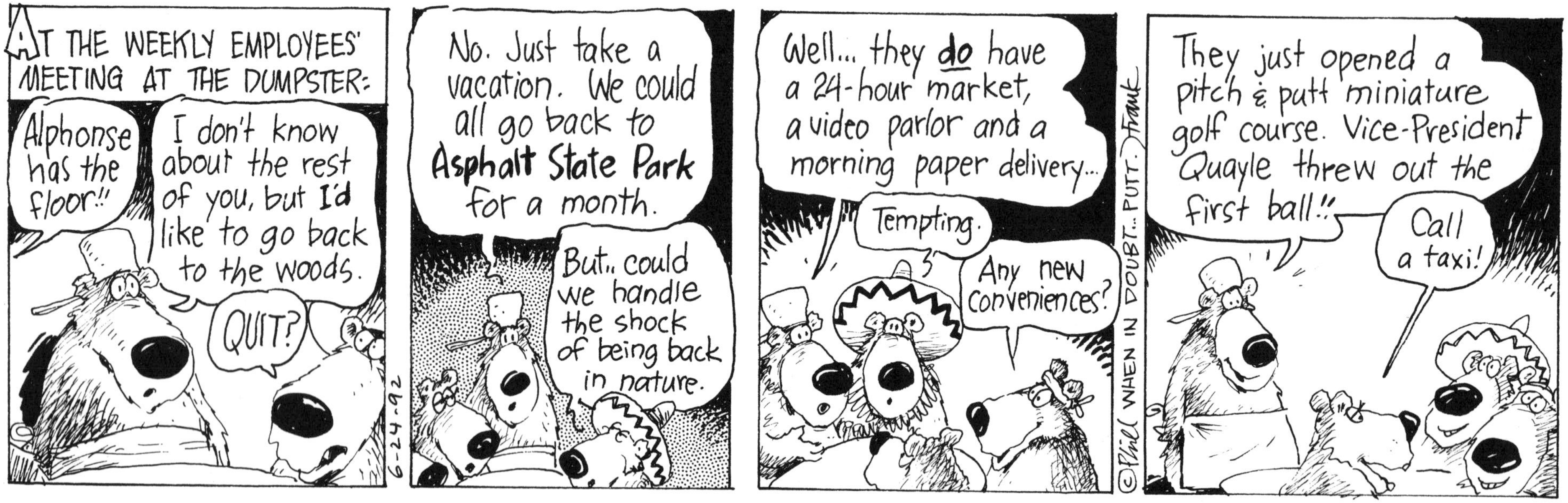

AT THE WEEKLY EMPLOYEES' MEETING AT THE DUMPSTER:
Alphonse has the floor!!
I don't know about the rest of you, but I'd like to go back to the woods.
QUIT?
6-24-92
No. Just take a vacation. We could all go back to Asphalt State Park for a month.
But.. could we handle the shock of being back in nature.
Well... they do have a 24-hour market, a video parlor and a morning paper delivery...
Tempting.
Any new conveniences?
© Phil WHEN IN DOUBT... PUTT. Frank
They just opened a pitch & putt miniature golf course. Vice-President Quayle threw out the first ball!!
Call a taxi!

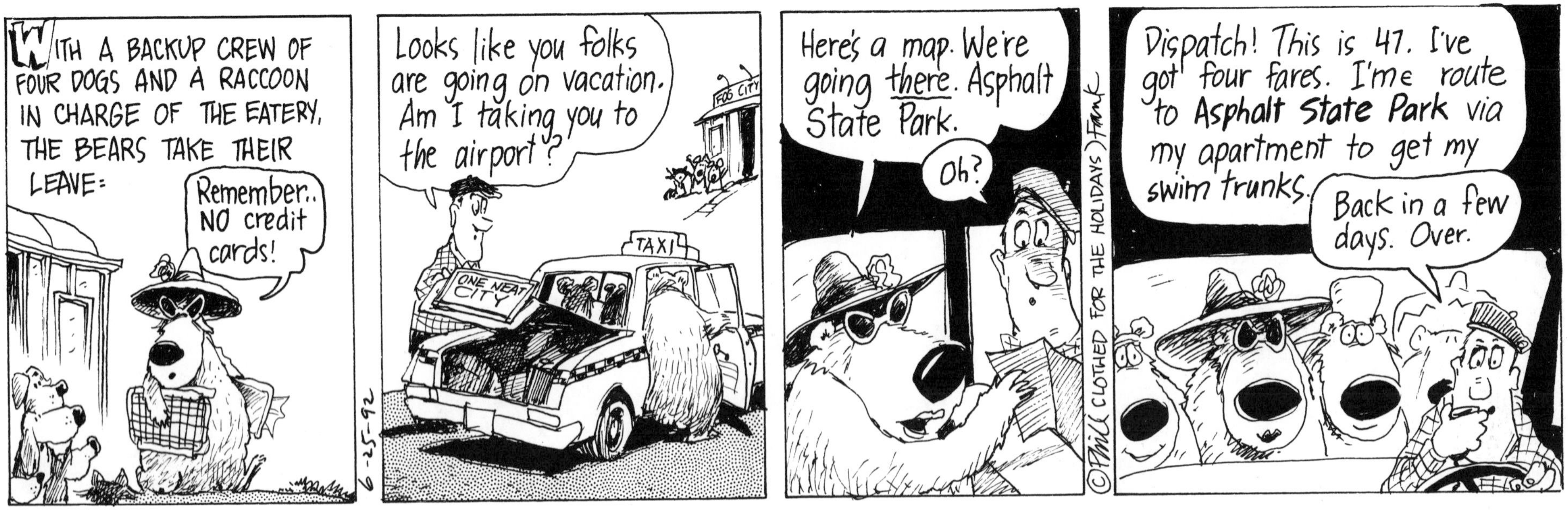
WITH A BACKUP CREW OF FOUR DOGS AND A RACCOON IN CHARGE OF THE EATERY, THE BEARS TAKE THEIR LEAVE:
Remember.. NO credit cards!
6-25-92
Looks like you folks are going on vacation. Am I taking you to the airport?
FOG CITY
TAXI
ONE NEAT CITY
Here's a map. We're going there. Asphalt State Park.
Oh?
©Phil CLOTHED FOR THE HOLIDAYS) Frank
Dispatch! This is 47. I've got four fares. I'mɛ route to **Asphalt State Park** via my apartment to get my swim trunks.
Back in a few days. Over.

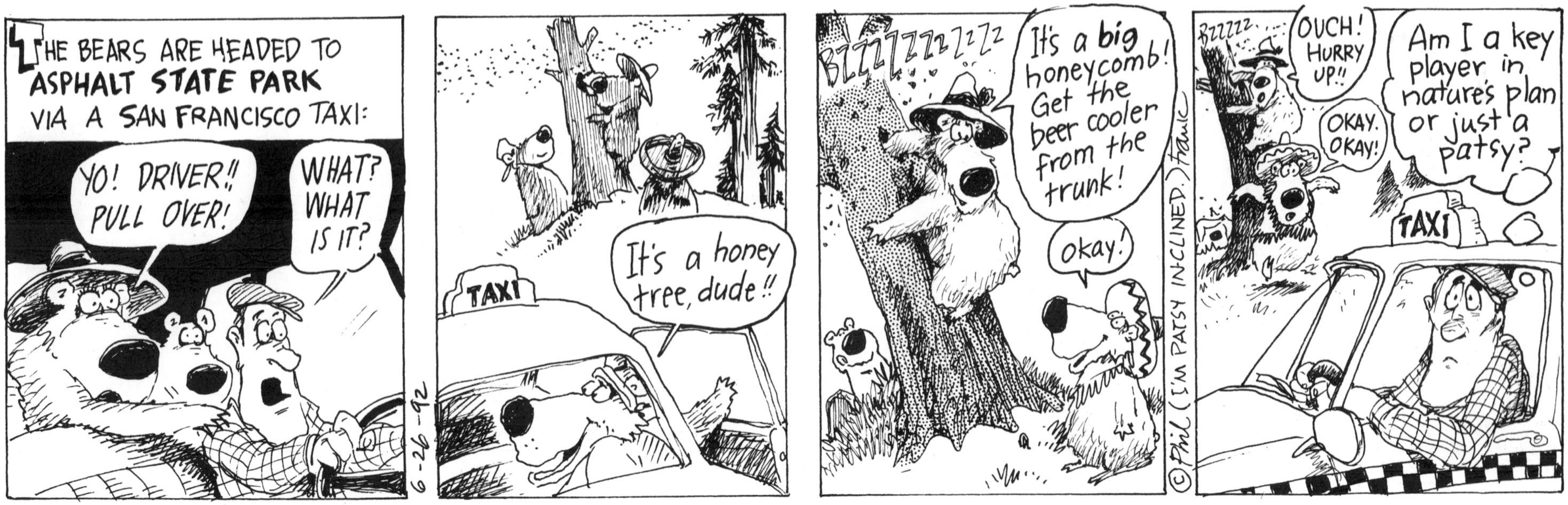
THE BEARS ARE HEADED TO **ASPHALT STATE PARK** VIA A SAN FRANCISCO TAXI:
YO! DRIVER!! PULL OVER!
WHAT? WHAT IS IT?
6-26-92
TAXI
It's a honey tree, dude!!
BZZZZZZZZZZ
It's a **big** honeycomb! Get the beer cooler from the trunk!
Okay!
©Phil (I'M PATSY INCLINED.) Frank
BZZZZZ
OUCH! HURRY UP!!
OKAY. OKAY!
Am I a key player in nature's plan or just a patsy?
TAXI

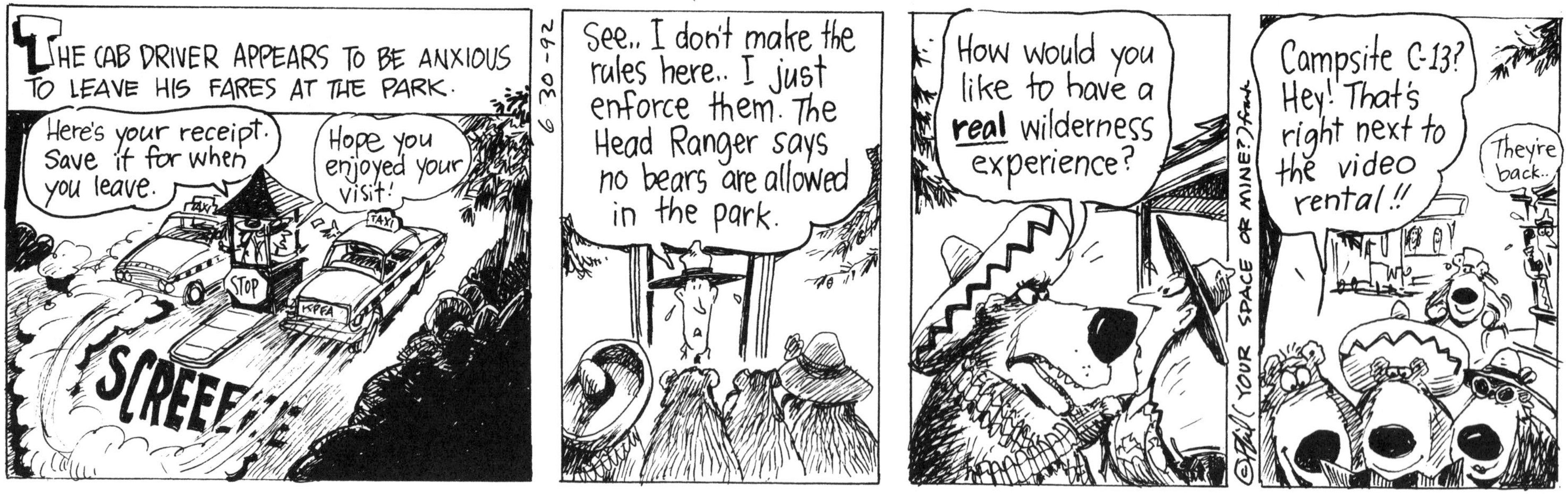
THE CAB DRIVER APPEARS TO BE ANXIOUS TO LEAVE HIS FARES AT THE PARK.
Here's your receipt. Save it for when you leave.
Hope you enjoyed your visit!
TAXI
STOP
SCREEE..
6-30-92
See.. I don't make the rules here.. I just enforce them. The Head Ranger says no bears are allowed in the park.
How would you like to have a **real** wilderness experience?
©Phil (YOUR SPACE OR MINE?) Frank
Campsite C-13? Hey! That's right next to the video rental!!
They're back..

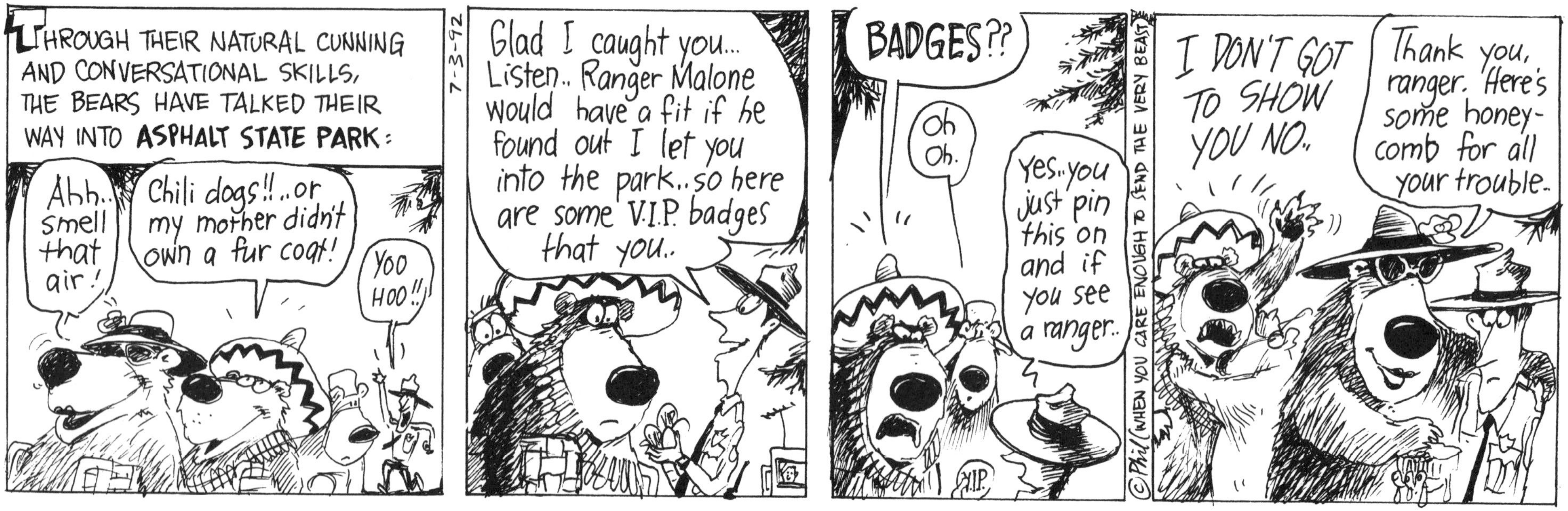
THROUGH THEIR NATURAL CUNNING AND CONVERSATIONAL SKILLS, THE BEARS HAVE TALKED THEIR WAY INTO **ASPHALT STATE PARK**:
Ahh.. smell that air!
Chili dogs!! ..or my mother didn't own a fur coat!
YOO HOO!!
7-3-92
Glad I caught you... Listen.. Ranger Malone would have a fit if he found out I let you into the park.. so here are some V.I.P. badges that you..
BADGES??
Oh Oh.
Yes.. you just pin this on and if you see a ranger..
V.I.P.
©Phil (WHEN YOU CARE ENOUGH TO SEND THE VERY BEAST
I DON'T GOT TO SHOW YOU NO..
Thank you, ranger. Here's some honey-comb for all your trouble.

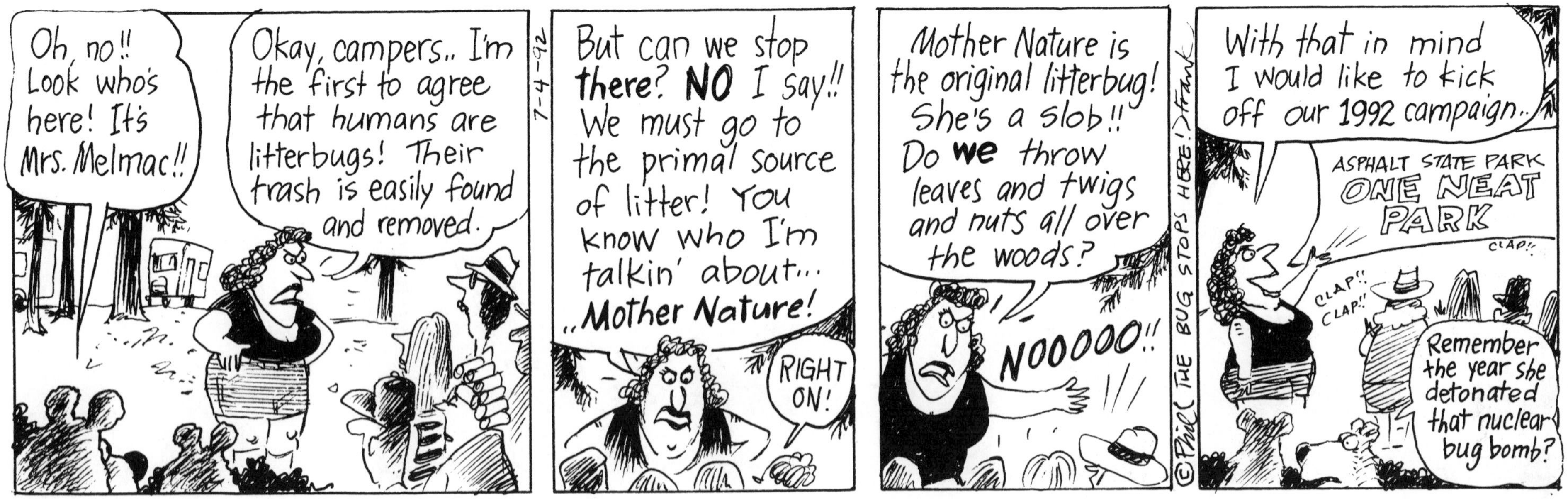
Oh, no!! Look who's here! It's Mrs. Melmac!!
Okay, campers.. I'm the first to agree that humans are litterbugs! Their trash is easily found and removed.
7-4-92
But can we stop there? NO I say!! We must go to the primal source of litter! You know who I'm talkin' about... ..Mother Nature!
RIGHT ON!
Mother Nature is the original litterbug! She's a slob!! Do we throw leaves and twigs and nuts all over the woods?
NOOOOO!!
©Phil (THE BUG STOPS HERE!) Frank
With that in mind I would like to kick off our 1992 campaign..
ASPHALT STATE PARK
ONE NEAT PARK
CLAP!!
CLAP!! CLAP!!
Remember the year she detonated that nuclear bug bomb?

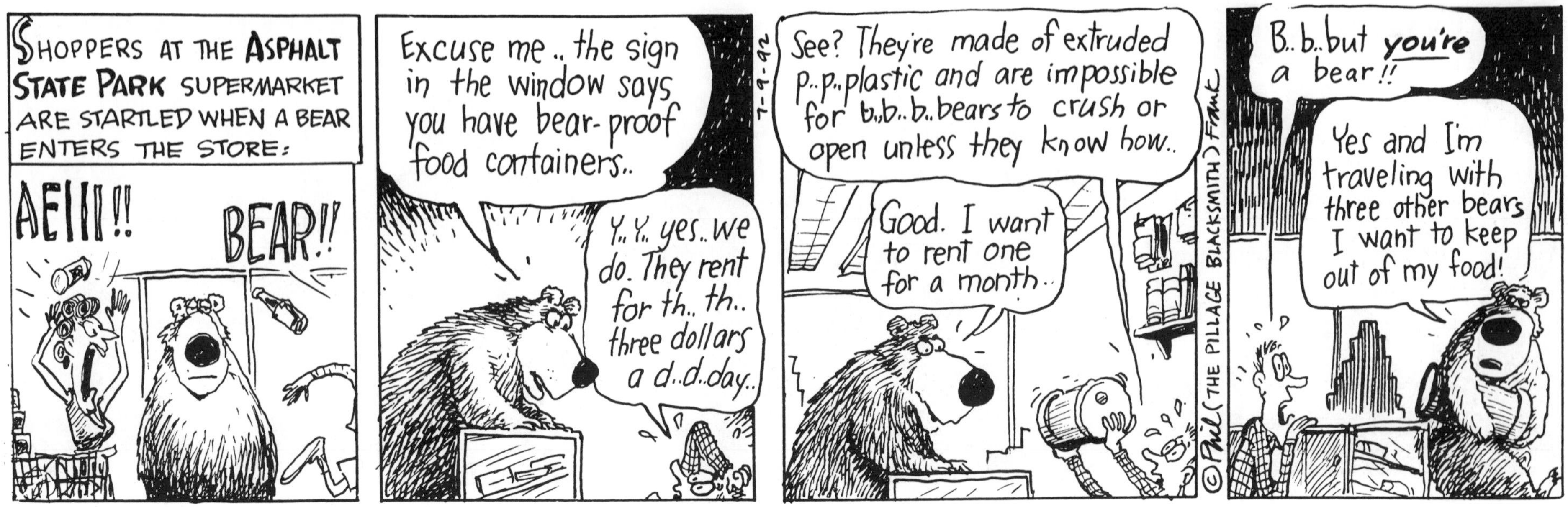
SHOPPERS AT THE ASPHALT STATE PARK SUPERMARKET ARE STARTLED WHEN A BEAR ENTERS THE STORE:
AEIII!!
BEAR!!
Excuse me.. the sign in the window says you have bear-proof food containers..
Y..Y.. yes.. we do. They rent for th.. th.. three dollars a d..d..day..
See? They're made of extruded p..p..plastic and are impossible for b..b..b..bears to crush or open unless they know how..
Good. I want to rent one for a month..
©Phil (THE PILLAGE BLACKSMITH) Frank
B..b..but you're a bear!!
Yes and I'm traveling with three other bears I want to keep out of my food!

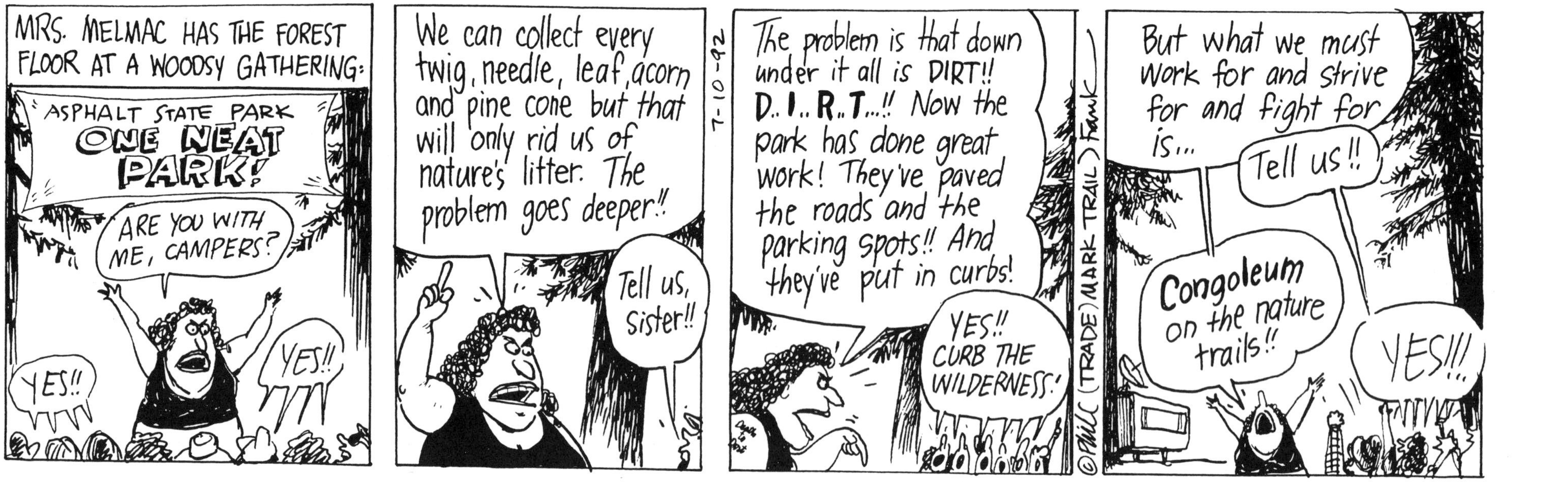
MRS. MELMAC HAS THE FOREST FLOOR AT A WOODSY GATHERING:
ASPHALT STATE PARK
ONE NEAT PARK!
ARE YOU WITH ME, CAMPERS?
YES!!
YES!!
We can collect every twig, needle, leaf, acorn and pine cone but that will only rid us of nature's litter. The problem goes deeper!!
Tell us, sister!!
7-10-92
The problem is that down under it all is DIRT!! D..I..R..T...!! Now the park has done great work! They've paved the roads and the parking spots!! And they've put in curbs!
YES!! CURB THE WILDERNESS!
©Phil (TRADE) MARK TRAIL) Frank
But what we must work for and strive for and fight for is...
Tell us!!
Congoleum on the nature trails!!
YES!!!

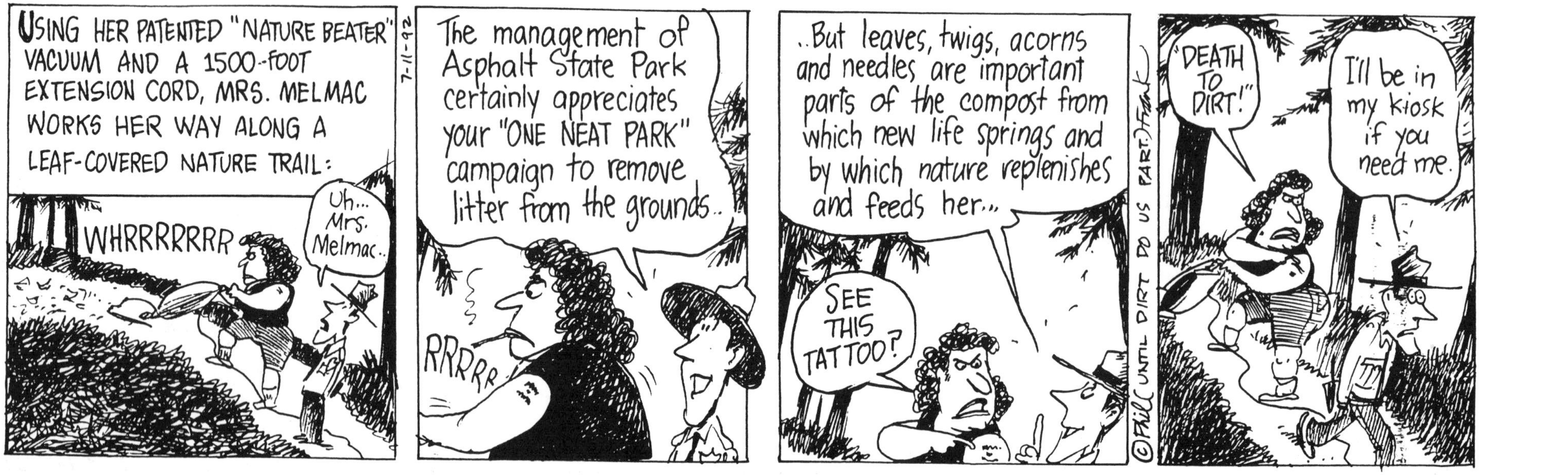
USING HER PATENTED "NATURE BEATER" VACUUM AND A 1500-FOOT EXTENSION CORD, MRS. MELMAC WORKS HER WAY ALONG A LEAF-COVERED NATURE TRAIL:
7-11-92
WHRRRRRRR
Uh... Mrs. Melmac..
The management of Asphalt State Park certainly appreciates your "ONE NEAT PARK" campaign to remove litter from the grounds..
RRRRR
..But leaves, twigs, acorns and needles are important parts of the compost from which new life springs and by which nature replenishes and feeds her...
SEE THIS TATTOO?
©Phil UNTIL DIRT DO US PART.) Frank
"DEATH TO DIRT!"
I'll be in my kiosk if you need me.

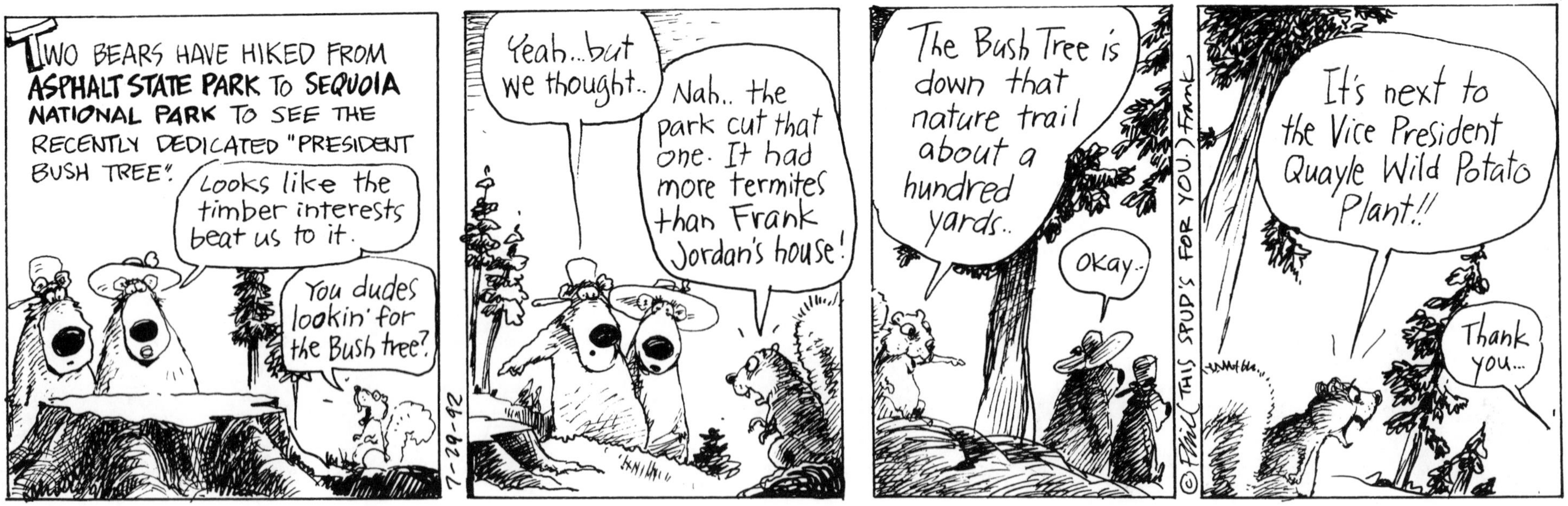
TWO BEARS HAVE HIKED FROM ASPHALT STATE PARK TO SEQUOIA NATIONAL PARK TO SEE THE RECENTLY DEDICATED "PRESIDENT BUSH TREE".
Looks like the timber interests beat us to it.
You dudes lookin' for the Bush tree?
7-29-92
Yeah...but we thought..
Nah.. the park cut that one. It had more termites than Frank Jordan's house!
The Bush Tree is down that nature trail about a hundred yards..
Okay..
© Phil (THIS SPUD'S FOR YOU.) Frank
It's next to the Vice President Quayle Wild Potato Plant!!
Thank you...

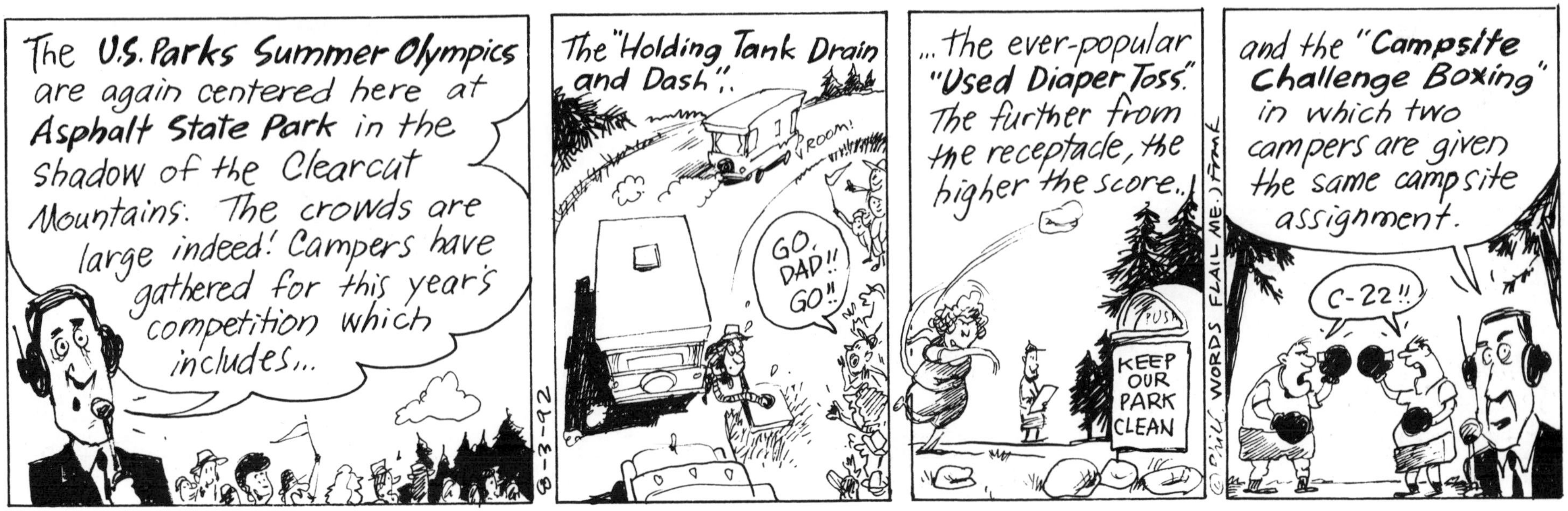
The U.S. Parks Summer Olympics are again centered here at Asphalt State Park in the shadow of the Clearcut Mountains. The crowds are large indeed! Campers have gathered for this year's competition which includes...
8-3-92
The "Holding Tank Drain and Dash"..
VROOM!
GO, DAD!! GO!!
...the ever-popular "Used Diaper Toss". The further from the receptacle, the higher the score..
PUSH
KEEP OUR PARK CLEAN
© Phil (WORDS FAIL ME.) Frank
and the "Campsite Challenge Boxing" in which two campers are given the same campsite assignment.
C-22!!

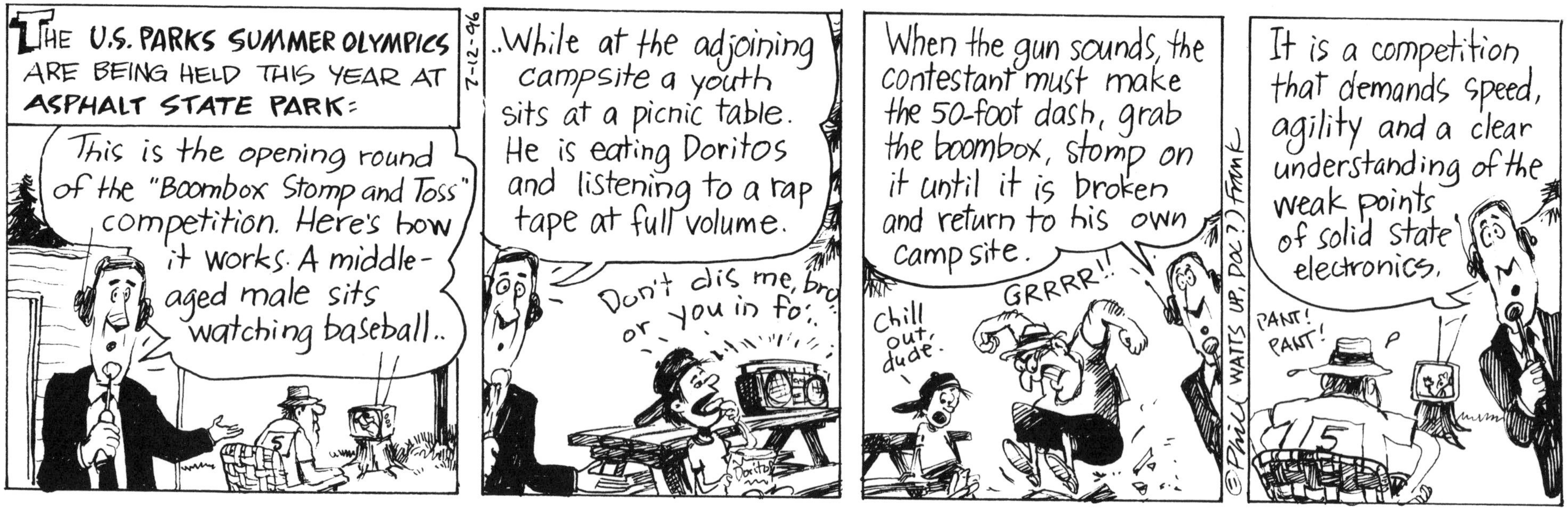
THE U.S. PARKS SUMMER OLYMPICS ARE BEING HELD THIS YEAR AT ASPHALT STATE PARK:
This is the opening round of the "Boombox Stomp and Toss" competition. Here's how it works. A middle-aged male sits watching baseball..
7-12-96
..While at the adjoining campsite a youth sits at a picnic table. He is eating Doritos and listening to a rap tape at full volume.
Don't dis me, bro or you in fo'..
Doritos
When the gun sounds, the contestant must make the 50-foot dash, grab the boombox, stomp on it until it is broken and return to his own camp site.
GRRRR!!
Chill out, dude.
© Phil (WATTS UP, DOC?) Frank
It is a competition that demands speed, agility and a clear understanding of the weak points of solid state electronics.
PANT! PANT!
15

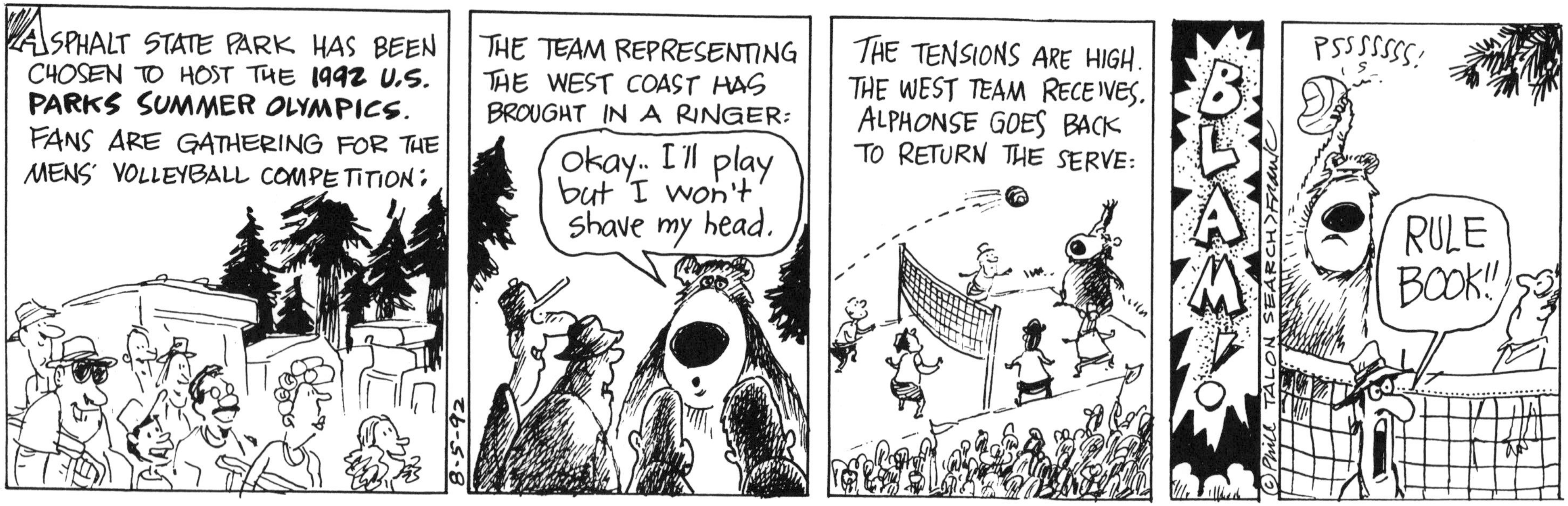
ASPHALT STATE PARK HAS BEEN CHOSEN TO HOST THE 1992 U.S. PARKS SUMMER OLYMPICS. FANS ARE GATHERING FOR THE MENS' VOLLEYBALL COMPETITION:
8-5-92
THE TEAM REPRESENTING THE WEST COAST HAS BROUGHT IN A RINGER:
Okay.. I'll play but I won't shave my head.
THE TENSIONS ARE HIGH. THE WEST TEAM RECEIVES. ALPHONSE GOES BACK TO RETURN THE SERVE:
BLAM!
© Phil (TALON SEARCH) Frank
PSSSSSSS!
RULE BOOK!!

THE U.S. PARKS SUMMER OLYMPICS continue here at beautiful Asphalt State Park We're in the last heat of the "Beach Space Stake and Claim" Competition.
GO!! GO!! GO!
BANG!!
8-6-92
Winners are judged on the size of their space, the speed with which they define its perimeters and its location relative to snack bar and toilets.
5
6
5
2
This final heat finds Mr. Brad Watson representing the East. I see youre wearing your Florsheim Competition Wingtips, Brad.
You betcha!
122
©Phil Frank HERE'S SAND IN YOUR EYE!
His opponent, representing the Western states, is, of course, the undefeated title holder, Mrs. Velma "Move It Or Lose It" Melmac weighing in at...
GRRR.
Uh.. Can I concede?
48

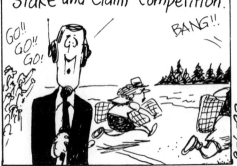

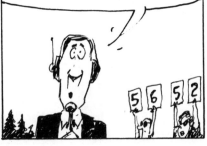

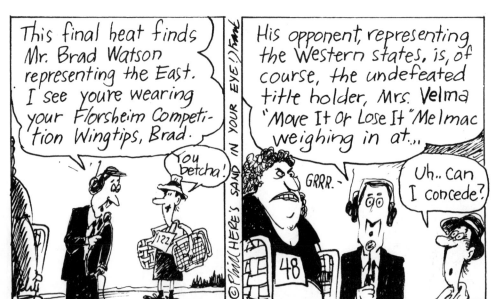

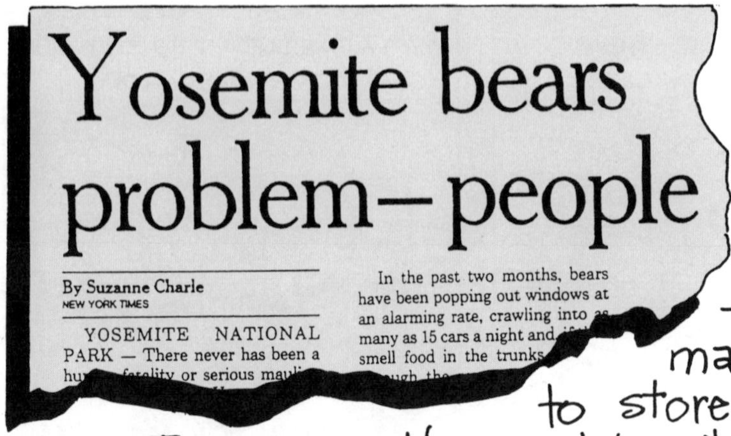

Yosemite bears problem—people

By Suzanne Charle
NEW YORK TIMES

YOSEMITE NATIONAL PARK — There never has been a hu...

In the past two months, bears have been popping out windows at an alarming rate, crawling into as many as 15 cars a night and, if they smell food in the trunks...

Bears have caused problems in many national parks. What most people fail to realize is that the bears make trouble because of visitors' bad habits. The problem is acute in Yosemite because so many of the urban visitors are concentrated in the Valley, a very small part of the park. Many people ignore park warnings, making for easy pickings for the bears. Visitors fail to store food properly and are easily victimized.

Steve Thompson, the park's wildlife biologist sums it up best: "Bears are smart and some are very smart. My problems start when the smarter bears and the dumber visitors interact."

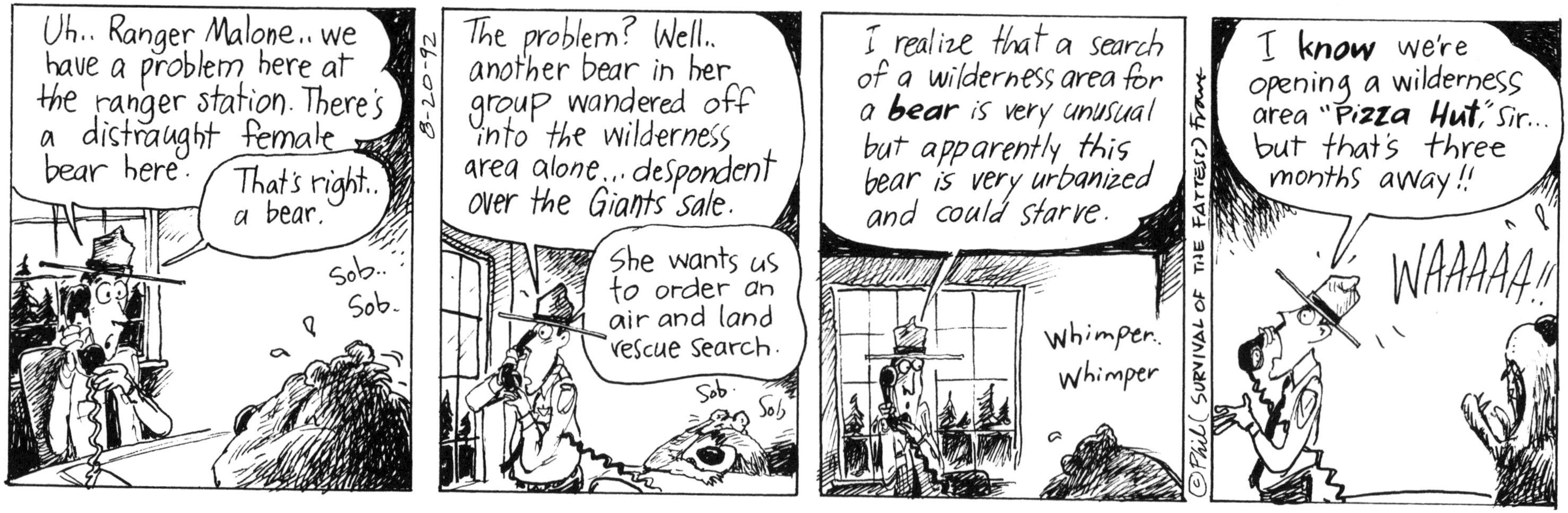

Uh.. Ranger Malone.. we have a problem here at the ranger station. There's a distraught female bear here.
That's right.. a bear.
Sob.. Sob.
8-20-92
The problem? Well.. another bear in her group wandered off into the wilderness area alone... despondent over the Giants sale.
She wants us to order an air and land rescue search.
Sob Sob
I realize that a search of a wilderness area for a **bear** is very unusual but apparently this bear is very urbanized and could starve.
Whimper.. Whimper
© Phil (SURVIVAL OF THE FATTEST) Frank
I **know** we're opening a wilderness area "**Pizza Hut**," Sir... but that's three months away!!
WAAAAA!!

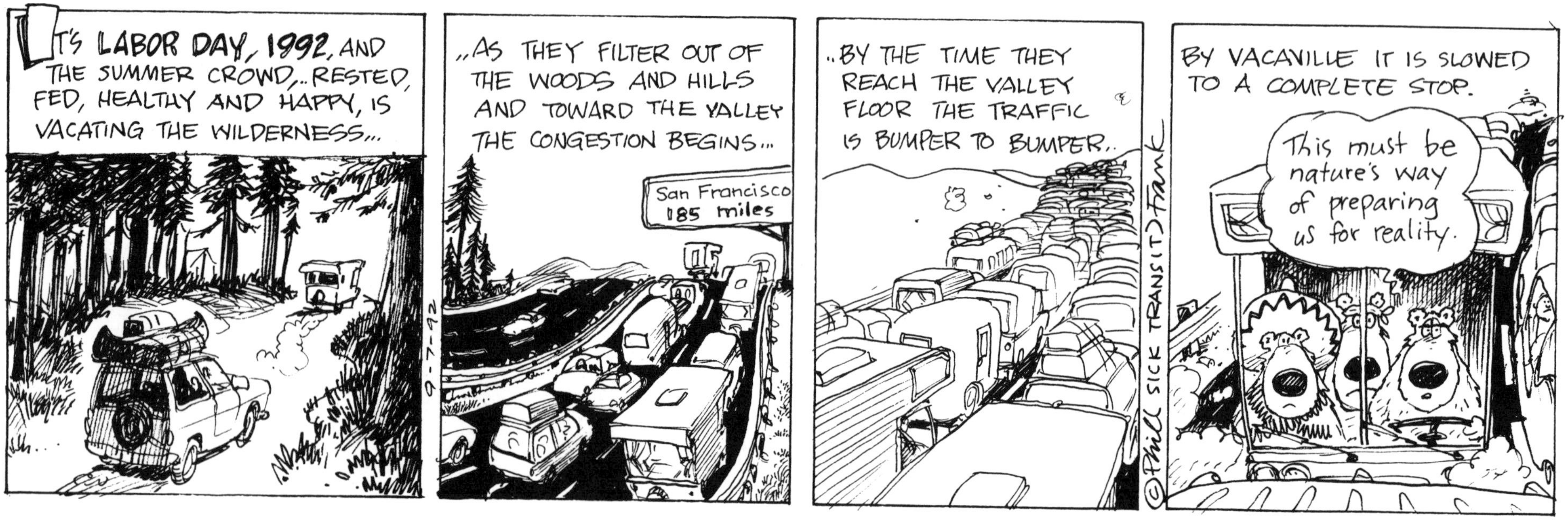

IT'S **LABOR DAY, 1992**, AND THE SUMMER CROWD,.. RESTED, FED, HEALTHY AND HAPPY, IS VACATING THE WILDERNESS...
..AS THEY FILTER OUT OF THE WOODS AND HILLS AND TOWARD THE VALLEY THE CONGESTION BEGINS...
San Francisco 185 miles
9-7-92
..BY THE TIME THEY REACH THE VALLEY FLOOR THE TRAFFIC IS BUMPER TO BUMPER..
© Phil (SICK TRANSIT) Frank
BY VACAVILLE IT IS SLOWED TO A COMPLETE STOP.
This must be nature's way of preparing us for reality.

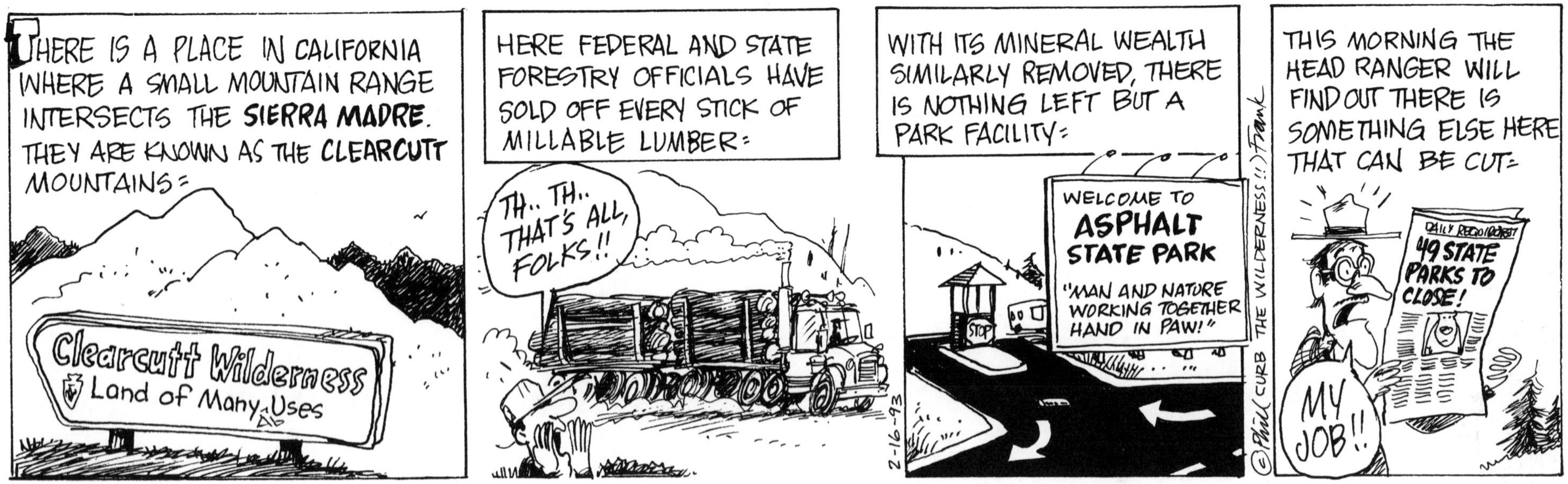
THERE IS A PLACE IN CALIFORNIA WHERE A SMALL MOUNTAIN RANGE INTERSECTS THE SIERRA MADRE. THEY ARE KNOWN AS THE CLEARCUTT MOUNTAINS=
Clearcutt Wilderness
Land of Many Uses
HERE FEDERAL AND STATE FORESTRY OFFICIALS HAVE SOLD OFF EVERY STICK OF MILLABLE LUMBER=
TH.. TH.. THAT'S ALL, FOLKS!!
WITH ITS MINERAL WEALTH SIMILARLY REMOVED, THERE IS NOTHING LEFT BUT A PARK FACILITY=
WELCOME TO
ASPHALT STATE PARK
"MAN AND NATURE WORKING TOGETHER HAND IN PAW!"
STOP
2-16-93
© Phil Frank CURB THE WILDERNESS!!
THIS MORNING THE HEAD RANGER WILL FIND OUT THERE IS SOMETHING ELSE HERE THAT CAN BE CUT=
49 STATE PARKS TO CLOSE!
MY JOB!!

It's February and Ranger Horace Malone is on the carpet.

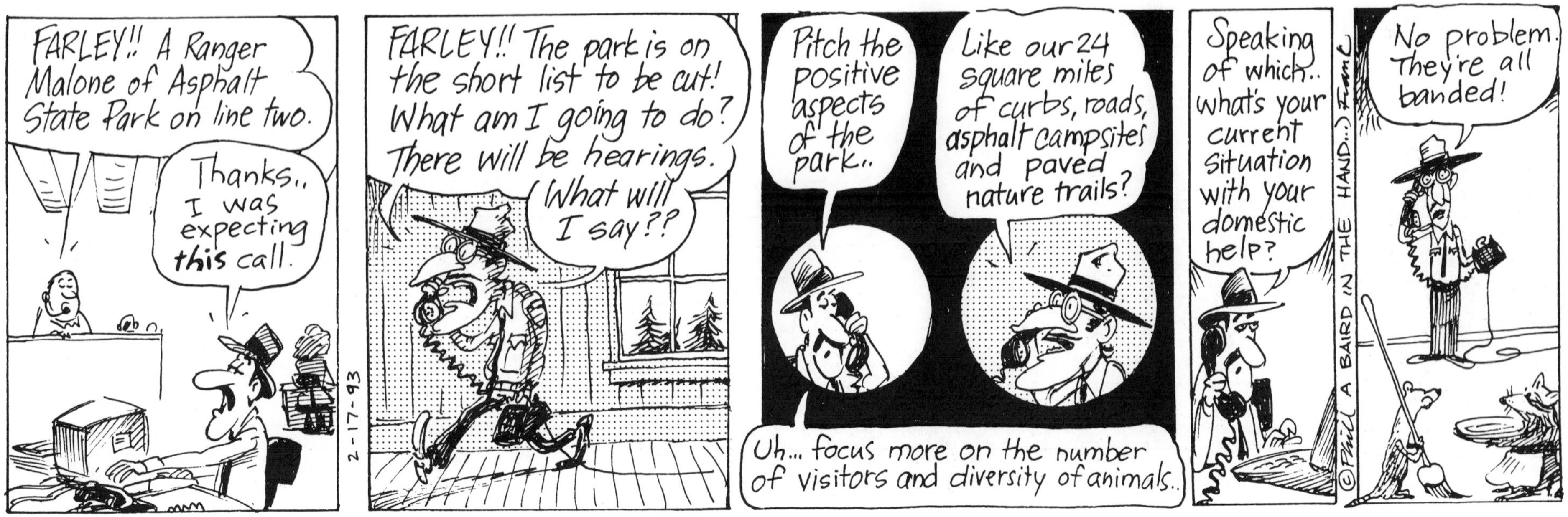
FARLEY!! A Ranger Malone of Asphalt State Park on line two.
Thanks.. I was expecting this call.
2-17-93
FARLEY!! The park is on the short list to be cut! What am I going to do? There will be hearings.
What will I say??
Pitch the positive aspects of the park..
Like our 24 square miles of curbs, roads, asphalt campsites and paved nature trails?
Uh... focus more on the number of visitors and diversity of animals..
Speaking of which.. what's your current situation with your domestic help?
© Phil Frank A BAIRD IN THE HAND...
No problem. They're all banded!

Horace Malone: Chief Bureaucrat

A WILDERNESS BUREAUCRAT WAS NEEDED FOR THE COMIC STRIP. CHIEF RANGER **HORACE MALONE** STEPPED FORWARD. HE IS ALLERGIC TO POLLEN, FLOWERS, BUGS, PINE NEEDLES...BASICALLY ANYTHING THAT IS OUTDOORS. SO HE STAYS INDOORS – IN AN OAK-PANELED CONCRETE BUNKER FROM WHICH HE SENDS OUT MEMOS THAT THE STAFF AND CAMPERS IGNORE. IN 1977 HORACE OFFERED FARLEY A SEASONAL RANGER POSITION TO WORK WITH THE UNRULY PARK BEARS. APPARENTLY HORACE IS ALLERGIC TO THE BEARS, TOO.

Horace Malone has always felt that whatever state or national park he was assigned to was a park that was underutilized.

He eliminated all threat of forest fires by cutting down all the trees. He controlled the spread of poison oak by paving large sections of park land.

By far, the concept which received the most attention in the national press was Horace's "**Curb the Wilderness**" plan.

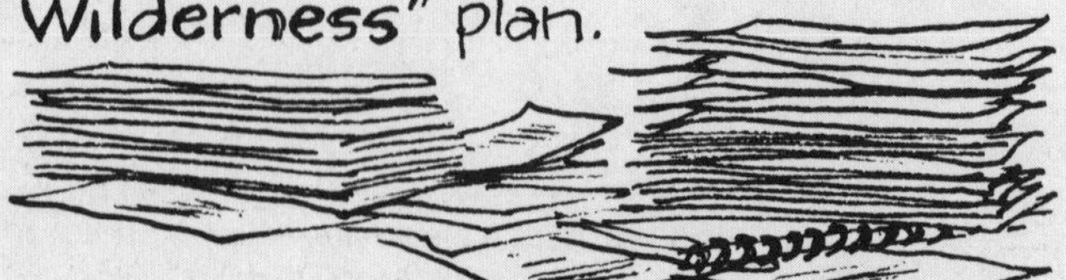

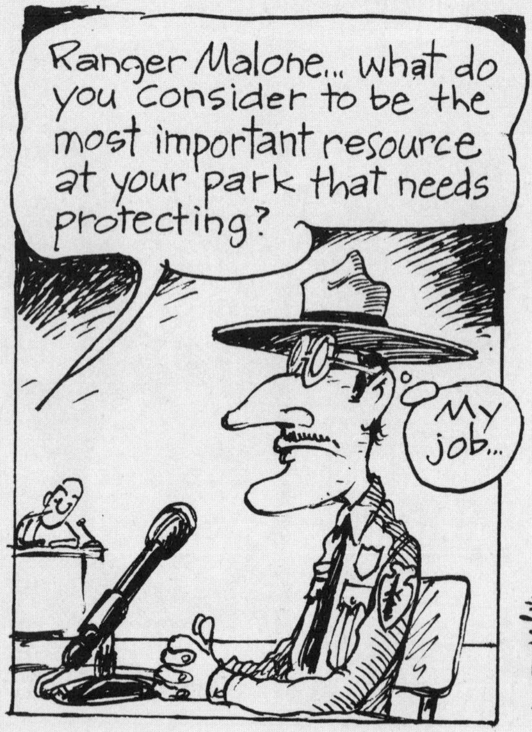
Ranger Malone... what do you consider to be the most important resource at your park that needs protecting?
My job...

The plan was really a dream... a dream that one day every wilderness trail, fire road and deer path in every park would have concrete curbs. Dreams like this do not die easily.

Horace introduced cable TV hook-ups to campsites and offered morning newspaper delivery. His crowning achievement was the construction of a 220 site campground on a formerly useless egret nesting area.

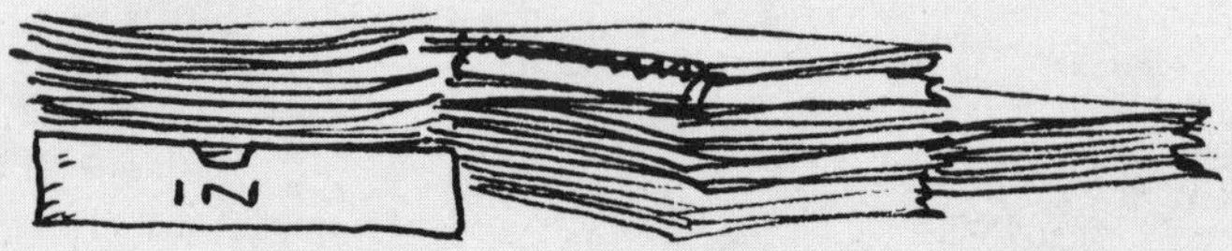
IN

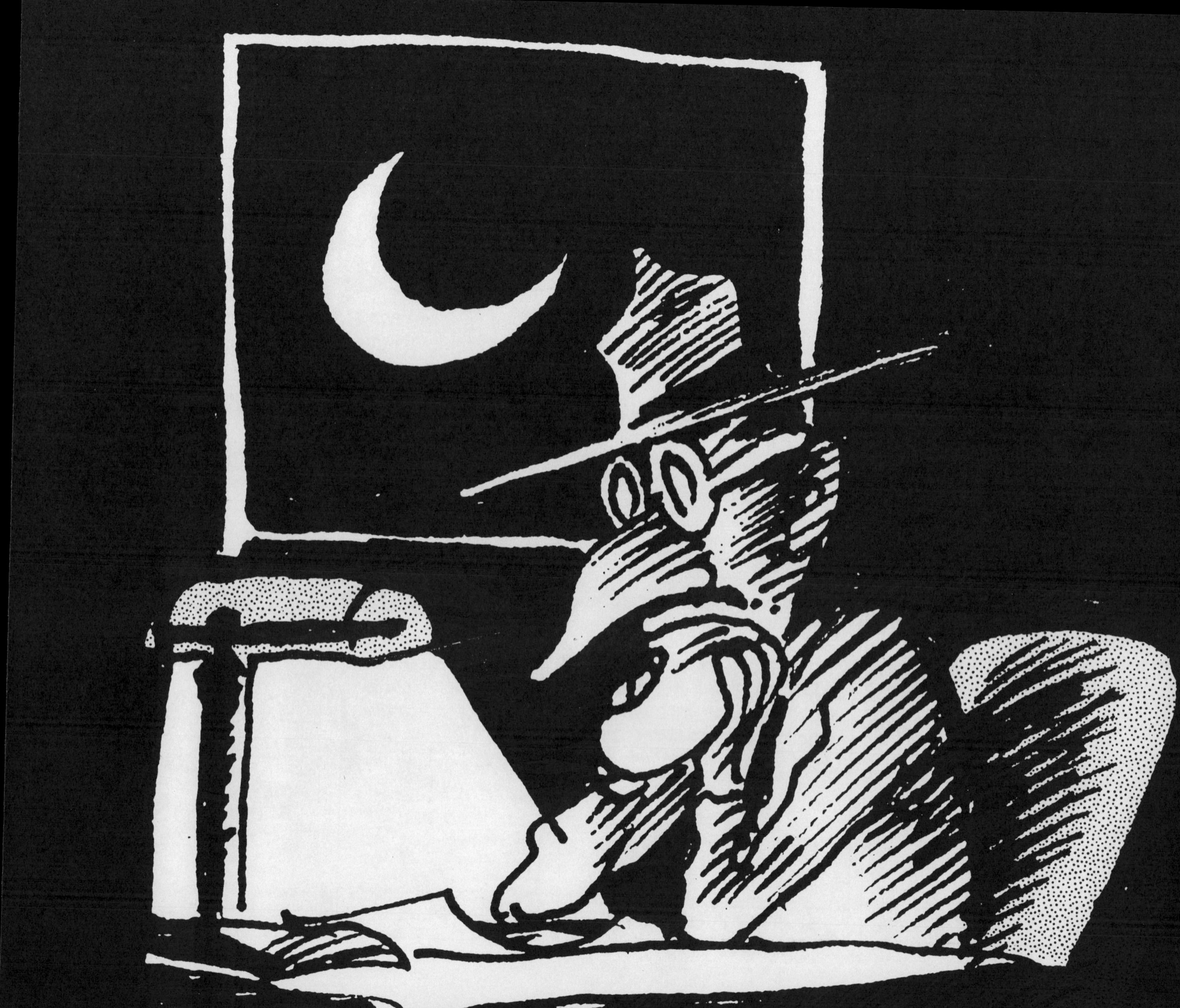

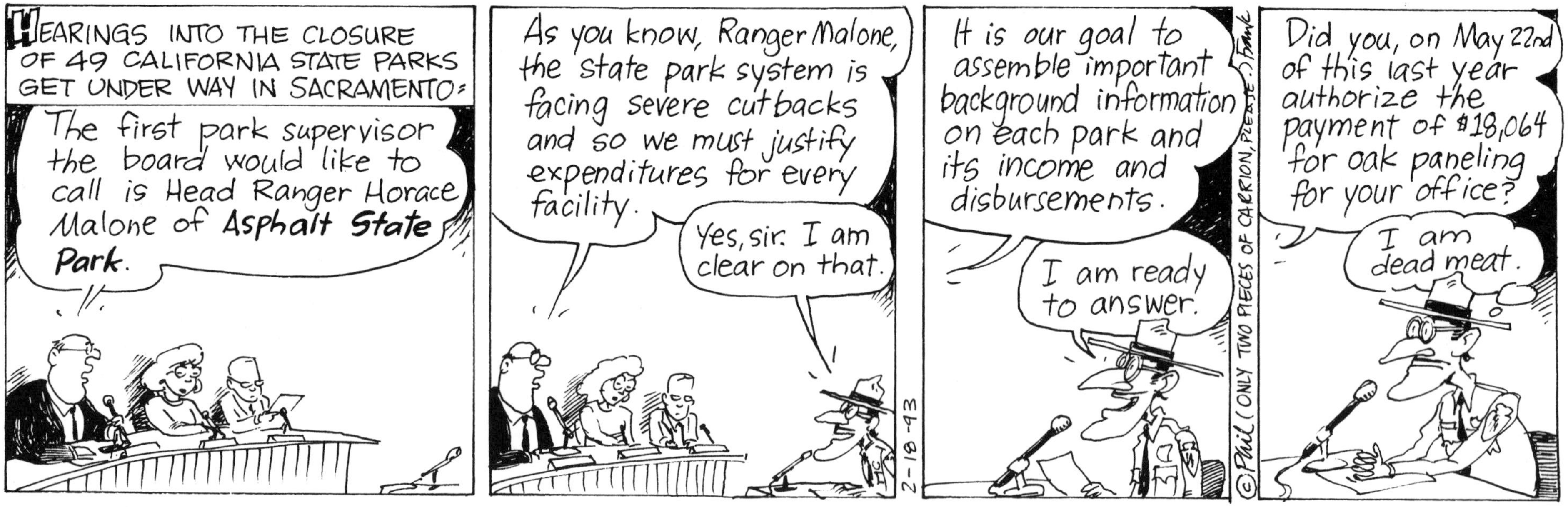
HEARINGS INTO THE CLOSURE OF 49 CALIFORNIA STATE PARKS GET UNDER WAY IN SACRAMENTO:
The first park supervisor the board would like to call is Head Ranger Horace Malone of **Asphalt State Park**.
As you know, Ranger Malone, the state park system is facing severe cutbacks and so we must justify expenditures for every facility.
Yes, sir. I am clear on that.
2-18-93
It is our goal to assemble important background information on each park and its income and disbursements.
I am ready to answer.
© Phil (ONLY TWO PIECES OF CARRION, PLEASE) Frank
Did you, on May 22nd of this last year authorize the payment of $18,064 for oak paneling for your office?
I am dead meat.

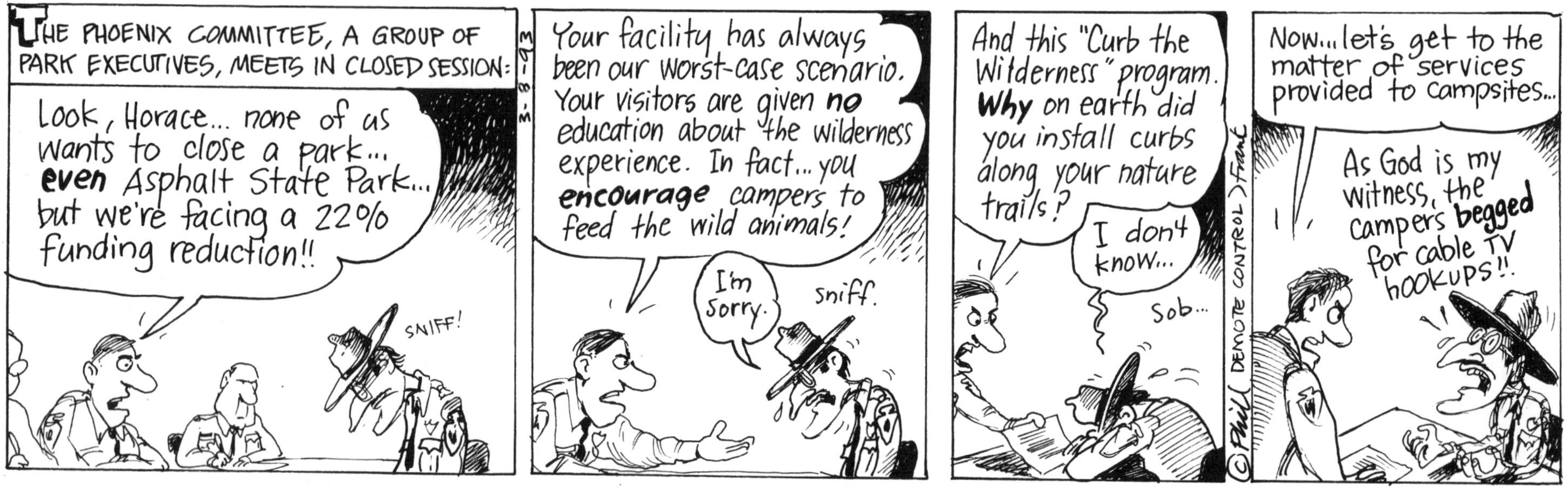
THE PHOENIX COMMITTEE, A GROUP OF PARK EXECUTIVES, MEETS IN CLOSED SESSION:
Look, Horace... none of us wants to close a park... **even** Asphalt State Park... but we're facing a 22% funding reduction!!
SNIFF!
3-8-93
Your facility has always been our worst-case scenario. Your visitors are given **no** education about the wilderness experience. In fact... you **encourage** campers to feed the wild animals!
I'm sorry.
sniff.
And this "Curb the Wilderness" program. **Why** on earth did you install curbs along your nature trails?
I don't know...
Sob...
© Phil (DEMOTE CONTROL) Frank
Now... let's get to the matter of services provided to campsites...
As God is my witness, the campers **begged** for cable TV hookups!!

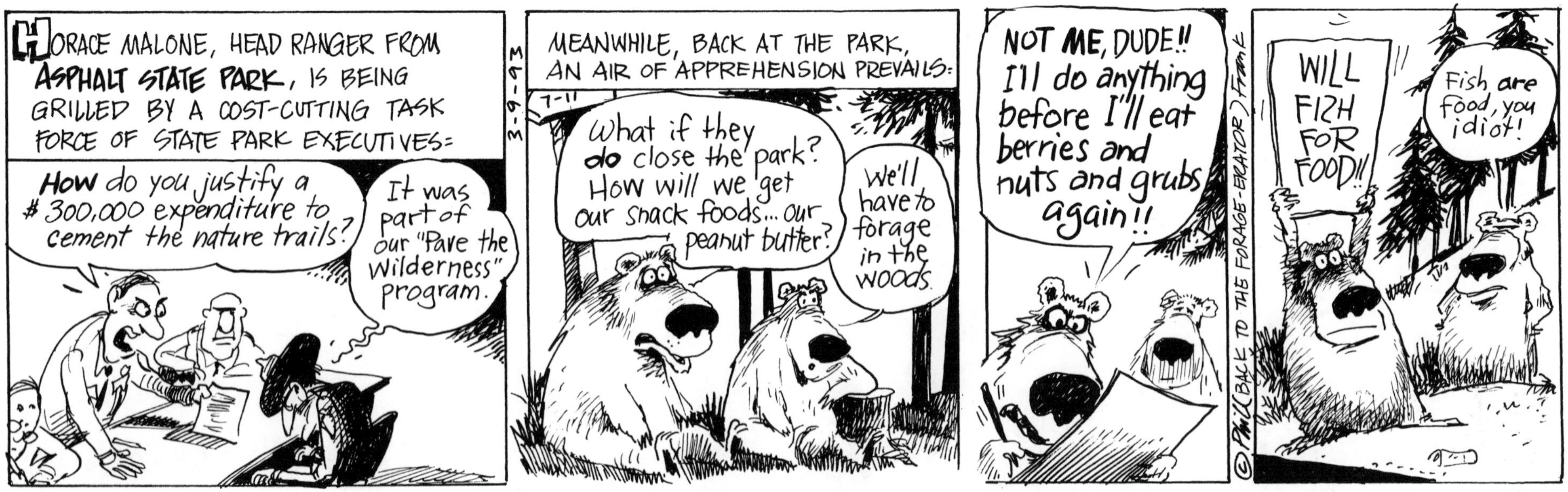
HORACE MALONE, HEAD RANGER FROM ASPHALT STATE PARK, IS BEING GRILLED BY A COST-CUTTING TASK FORCE OF STATE PARK EXECUTIVES:
HOW do you justify a # 300,000 expenditure to cement the nature trails?
It was part of our "Pave the Wilderness" program.
3-9-93
MEANWHILE, BACK AT THE PARK, AN AIR OF APPREHENSION PREVAILS:
What if they do close the park? How will we get our snack foods... our peanut butter?
We'll have to forage in the woods.
NOT ME, DUDE!! I'll do anything before I'll eat berries and nuts and grubs again!!
© Phil (BACK TO THE FORAGE-ERATOR) Frank
WILL FISH FOR FOOD!!
Fish are food, you idiot!

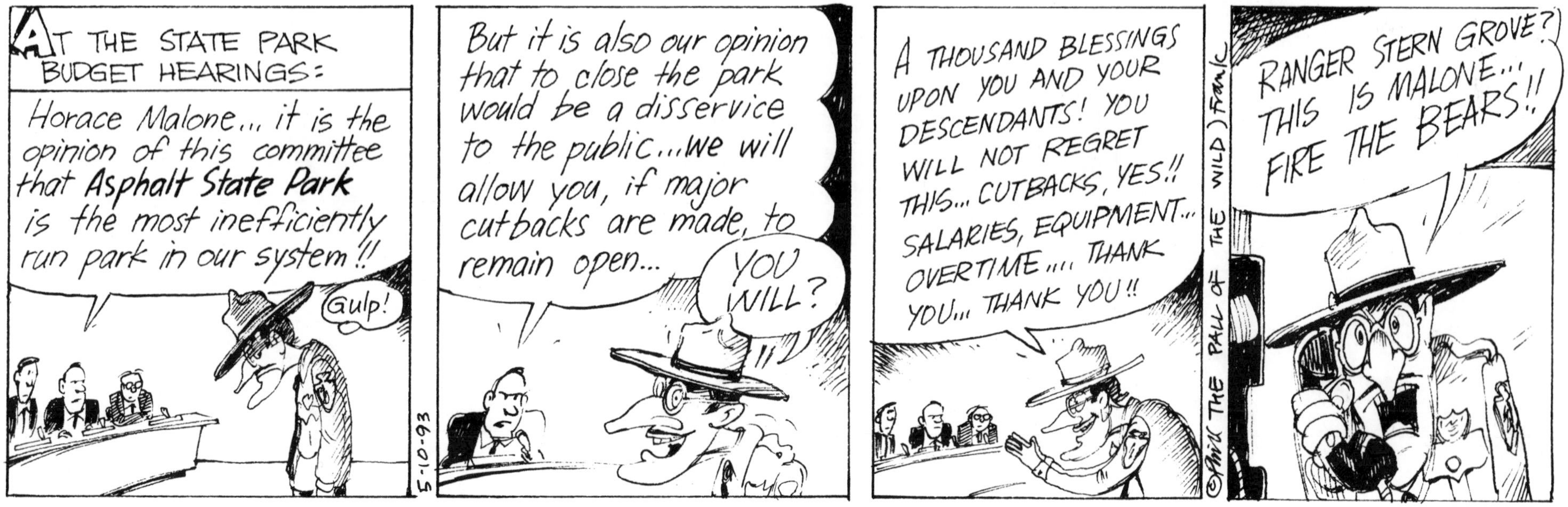
AT THE STATE PARK BUDGET HEARINGS:
Horace Malone... it is the opinion of this committee that Asphalt State Park is the most inefficiently run park in our system!!
Gulp!
5-10-93
But it is also our opinion that to close the park would be a disservice to the public... we will allow you, if major cutbacks are made, to remain open...
YOU WILL?
A THOUSAND BLESSINGS UPON YOU AND YOUR DESCENDANTS! YOU WILL NOT REGRET THIS... CUTBACKS, YES!! SALARIES, EQUIPMENT... OVERTIME.... THANK YOU... THANK YOU!!
© Phil (THE FALL OF THE WILD) Frank
RANGER STERN GROVE? THIS IS MALONE... FIRE THE BEARS!!

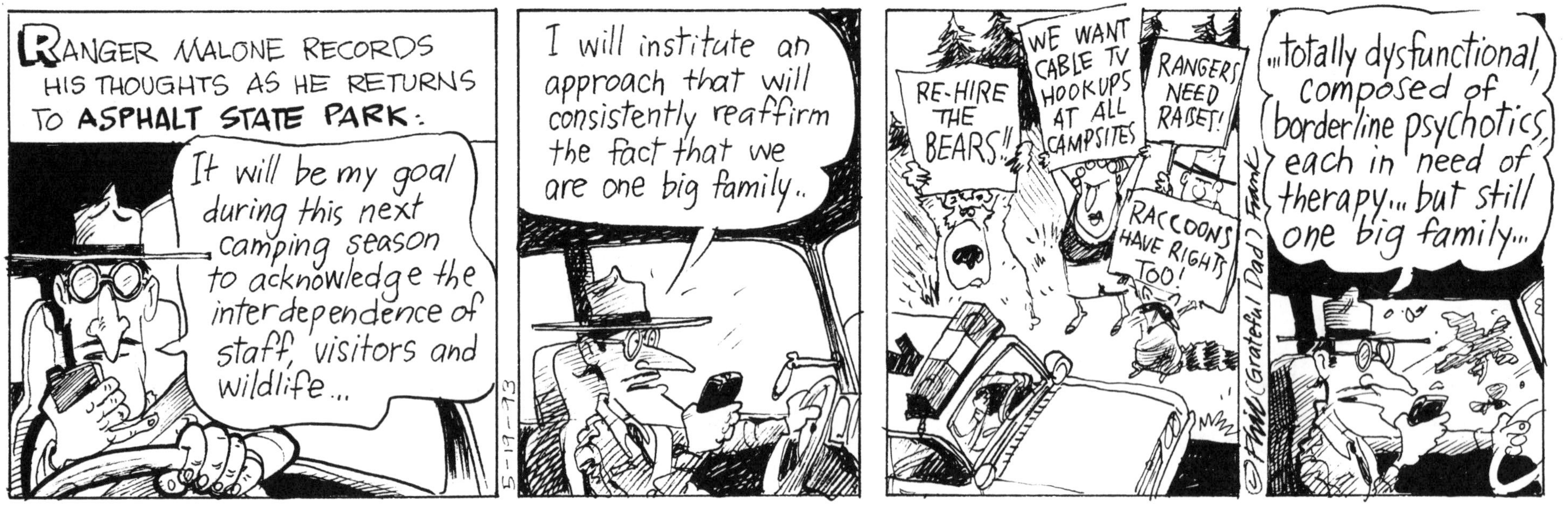
RANGER MALONE RECORDS HIS THOUGHTS AS HE RETURNS TO ASPHALT STATE PARK:
It will be my goal during this next camping season to acknowledge the interdependence of staff, visitors and wildlife...
5-19-93
I will institute an approach that will consistently reaffirm the fact that we are one big family..
RE-HIRE THE BEARS!!
WE WANT CABLE TV HOOKUPS AT ALL CAMPSITES
RANGERS NEED RAISES!
RACCOONS HAVE RIGHTS TOO!
©Phil (Grateful Dad) Frank
...totally dysfunctional, composed of borderline psychotics, each in need of therapy... but still one big family...

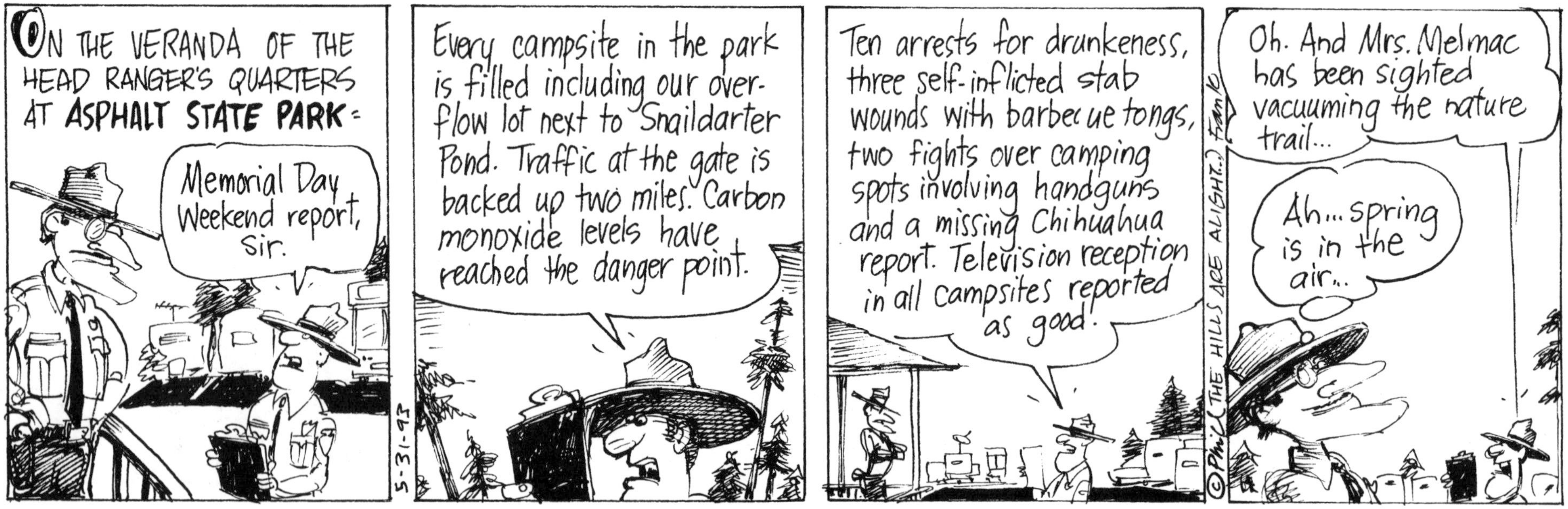
ON THE VERANDA OF THE HEAD RANGER'S QUARTERS AT ASPHALT STATE PARK:
Memorial Day Weekend report, sir.
5-31-93
Every campsite in the park is filled including our overflow lot next to Snaildarter Pond. Traffic at the gate is backed up two miles. Carbon monoxide levels have reached the danger point.
Ten arrests for drunkeness, three self-inflicted stab wounds with barbecue tongs, two fights over camping spots involving handguns and a missing Chihuahua report. Television reception in all campsites reported as good.
©Phil (THE HILLS ARE ALIGHT..) Frank
Oh. And Mrs. Melmac has been sighted vacuuming the nature trail...
Ah... spring is in the air..

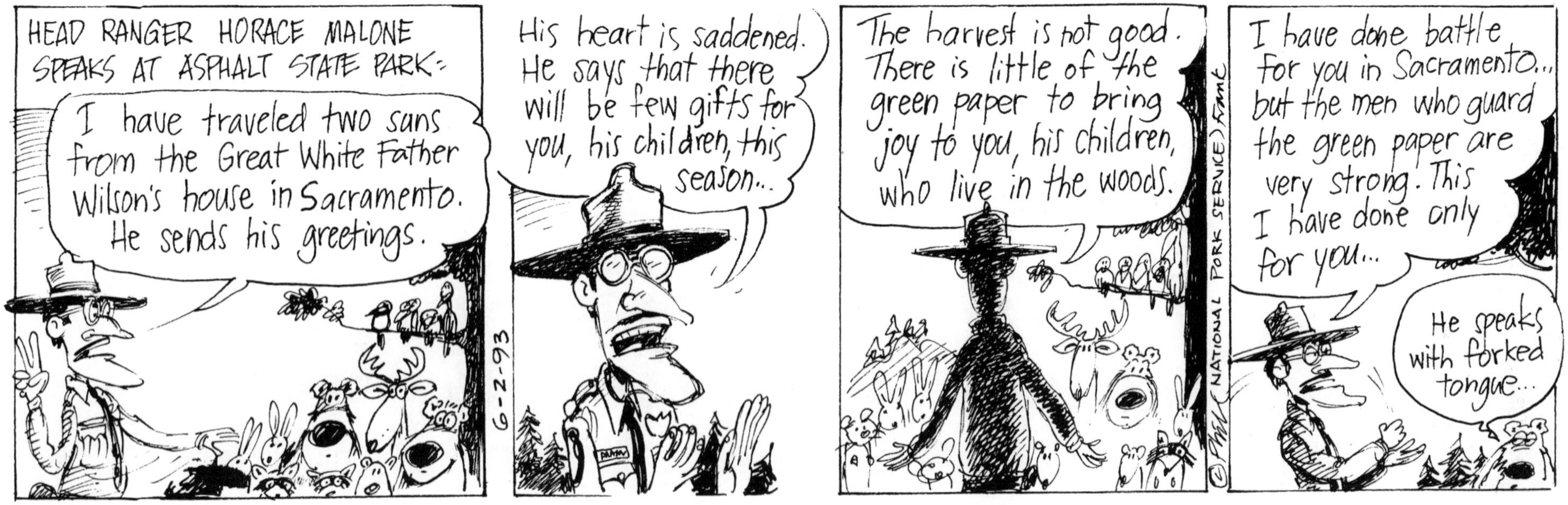
HEAD RANGER HORACE MALONE SPEAKS AT ASPHALT STATE PARK:
I have traveled two suns from the Great White Father Wilson's house in Sacramento. He sends his greetings.
6-2-93
His heart is saddened. He says that there will be few gifts for you, his children, this season..
The harvest is not good. There is little of the green paper to bring joy to you, his children, who live in the woods.
© Pirie (NATIONAL PORK SERVICE) Frank
I have done battle for you in Sacramento... but the men who guard the green paper are very strong. This I have done only for you...
He speaks with forked tongue...

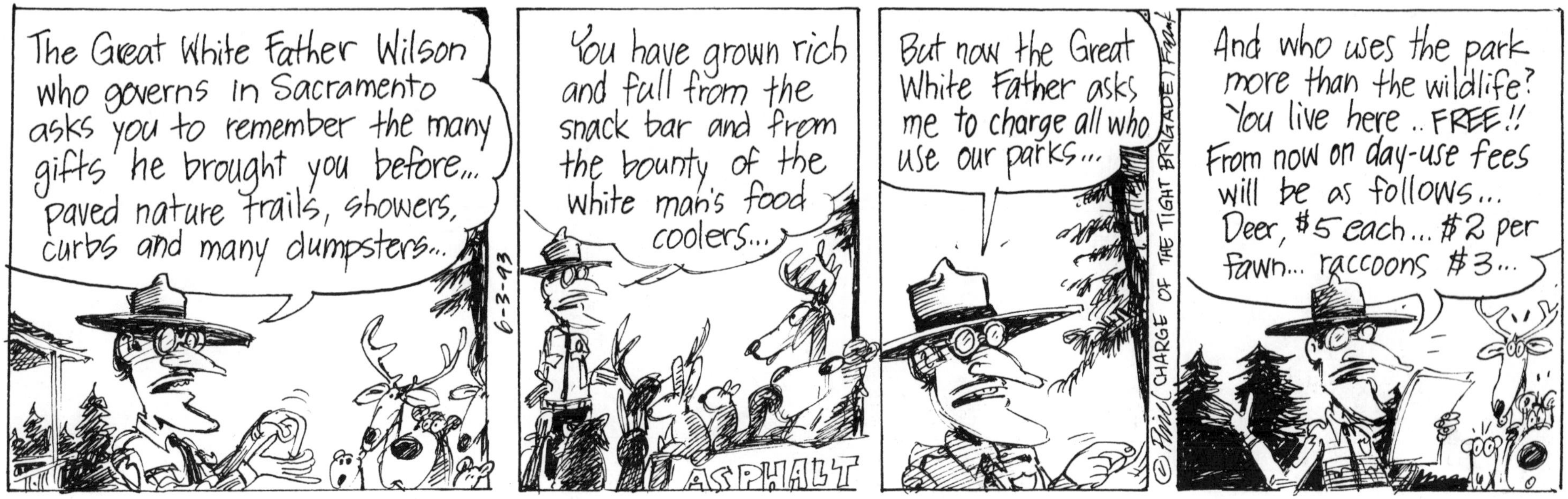
The Great White Father Wilson who governs in Sacramento asks you to remember the many gifts he brought you before... paved nature trails, showers, curbs and many dumpsters...
6-3-93
You have grown rich and full from the snack bar and from the bounty of the white man's food coolers...
ASPHALT
But now the Great White Father asks me to charge all who use our parks...
© Pirie (CHARGE OF THE TIGHT BRIGADE) Frank
And who uses the park more than the wildlife? You live here .. FREE!! From now on day-use fees will be as follows... Deer, $5 each... $2 per fawn... raccoons $3...

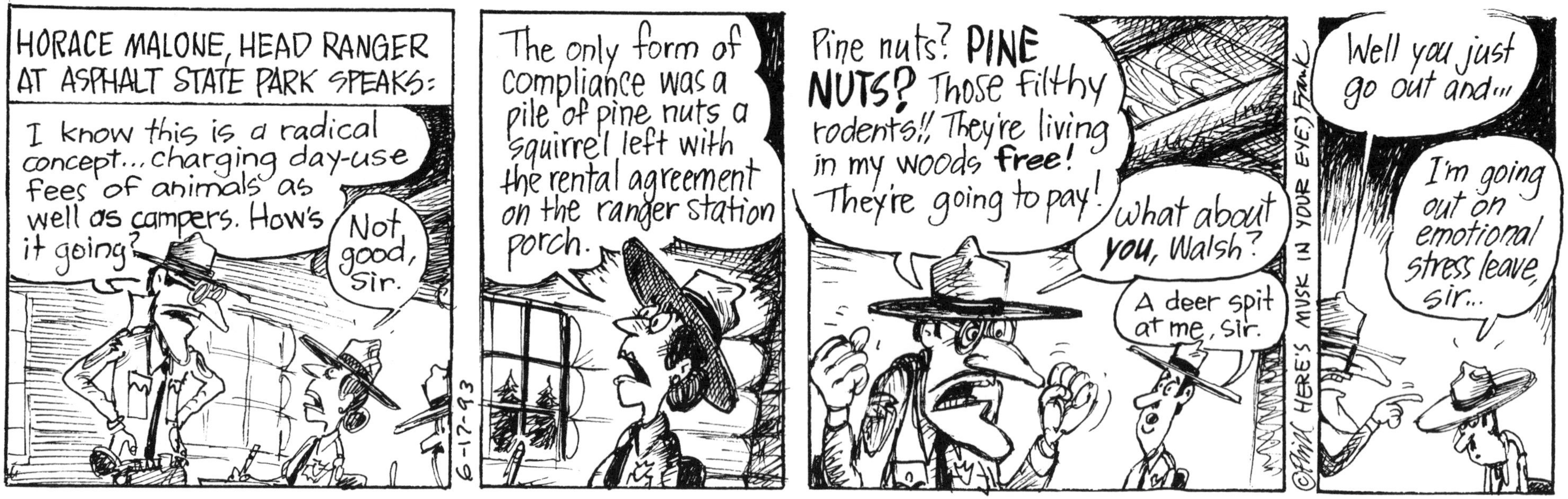
HORACE MALONE, HEAD RANGER AT ASPHALT STATE PARK SPEAKS:
I know this is a radical concept... charging day-use fees of animals as well as campers. How's it going?
Not good, sir.
6-17-93
The only form of compliance was a pile of pine nuts a squirrel left with the rental agreement on the ranger station porch.
Pine nuts? PINE NUTS? Those filthy rodents!! They're living in my woods free! They're going to pay!
What about YOU, Walsh?
A deer spit at me, sir.
©Phil (HERE'S MUSK IN YOUR EYE) Frank
Well you just go out and...
I'm going out on emotional stress leave, sir...

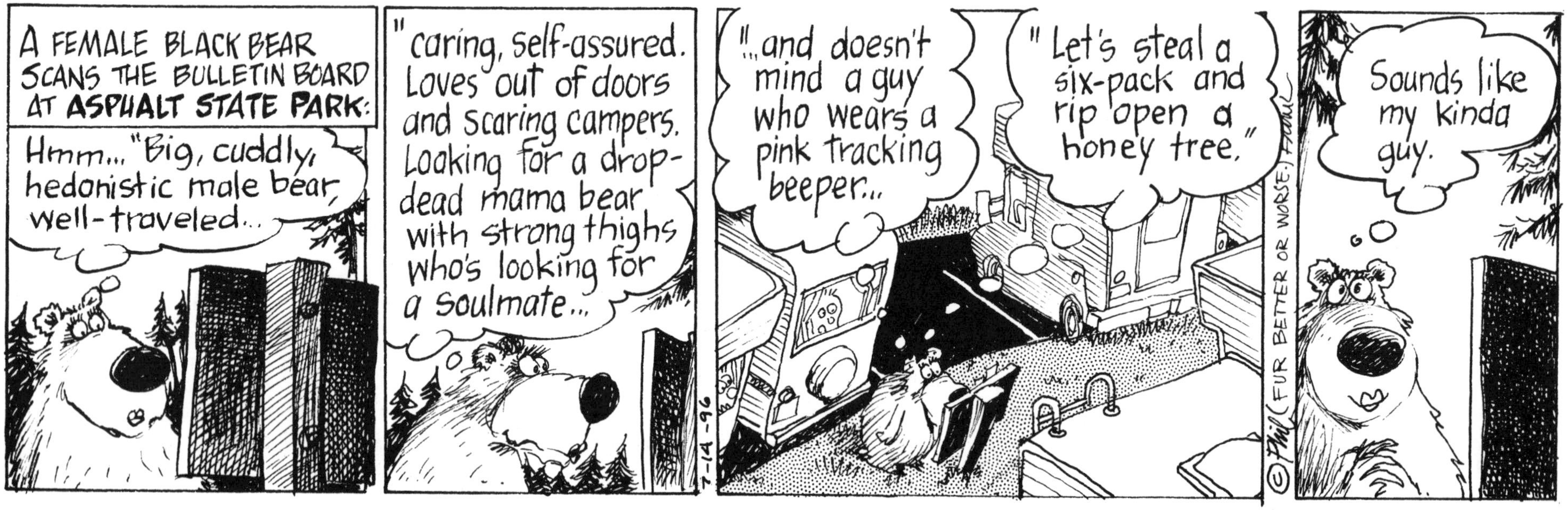
A FEMALE BLACK BEAR SCANS THE BULLETIN BOARD AT ASPHALT STATE PARK:
Hmm... "Big, cuddly, hedonistic male bear, well-traveled...
"caring, self-assured. Loves out of doors and scaring campers. Looking for a drop-dead mama bear with strong thighs who's looking for a soulmate...
7-14-96
"...and doesn't mind a guy who wears a pink tracking beeper...
"Let's steal a six-pack and rip open a honey tree."
© Phil (FUR BETTER OR WORSE) Frank
Sounds like my kinda guy.

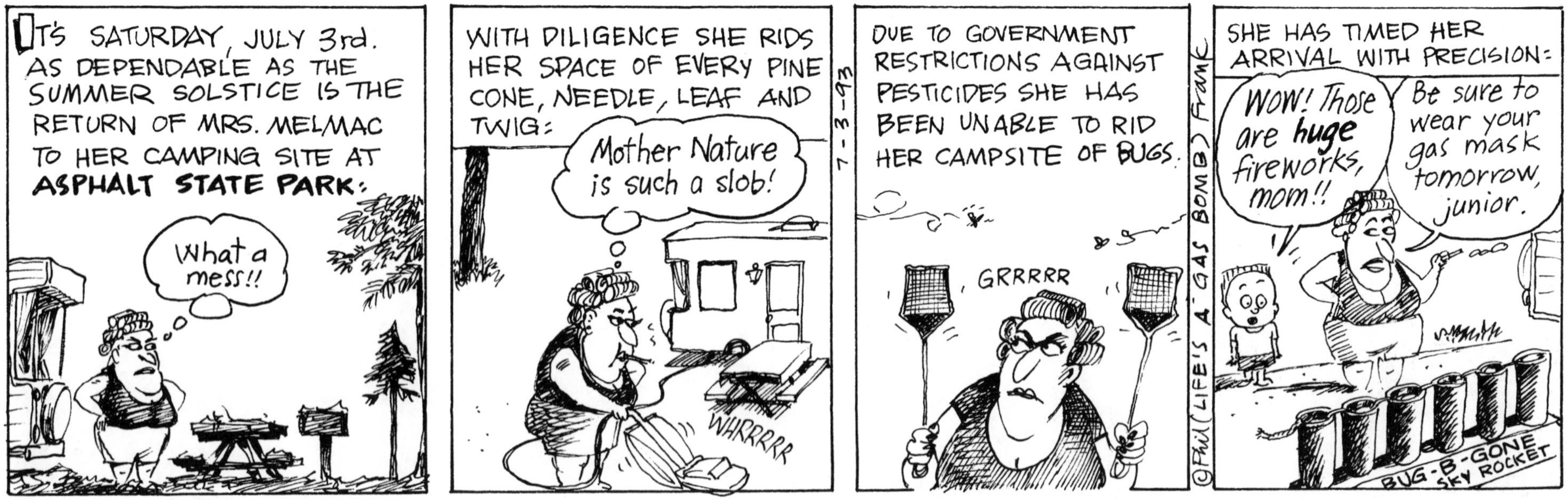
IT'S SATURDAY, JULY 3rd. AS DEPENDABLE AS THE SUMMER SOLSTICE IS THE RETURN OF MRS. MELMAC TO HER CAMPING SITE AT ASPHALT STATE PARK:
What a mess!!
WITH DILIGENCE SHE RIDS HER SPACE OF EVERY PINE CONE, NEEDLE, LEAF AND TWIG:
Mother Nature is such a slob!
WHRRRRR
7-3-93
DUE TO GOVERNMENT RESTRICTIONS AGAINST PESTICIDES SHE HAS BEEN UNABLE TO RID HER CAMPSITE OF BUGS.
GRRRRR
©Phil (LIFE'S A GAS BOMB) Frank
SHE HAS TIMED HER ARRIVAL WITH PRECISION:
WOW! Those are huge fireworks, mom!!
Be sure to wear your gas mask tomorrow, junior.
BUG-B-GONE SKY ROCKET

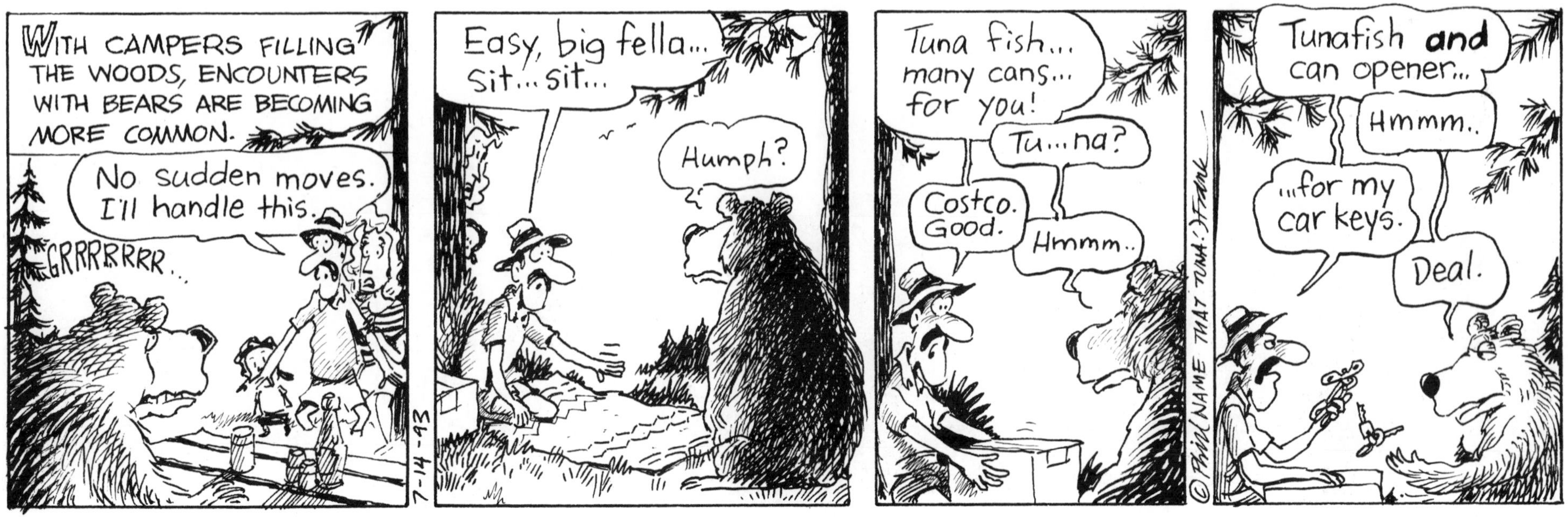
WITH CAMPERS FILLING THE WOODS, ENCOUNTERS WITH BEARS ARE BECOMING MORE COMMON.
No sudden moves. I'll handle this.
GRRRRRRR...
7-14-93
Easy, big fella... sit... sit...
Humph?
Tuna fish... many cans... for you!
Tu...na?
Costco. Good.
Hmmm..
©Phil (NAME THAT TUNA!) Frank
Tunafish and can opener...
Hmmm..
...for my car keys.
Deal.

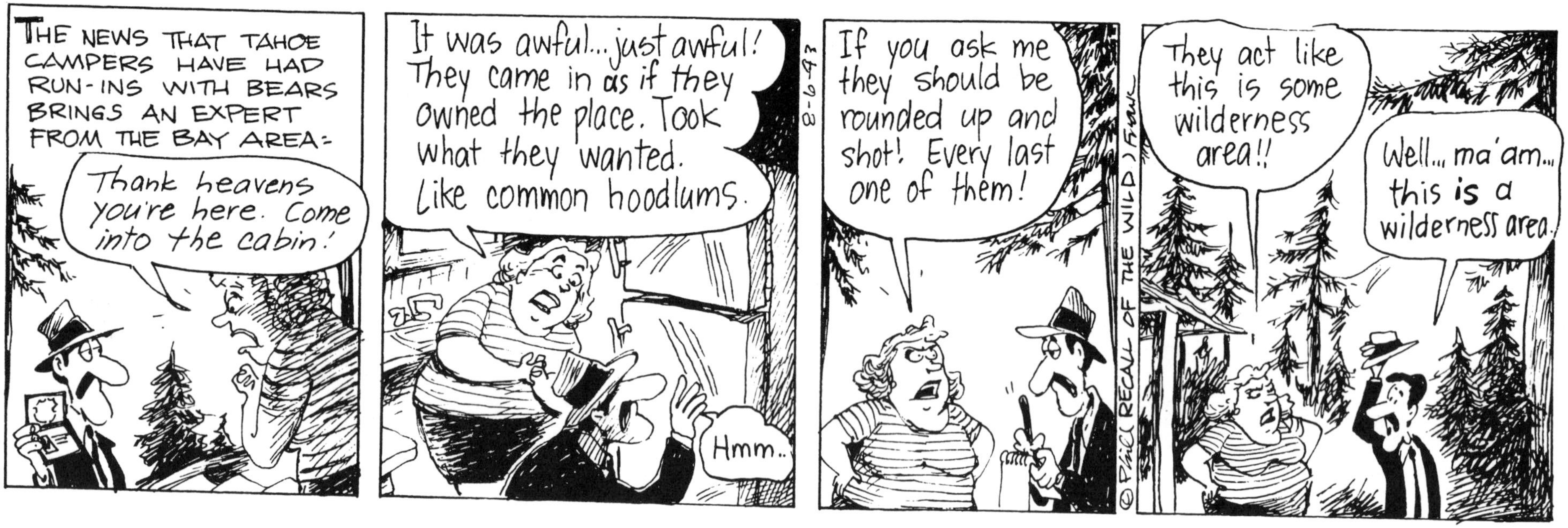
THE NEWS THAT TAHOE CAMPERS HAVE HAD RUN-INS WITH BEARS BRINGS AN EXPERT FROM THE BAY AREA:
Thank heavens you're here. Come into the cabin!
It was awful...just awful! They came in as if they owned the place. Took what they wanted. Like common hoodlums.
Hmm..
8-6-93
If you ask me they should be rounded up and shot! Every last one of them!
© Phil (RECALL OF THE WILD) Frank
They act like this is some wilderness area!!
Well... ma'am... this **is** a wilderness area.

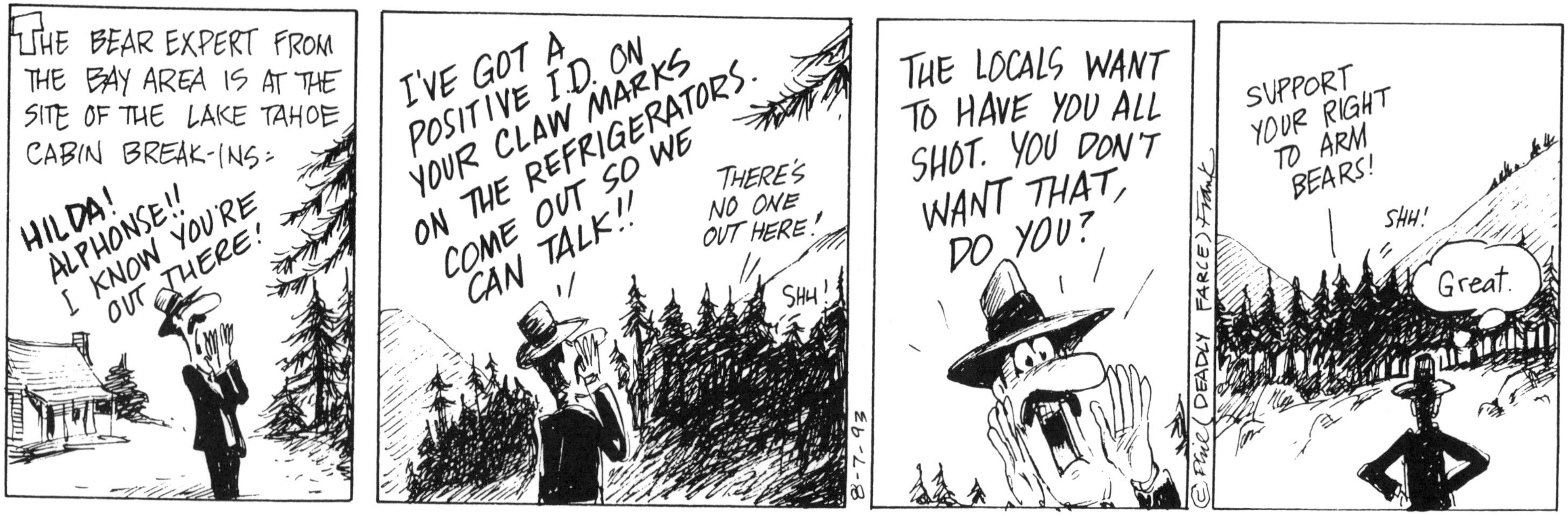
THE BEAR EXPERT FROM THE BAY AREA IS AT THE SITE OF THE LAKE TAHOE CABIN BREAK-INS:
HILDA! ALPHONSE!! I KNOW YOU'RE OUT THERE!
I'VE GOT A POSITIVE I.D. ON YOUR CLAW MARKS ON THE REFRIGERATORS. COME OUT SO WE CAN TALK!!
THERE'S NO ONE OUT HERE!
SHH!
8-7-93
THE LOCALS WANT TO HAVE YOU ALL SHOT. YOU DON'T WANT THAT, DO YOU?
© Phil (DEADLY FARCE) Frank
SUPPORT YOUR RIGHT TO ARM BEARS!
SHH!
Great.

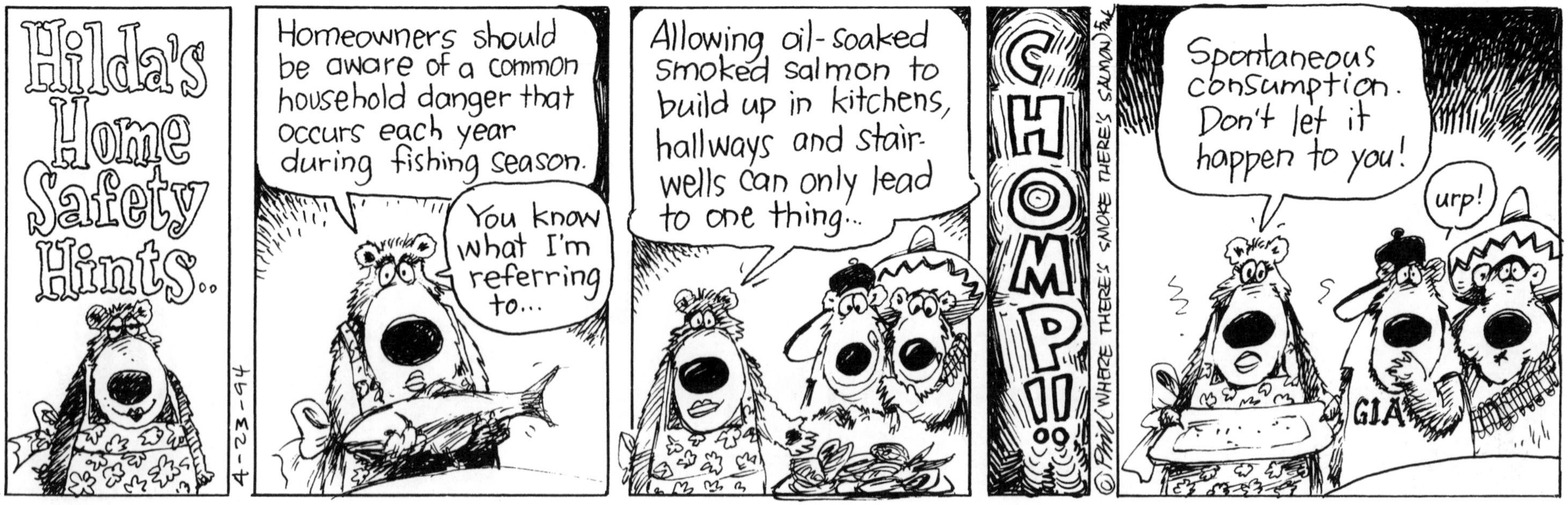

Hilda's Home Safety Hints..
4-23-94
Homeowners should be aware of a common household danger that occurs each year during fishing season.
You know what I'm referring to...
Allowing oil-soaked smoked salmon to build up in kitchens, hallways and stairwells can only lead to one thing...
CHOMP!!
(WHERE THERE'S SMOKE THERE'S SALMON)
Spontaneous consumption. Don't let it happen to you!
urp!
GIA

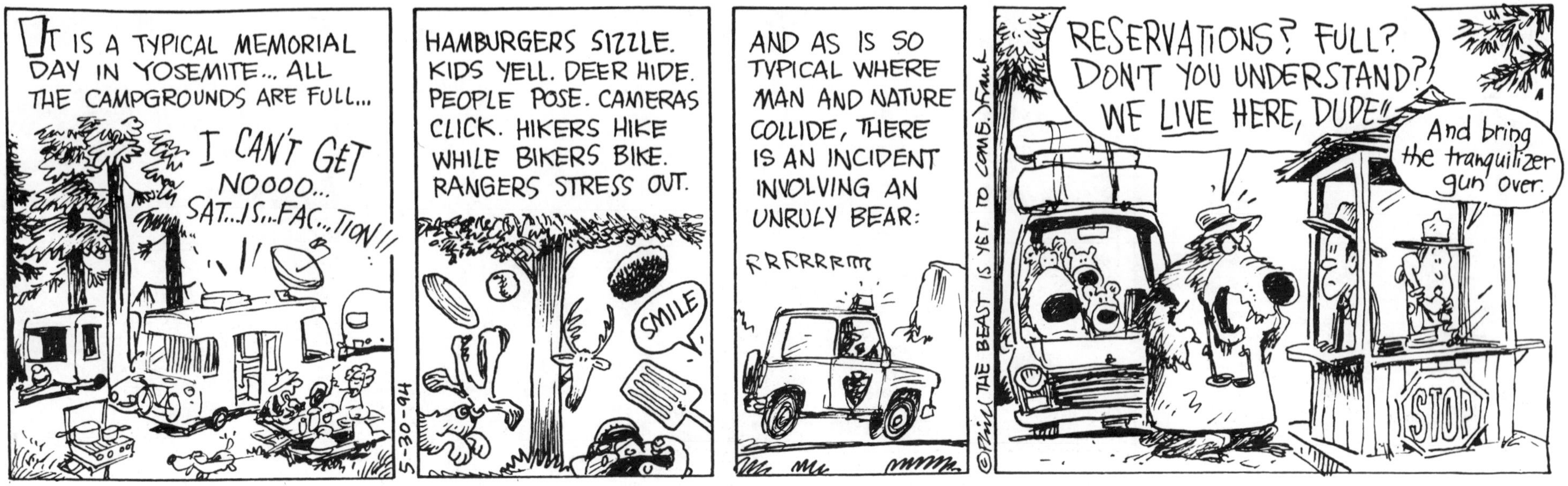

IT IS A TYPICAL MEMORIAL DAY IN YOSEMITE... ALL THE CAMPGROUNDS ARE FULL...
I CAN'T GET NOOOO... SAT...IS...FAC...TION!
5-30-94
HAMBURGERS SIZZLE. KIDS YELL. DEER HIDE. PEOPLE POSE. CAMERAS CLICK. HIKERS HIKE WHILE BIKERS BIKE. RANGERS STRESS OUT.
SMILE
AND AS IS SO TYPICAL WHERE MAN AND NATURE COLLIDE, THERE IS AN INCIDENT INVOLVING AN UNRULY BEAR:
RRRRRRRM
(THE BEAST IS YET TO COME.)
RESERVATIONS? FULL? DON'T YOU UNDERSTAND? WE LIVE HERE, DUDE!!
And bring the tranquilizer gun over.
STOP

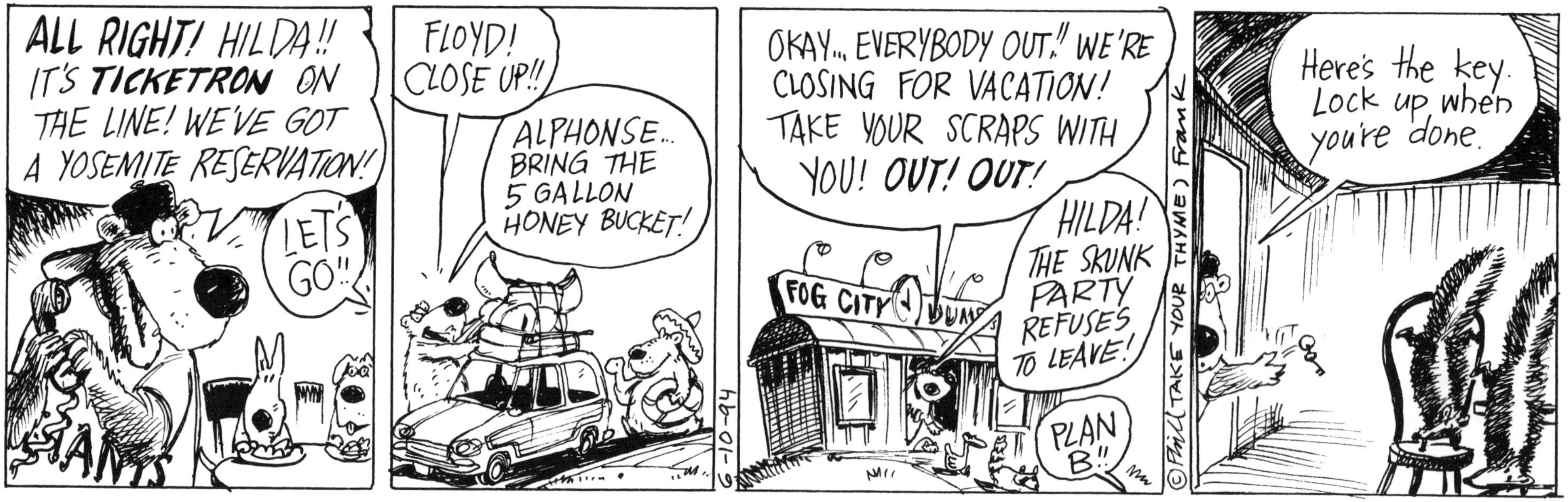
ALL RIGHT! HILDA!! IT'S TICKETRON ON THE LINE! WE'VE GOT A YOSEMITE RESERVATION!
LET'S GO!!
FLOYD! CLOSE UP!!
ALPHONSE... BRING THE 5 GALLON HONEY BUCKET!
6-10-94
OKAY... EVERYBODY OUT!! WE'RE CLOSING FOR VACATION! TAKE YOUR SCRAPS WITH YOU! OUT! OUT!
FOG CITY DUMP
HILDA! THE SKUNK PARTY REFUSES TO LEAVE!
PLAN B!!
© Phil (TAKE YOUR THYME) Frank
Here's the key. Lock up when you're done.

The bears close up the Dumpster and head for the hills.

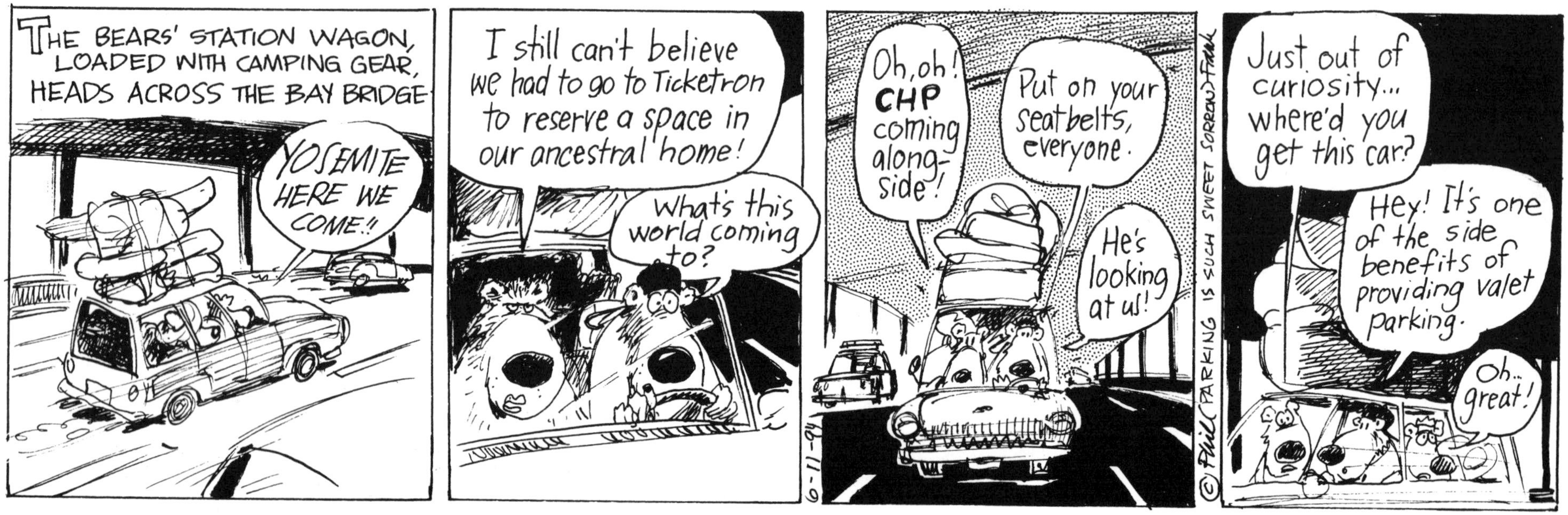
THE BEARS' STATION WAGON, LOADED WITH CAMPING GEAR, HEADS ACROSS THE BAY BRIDGE
YOSEMITE HERE WE COME!!
I still can't believe we had to go to Ticketron to reserve a space in our ancestral home!
What's this world coming to?
6-11-94
Oh, oh! CHP coming along-side!
Put on your seatbelts, everyone.
He's looking at us!
© Phil (PARKING IS SUCH SWEET SORROW) Frank
Just out of curiosity... where'd you get this car?
Hey! It's one of the side benefits of providing valet parking.
Oh... great!

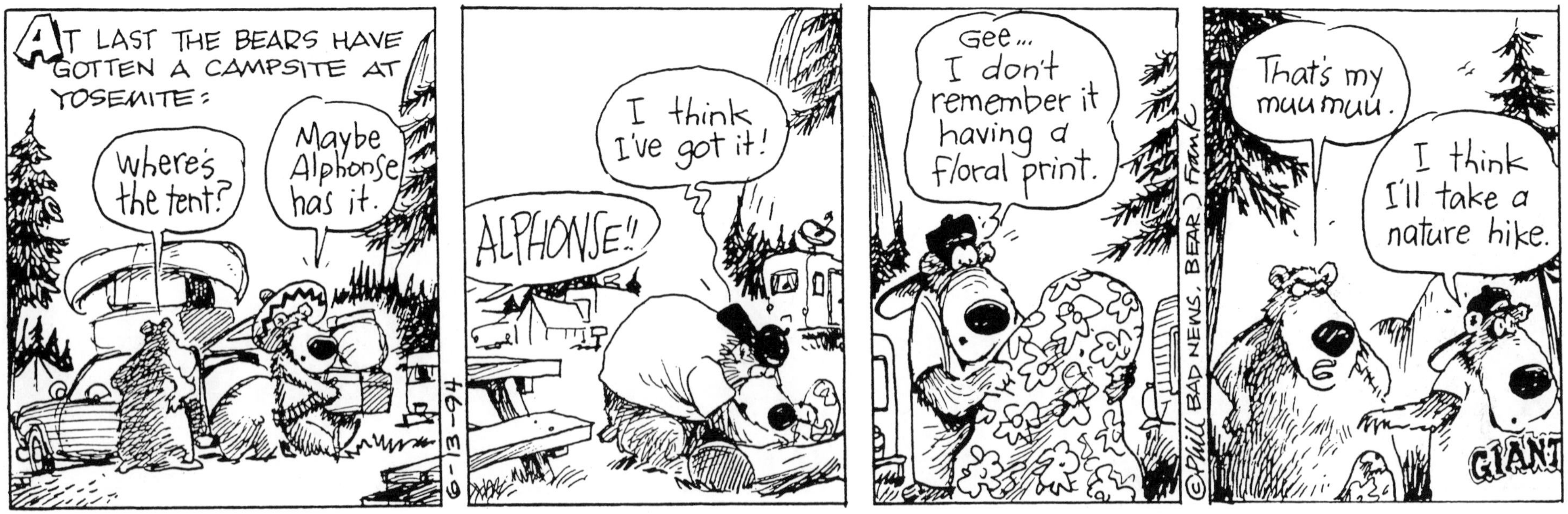
AT LAST THE BEARS HAVE GOTTEN A CAMPSITE AT YOSEMITE:
Where's the tent?
Maybe Alphonse has it.
6-13-94
ALPHONSE!!
I think I've got it!
Gee... I don't remember it having a floral print.
©Phill (BAD NEWS, BEAR) Frank
That's my muumuu.
I think I'll take a nature hike.
GIANT

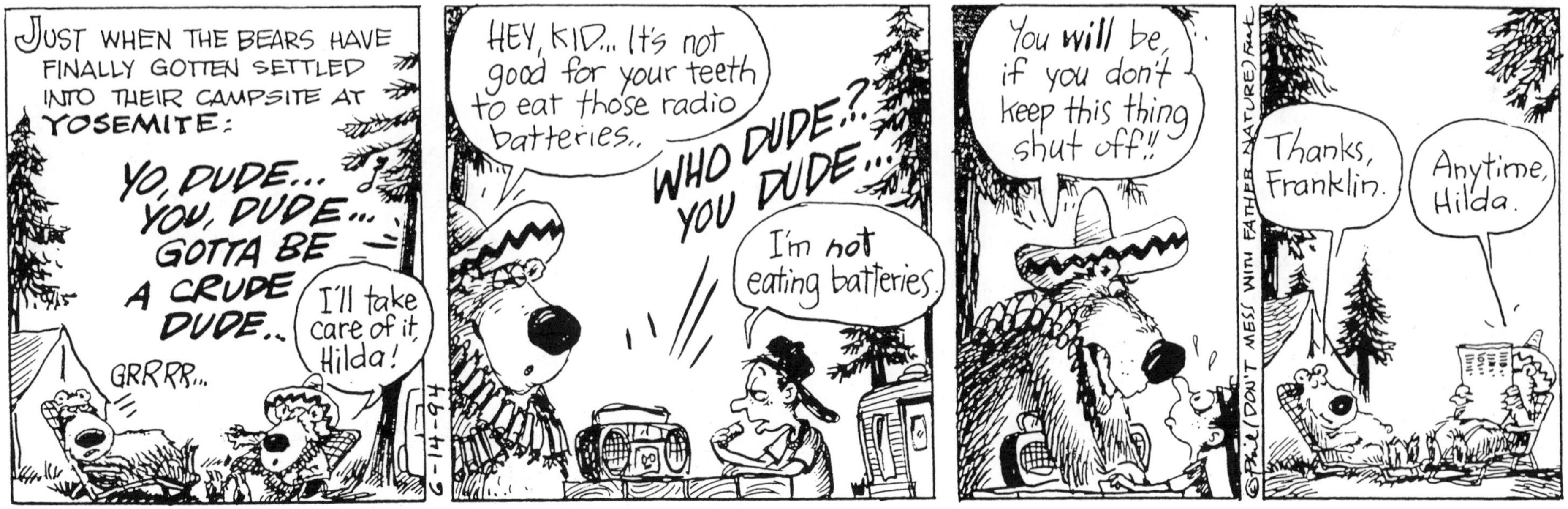
JUST WHEN THE BEARS HAVE FINALLY GOTTEN SETTLED INTO THEIR CAMPSITE AT YOSEMITE:
YO, DUDE... YOU, DUDE... GOTTA BE A CRUDE DUDE...
GRRRR...
I'll take care of it, Hilda!
6-14-94
HEY, KID... It's not good for your teeth to eat those radio batteries..
WHO DUDE?.. YOU DUDE...
I'm not eating batteries.
You will be, if you don't keep this thing shut off!!
©Phill (DON'T MESS WITH FATHER NATURE) Frank
Thanks, Franklin.
Anytime, Hilda.

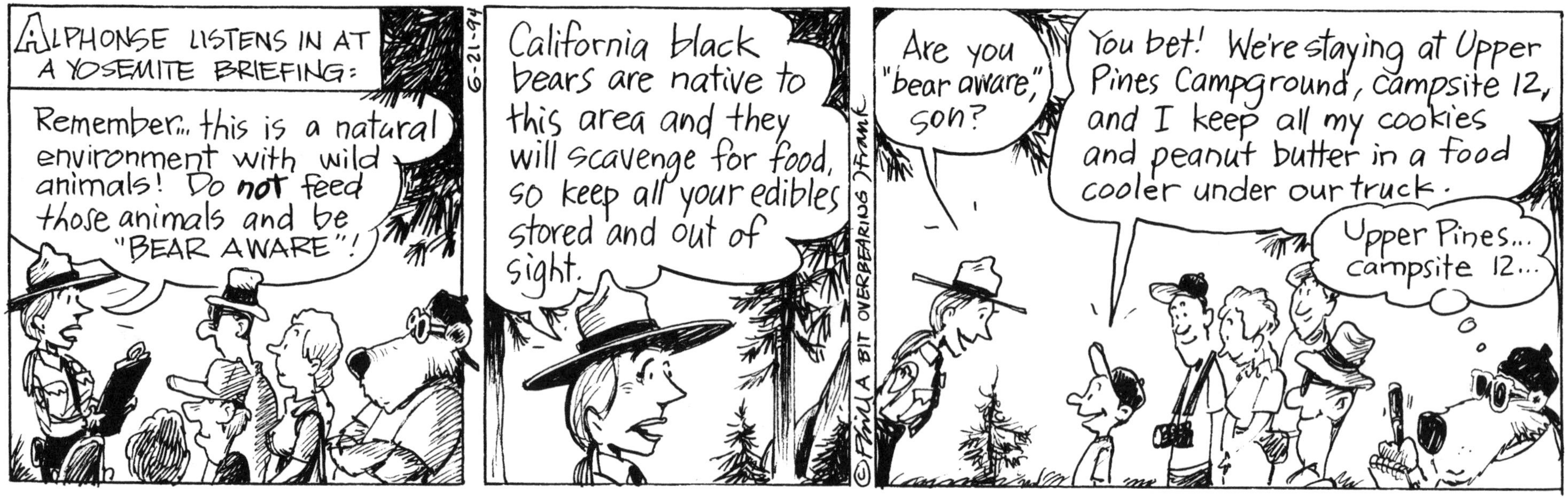
ALPHONSE LISTENS IN AT A YOSEMITE BRIEFING:
Remember... this is a natural environment with wild animals! Do **not** feed those animals and be "BEAR AWARE"!
6-21-94
California black bears are native to this area and they will scavenge for food, so keep all your edibles stored and out of sight.
©PHIL A BIT OVERBEARING Frank
Are you "bear aware," son?
You bet! We're staying at Upper Pines Campground, campsite 12, and I keep all my cookies and peanut butter in a food cooler under our truck.
Upper Pines... campsite 12...

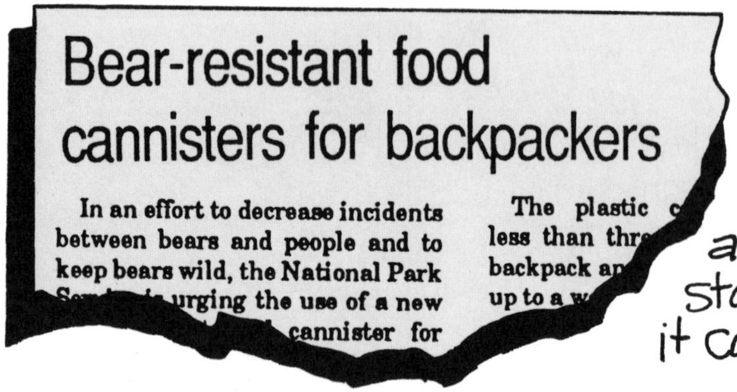

Bear-resistant food cannisters for backpackers

In an effort to decrease incidents between bears and people and to keep bears wild, the National Park ... urging the use of a new ... cannister for

The plastic c... less than thr... backpack a... up to a w...

When I started doing the comic strip twenty-four years ago, I picked bears as ideal cartoon characters because of their human-like habits and thinking processes. Every wildlife technician and bear expert I've spoken with has numerous stories about the creativity of these animals when it comes to getting at human food.

The Park Service was certain it had found a way to keep bears away from campers' food with its new bear-proof canister. When a press conference was held to announce a secure canister, which would be available to rent or purchase at Yosemite, it was grist for the cartoonist's mill.

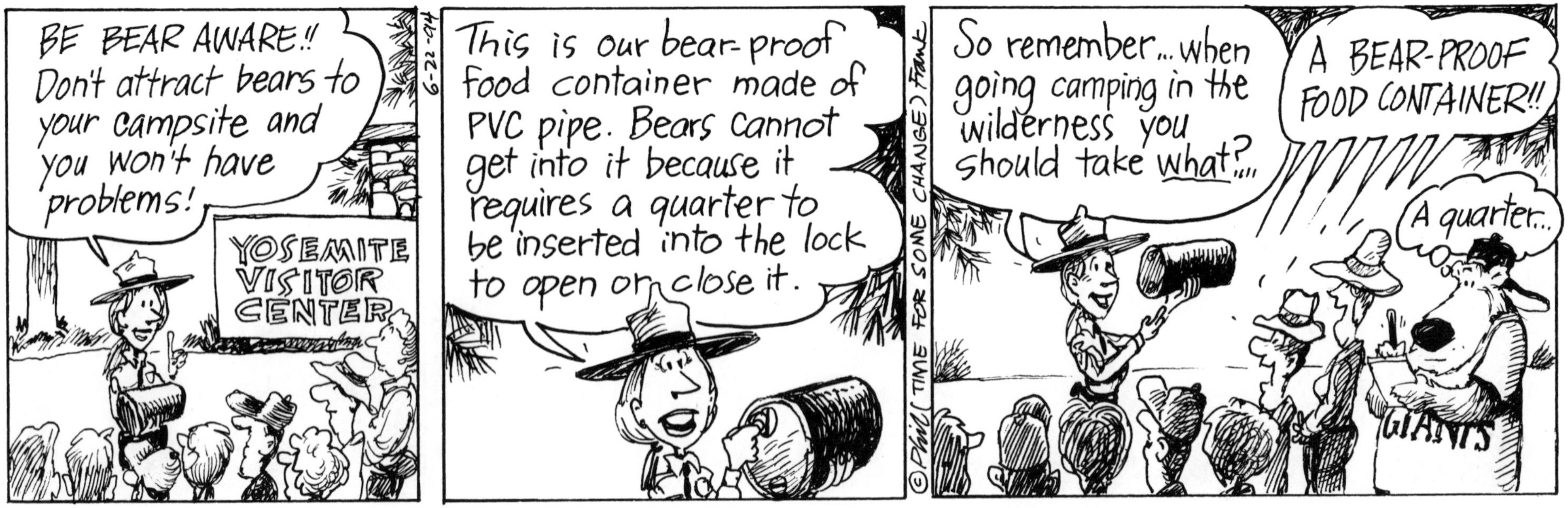
6-22-94
BE BEAR AWARE!! Don't attract bears to your campsite and you won't have problems!
YOSEMITE VISITOR CENTER
This is our bear-proof food container made of PVC pipe. Bears cannot get into it because it requires a quarter to be inserted into the lock to open or close it.
© Phil (TIME FOR SOME CHANGE) Frank
So remember... when going camping in the wilderness you should take what?...
A BEAR-PROOF FOOD CONTAINER!!
A quarter...
GIANTS

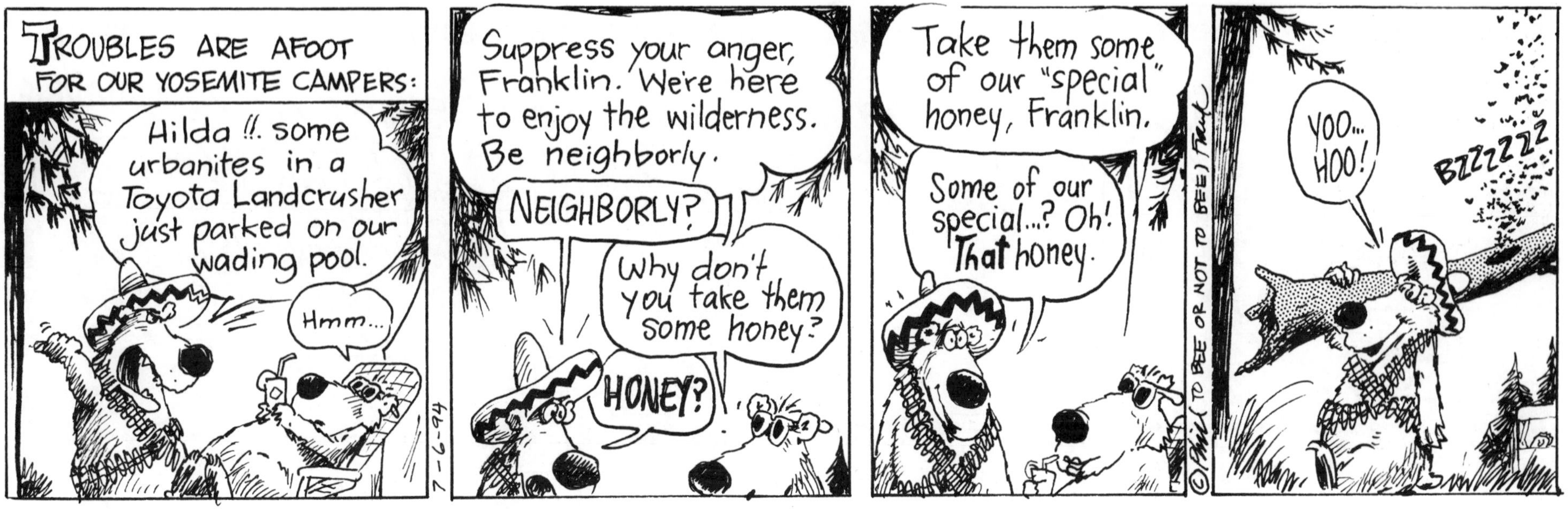
TROUBLES ARE AFOOT FOR OUR YOSEMITE CAMPERS:
Hilda!!. some urbanites in a Toyota Landcrusher just parked on our wading pool.
Hmm...
7-6-94
Suppress your anger, Franklin. We're here to enjoy the wilderness. Be neighborly.
NEIGHBORLY?
Why don't you take them some honey?
HONEY?
Take them some of our "special" honey, Franklin.
Some of our special...? Oh! That honey.
© Phil (TO BEE OR NOT TO BEE) Frank
YOO... HOO!
BZZZZZZ

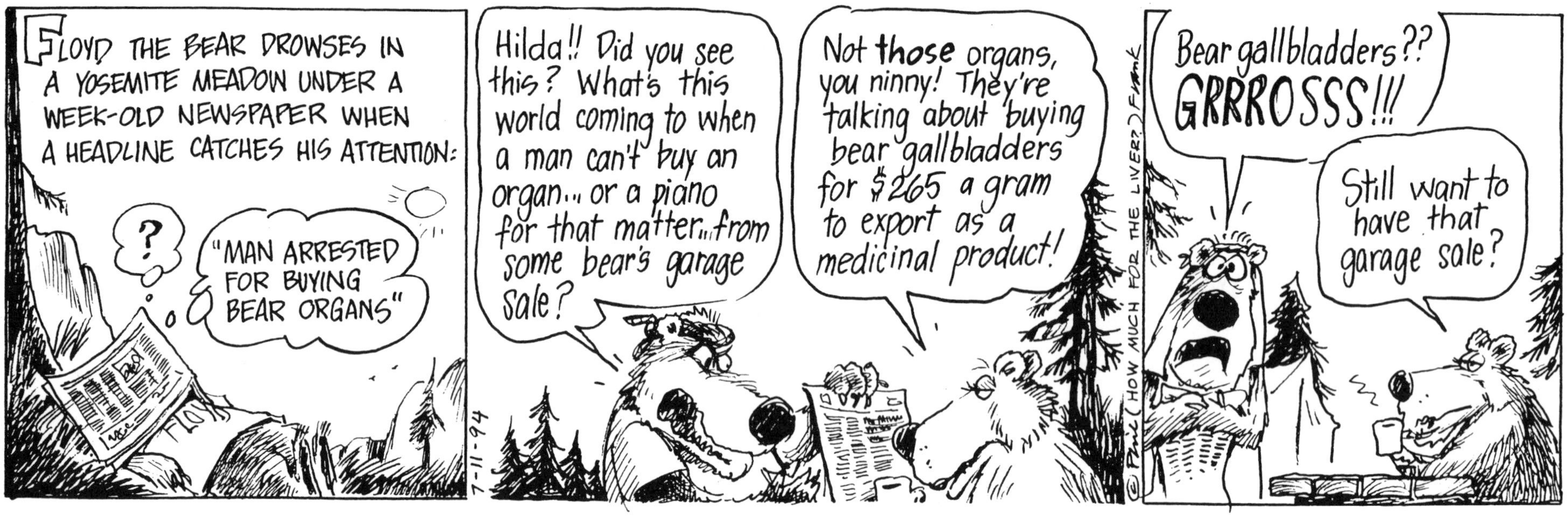
FLOYD THE BEAR DROWSES IN A YOSEMITE MEADOW UNDER A WEEK-OLD NEWSPAPER WHEN A HEADLINE CATCHES HIS ATTENTION:
?
"MAN ARRESTED FOR BUYING BEAR ORGANS"
7-11-94
Hilda!! Did you see this? What's this world coming to when a man can't buy an organ... or a piano for that matter... from some bear's garage sale?
Not those organs, you ninny! They're talking about buying bear gallbladders for $265 a gram to export as a medicinal product!
© Phil (HOW MUCH FOR THE LIVER?) Frank
Bear gallbladders?? GRRROSSS!!!
Still want to have that garage sale?

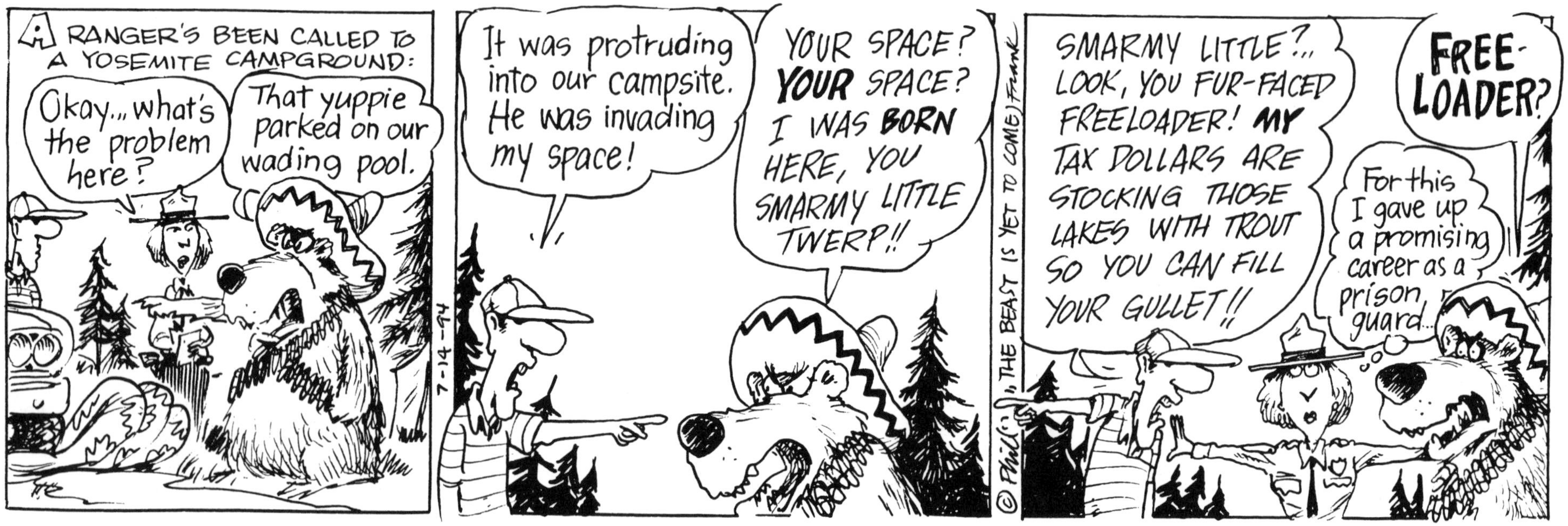
A RANGER'S BEEN CALLED TO A YOSEMITE CAMPGROUND:
Okay... what's the problem here?
That yuppie parked on our wading pool.
7-14-94
It was protruding into our campsite. He was invading my space!
YOUR SPACE? YOUR SPACE? I WAS BORN HERE, YOU SMARMY LITTLE TWERP!!
© Phil THE BEAST IS YET TO COME Frank
SMARMY LITTLE?... LOOK, YOU FUR-FACED FREELOADER! MY TAX DOLLARS ARE STOCKING THOSE LAKES WITH TROUT SO YOU CAN FILL YOUR GULLET!!
FREE-LOADER?
For this I gave up a promising career as a prison guard...

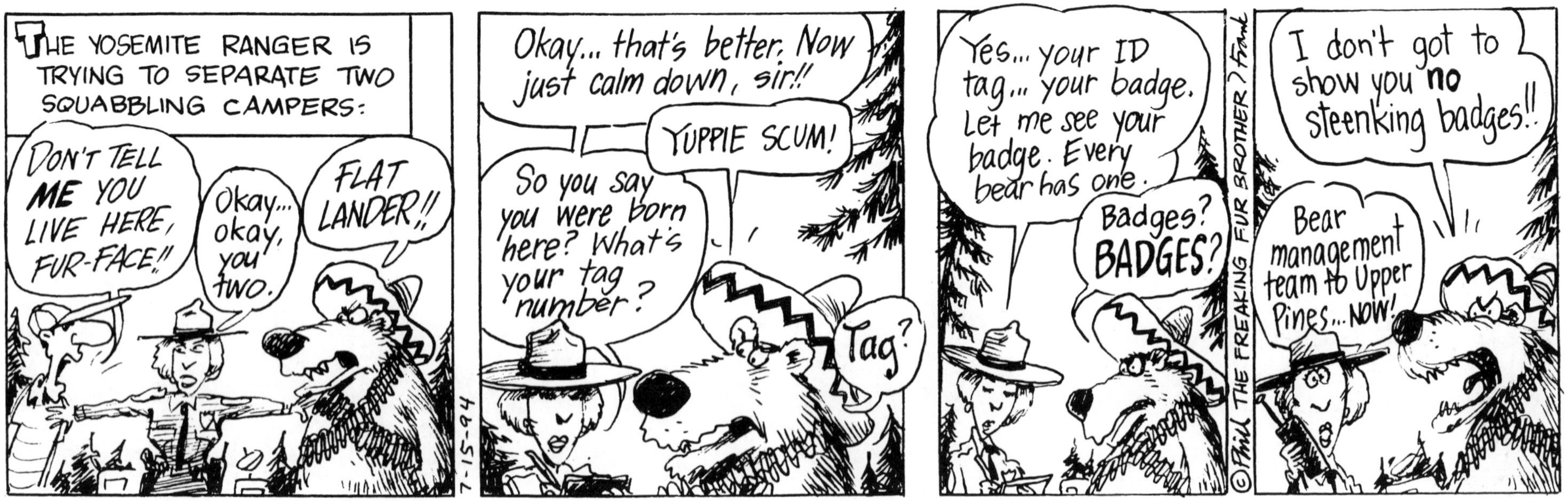
THE YOSEMITE RANGER IS TRYING TO SEPARATE TWO SQUABBLING CAMPERS:
DON'T TELL ME YOU LIVE HERE, FUR-FACE!!
Okay... okay, you two.
FLAT LANDER!!
7-15-94
Okay... that's better. Now just calm down, sir!!
YUPPIE SCUM!
So you say you were born here? What's your tag number?
Tag?
Yes... your ID tag... your badge. Let me see your badge. Every bear has one.
Badges? BADGES?
© Phil THE FREAKING FUR BROTHER? Frank
I don't got to show you no steenking badges!!
Bear management team to Upper Pines... NOW!

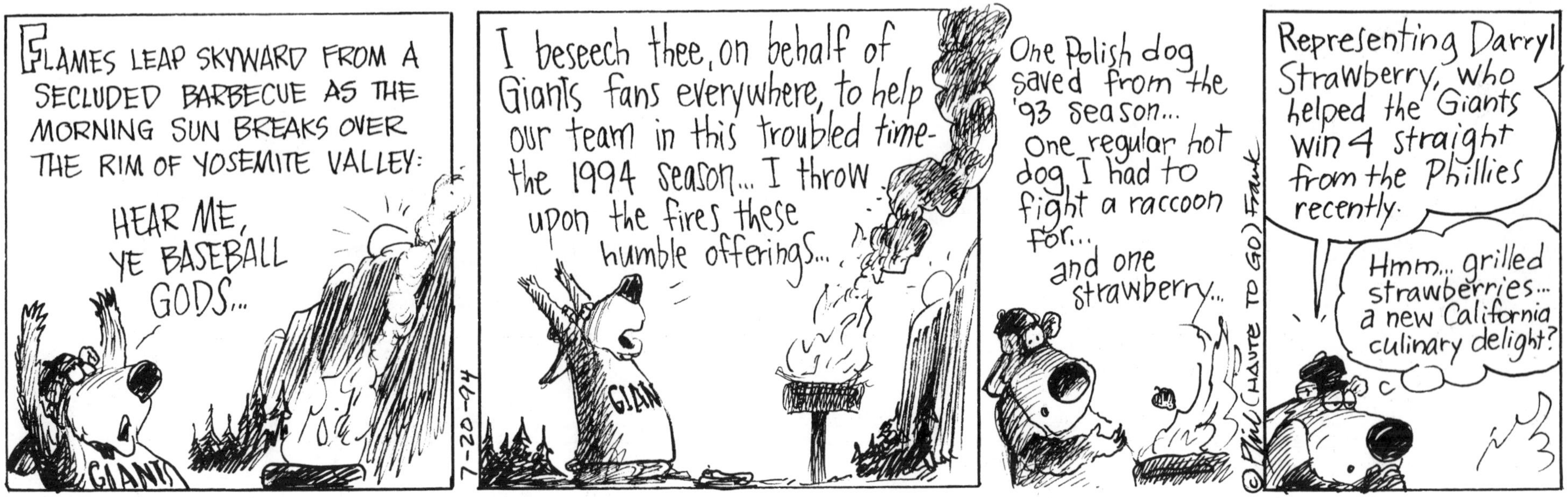
FLAMES LEAP SKYWARD FROM A SECLUDED BARBECUE AS THE MORNING SUN BREAKS OVER THE RIM OF YOSEMITE VALLEY:
HEAR ME, YE BASEBALL GODS...
GIANTS
7-20-94
I beseech thee, on behalf of Giants fans everywhere, to help our team in this troubled time- the 1994 season... I throw upon the fires these humble offerings...
One Polish dog saved from the '93 season...
One regular hot dog I had to fight a raccoon for...
and one strawberry...
© Phil (HAUTE TO GO) Frank
Representing Darryl Strawberry, who helped the Giants win 4 straight from the Phillies recently.
Hmm... grilled strawberries... a new California culinary delight?

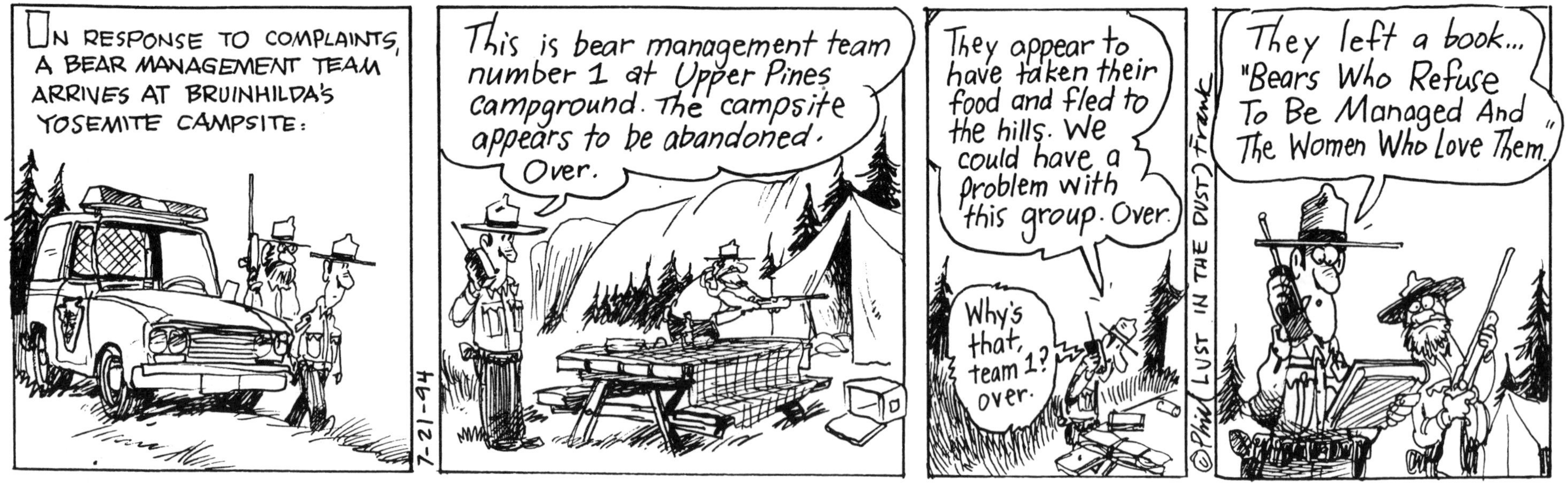
IN RESPONSE TO COMPLAINTS, A BEAR MANAGEMENT TEAM ARRIVES AT BRUINHILDA'S YOSEMITE CAMPSITE:
7-21-94
This is bear management team number 1 at Upper Pines campground. The campsite appears to be abandoned. Over.
They appear to have taken their food and fled to the hills. We could have a problem with this group. Over.
Why's that, team 1? over.
©Phil (LUST IN THE DUST) Frank
They left a book... "Bears Who Refuse To Be Managed And The Women Who Love Them."

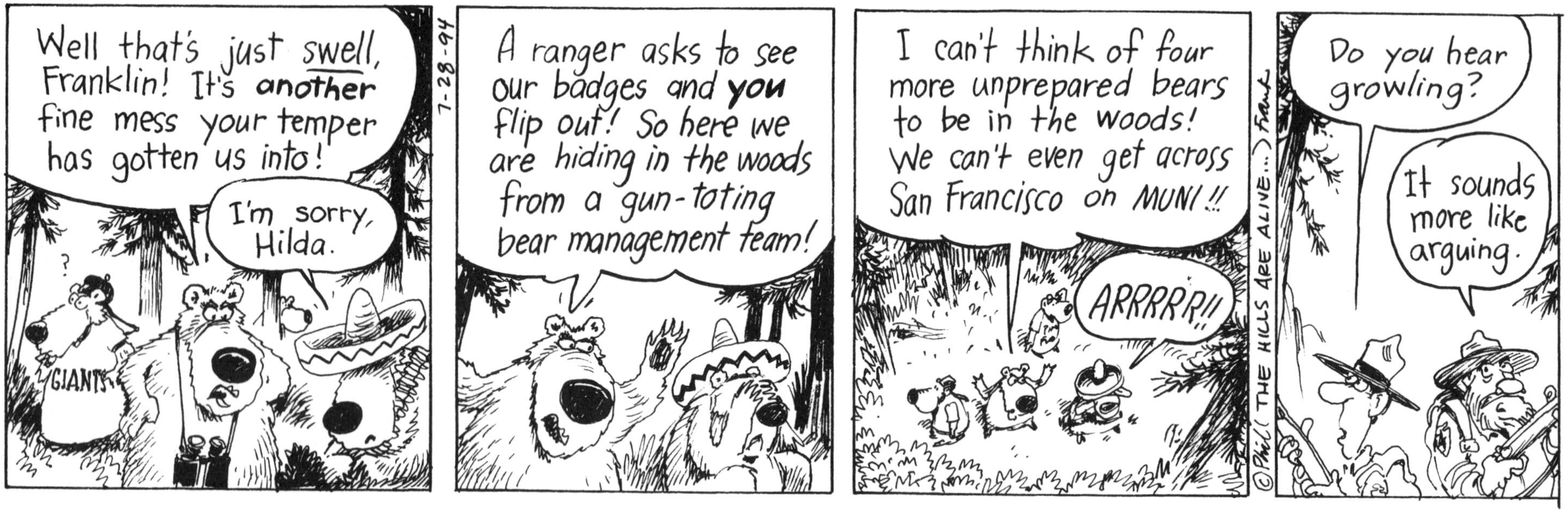
Well that's just swell, Franklin! It's **another** fine mess your temper has gotten us into!
I'm sorry, Hilda.
?
GIANTS
7-28-94
A ranger asks to see our badges and **you** flip out! So here we are hiding in the woods from a gun-toting bear management team!
I can't think of four more unprepared bears to be in the woods! We can't even get across San Francisco on MUNI!!
ARRRRR!!
©Phil (THE HILLS ARE ALIVE...) Frank
Do you hear growling?
It sounds more like arguing.

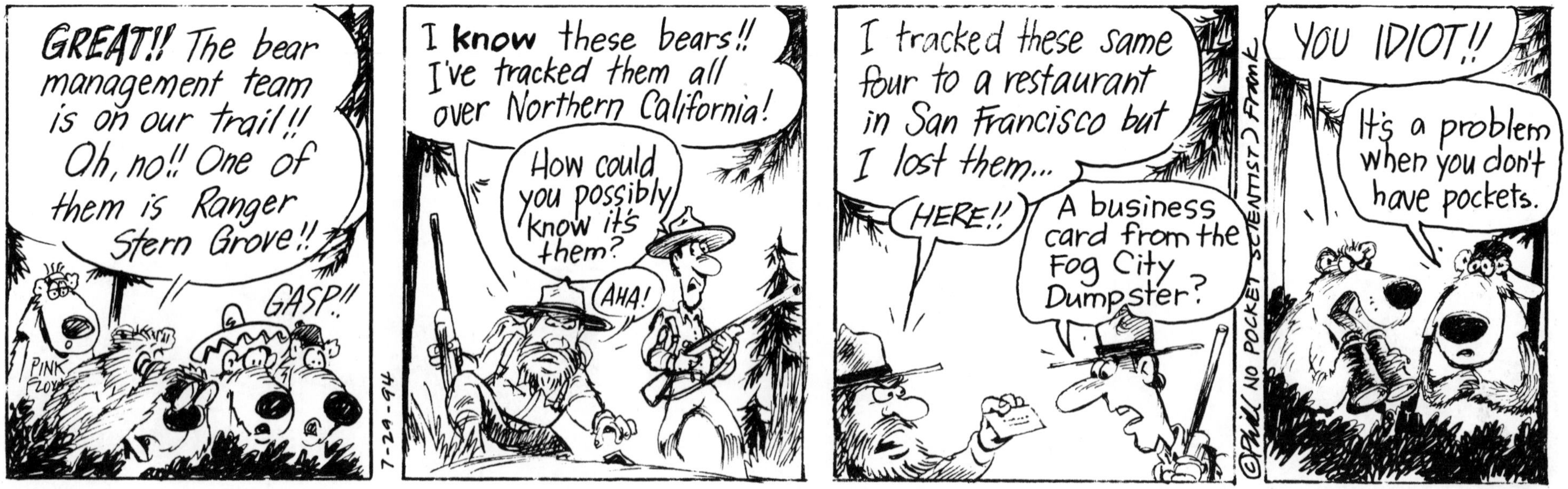

GREAT!! The bear management team is on our trail!! Oh, no!! One of them is Ranger Stern Grove!!
GASP!!
PINK FLOYD
7-29-94
I know these bears!! I've tracked them all over Northern California!
How could you possibly know it's them?
AHA!
I tracked these same four to a restaurant in San Francisco but I lost them...
HERE!!
A business card from the Fog City Dumpster?
©Phil Frank (NO POCKET SCIENTIST)
YOU IDIOT!!
It's a problem when you don't have pockets.

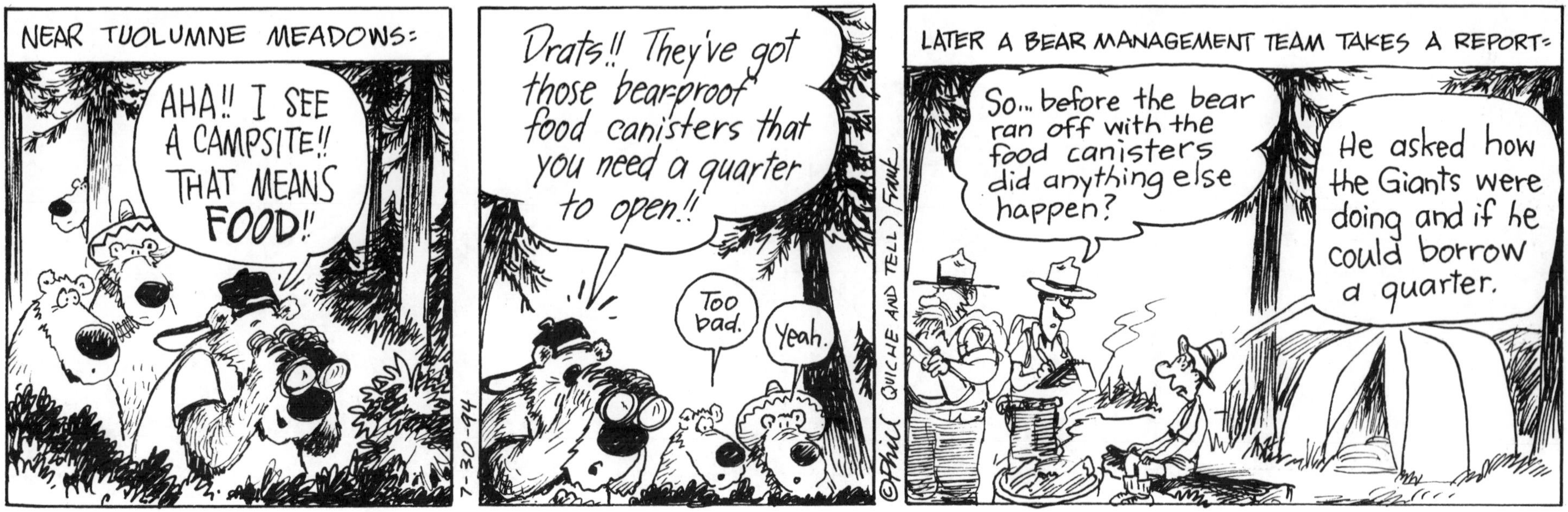

NEAR TUOLUMNE MEADOWS:
AHA!! I SEE A CAMPSITE!! THAT MEANS FOOD!!
7-30-94
Drats!! They've got those bearproof food canisters that you need a quarter to open!!
Too bad.
Yeah.
©Phil Frank (QUICHE AND TELL)
LATER A BEAR MANAGEMENT TEAM TAKES A REPORT:
So... before the bear ran off with the food canisters did anything else happen?
He asked how the Giants were doing and if he could borrow a quarter.

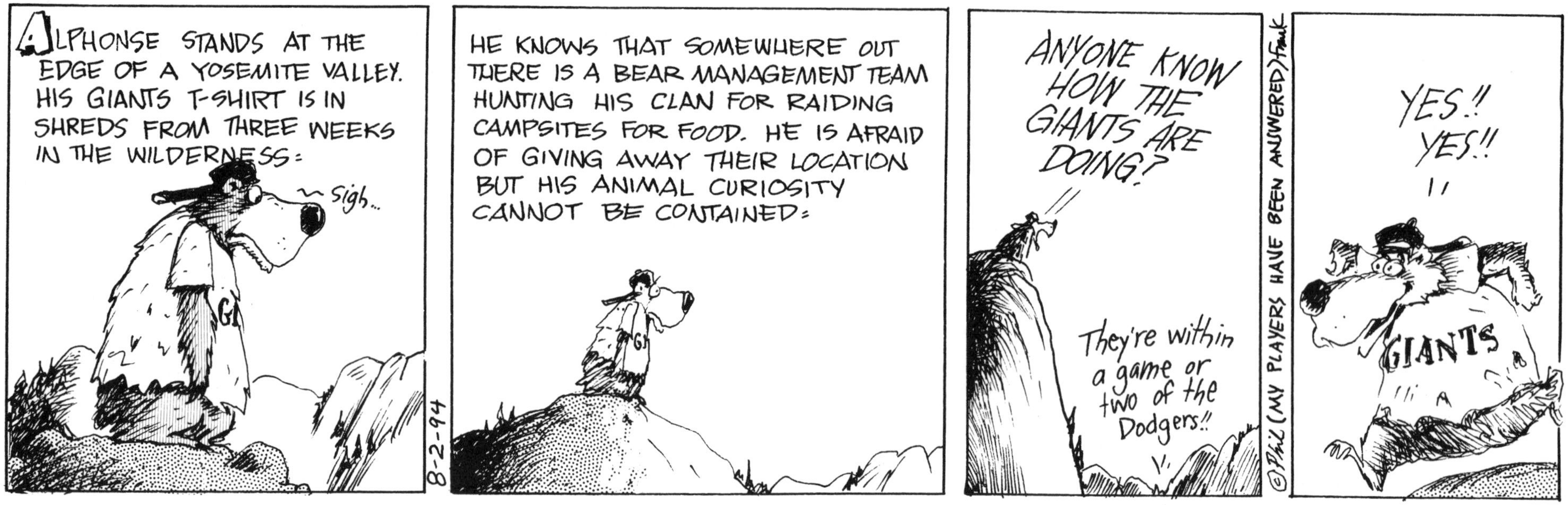
ALPHONSE STANDS AT THE EDGE OF A YOSEMITE VALLEY. HIS GIANTS T-SHIRT IS IN SHREDS FROM THREE WEEKS IN THE WILDERNESS.
~ Sigh...
8-2-94
HE KNOWS THAT SOMEWHERE OUT THERE IS A BEAR MANAGEMENT TEAM HUNTING HIS CLAN FOR RAIDING CAMPSITES FOR FOOD. HE IS AFRAID OF GIVING AWAY THEIR LOCATION BUT HIS ANIMAL CURIOSITY CANNOT BE CONTAINED.
ANYONE KNOW HOW THE GIANTS ARE DOING?
They're within a game or two of the Dodgers!!
© Phil (MY PLAYERS HAVE BEEN ANSWERED) Frank
YES!! YES!!
GIANTS

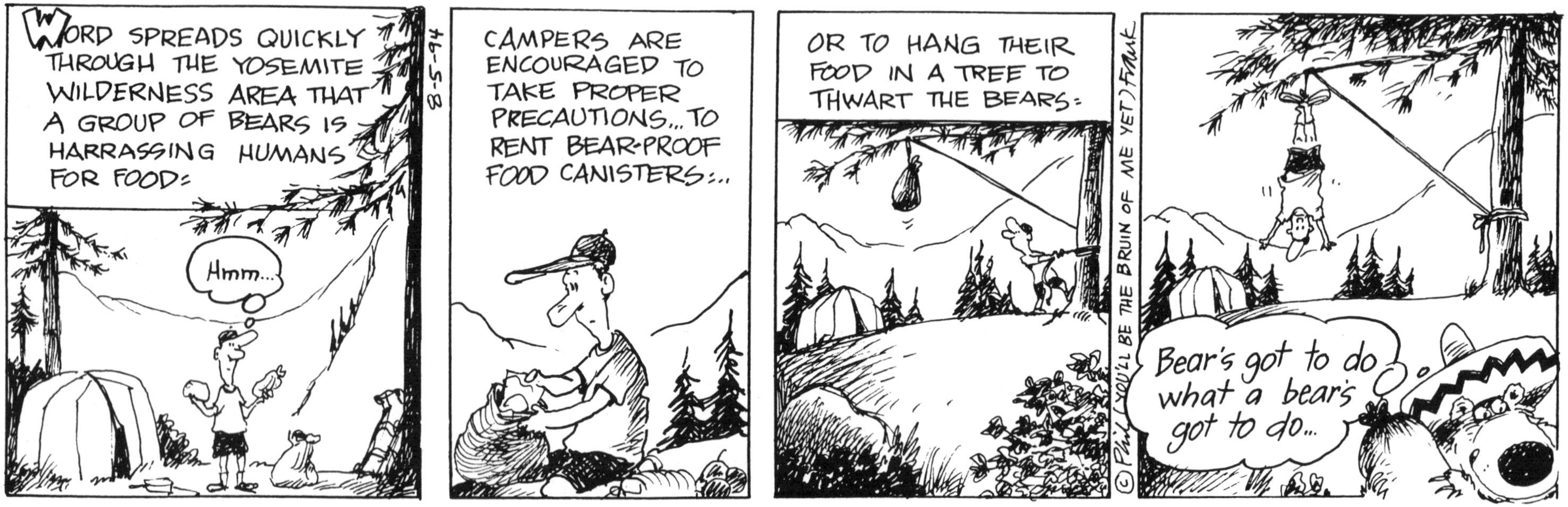
WORD SPREADS QUICKLY THROUGH THE YOSEMITE WILDERNESS AREA THAT A GROUP OF BEARS IS HARRASSING HUMANS FOR FOOD.
Hmm...
8-5-94
CAMPERS ARE ENCOURAGED TO TAKE PROPER PRECAUTIONS... TO RENT BEAR-PROOF FOOD CANISTERS...
OR TO HANG THEIR FOOD IN A TREE TO THWART THE BEARS.
© Phil (YOU'LL BE THE BRUIN OF ME YET) Frank
Bear's got to do what a bear's got to do...

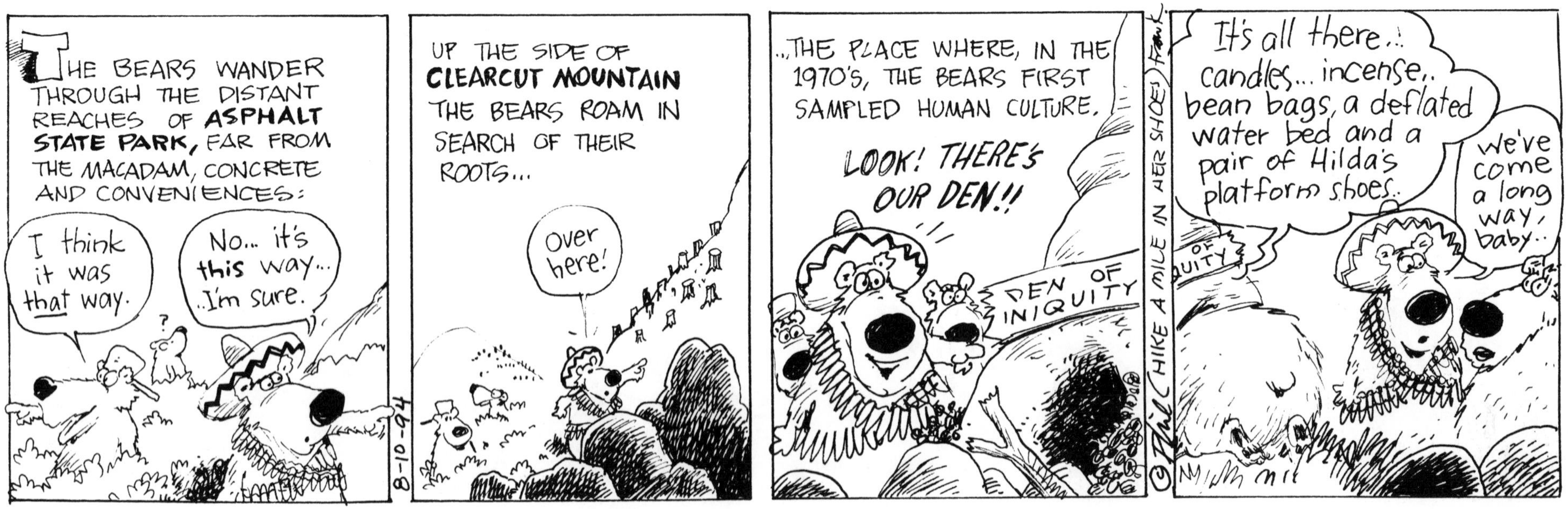
THE BEARS WANDER THROUGH THE DISTANT REACHES OF ASPHALT STATE PARK, FAR FROM THE MACADAM, CONCRETE AND CONVENIENCES:
I think it was that way.
No... it's this way... ..I'm sure.
8-10-94
UP THE SIDE OF CLEARCUT MOUNTAIN THE BEARS ROAM IN SEARCH OF THEIR ROOTS...
Over here!
..THE PLACE WHERE, IN THE 1970'S, THE BEARS FIRST SAMPLED HUMAN CULTURE.
LOOK! THERE'S OUR DEN!!
DEN OF INIQUITY
© Phil Frank
HIKE A MILE IN HER SHOES
It's all there..! candles... incense.. bean bags, a deflated water bed and a pair of Hilda's platform shoes..
We've come a long way, baby..
OF UITY

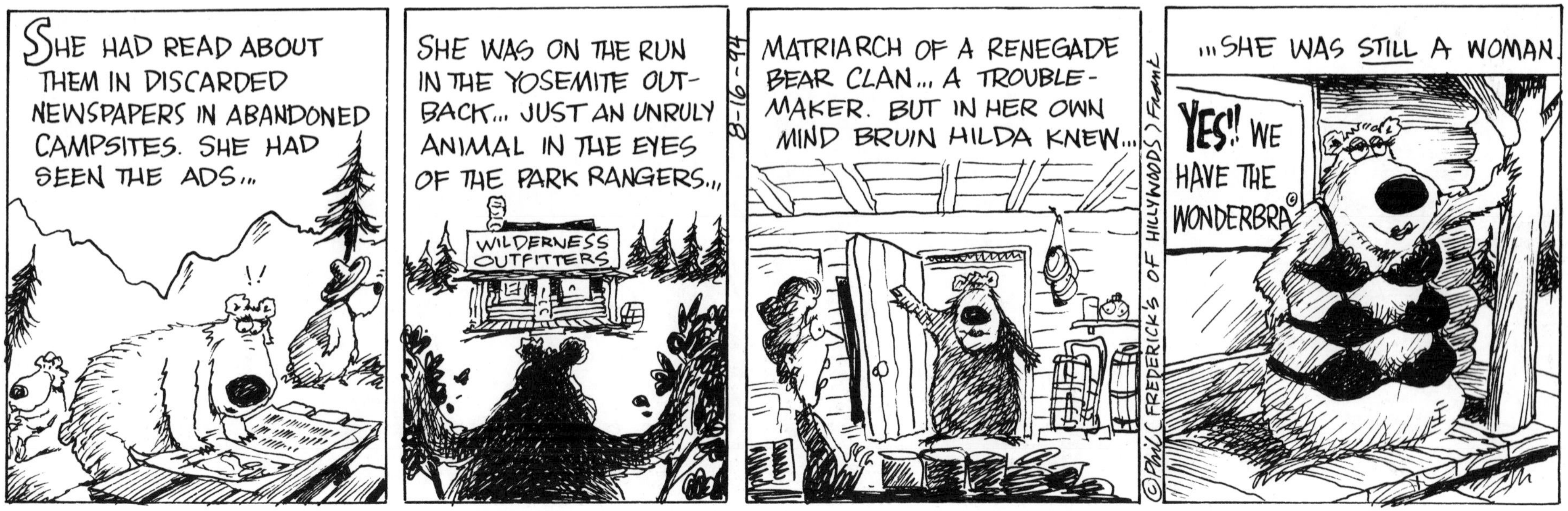
SHE HAD READ ABOUT THEM IN DISCARDED NEWSPAPERS IN ABANDONED CAMPSITES. SHE HAD SEEN THE ADS...
SHE WAS ON THE RUN IN THE YOSEMITE OUT-BACK... JUST AN UNRULY ANIMAL IN THE EYES OF THE PARK RANGERS...
WILDERNESS OUTFITTERS
8-16-94
MATRIARCH OF A RENEGADE BEAR CLAN... A TROUBLE-MAKER. BUT IN HER OWN MIND BRUIN HILDA KNEW...
© Phil (FREDERICK'S OF HILLYWOODS) Frank
...SHE WAS STILL A WOMAN.
YES!! WE HAVE THE WONDERBRA®

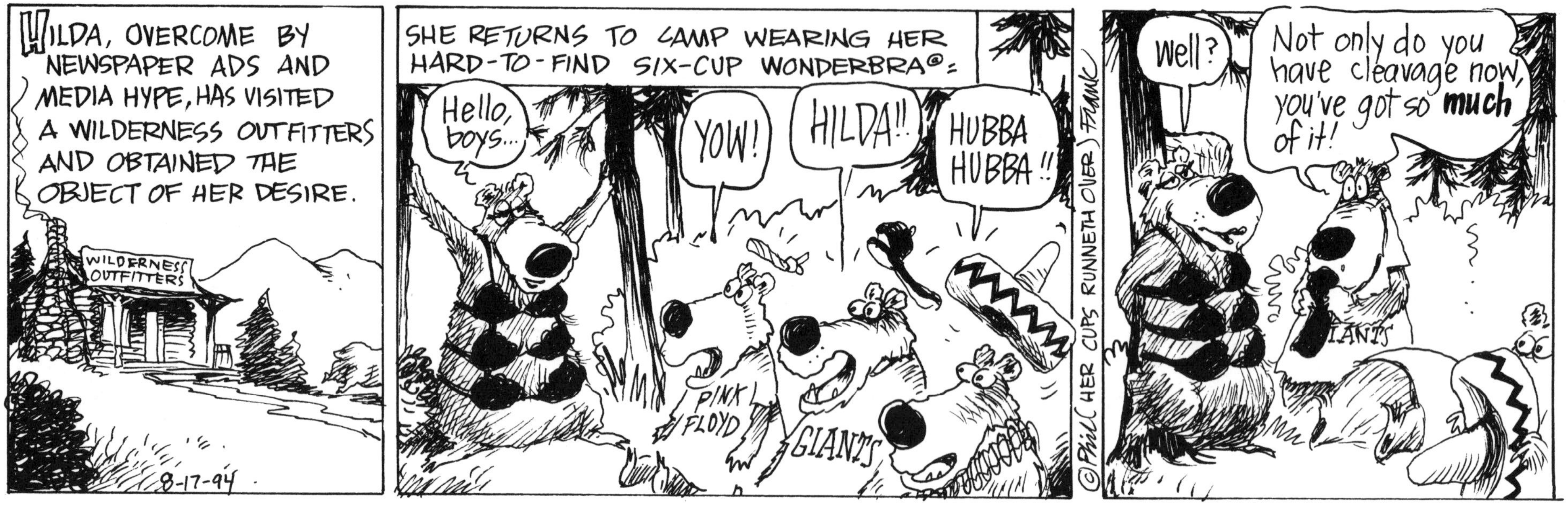
HILDA, OVERCOME BY NEWSPAPER ADS AND MEDIA HYPE, HAS VISITED A WILDERNESS OUTFITTERS AND OBTAINED THE OBJECT OF HER DESIRE.
WILDERNESS OUTFITTERS
8-17-94
SHE RETURNS TO CAMP WEARING HER HARD-TO-FIND SIX-CUP WONDERBRA®:
Hello, boys...
YOW!
HILDA!!
HUBBA HUBBA!!
PINK FLOYD
GIANTS
©Phil (HER CUPS RUNNETH OVER) Frank
Well?
Not only do you have cleavage now, you've got so **much** of it!

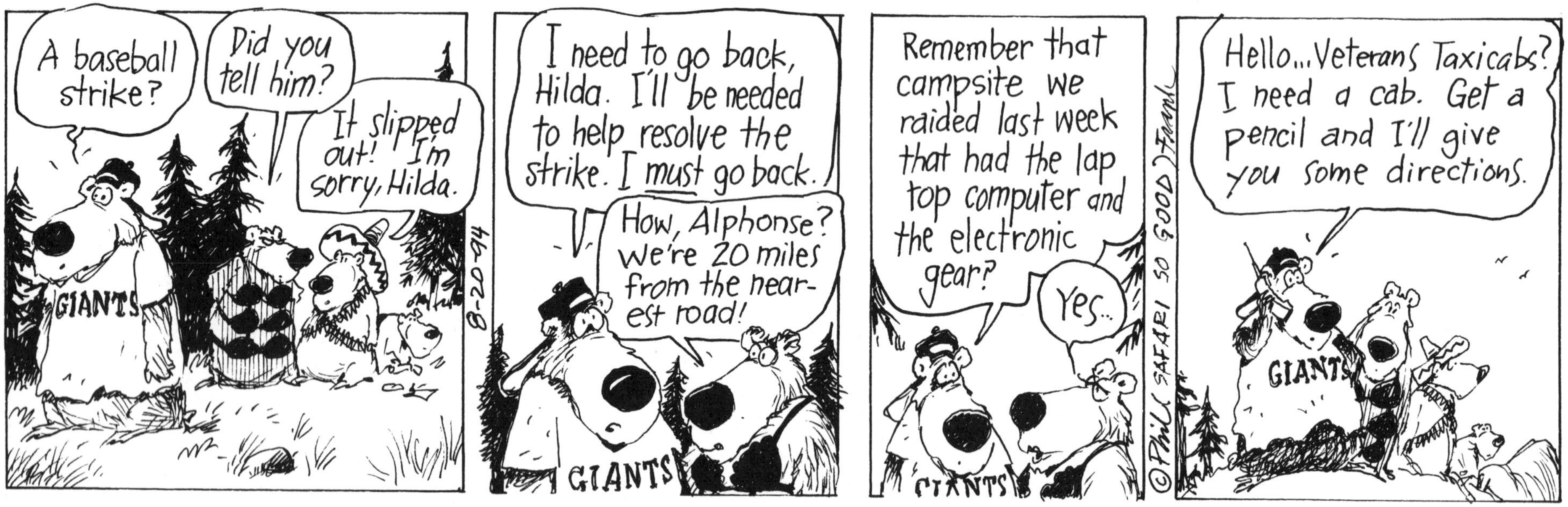
A baseball strike?
Did you tell him?
It slipped out! I'm sorry, Hilda.
GIANTS
8-20-94
I need to go back, Hilda. I'll be needed to help resolve the strike. I must go back.
How, Alphonse? We're 20 miles from the nearest road!
GIANTS
Remember that campsite we raided last week that had the lap top computer and the electronic gear?
Yes...
©Phil (SAFARI SO GOOD) Frank
Hello... Veterans Taxicabs? I need a cab. Get a pencil and I'll give you some directions.
GIANTS

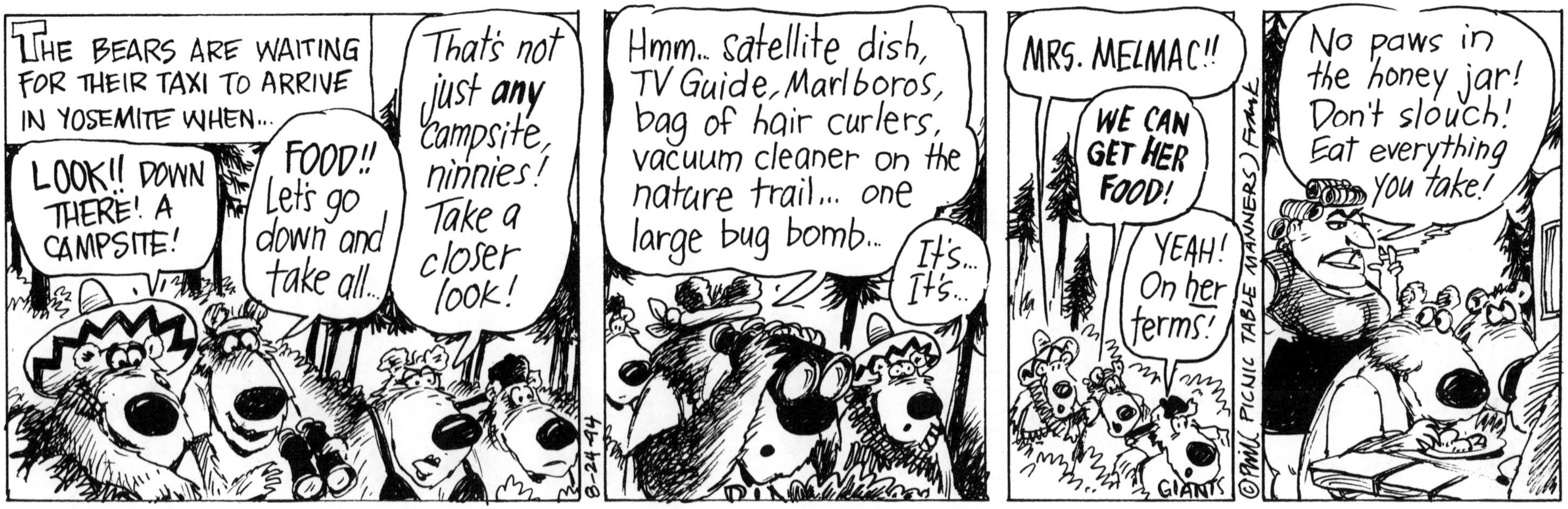
THE BEARS ARE WAITING FOR THEIR TAXI TO ARRIVE IN YOSEMITE WHEN...
LOOK!! DOWN THERE! A CAMPSITE!
FOOD!! Let's go down and take all...
That's not just any campsite, ninnies! Take a closer look!
8-24-94
Hmm.. satellite dish, TV Guide, Marlboros, bag of hair curlers, vacuum cleaner on the nature trail... one large bug bomb...
It's... It's...
MRS. MELMAC!!
WE CAN GET HER FOOD!
YEAH! On her terms!
GIANTS
©Phil (PICNIC TABLE MANNERS) Frank
No paws in the honey jar! Don't slouch! Eat everything you take!

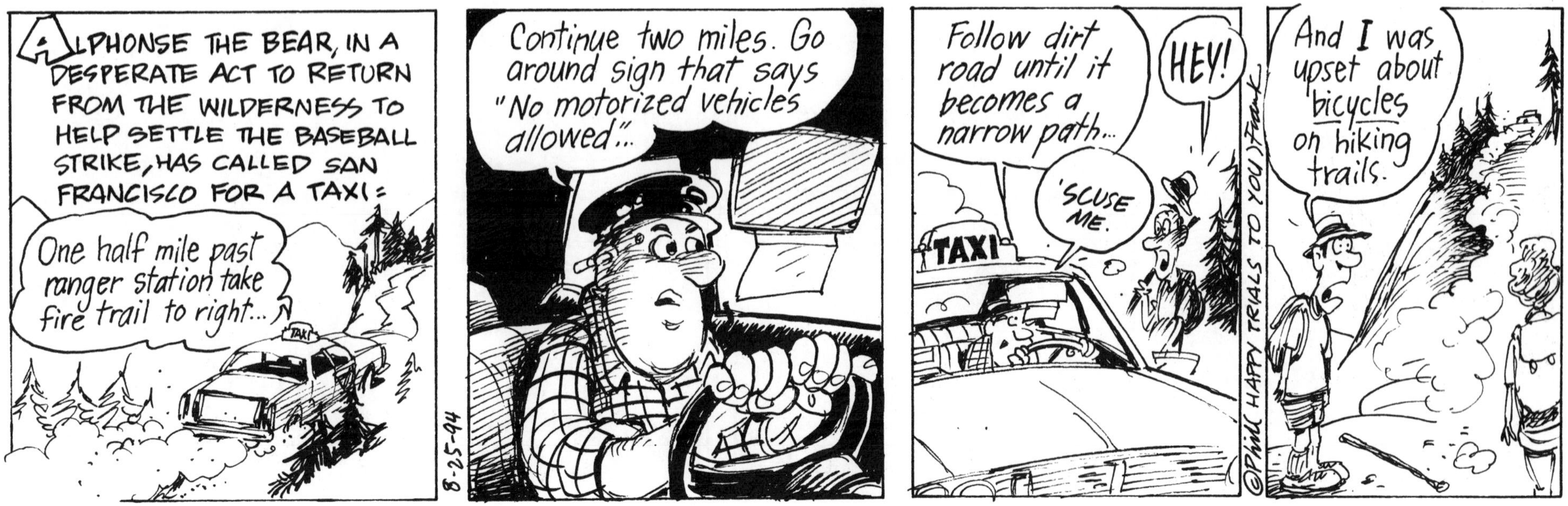
ALPHONSE THE BEAR, IN A DESPERATE ACT TO RETURN FROM THE WILDERNESS TO HELP SETTLE THE BASEBALL STRIKE, HAS CALLED SAN FRANCISCO FOR A TAXI:
One half mile past ranger station take fire trail to right...
TAXI
8-25-94
Continue two miles. Go around sign that says "No motorized vehicles allowed"...
Follow dirt road until it becomes a narrow path...
HEY!
TAXI
'SCUSE ME.
©Phil (HAPPY TRIALS TO YOU) Frank
And I was upset about bicycles on hiking trails.

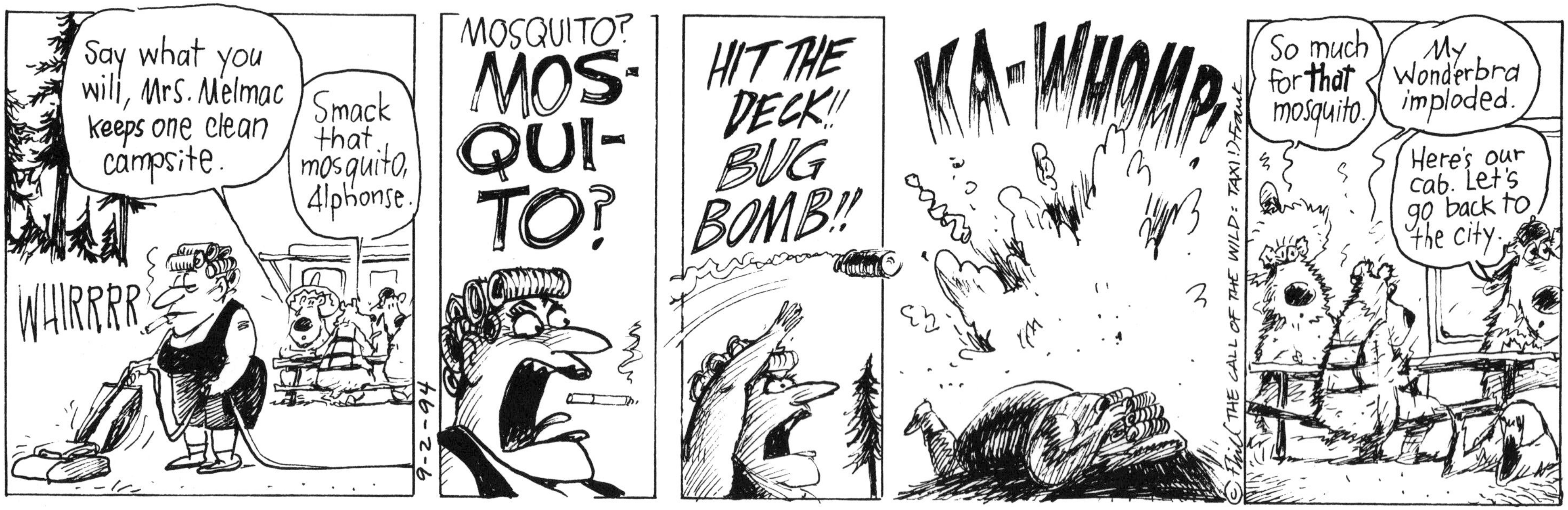
Say what you will, Mrs. Melmac **keeps** one clean campsite.
WHIRRRR
Smack that mosquito, Alphonse.
9-2-94
MOSQUITO? MOS-QUI-TO?
HIT THE DECK!! BUG BOMB!!
KA-WHOMP!
© Phil (THE CALL OF THE WILD: TAXI!) Frank
So much for **that** mosquito.
My Wonderbra imploded.
Here's our cab. Let's go back to the city.

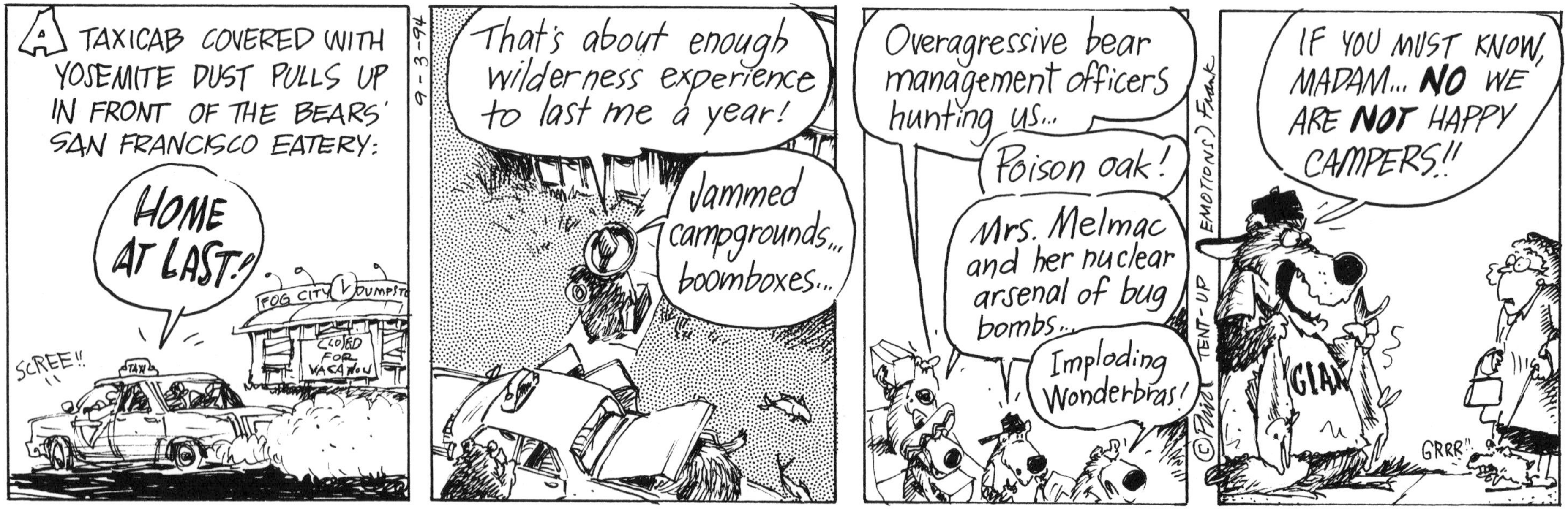
A TAXICAB COVERED WITH YOSEMITE DUST PULLS UP IN FRONT OF THE BEARS' SAN FRANCISCO EATERY:
HOME AT LAST!
SCREE!!
TAXI
9-3-94
That's about enough wilderness experience to last me a year!
Jammed campgrounds... boomboxes...
Overagressive bear management officers hunting us...
Poison oak!
Mrs. Melmac and her nuclear arsenal of bug bombs...
Imploding Wonderbras!
© Phil (TENT-UP EMOTIONS) Frank
IF YOU MUST KNOW, MADAM... **NO** WE ARE **NOT** HAPPY CAMPERS!!
GRRR!!

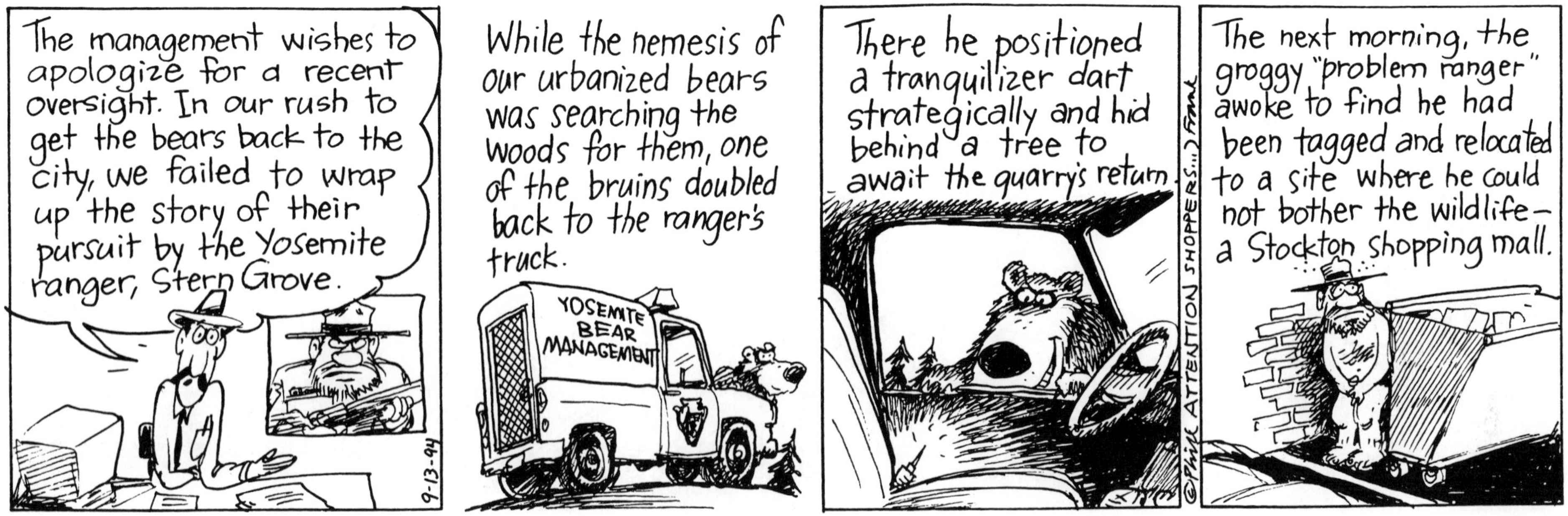
The management wishes to apologize for a recent oversight. In our rush to get the bears back to the city, we failed to wrap up the story of their pursuit by the Yosemite ranger, Stern Grove.
9-13-94
While the nemesis of our urbanized bears was searching the woods for them, one of the bruins doubled back to the ranger's truck.
YOSEMITE BEAR MANAGEMENT
There he positioned a tranquilizer dart strategically and hid behind a tree to await the quarry's return.
©Phil ATTENTION SHOPPERS...) Frank
The next morning, the groggy "problem ranger" awoke to find he had been tagged and relocated to a site where he could not bother the wildlife— a Stockton shopping mall.

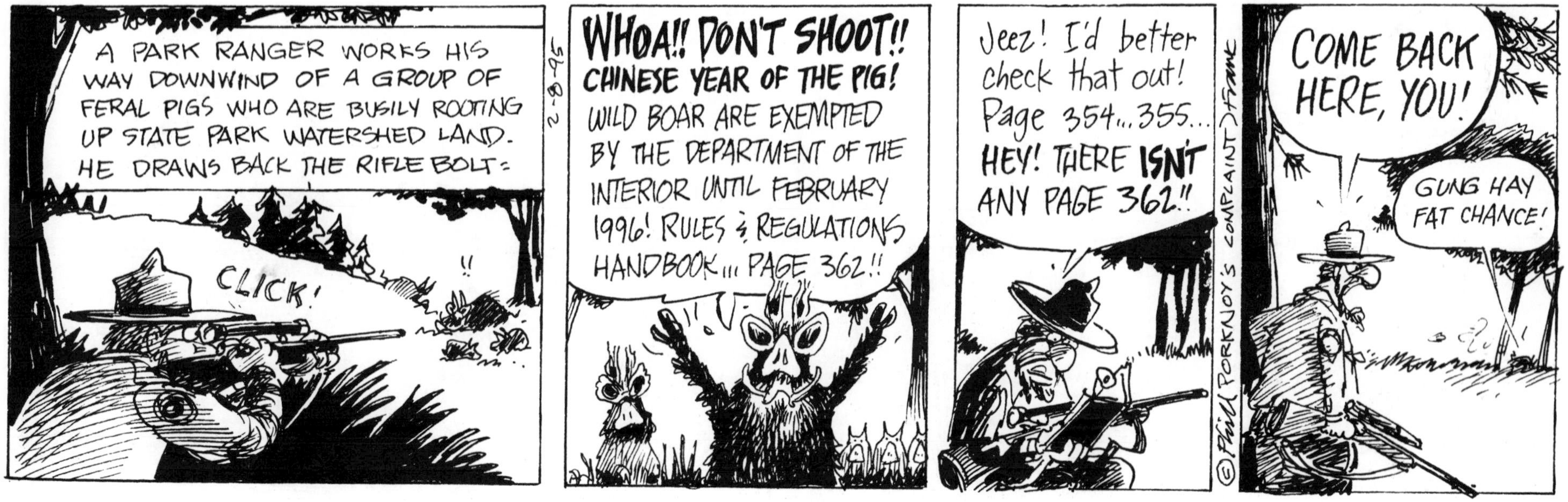
A PARK RANGER WORKS HIS WAY DOWNWIND OF A GROUP OF FERAL PIGS WHO ARE BUSILY ROOTING UP STATE PARK WATERSHED LAND. HE DRAWS BACK THE RIFLE BOLT=
CLICK!
!!
2-8-95
WHOA!! DON'T SHOOT!! CHINESE YEAR OF THE PIG! WILD BOAR ARE EXEMPTED BY THE DEPARTMENT OF THE INTERIOR UNTIL FEBRUARY 1996! RULES & REGULATIONS HANDBOOK... PAGE 362!!
Jeez! I'd better check that out! Page 354...355... HEY! THERE ISN'T ANY PAGE 362!!
©Phil PORKNOY'S COMPLAINT) Frank
COME BACK HERE, YOU!
GUNG HAY FAT CHANCE!

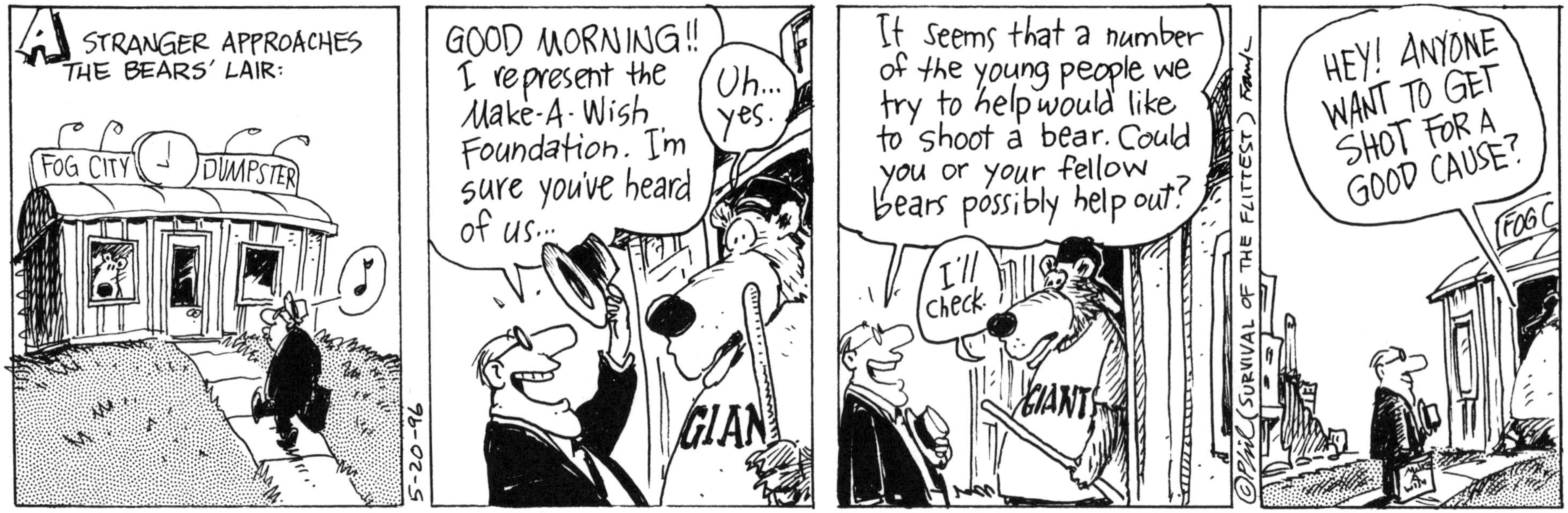
A STRANGER APPROACHES THE BEARS' LAIR:
FOG CITY DUMPSTER
5-20-96
GOOD MORNING!! I represent the Make-A-Wish Foundation. I'm sure you've heard of us...
Oh... yes.
GIAN
It seems that a number of the young people we try to help would like to shoot a bear. Could you or your fellow bears possibly help out?
I'll check.
GIANT
©Phil (SURVIVAL OF THE FLITTEST) Frank
HEY! ANYONE WANT TO GET SHOT FOR A GOOD CAUSE?
FOG C

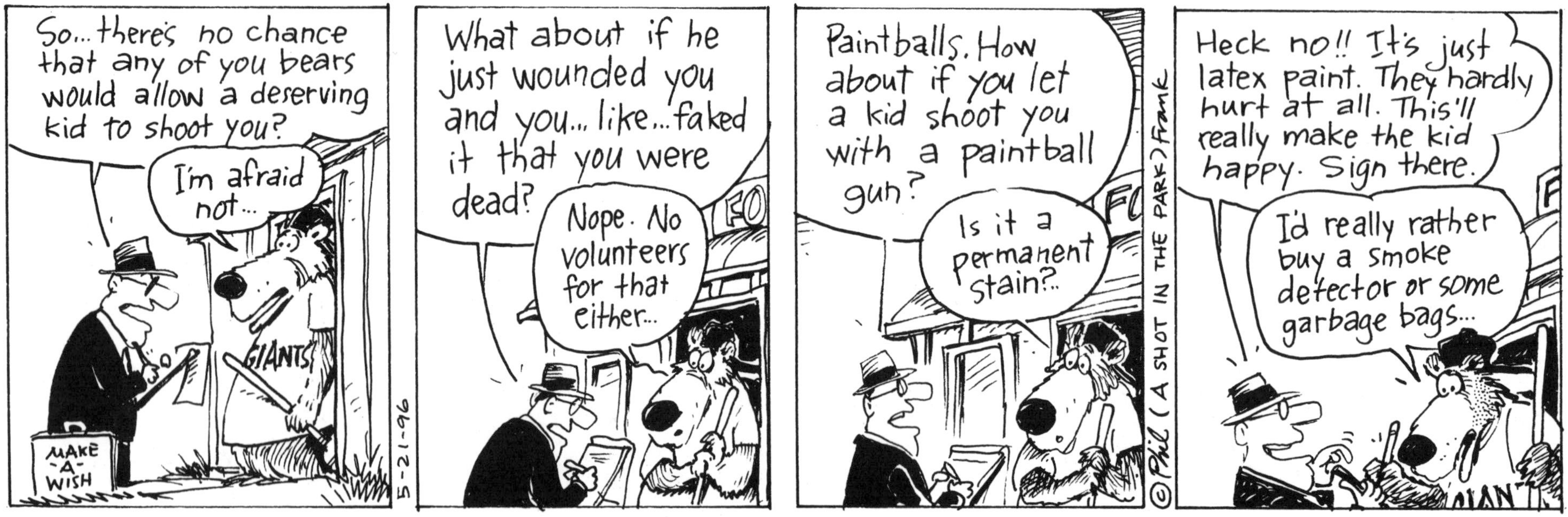
So... there's no chance that any of you bears would allow a deserving kid to shoot you?
I'm afraid not...
GIANTS
MAKE -A- WISH
5-21-96
What about if he just wounded you and you... like... faked it that you were dead?
Nope. No volunteers for that either...
FO
Paintballs. How about if you let a kid shoot you with a paintball gun?
Is it a permanent stain?..
©Phil (A SHOT IN THE PARK) Frank
Heck no!! It's just latex paint. They hardly hurt at all. This'll really make the kid happy. Sign there.
I'd really rather buy a smoke detector or some garbage bags...

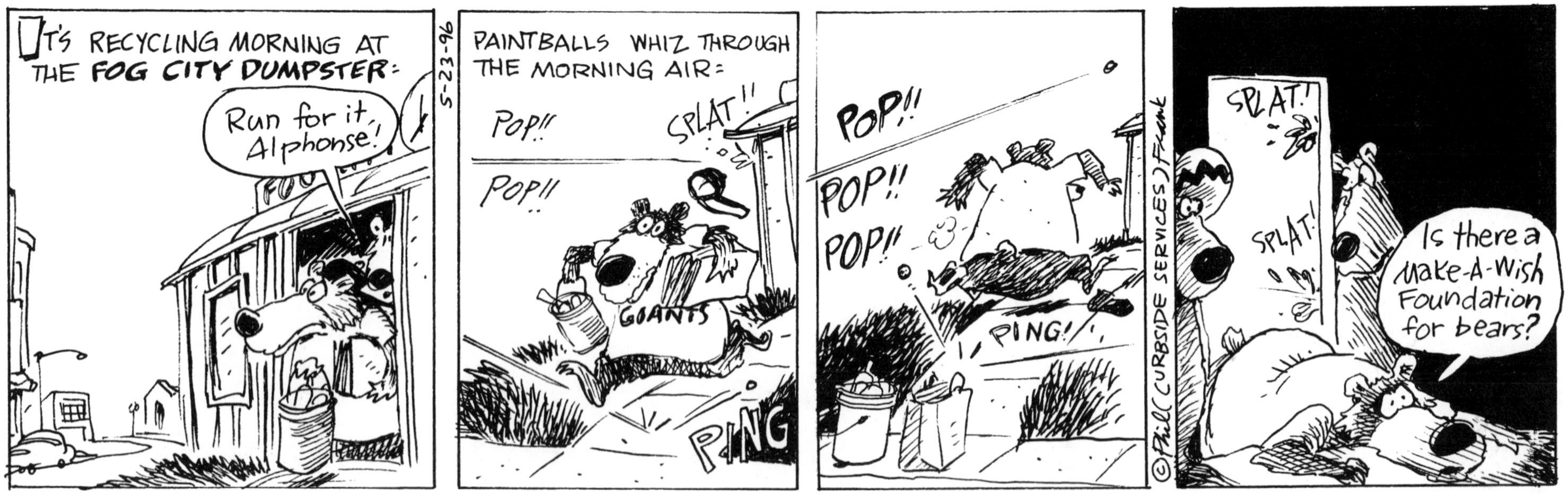
IT'S RECYCLING MORNING AT THE FOG CITY DUMPSTER:
Run for it, Alphonse!
5-23-96
PAINTBALLS WHIZ THROUGH THE MORNING AIR:
POP!!
SPLAT!!
POP!!
GIANTS
PING
POP!!
POP!!
POP!!
PING!
©Phil (CURBSIDE SERVICES) Frank
SPLAT!
SPLAT!
Is there a Make-A-Wish Foundation for bears?

It's time for the State Park Summer Olympics. Farley's on the job.

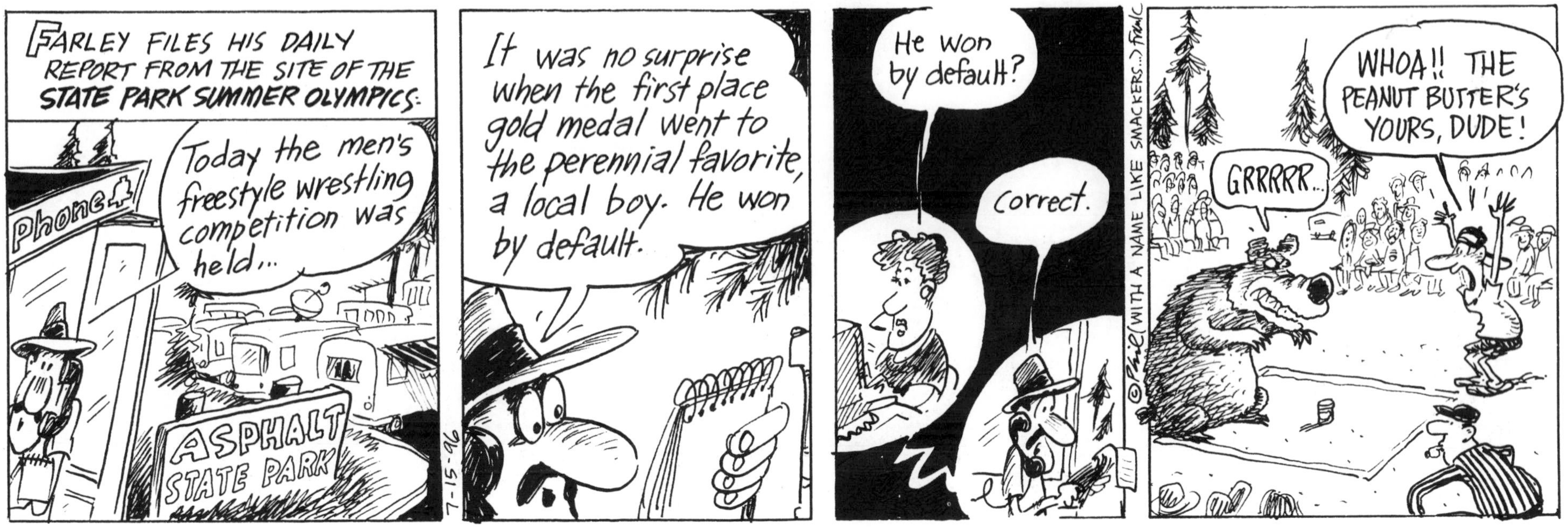
FARLEY FILES HIS DAILY REPORT FROM THE SITE OF THE STATE PARK SUMMER OLYMPICS:
Phone
Today the men's freestyle wrestling competition was held...
ASPHALT STATE PARK
7-15-96
It was no surprise when the first place gold medal went to the perennial favorite, a local boy. He won by default.
He won by default?
Correct.
©Phil (WITH A NAME LIKE SMACKERS...) Frank
GRRRRR...
WHOA!! THE PEANUT BUTTER'S YOURS, DUDE!

Farley: Do-Good Ranger

FARLEY WAS A BACKPACKING CARTOON CHARACTER IN 1976. AT THE TIME THE COMIC STRIP WAS SYNDICATED NATIONWIDE. ONE DAY HE STROLLED INTO **ASPHALT STATE PARK**, WHILE ON A CROSS-COUNTRY ODYSSEY, SEARCHING FOR THE HEART OF AMERICA. HE WAS LOOKING FOR A PLACE TO CAMP. HE FOUND THAT AND A GROUP OF CHARACTERS THAT REMAINED A MAINSTAY OF THE COMIC STRIP.— FOUR CONNIVING BLACK BEARS AND A CHIEF PARK RANGER WHO WAS ALLERGIC TO TREES. WHEN THE STRIP LOCALIZED IN 1986 TO **SAN FRANCISCO**, **ASPHALT STATE PARK** BECAME **YOSEMITE**.

Farley, a thinly disguised take on the creator of the comic strip, has, as of 1999 been in print for 24 years. He shares the artist's view of the modern-day world.

The world has gone hi-tech but Farley remains a lo-tech kind of guy. He spurns trends...wears no clothing that declares a brand name nor T-shirts with messages, refuses to be paged and watches in bemused amazement as a panoply of humanity passes by. He works as a reporter for the **Daily Requirement**, a San Francisco daily paper. He lives in a loft with a raven for a roommate, dates a meter maid and continually fends off the advances of Bruinhilda, matriarch of the bear clan. (He doesn't date outside his species).

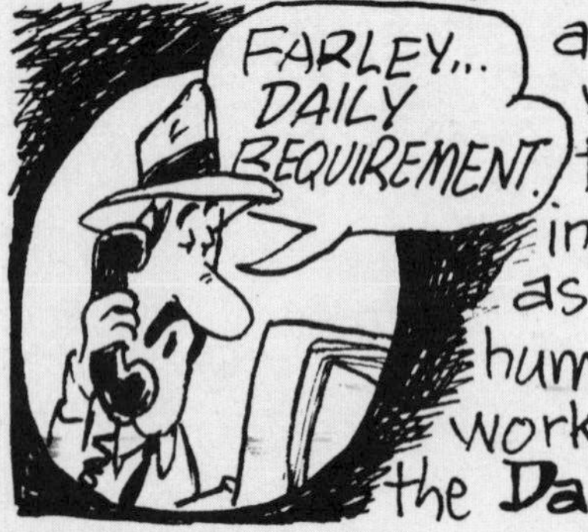
FARLEY... DAILY REQUIREMENT.

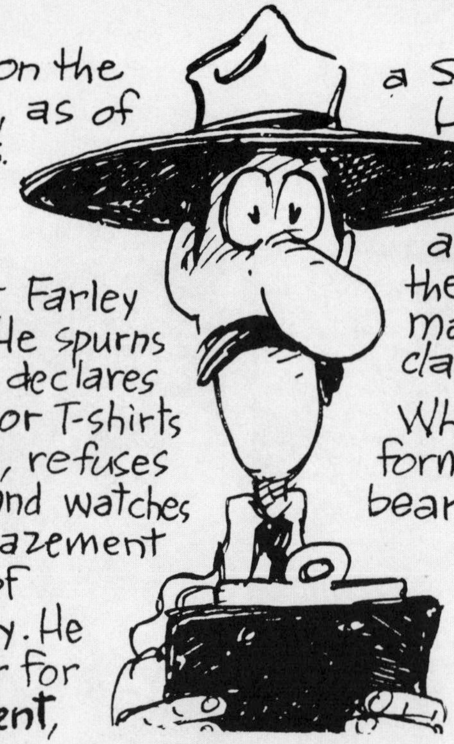

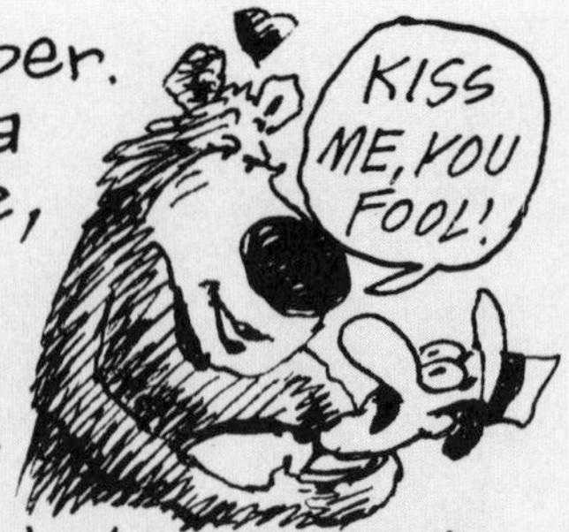
KISS ME, YOU FOOL!

When the strip departed its national format and localized, the quartet of bears followed Farley to San Francisco.

On occasion, Farley will return to the parks and his job as a ranger just to witness the collision of man and nature in a wilderness setting.

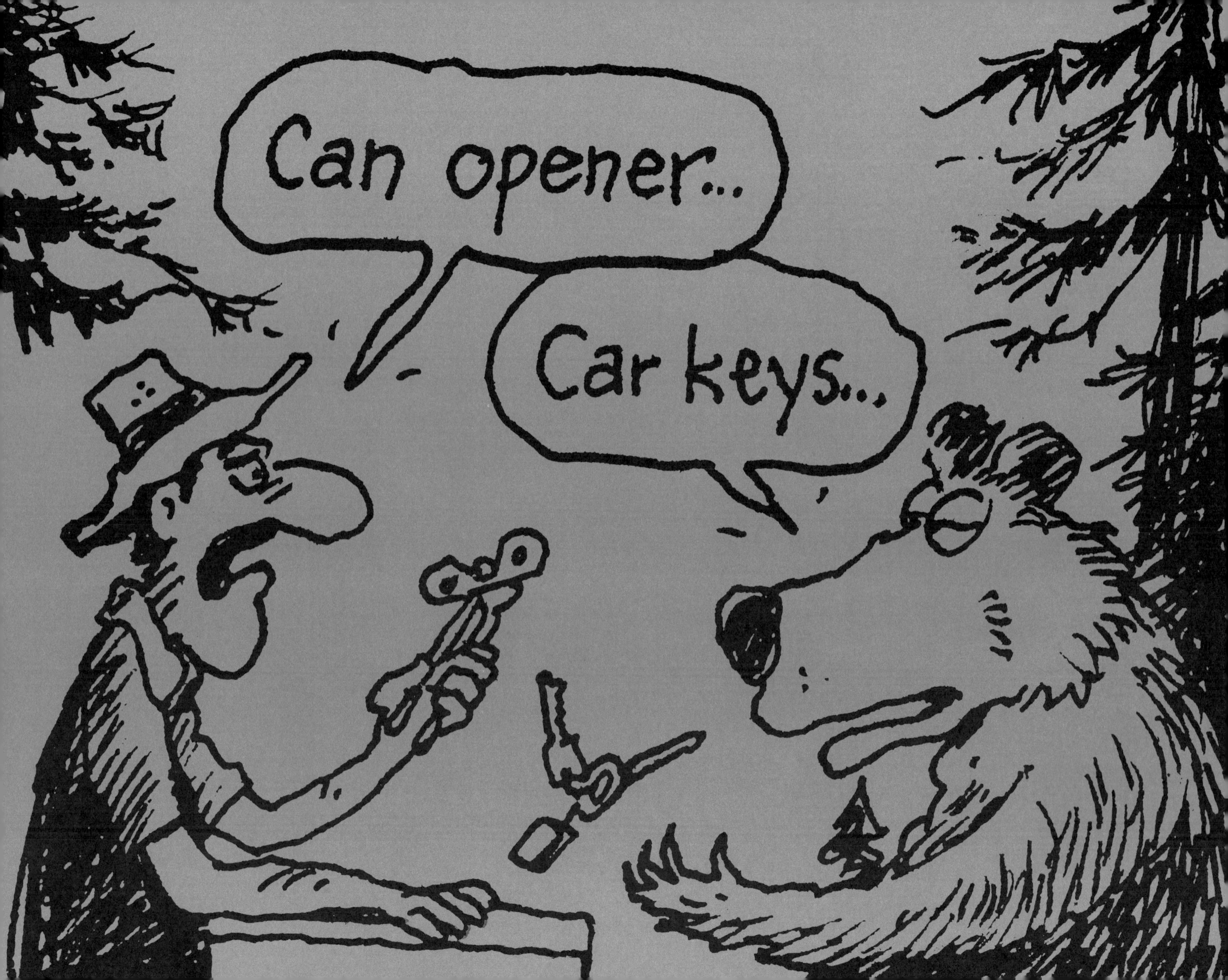
Can opener...
Car keys...

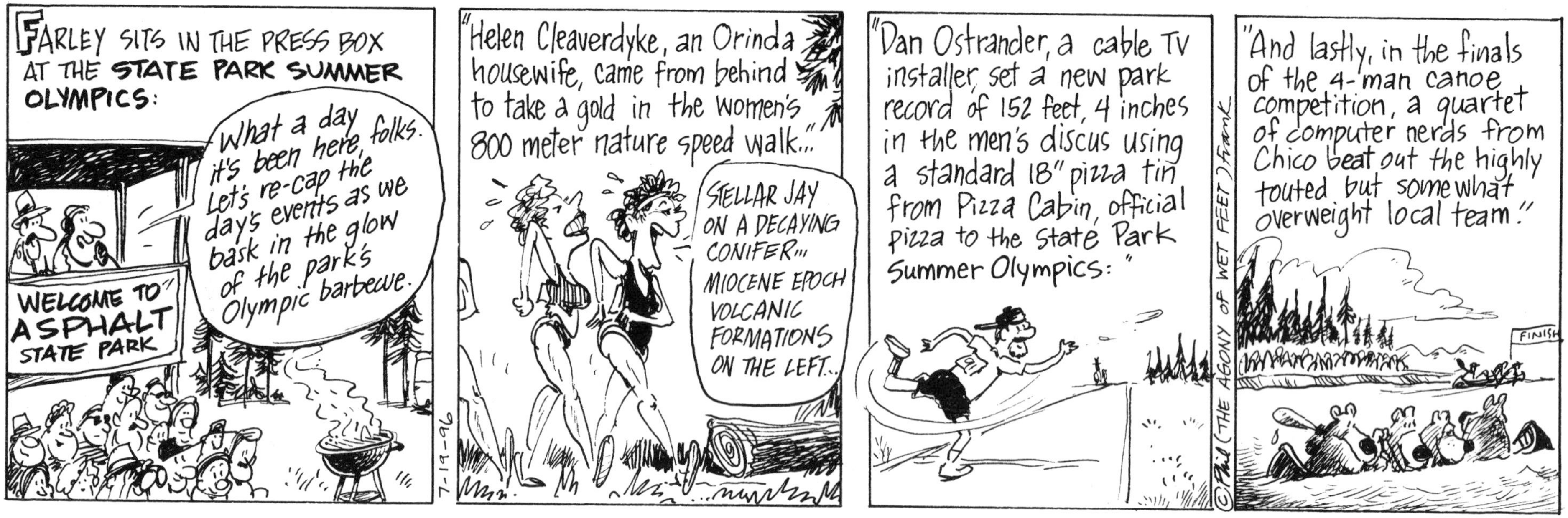
FARLEY SITS IN THE PRESS BOX AT THE STATE PARK SUMMER OLYMPICS:
What a day it's been here, folks. Let's re-cap the day's events as we bask in the glow of the park's Olympic barbecue.
WELCOME TO ASPHALT STATE PARK
"Helen Cleaverdyke, an Orinda housewife, came from behind to take a gold in the women's 800 meter nature speed walk..."
STELLAR JAY ON A DECAYING CONIFER... MIOCENE EPOCH VOLCANIC FORMATIONS ON THE LEFT...
"Dan Ostrander, a cable TV installer, set a new park record of 152 feet, 4 inches in the men's discus using a standard 18" pizza tin from Pizza Cabin, official pizza to the State Park Summer Olympics."
"And lastly, in the finals of the 4-man canoe competition, a quartet of computer nerds from Chico beat out the highly touted but somewhat overweight local team."
FINISH
7-19-96
© Phil (THE AGONY OF WET FEET) Frank

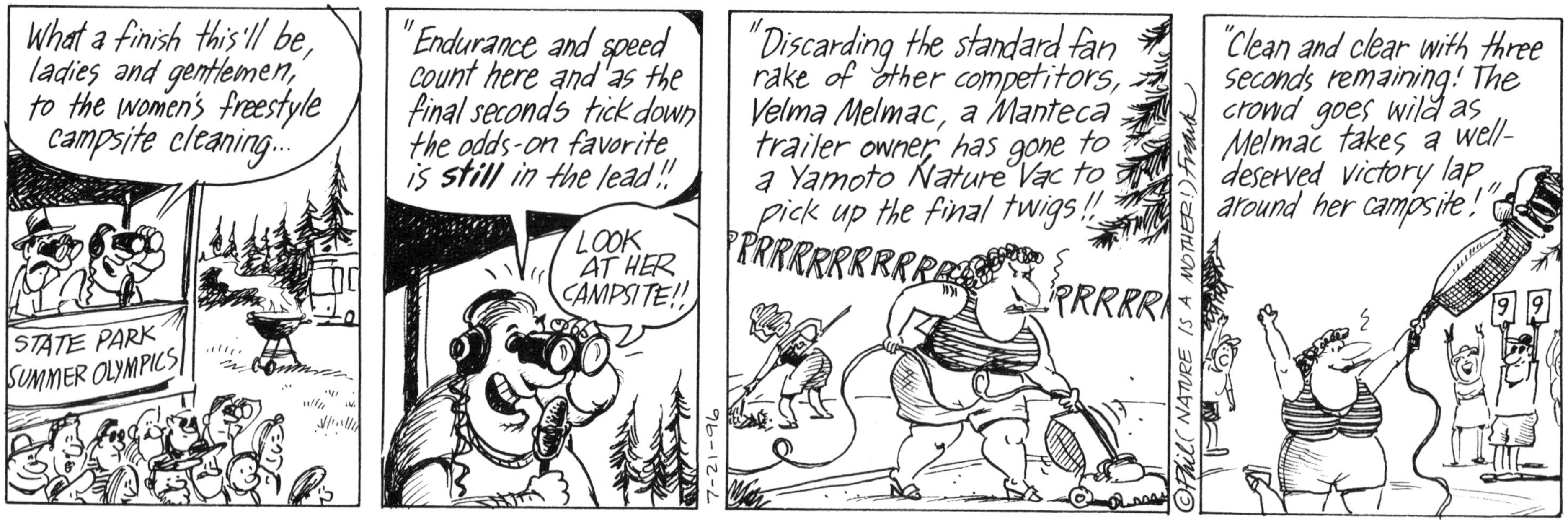
What a finish this'll be, ladies and gentlemen, to the women's freestyle campsite cleaning...
STATE PARK SUMMER OLYMPICS
"Endurance and speed count here and as the final seconds tick down the odds-on favorite is still in the lead!!
LOOK AT HER CAMPSITE!!
"Discarding the standard fan rake of other competitors, Velma Melmac, a Manteca trailer owner, has gone to a Yamoto Nature Vac to pick up the final twigs!!
PRRRRRRRRRRRR
PRRRRR
"Clean and clear with three seconds remaining! The crowd goes wild as Melmac takes a well-deserved victory lap around her campsite!"
9 9
7-21-96
© Phil (NATURE IS A MOTHER!) Frank

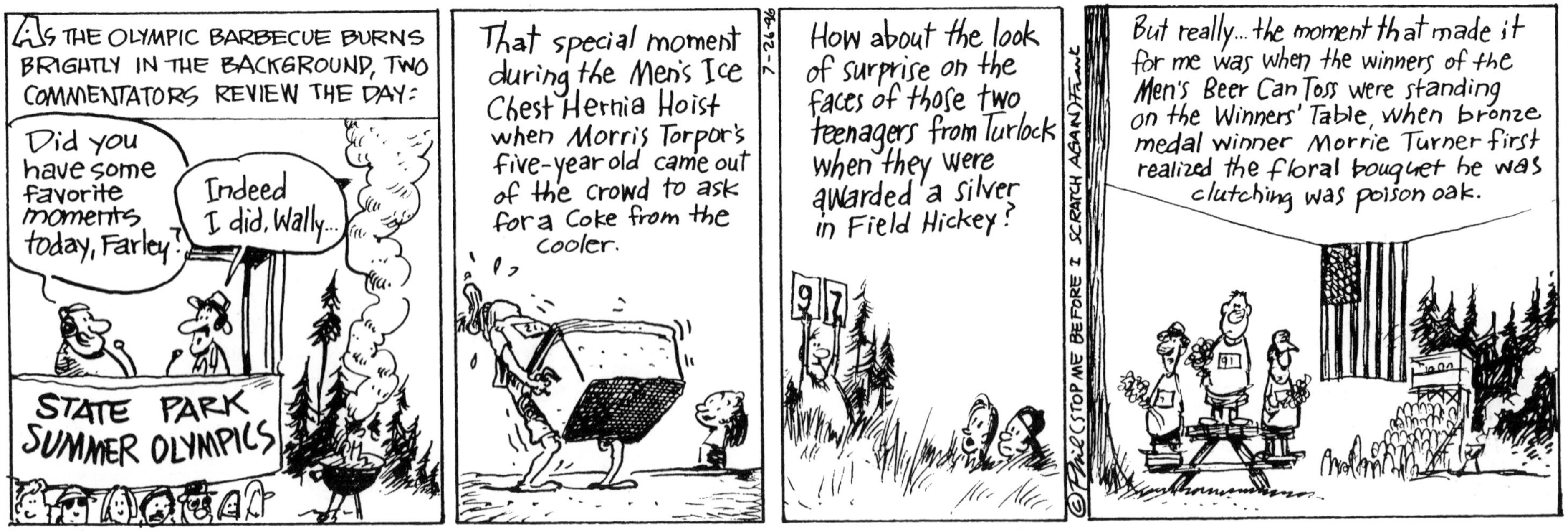
As the Olympic barbecue burns brightly in the background, two commentators review the day:
Did you have some favorite moments today, Farley?
Indeed I did, Wally...
STATE PARK SUMMER OLYMPICS
That special moment during the Men's Ice Chest Hernia Hoist when Morris Torpor's five-year old came out of the crowd to ask for a Coke from the cooler.
7-26-96
How about the look of surprise on the faces of those two teenagers from Turlock when they were awarded a silver in Field Hickey?
9
7
© Phil (STOP ME BEFORE I SCRATCH AGAIN) Frank
But really... the moment that made it for me was when the winners of the Men's Beer Can Toss were standing on the Winners' Table, when bronze medal winner Morrie Turner first realized the floral bouquet he was clutching was poison oak.

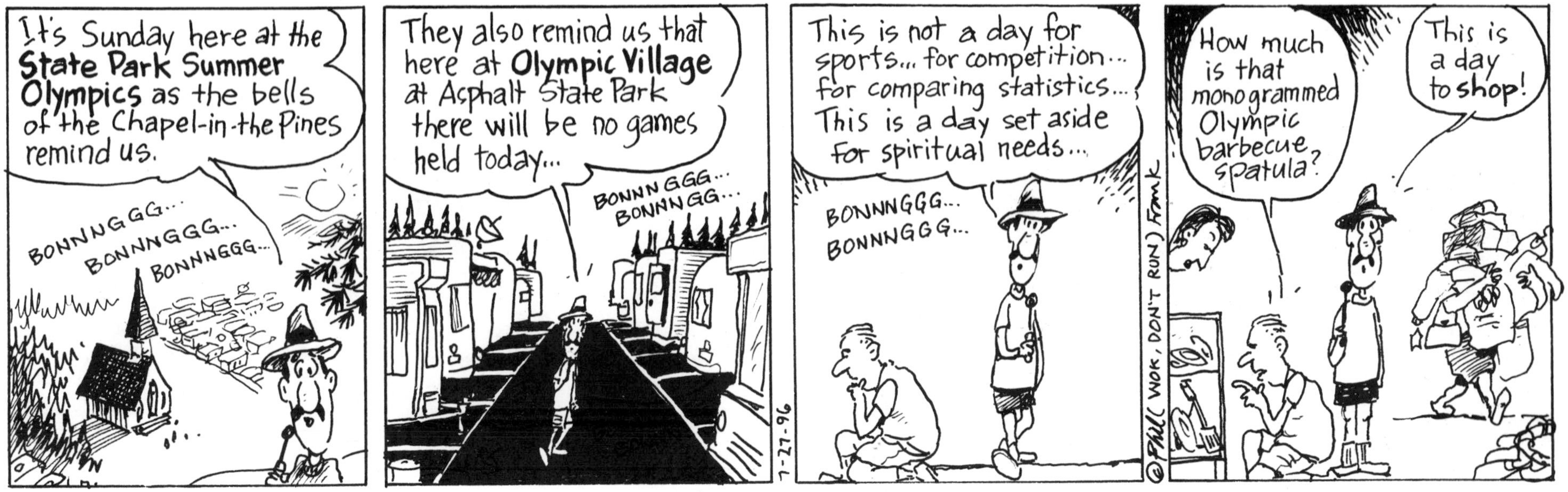
It's Sunday here at the State Park Summer Olympics as the bells of the Chapel-in-the Pines remind us.
BONNNGGG... BONNNGGG... BONNNGGG...
They also remind us that here at Olympic Village at Asphalt State Park there will be no games held today...
BONNNGGG... BONNNGG...
7-27-96
This is not a day for sports... for competition... for comparing statistics... This is a day set aside for spiritual needs...
BONNNGGG... BONNNGGG...
© Phil (WOK, DON'T RUN) Frank
How much is that monogrammed Olympic barbecue spatula?
This is a day to shop!

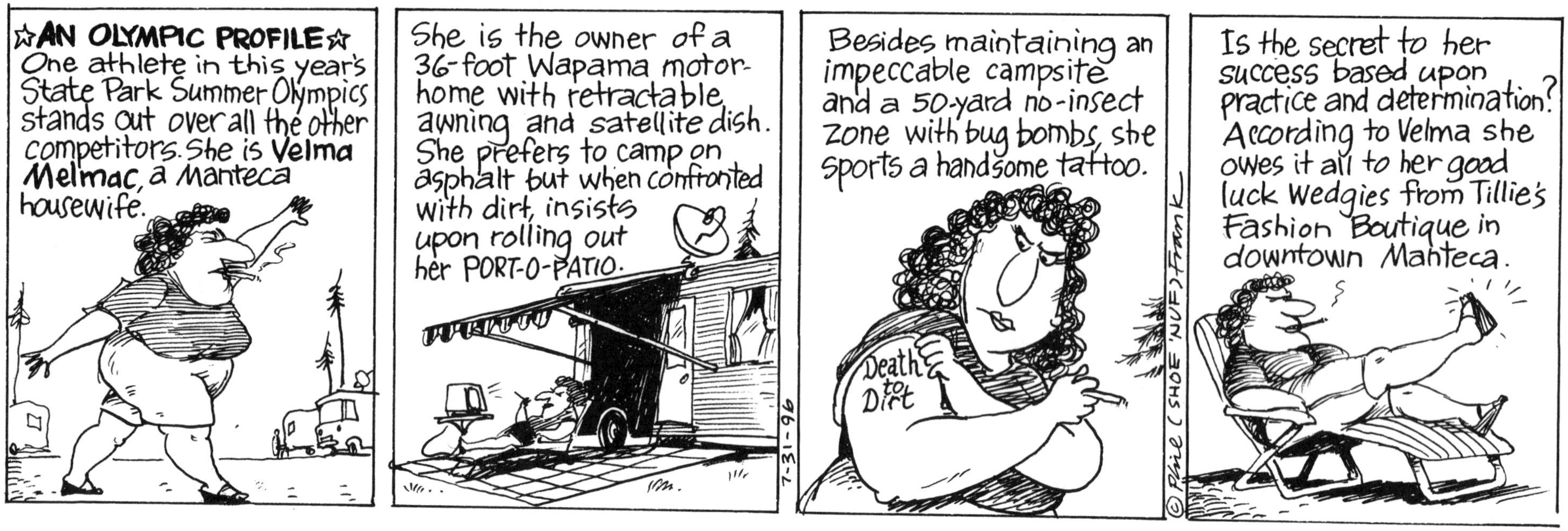
☆AN OLYMPIC PROFILE☆ One athlete in this year's State Park Summer Olympics stands out over all the other competitors. She is Velma Melmac, a Manteca housewife.
She is the owner of a 36-foot Wapama motor-home with retractable awning and satellite dish. She prefers to camp on asphalt but when confronted with dirt, insists upon rolling out her PORT-O-PATIO.
7-31-96
Besides maintaining an impeccable campsite and a 50-yard no-insect zone with bug bombs, she sports a handsome tattoo.
Death to Dirt
© Phil (SHOE 'NUF) Frank
Is the secret to her success based upon practice and determination? According to Velma she owes it all to her good luck Wedgies from Tillie's Fashion Boutique in downtown Manteca.

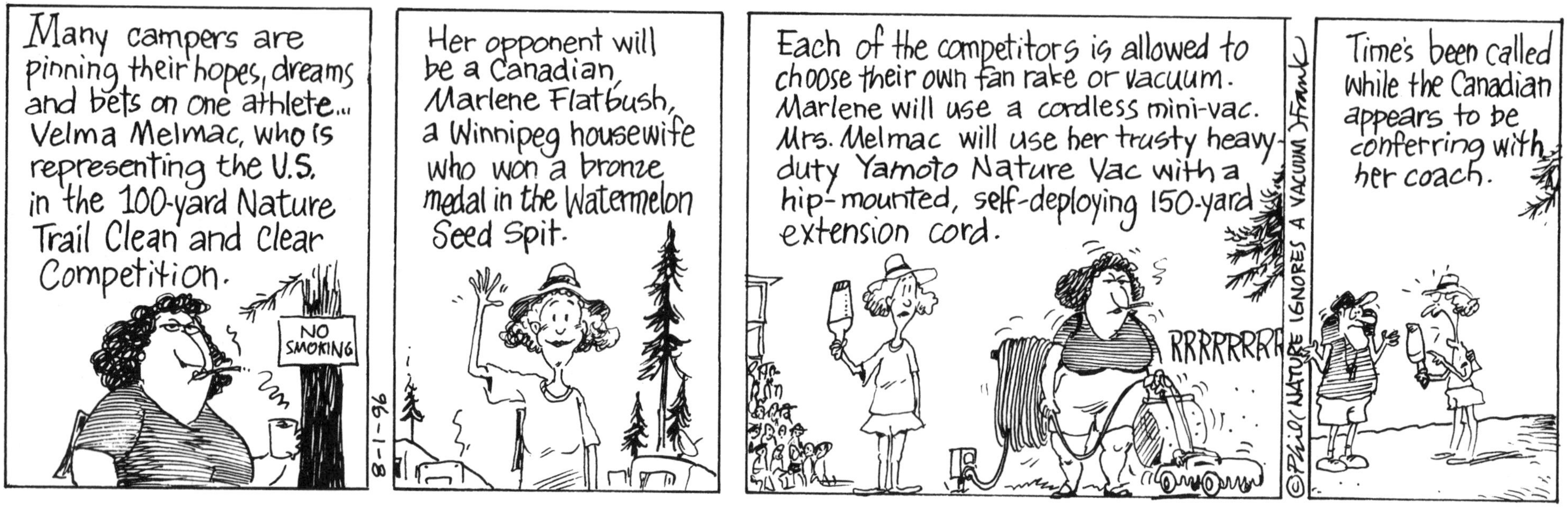
Many campers are pinning their hopes, dreams and bets on one athlete... Velma Melmac, who is representing the U.S. in the 100-yard Nature Trail Clean and Clear Competition.
NO SMOKING
8-1-96
Her opponent will be a Canadian, Marlene Flatbush, a Winnipeg housewife who won a bronze medal in the Watermelon Seed Spit.
Each of the competitors is allowed to choose their own fan rake or vacuum. Marlene will use a cordless mini-vac. Mrs. Melmac will use her trusty heavy-duty Yamoto Nature Vac with a hip-mounted, self-deploying 150-yard extension cord.
RRRRRRRR
© Phil (NATURE IGNORES A VACUUM) Frank
Time's been called while the Canadian appears to be conferring with her coach.

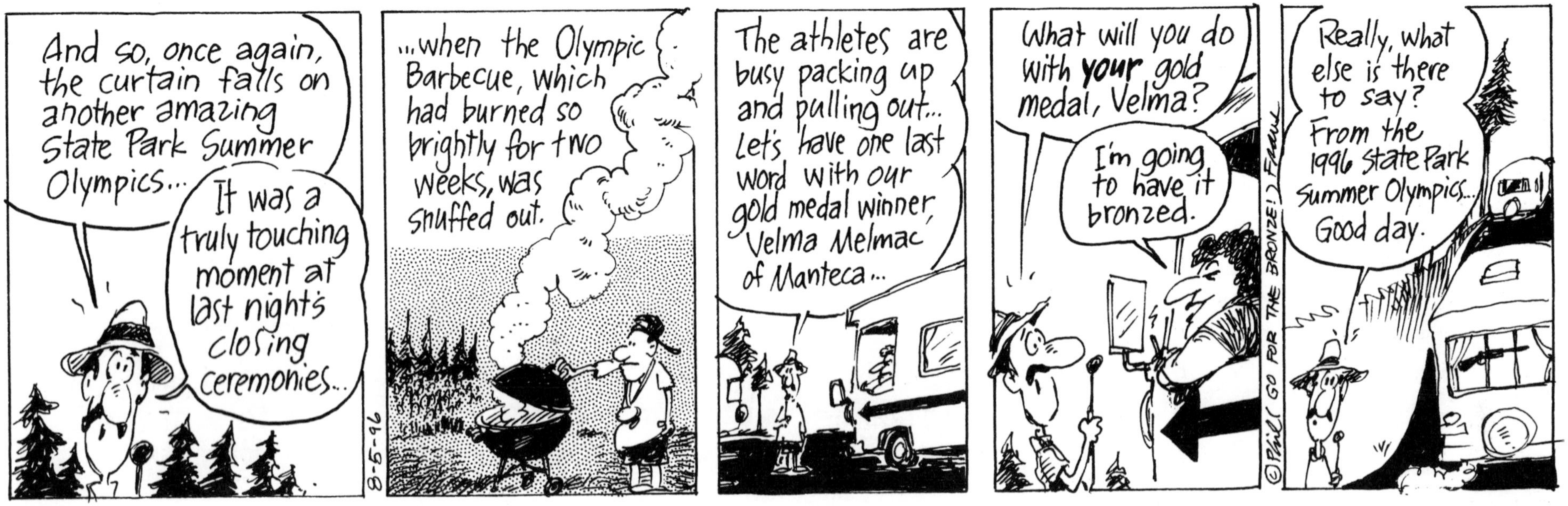
And so, once again, the curtain falls on another amazing State Park Summer Olympics...
It was a truly touching moment at last night's closing ceremonies...
8-5-96
...when the Olympic Barbecue, which had burned so brightly for two weeks, was snuffed out.
The athletes are busy packing up and pulling out... Let's have one last word with our gold medal winner, Velma Melmac of Manteca...
What will you do with **your** gold medal, Velma?
I'm going to have it bronzed.
©Phil's (GO FOR THE BRONZE!) Frank
Really, what else is there to say? From the 1996 State Park Summer Olympics... Good day.

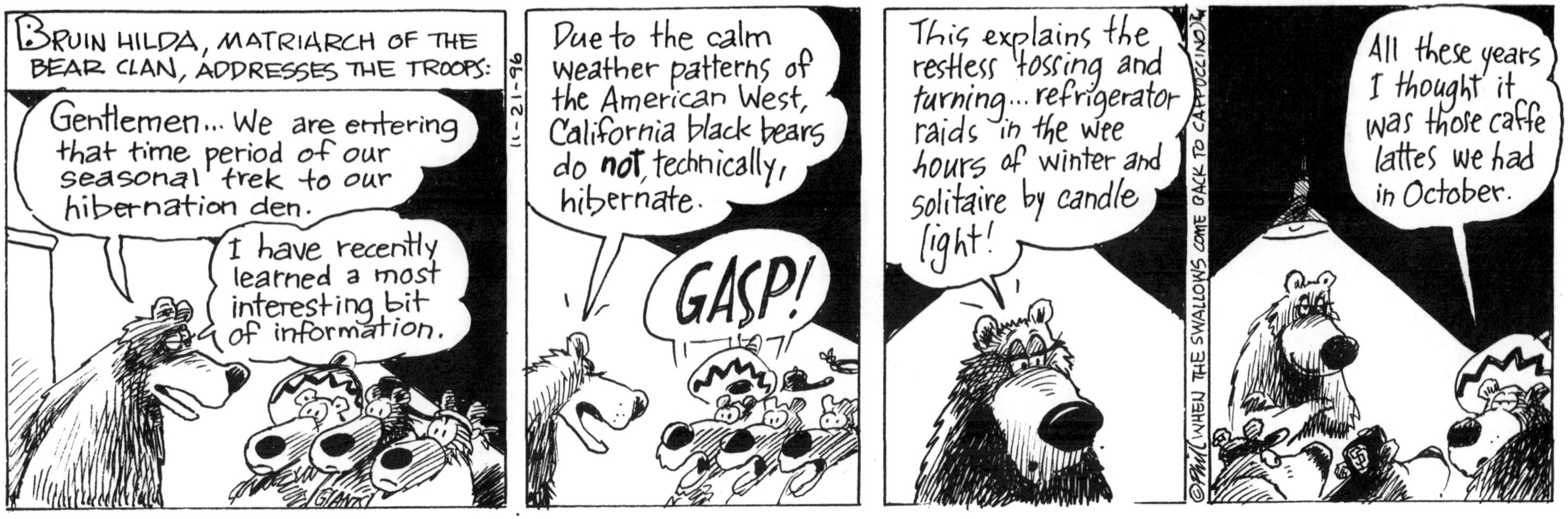
BRUIN HILDA, MATRIARCH OF THE BEAR CLAN, ADDRESSES THE TROOPS:
Gentlemen... We are entering that time period of our seasonal trek to our hibernation den.
I have recently learned a most interesting bit of information.
11-21-96
Due to the calm weather patterns of the American West, California black bears do **not**, technically, hibernate.
GASP!
This explains the restless tossing and turning... refrigerator raids in the wee hours of winter and solitaire by candle light!
©Phil (WHEN THE SWALLOWS COME BACK TO CAPPUCCINO)
All these years I thought it was those caffe lattes we had in October.

State's Worst Flooding Ever

Yosemite: Escape route cleared

Nature closed Yosemite in early January of 1997 when the flooding Merced River, fed by unexpected snow melt, washed away camping areas, stranded visitors, buckled highways and destroyed bridges. Crashing boulders being carried by the roaring river made so much noise in the Valley that it awakened hibernating bears who came out of their dens to find food lockers filled with campers' edibles torn open by the raging waters.

The park was closed while repairs to the infrastructure were being made. To help NPS with the massive project, I brought Mrs. Melmac out of **her** hibernation in Manteca. She fired up her Wapama motorhome and came to the rescue.

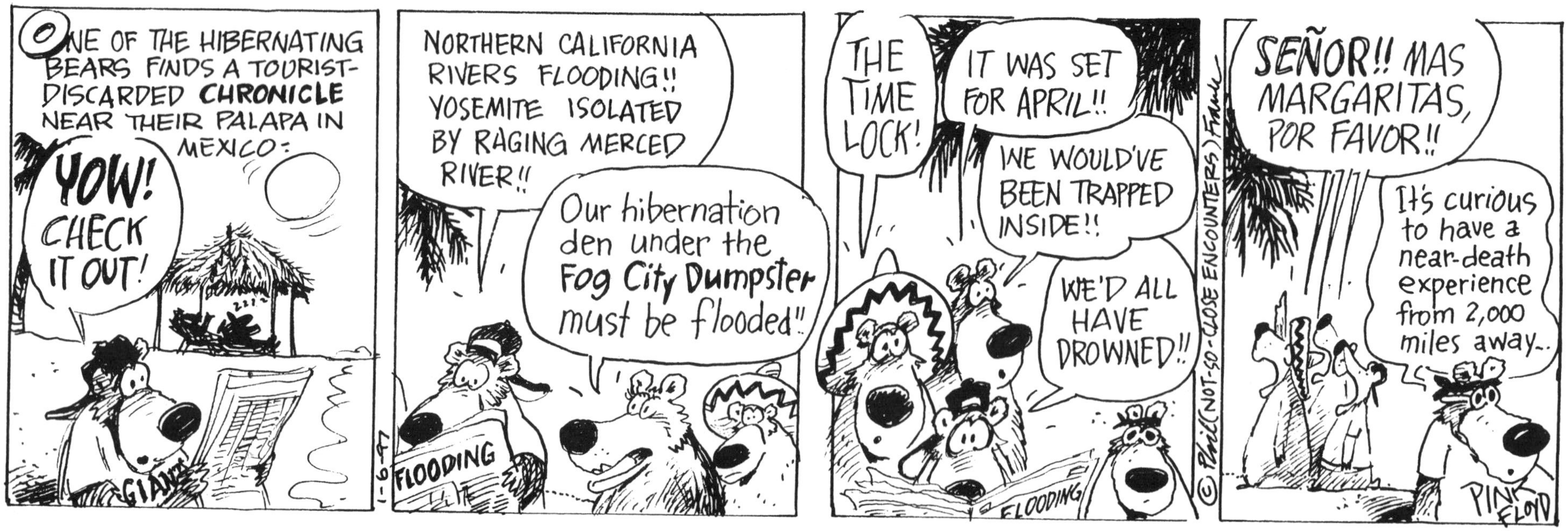
ONE OF THE HIBERNATING BEARS FINDS A TOURIST-DISCARDED CHRONICLE NEAR THEIR PALAPA IN MEXICO:
YOW! CHECK IT OUT!
1-6-97
NORTHERN CALIFORNIA RIVERS FLOODING!! YOSEMITE ISOLATED BY RAGING MERCED RIVER!!
Our hibernation den under the Fog City Dumpster must be flooded!!
FLOODING
THE TIME LOCK!
IT WAS SET FOR APRIL!!
WE WOULD'VE BEEN TRAPPED INSIDE!!
WE'D ALL HAVE DROWNED!!
FLOODING
© Phil (NOT-SO-CLOSE ENCOUNTERS) Frank
SEÑOR!! MAS MARGARITAS, POR FAVOR!!
It's curious to have a near-death experience from 2,000 miles away..
PINK FLOYD

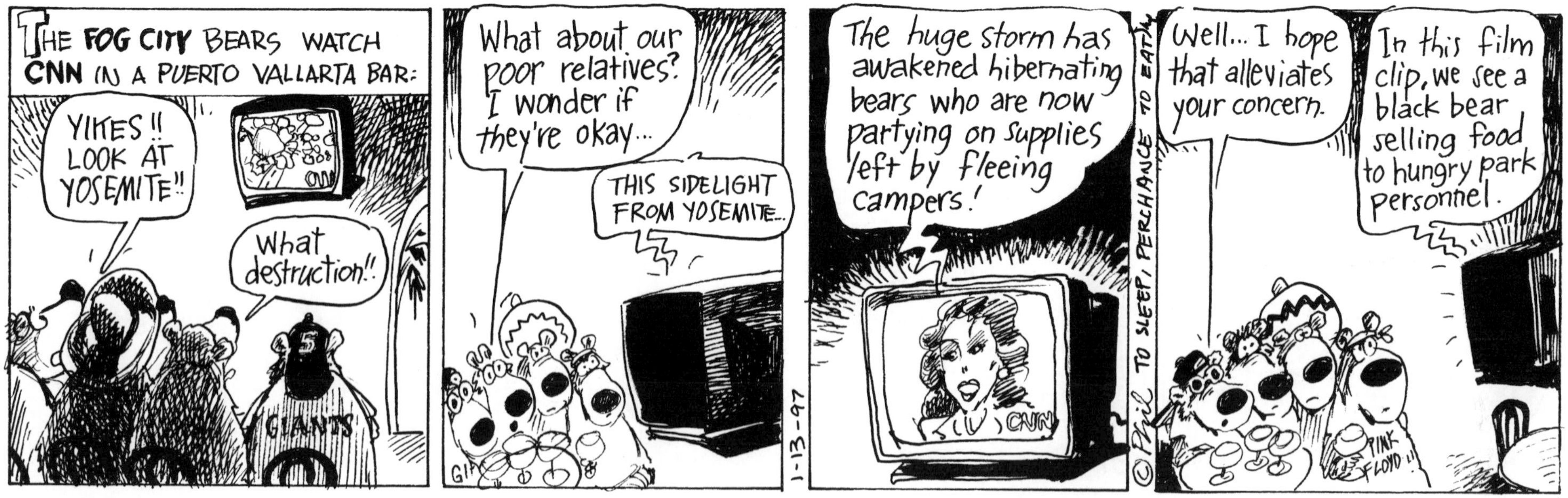

THE FOG CITY BEARS WATCH CNN IN A PUERTO VALLARTA BAR:
YIKES!! LOOK AT YOSEMITE!!
What destruction!!
GIANTS
What about our poor relatives? I wonder if they're okay...
THIS SIDELIGHT FROM YOSEMITE...
1-13-97
The huge storm has awakened hibernating bears who are now partying on supplies left by fleeing campers!
CNN
© Phil TO SLEEP, PERCHANCE TO EAT
Well... I hope that alleviates your concern.
In this film clip, we see a black bear selling food to hungry park personnel.
PINK FLOYD!!

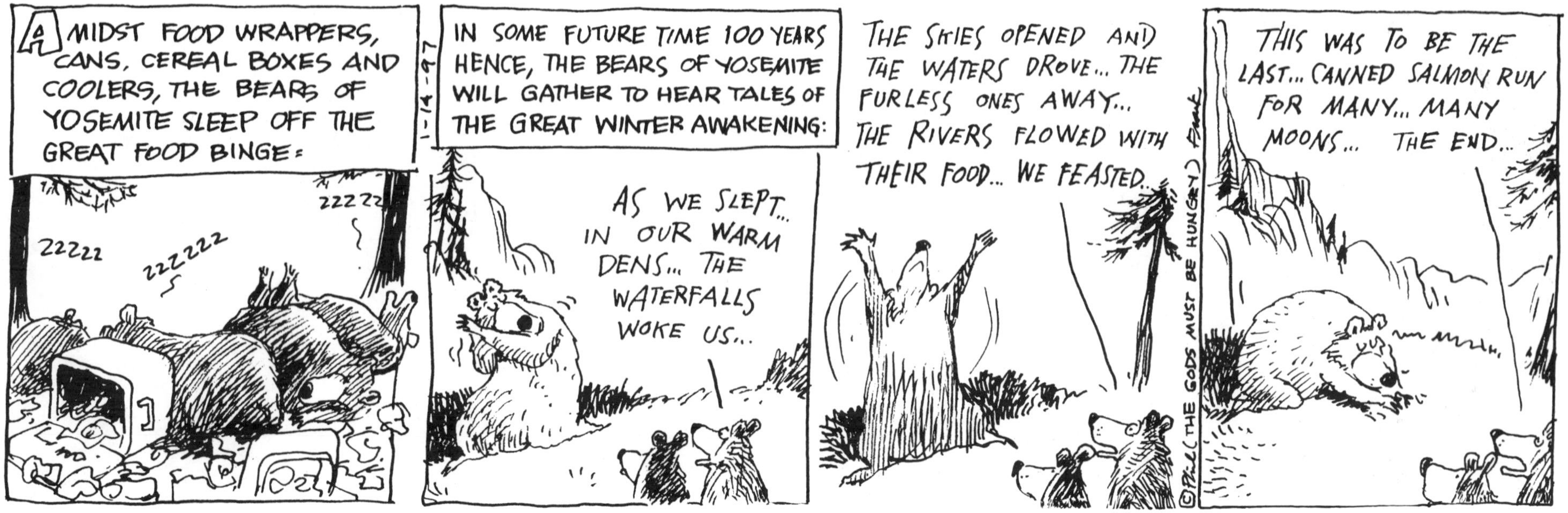

AMIDST FOOD WRAPPERS, CANS, CEREAL BOXES AND COOLERS, THE BEARS OF YOSEMITE SLEEP OFF THE GREAT FOOD BINGE:
ZZZZZ
ZZZZZZ
ZZZZZ
1-14-97
IN SOME FUTURE TIME 100 YEARS HENCE, THE BEARS OF YOSEMITE WILL GATHER TO HEAR TALES OF THE GREAT WINTER AWAKENING:
AS WE SLEPT... IN OUR WARM DENS... THE WATERFALLS WOKE US...
THE SKIES OPENED AND THE WATERS DROVE... THE FURLESS ONES AWAY... THE RIVERS FLOWED WITH THEIR FOOD... WE FEASTED...
© Phil (THE GODS MUST BE HUNGRY) Frank
THIS WAS TO BE THE LAST... CANNED SALMON RUN FOR MANY... MANY MOONS... THE END...

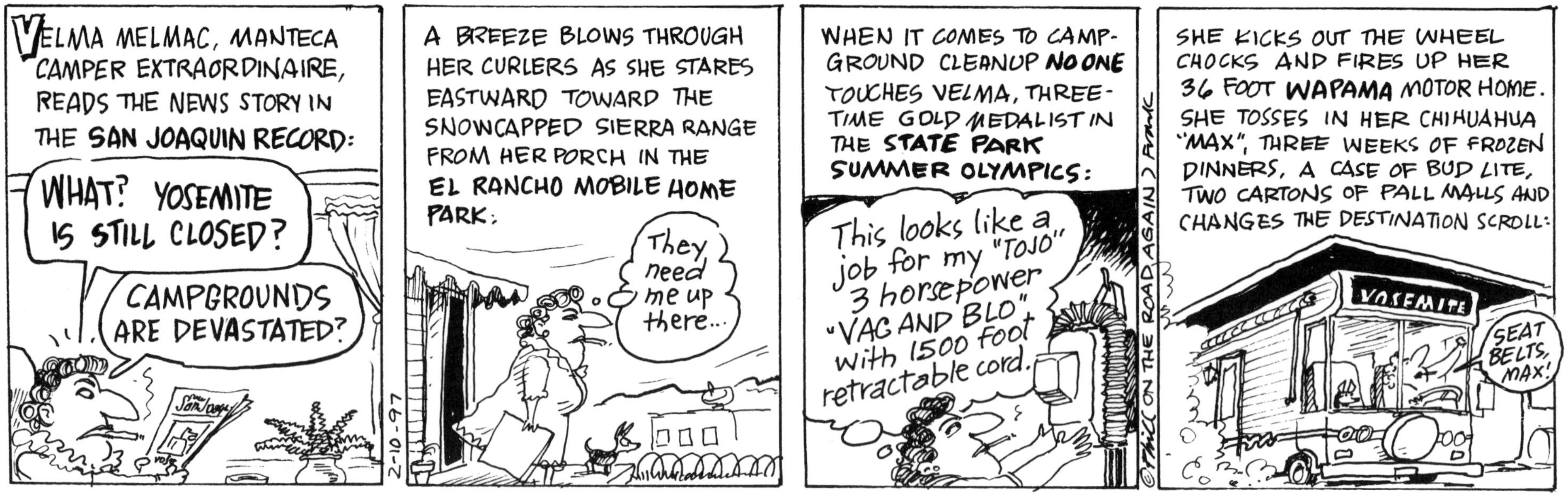
VELMA MELMAC, MANTECA CAMPER EXTRAORDINAIRE, READS THE NEWS STORY IN THE SAN JOAQUIN RECORD:
WHAT? YOSEMITE IS STILL CLOSED?
CAMPGROUNDS ARE DEVASTATED?
A BREEZE BLOWS THROUGH HER CURLERS AS SHE STARES EASTWARD TOWARD THE SNOWCAPPED SIERRA RANGE FROM HER PORCH IN THE EL RANCHO MOBILE HOME PARK:
They need me up there...
2-10-97
WHEN IT COMES TO CAMPGROUND CLEANUP NO ONE TOUCHES VELMA, THREE-TIME GOLD MEDALIST IN THE STATE PARK SUMMER OLYMPICS:
This looks like a job for my "TOJO" 3 horsepower "VAC AND BLO" with 1500 foot retractable cord.
©Phil (ON THE ROAD AGAIN) Frank
SHE KICKS OUT THE WHEEL CHOCKS AND FIRES UP HER 36 FOOT WAPAMA MOTOR HOME. SHE TOSSES IN HER CHIHUAHUA "MAX", THREE WEEKS OF FROZEN DINNERS, A CASE OF BUD LITE, TWO CARTONS OF PALL MALLS AND CHANGES THE DESTINATION SCROLL:
YOSEMITE
SEAT BELTS, MAX!

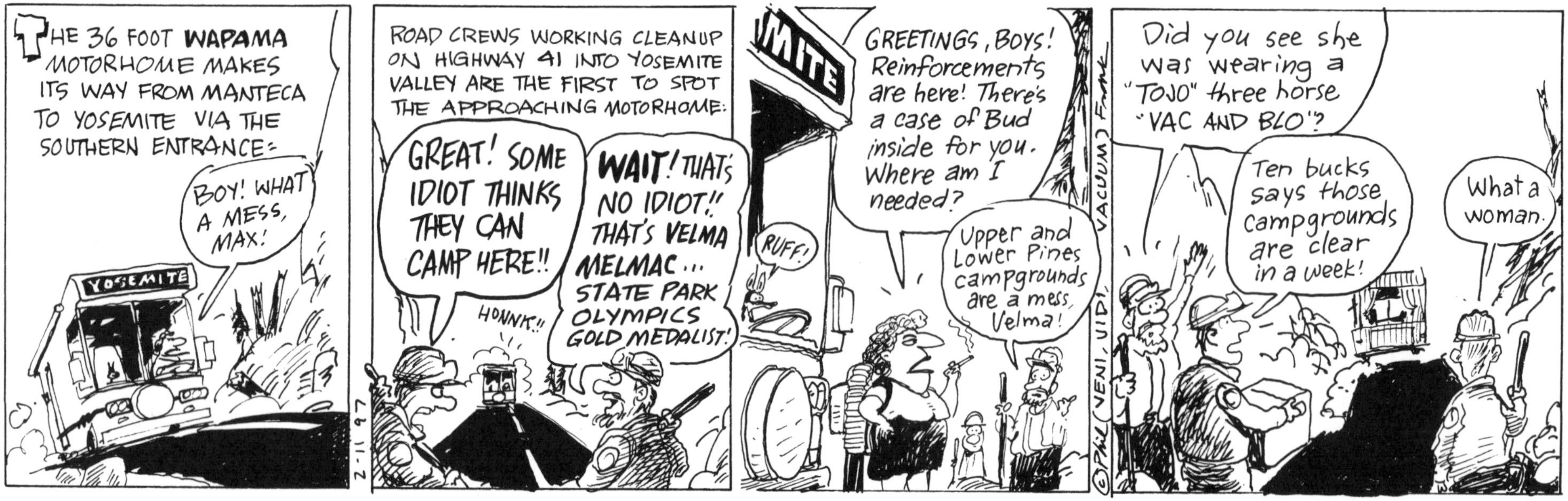
THE 36 FOOT WAPAMA MOTORHOME MAKES ITS WAY FROM MANTECA TO YOSEMITE VIA THE SOUTHERN ENTRANCE:
BOY! WHAT A MESS, MAX!
YOSEMITE
2-11-97
ROAD CREWS WORKING CLEANUP ON HIGHWAY 41 INTO YOSEMITE VALLEY ARE THE FIRST TO SPOT THE APPROACHING MOTORHOME:
GREAT! SOME IDIOT THINKS THEY CAN CAMP HERE!!
WAIT! THAT'S NO IDIOT!! THAT'S VELMA MELMAC... STATE PARK OLYMPICS GOLD MEDALIST!
HONNK!!
MITE
GREETINGS, BOYS! Reinforcements are here! There's a case of Bud inside for you. Where am I needed?
RUFF!
Upper and Lower Pines campgrounds are a mess, Velma!
©Phil (VENI, VIDI, VACUUM) Frank
Did you see she was wearing a "TOJO" three horse "VAC AND BLO"?
Ten bucks says those campgrounds are clear in a week!
What a woman.

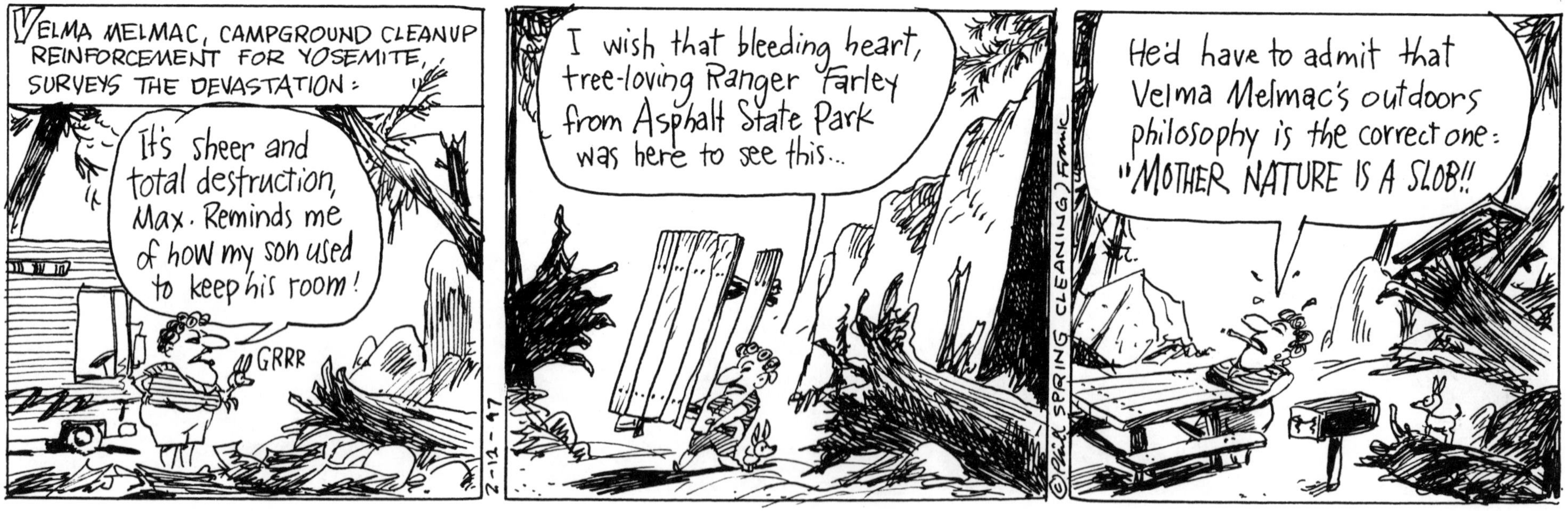
VELMA MELMAC, CAMPGROUND CLEANUP REINFORCEMENT FOR YOSEMITE, SURVEYS THE DEVASTATION:
It's sheer and total destruction, Max. Reminds me of how my son used to keep his room!
GRRR
2-12-97
I wish that bleeding heart, tree-loving Ranger Farley from Asphalt State Park was here to see this...
©Phil (SPRING CLEANING) Frank
He'd have to admit that Velma Melmac's outdoors philosophy is the correct one: "MOTHER NATURE IS A SLOB!!

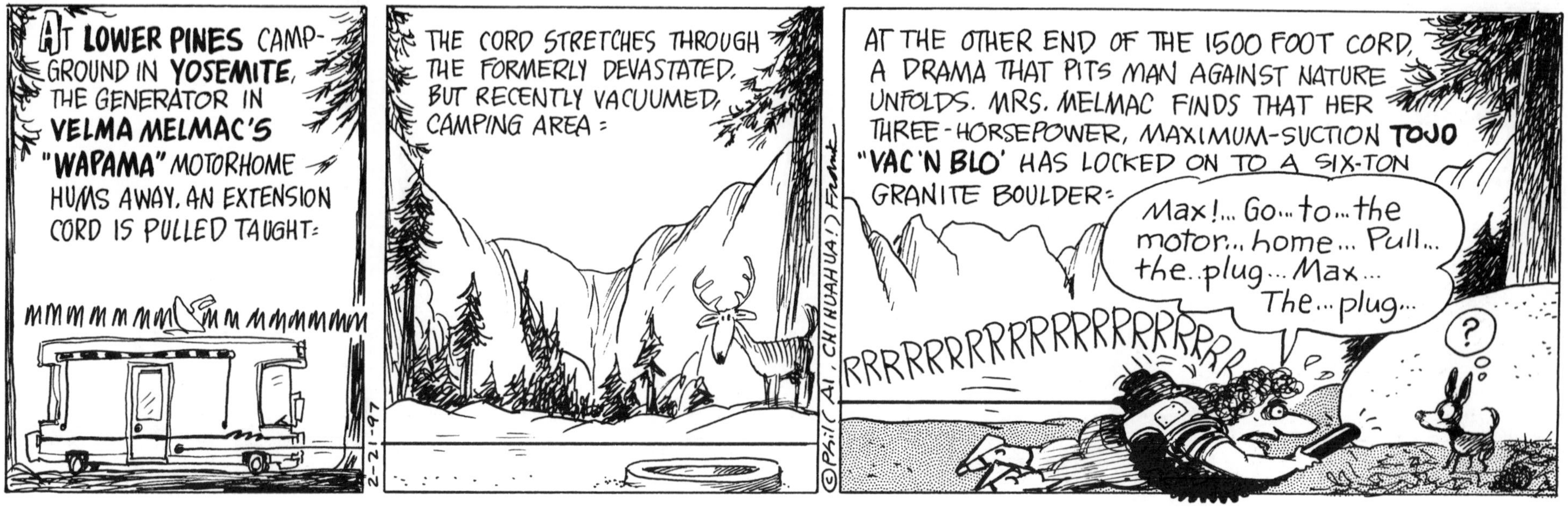
AT LOWER PINES CAMPGROUND IN YOSEMITE, THE GENERATOR IN VELMA MELMAC'S "WAPAMA" MOTORHOME HUMS AWAY. AN EXTENSION CORD IS PULLED TAUGHT:
MMMMMMMMMMMMMMMMMMMM
2-21-97
THE CORD STRETCHES THROUGH THE FORMERLY DEVASTATED, BUT RECENTLY VACUUMED, CAMPING AREA:
©Phil (AI, CHIHUAHUA!) Frank
AT THE OTHER END OF THE 1500 FOOT CORD, A DRAMA THAT PITS MAN AGAINST NATURE UNFOLDS. MRS. MELMAC FINDS THAT HER THREE-HORSEPOWER, MAXIMUM-SUCTION TOJO "VAC'N BLO' HAS LOCKED ON TO A SIX-TON GRANITE BOULDER:
Max!... Go... to... the motor... home... Pull... the.. plug... Max... The... plug...
RRRRRRRRRRRRRRRRRRRRRR
?

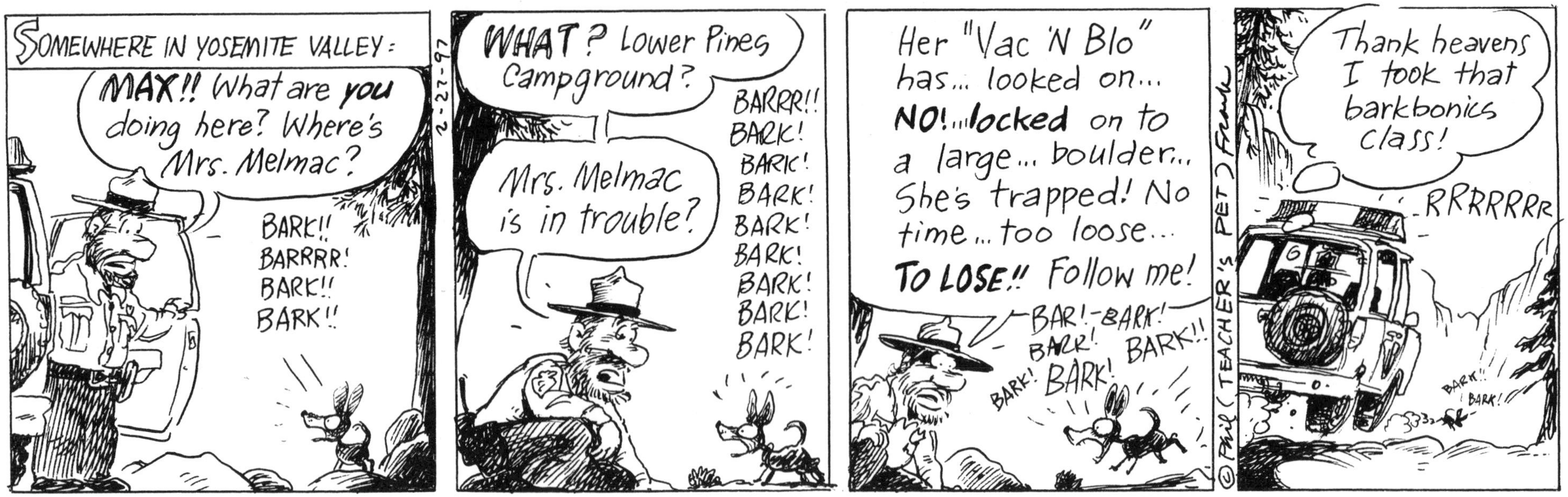
SOMEWHERE IN YOSEMITE VALLEY:
MAX!! What are you doing here? Where's Mrs. Melmac?
BARK!! BARRRR! BARK!! BARK!!
2-27-97
WHAT? Lower Pines Campground?
Mrs. Melmac is in trouble?
BARRR!! BARK! BARK! BARK! BARK! BARK! BARK! BARK! BARK!
Her "Vac 'N Blo" has... looked on... NO!...locked on to a large... boulder... She's trapped! No time... too loose... TO LOSE!! Follow me!
BAR!-BARK! BARK! BARK! BARK! BARK!!
© Phil (TEACHER'S PET) Frank
Thank heavens I took that barkbonics class!
RRRRRRR
BARK!! BARK!

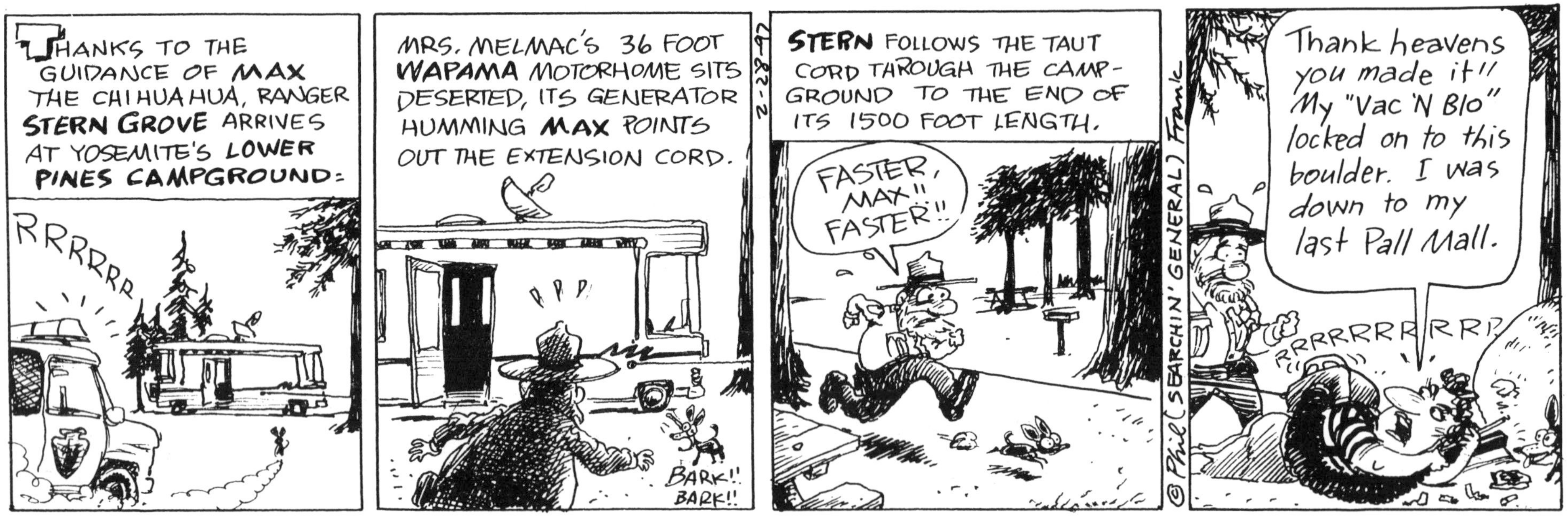
THANKS TO THE GUIDANCE OF MAX THE CHIHUAHUA, RANGER STERN GROVE ARRIVES AT YOSEMITE'S LOWER PINES CAMPGROUND:
RRRRRRR
MRS. MELMAC'S 36 FOOT WAPAMA MOTORHOME SITS DESERTED, ITS GENERATOR HUMMING MAX POINTS OUT THE EXTENSION CORD.
BARK!! BARK!!
2-28-97
STERN FOLLOWS THE TAUT CORD THROUGH THE CAMPGROUND TO THE END OF ITS 1500 FOOT LENGTH.
FASTER, MAX!! FASTER!!
© Phil (SEARCHIN' GENERAL) Frank
Thank heavens you made it!! My "Vac 'N Blo" locked on to this boulder. I was down to my last Pall Mall.
RRRRRRRRRRRP

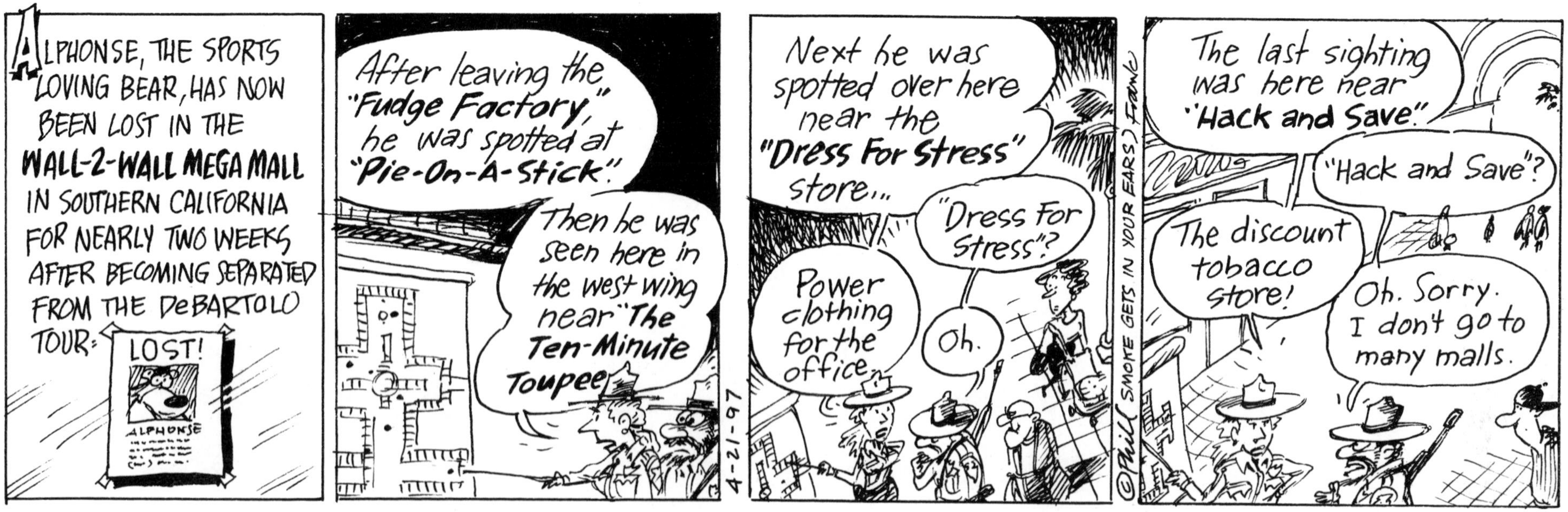
ALPHONSE, THE SPORTS LOVING BEAR, HAS NOW BEEN LOST IN THE **WALL-2-WALL MEGA MALL** IN SOUTHERN CALIFORNIA FOR NEARLY TWO WEEKS AFTER BECOMING SEPARATED FROM THE DeBARTOLO TOUR:
LOST!
ALPHONSE
After leaving the "**Fudge Factory**," he was spotted at "**Pie-On-A-Stick**."
Then he was seen here in the west wing near "**The Ten-Minute Toupee**."
4-21-97
Next he was spotted over here near the "**Dress For Stress**" store...
"Dress For Stress"?
Power clothing for the office.
Oh.
©Phil (SMOKE GETS IN YOUR EARS) Frank
The last sighting was here near "**Hack and Save**."
"Hack and Save"?
The discount tobacco store!
Oh. Sorry. I don't go to many malls.

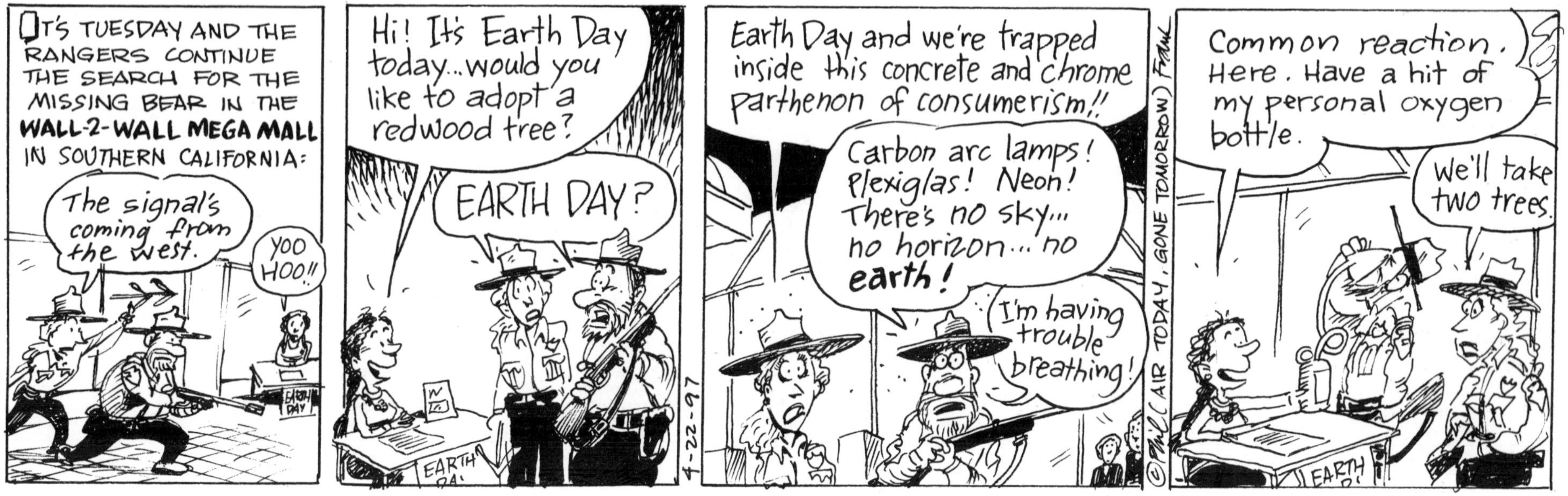
IT'S TUESDAY AND THE RANGERS CONTINUE THE SEARCH FOR THE MISSING BEAR IN THE **WALL-2-WALL MEGA MALL** IN SOUTHERN CALIFORNIA:
The signal's coming from the west.
YOO HOO!!
EARTH DAY
Hi! It's Earth Day today... would you like to adopt a redwood tree?
EARTH DAY?
4-22-97
Earth Day and we're trapped inside this concrete and chrome parthenon of consumerism!!
Carbon arc lamps! Plexiglas! Neon! There's no sky... no horizon... no **earth!**
I'm having trouble breathing!
©Phil (AIR TODAY, GONE TOMORROW) Frank
Common reaction. Here. Have a hit of my personal oxygen bottle.
We'll take two trees.

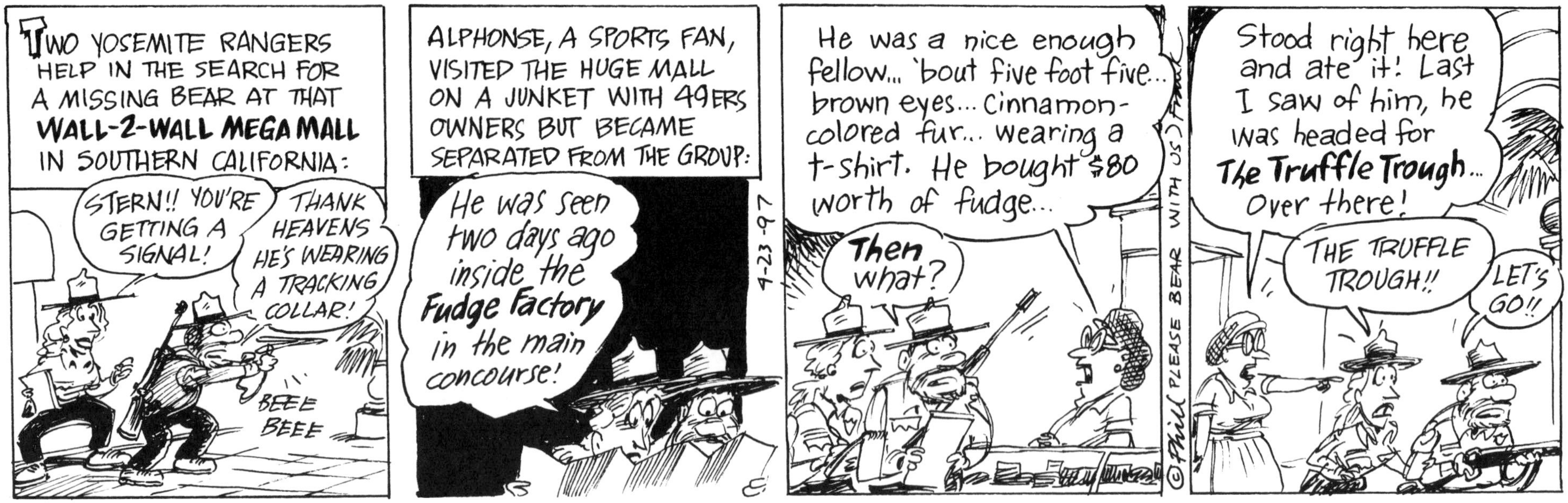
TWO YOSEMITE RANGERS HELP IN THE SEARCH FOR A MISSING BEAR AT THAT **WALL-2-WALL MEGA MALL** IN SOUTHERN CALIFORNIA:
STERN!! YOU'RE GETTING A SIGNAL!
THANK HEAVENS HE'S WEARING A TRACKING COLLAR!
BEEE BEEE
ALPHONSE, A SPORTS FAN, VISITED THE HUGE MALL ON A JUNKET WITH 49ERS OWNERS BUT BECAME SEPARATED FROM THE GROUP:
He was seen two days ago inside the **Fudge Factory** in the main concourse!
4-23-97
He was a nice enough fellow... 'bout five foot five... brown eyes... cinnamon-colored fur... wearing a t-shirt. He bought $80 worth of fudge...
Then what?
©Phil Frank (PLEASE BEAR WITH US)
Stood right here and ate it! Last I saw of him, he was headed for **The Truffle Trough**... Over there!
THE TRUFFLE TROUGH!!
LET'S GO!!

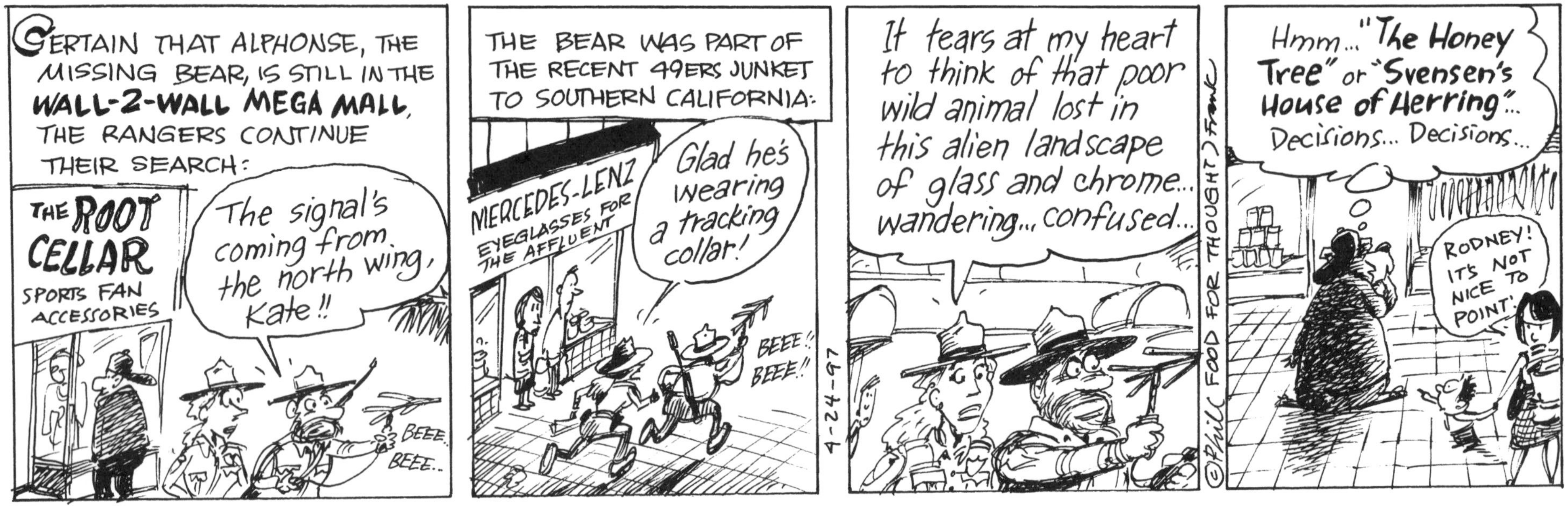
CERTAIN THAT ALPHONSE, THE MISSING BEAR, IS STILL IN THE **WALL-2-WALL MEGA MALL**, THE RANGERS CONTINUE THEIR SEARCH:
THE ROOT CELLAR SPORTS FAN ACCESSORIES
The signal's coming from the north wing, Kate!!
BEEE.. BEEE..
THE BEAR WAS PART OF THE RECENT 49ERS JUNKET TO SOUTHERN CALIFORNIA:
MERCEDES-LENZ EYEGLASSES FOR THE AFFLUENT
Glad he's wearing a tracking collar!
BEEE!! BEEE!!
4-24-97
It tears at my heart to think of that poor wild animal lost in this alien landscape of glass and chrome... wandering... confused...
©Phil Frank (FOOD FOR THOUGHT)
Hmm... "**The Honey Tree**" or "**Svensen's House of Herring**"... Decisions... Decisions...
RODNEY! IT'S NOT NICE TO POINT!

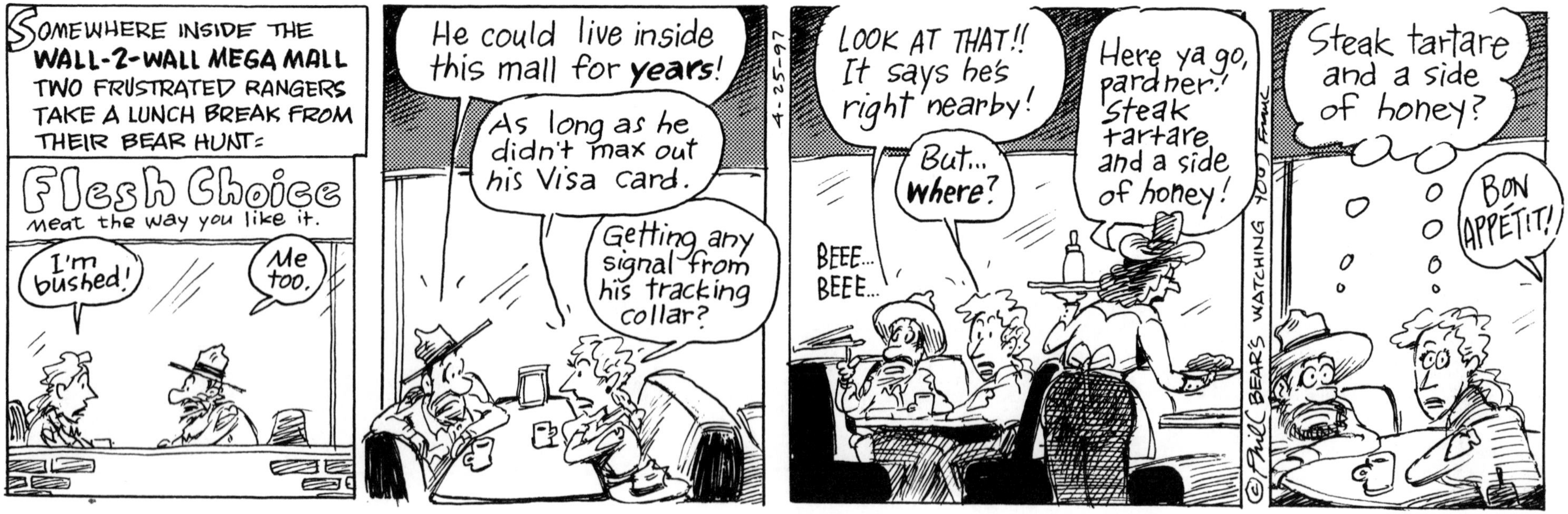

SOMEWHERE INSIDE THE **WALL-2-WALL MEGA MALL** TWO FRUSTRATED RANGERS TAKE A LUNCH BREAK FROM THEIR BEAR HUNT:
Flesh Choice
meat the way you like it.
I'm bushed!
Me too.
He could live inside this mall for **years**!
As long as he didn't max out his Visa card.
Getting any signal from his tracking collar?
4-25-97
LOOK AT THAT!! It says he's right nearby!
BEEE... BEEE...
But... **where**?
Here ya go, pardner! Steak tartare and a side of honey!
© Phil Frank BEAR'S WATCHING YOU
Steak tartare and a side of honey?
BON APPÉTIT!

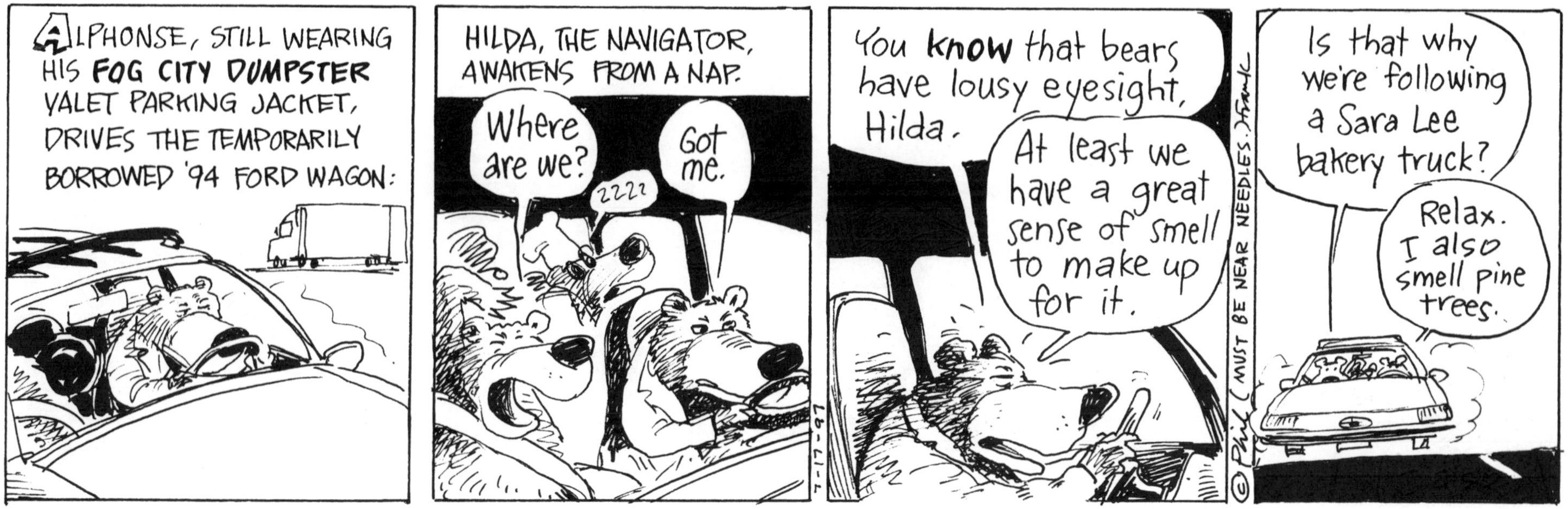

ALPHONSE, STILL WEARING HIS **FOG CITY DUMPSTER** VALET PARKING JACKET, DRIVES THE TEMPORARILY BORROWED '94 FORD WAGON:
HILDA, THE NAVIGATOR, AWAKENS FROM A NAP.
Where are we?
ZZZZ
Got me.
7-17-97
You **know** that bears have lousy eyesight, Hilda.
At least we have a great sense of smell to make up for it.
© Phil Frank MUST BE NEAR NEEDLES.
Is that why we're following a Sara Lee bakery truck?
Relax. I also smell pine trees.

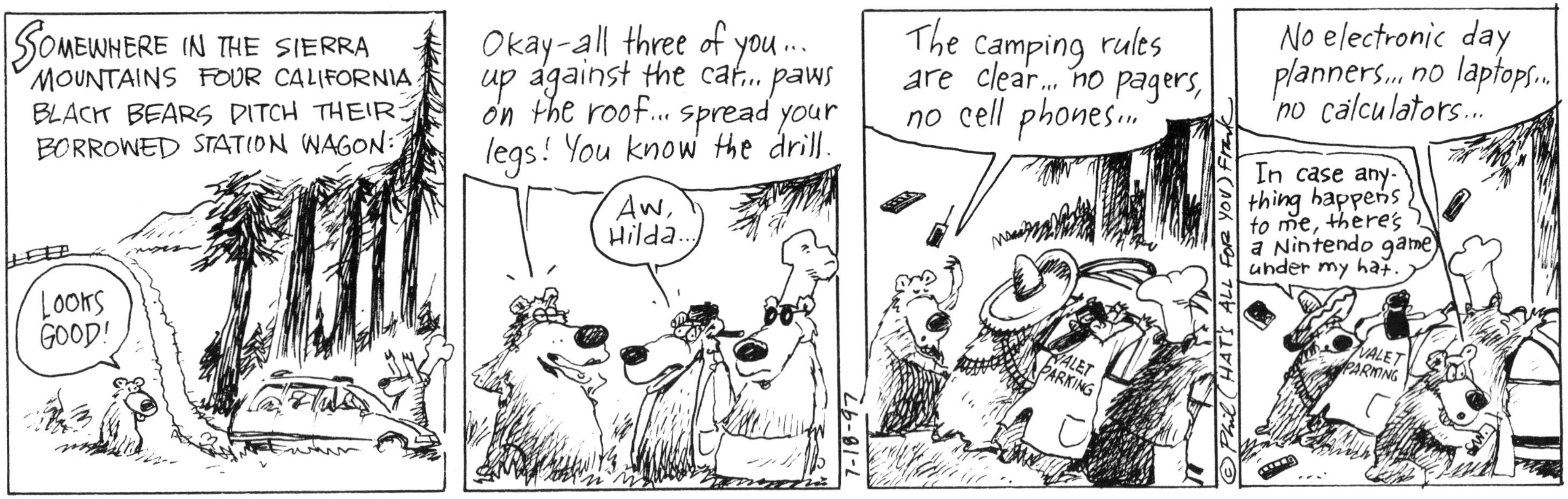
SOMEWHERE IN THE SIERRA MOUNTAINS FOUR CALIFORNIA BLACK BEARS DITCH THEIR BORROWED STATION WAGON:
LOOKS GOOD!
Okay–all three of you... up against the car... paws on the roof... spread your legs! You know the drill.
Aw, Hilda...
7-18-97
The camping rules are clear... no pagers, no cell phones...
VALET PARKING
© Phil (HAT'S ALL FOR YOU) Frank
No electronic day planners... no laptops... no calculators...
In case anything happens to me, there's a Nintendo game under my hat.
VALET PARKING

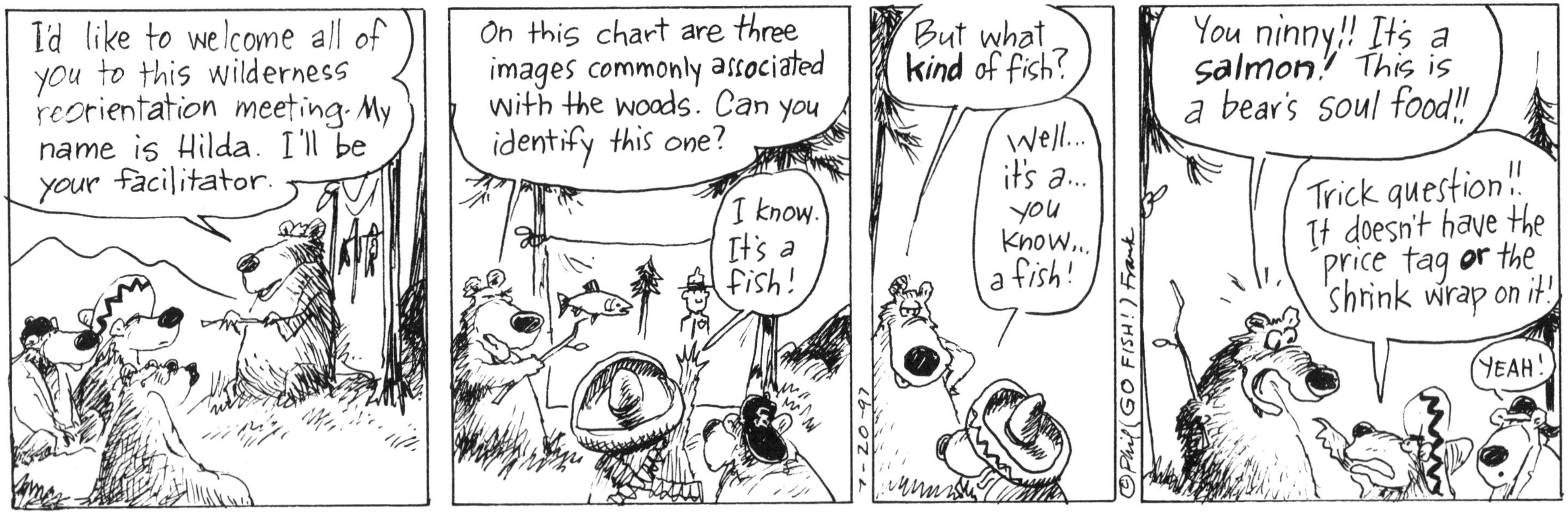
I'd like to welcome all of you to this wilderness reorientation meeting. My name is Hilda. I'll be your facilitator.
On this chart are three images commonly associated with the woods. Can you identify this one?
I know. It's a fish!
7-20-97
But what **kind** of fish?
Well... it's a... you know... a fish!
© Phil (GO FISH!) Frank
You ninny!! It's a **salmon**! This is a bear's soul food!!
Trick question!! It doesn't have the price tag **or** the shrink wrap on it!
YEAH!

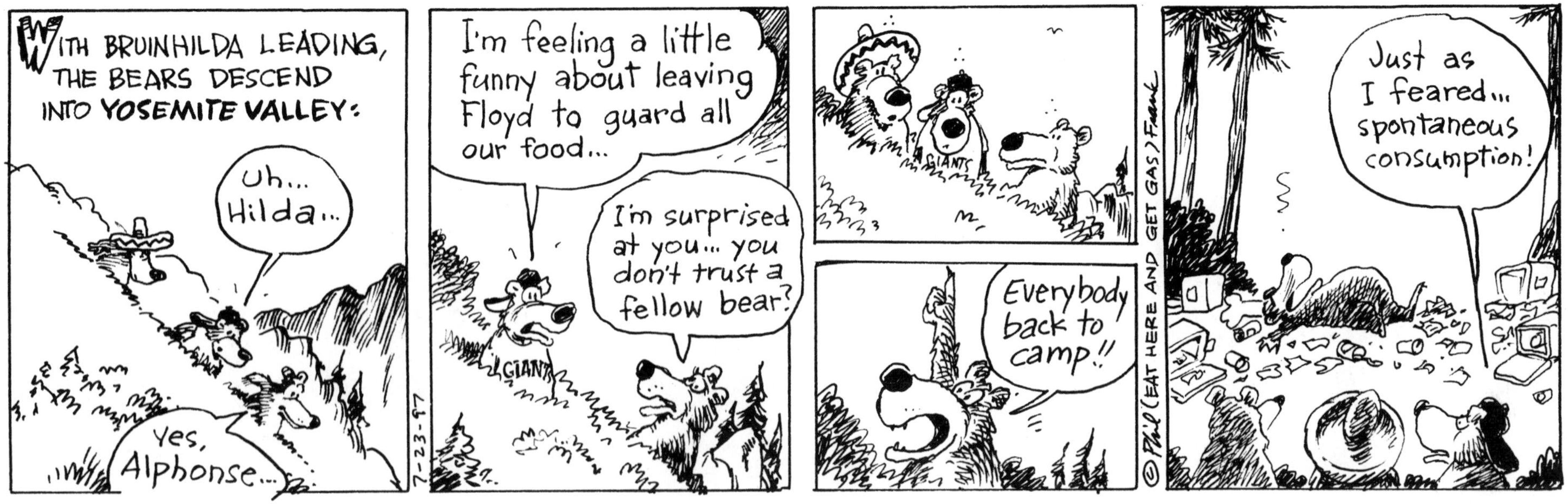
WITH BRUINHILDA LEADING, THE BEARS DESCEND INTO YOSEMITE VALLEY:
Uh... Hilda...
Yes, Alphonse...
7-23-97
I'm feeling a little funny about leaving Floyd to guard all our food...
GIANT
I'm surprised at you... you don't trust a fellow bear?
GIANTS
Everybody back to camp!!
© Phil (EAT HERE AND GET GAS) Frank
Just as I feared... spontaneous consumption!

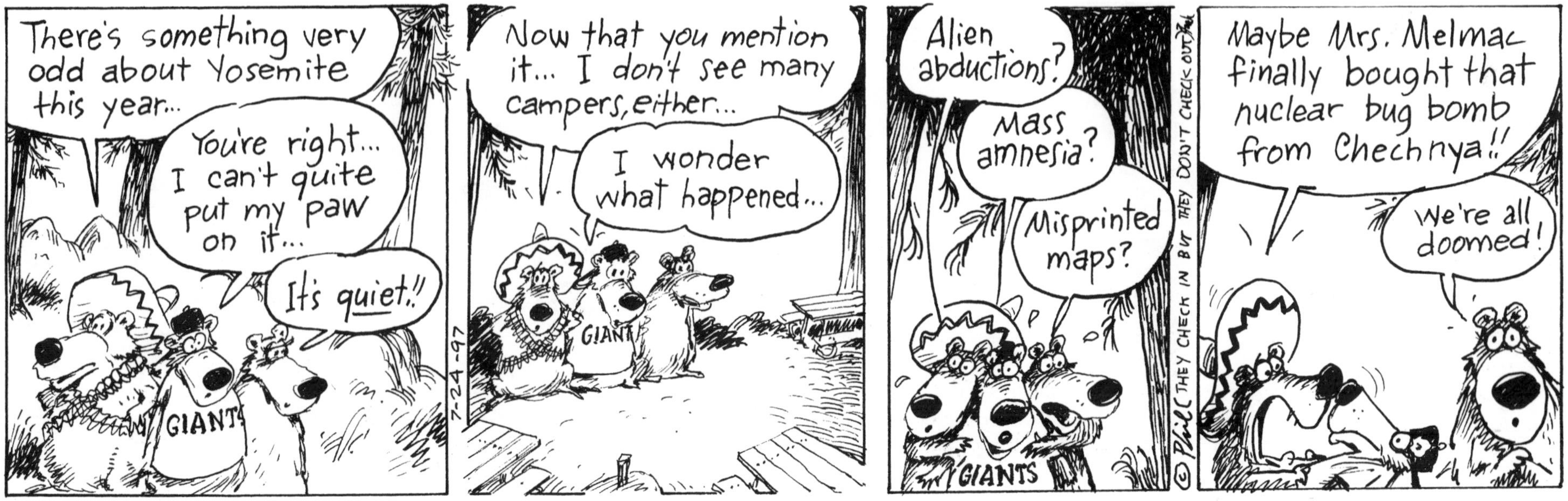
There's something very odd about Yosemite this year...
You're right... I can't quite put my paw on it...
It's quiet!!
GIANTS
Now that you mention it... I don't see many campers, either...
I wonder what happened...
GIANT
7-24-97
Alien abductions?
Mass amnesia?
Misprinted maps?
GIANTS
© Phil THEY CHECK IN BUT THEY DON'T CHECK OUT Frank
Maybe Mrs. Melmac finally bought that nuclear bug bomb from Chechnya!!
We're all doomed!

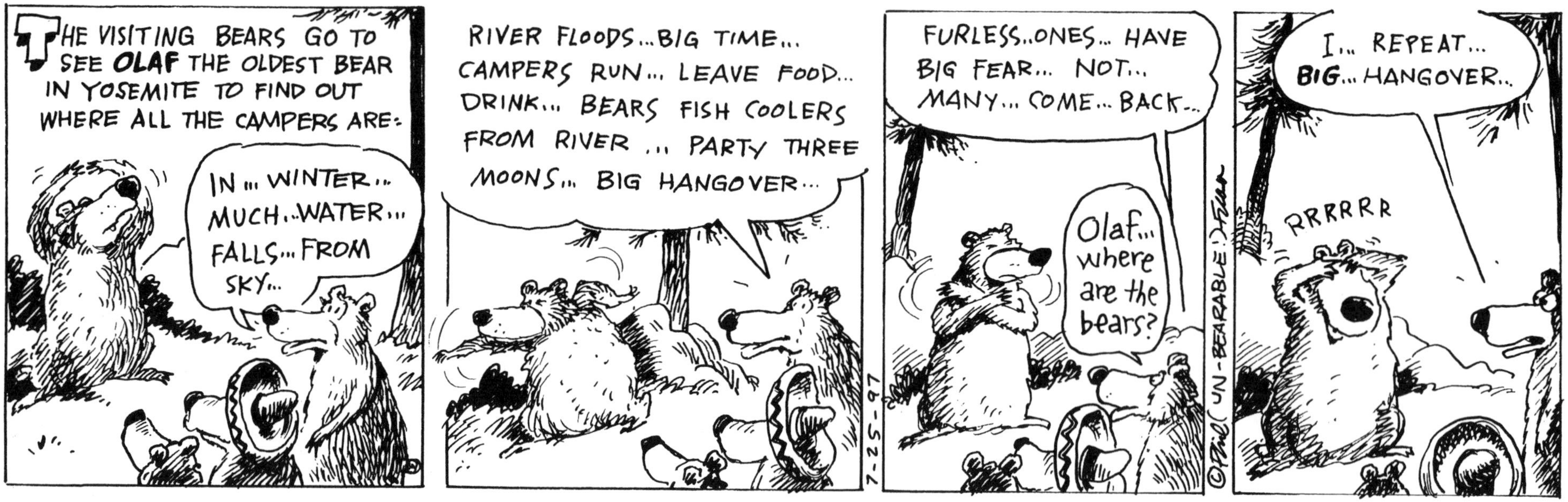
THE VISITING BEARS GO TO SEE OLAF THE OLDEST BEAR IN YOSEMITE TO FIND OUT WHERE ALL THE CAMPERS ARE:
IN... WINTER... MUCH...WATER... FALLS...FROM SKY...
RIVER FLOODS...BIG TIME... CAMPERS RUN... LEAVE FOOD... DRINK... BEARS FISH COOLERS FROM RIVER ... PARTY THREE MOONS... BIG HANGOVER...
7-25-97
FURLESS..ONES... HAVE BIG FEAR... NOT... MANY... COME... BACK...
Olaf... where are the bears?
©Phil (UN-BEARABLE!)
I... REPEAT... BIG... HANGOVER...
RRRRRR

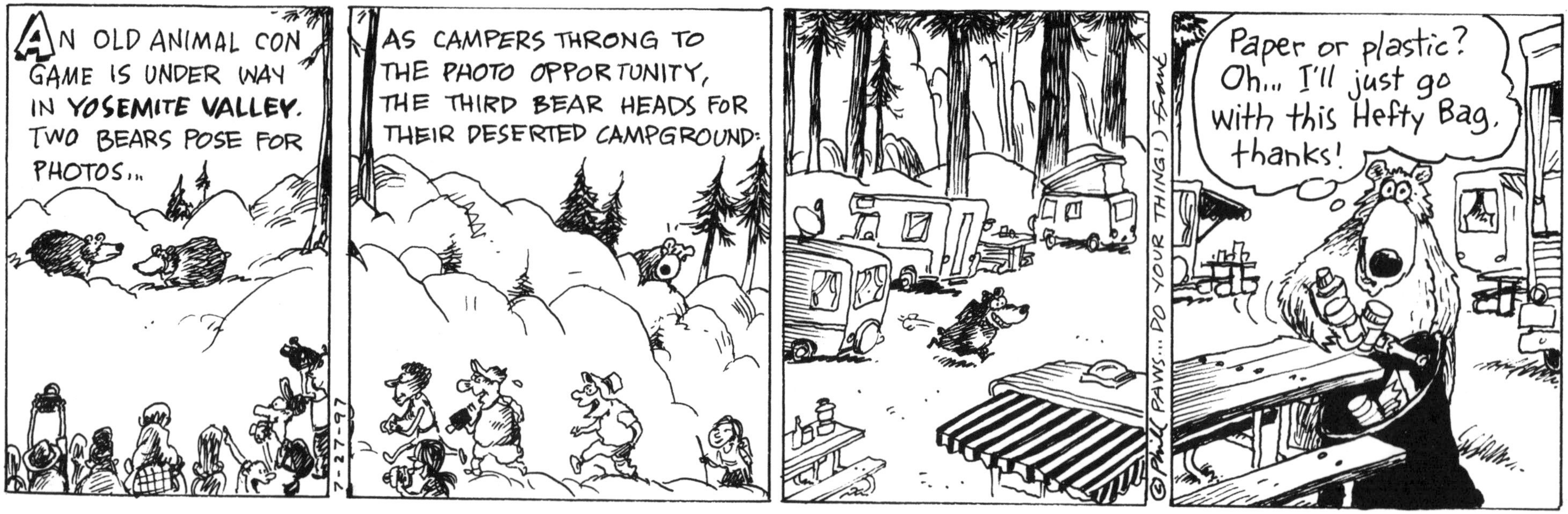
AN OLD ANIMAL CON GAME IS UNDER WAY IN YOSEMITE VALLEY. TWO BEARS POSE FOR PHOTOS...
7-27-97
AS CAMPERS THRONG TO THE PHOTO OPPORTUNITY, THE THIRD BEAR HEADS FOR THEIR DESERTED CAMPGROUND:
©Phil PAWS... DO YOUR THING!)
Paper or plastic? Oh... I'll just go with this Hefty Bag, thanks!

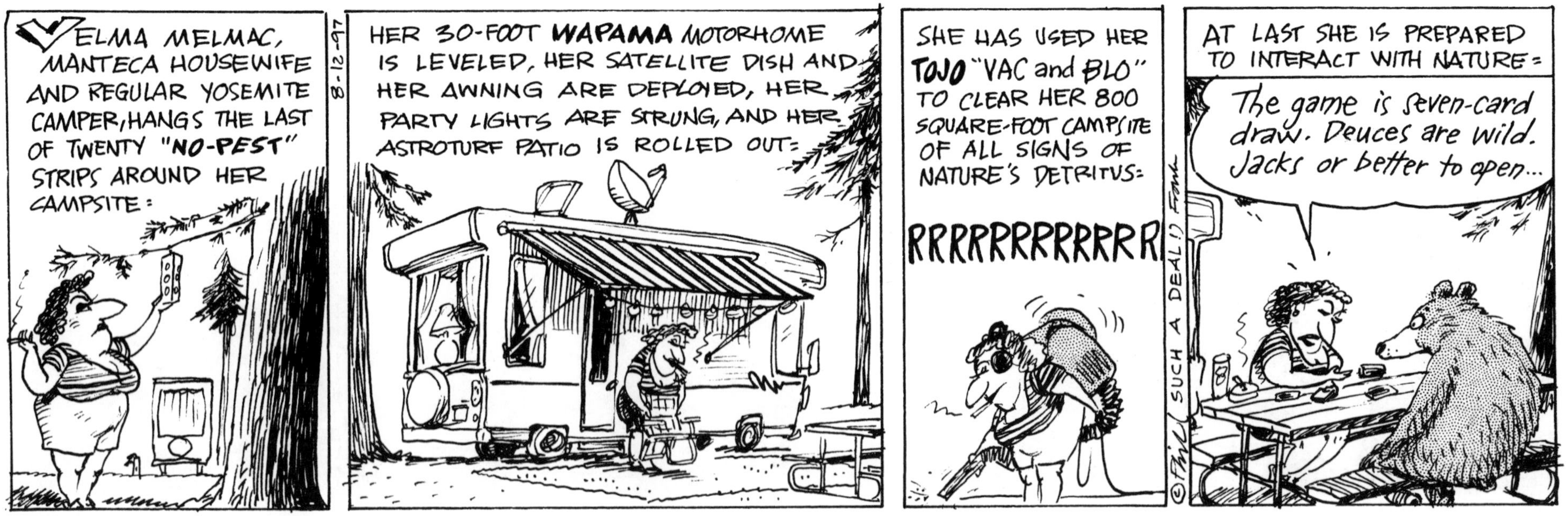
VELMA MELMAC, MANTECA HOUSEWIFE AND REGULAR YOSEMITE CAMPER, HANGS THE LAST OF TWENTY "NO-PEST" STRIPS AROUND HER CAMPSITE:
8-12-97
HER 30-FOOT WAPAMA MOTORHOME IS LEVELED, HER SATELLITE DISH AND HER AWNING ARE DEPLOYED, HER PARTY LIGHTS ARE STRUNG, AND HER ASTROTURF PATIO IS ROLLED OUT:
SHE HAS USED HER TOJO "VAC and BLO" TO CLEAR HER 800 SQUARE-FOOT CAMPSITE OF ALL SIGNS OF NATURE'S DETRITUS:
RRRRRRRRRRRR
©Phil (SUCH A DEAL!) Frank
AT LAST SHE IS PREPARED TO INTERACT WITH NATURE:
The game is seven-card draw. Deuces are wild. Jacks or better to open...

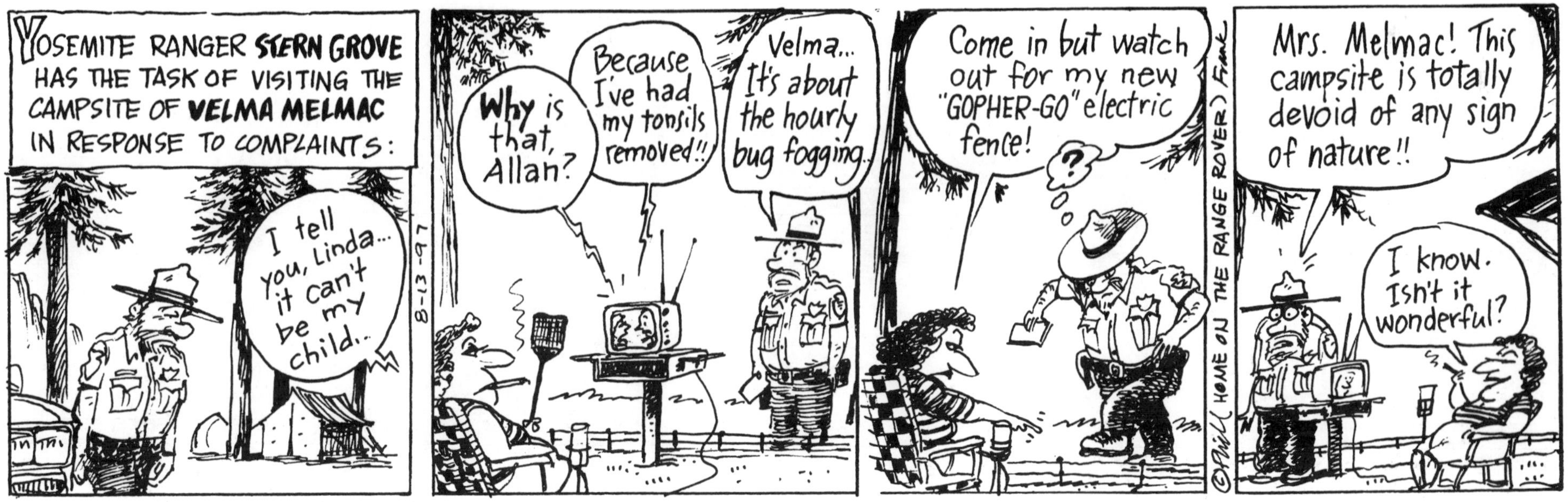
YOSEMITE RANGER STERN GROVE HAS THE TASK OF VISITING THE CAMPSITE OF VELMA MELMAC IN RESPONSE TO COMPLAINTS:
I tell you, Linda... it can't be my child..
8-13-97
Why is that, Allan?
Because I've had my tonsils removed!!
Velma... It's about the hourly bug fogging..
Come in but watch out for my new "GOPHER-GO" electric fence!
?
©Phil (HOME ON THE RANGE ROVER) Frank
Mrs. Melmac! This campsite is totally devoid of any sign of nature!!
I know. Isn't it wonderful?

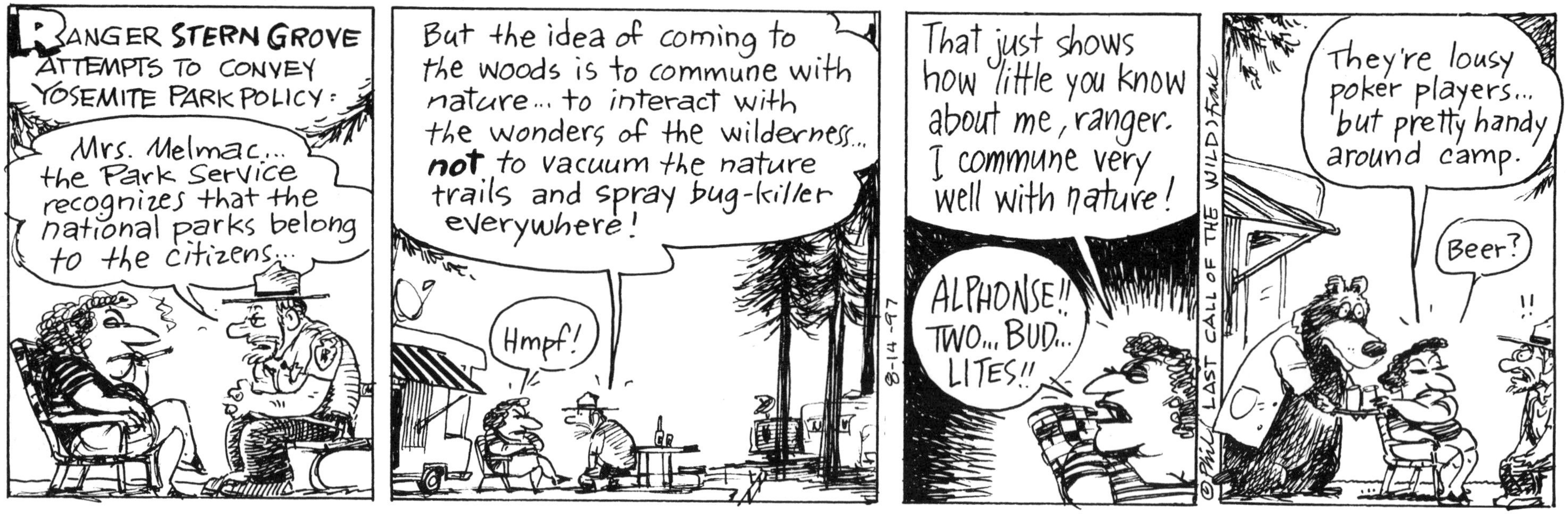
RANGER STERN GROVE ATTEMPTS TO CONVEY YOSEMITE PARK POLICY:
Mrs. Melmac... the Park Service recognizes that the national parks belong to the citizens...
But the idea of coming to the woods is to commune with nature... to interact with the wonders of the wilderness... **not** to vacuum the nature trails and spray bug-killer everywhere!
Hmpf!
8-14-97
That just shows how little you know about me, ranger. I commune very well with nature!
ALPHONSE!! TWO... BUD... LITES!!
© Phil (LAST CALL OF THE WILD) Frank
They're lousy poker players... but pretty handy around camp.
Beer?
!!

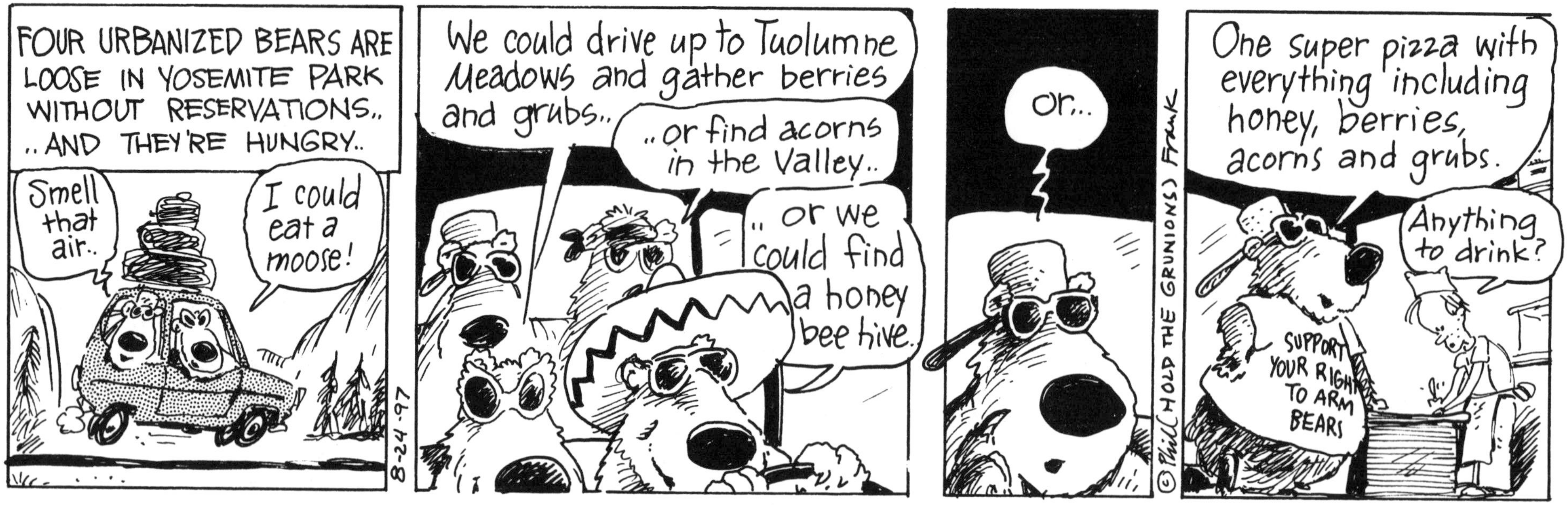
FOUR URBANIZED BEARS ARE LOOSE IN YOSEMITE PARK WITHOUT RESERVATIONS.. ..AND THEY'RE HUNGRY..
Smell that air..
I could eat a moose!
8-24-97
We could drive up to Tuolumne Meadows and gather berries and grubs..
..or find acorns in the Valley..
.. or we could find a honey bee hive.
or...
© Phil (HOLD THE GRUNIONS) Frank
One super pizza with everything including honey, berries, acorns and grubs.
Anything to drink?
SUPPORT YOUR RIGHT TO ARM BEARS

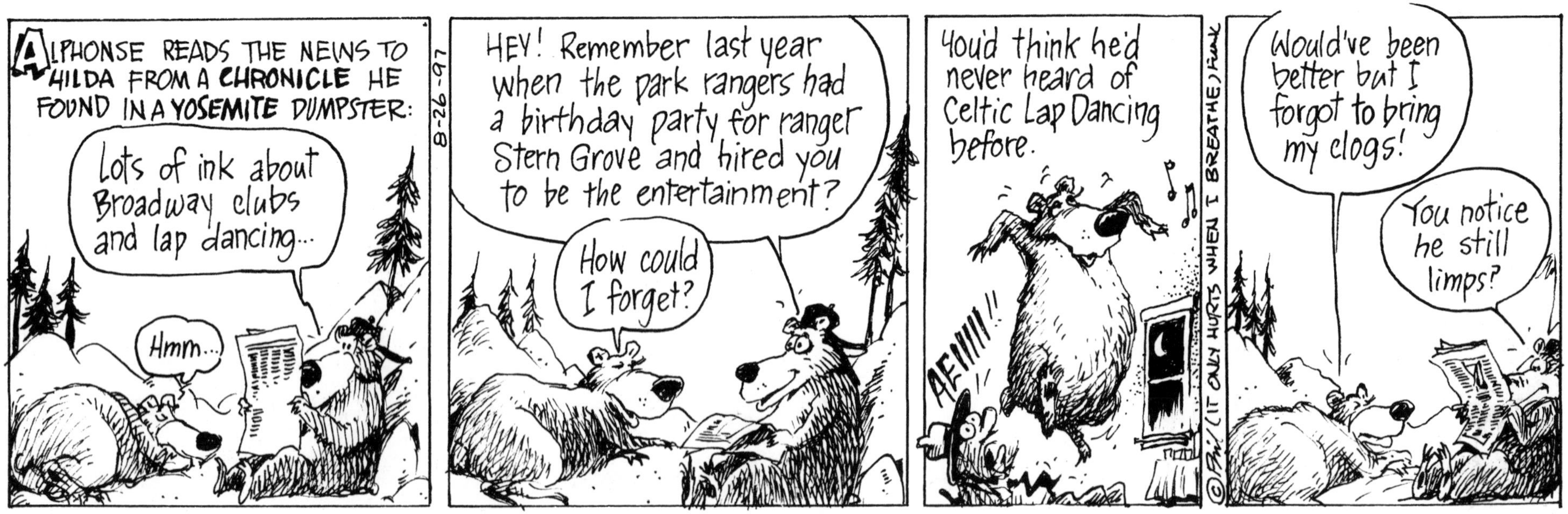
ALPHONSE READS THE NEWS TO HILDA FROM A CHRONICLE HE FOUND IN A YOSEMITE DUMPSTER:
Lots of ink about Broadway clubs and lap dancing...
Hmm...
8-26-97
HEY! Remember last year when the park rangers had a birthday party for ranger Stern Grove and hired you to be the entertainment?
How could I forget?
You'd think he'd never heard of Celtic Lap Dancing before.
AEIIIII!!
©Phil (IT ONLY HURTS WHEN I BREATHE) Frank
Would've been better but I forgot to bring my clogs!
You notice he still limps?

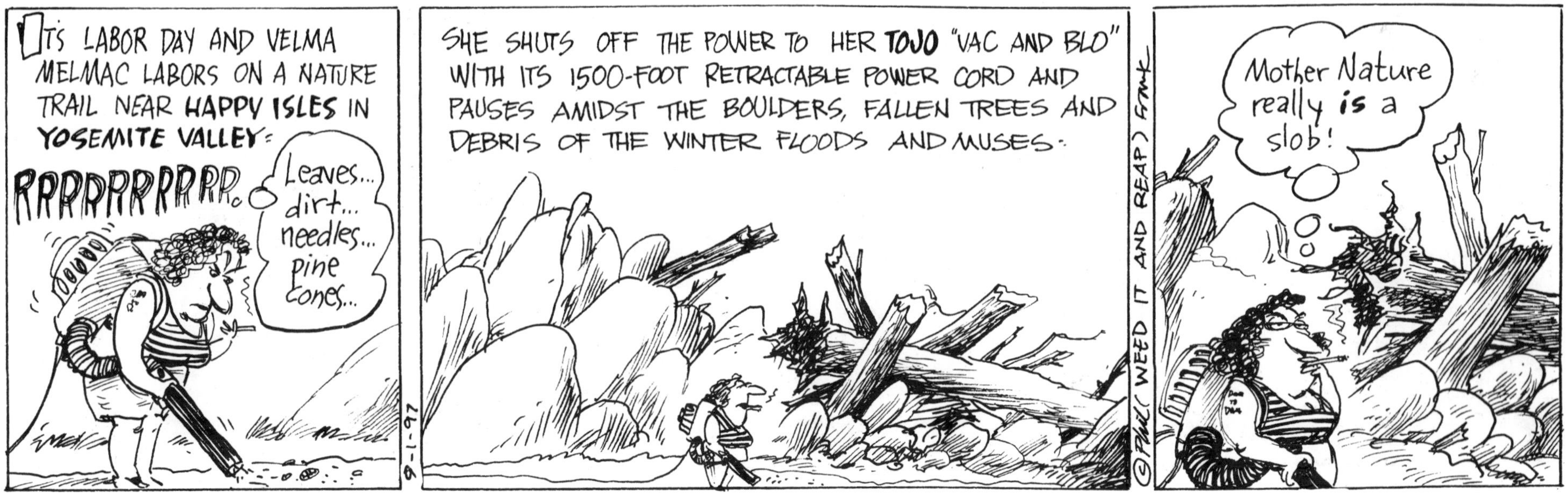
IT'S LABOR DAY AND VELMA MELMAC LABORS ON A NATURE TRAIL NEAR HAPPY ISLES IN YOSEMITE VALLEY:
RRRRRRRRRRR
Leaves... dirt... needles... pine cones...
9-1-97
SHE SHUTS OFF THE POWER TO HER TOJO "VAC AND BLO" WITH ITS 1500-FOOT RETRACTABLE POWER CORD AND PAUSES AMIDST THE BOULDERS, FALLEN TREES AND DEBRIS OF THE WINTER FLOODS AND MUSES:
©Phil (WEED IT AND REAP) Frank
Mother Nature really is a slob!

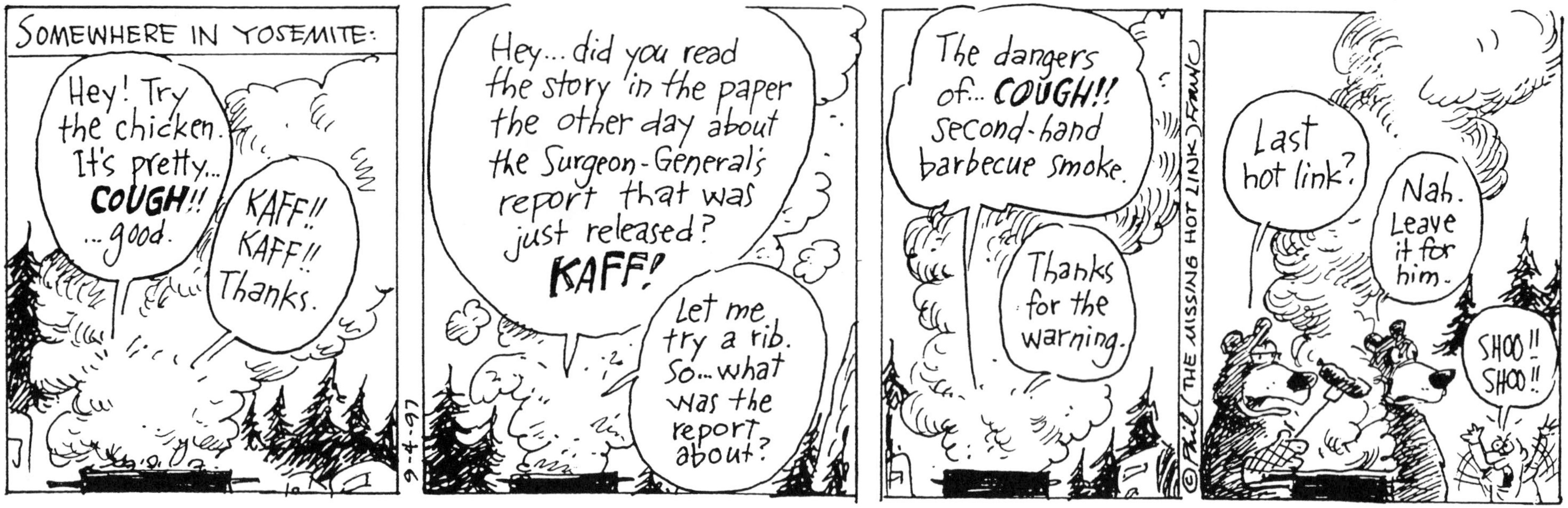
SOMEWHERE IN YOSEMITE:
Hey! Try the chicken. It's pretty... COUGH!! ...good.
KAFF!! KAFF!! Thanks.
9-4-97
Hey... did you read the story in the paper the other day about the Surgeon-General's report that was just released? KAFF!
Let me try a rib. So... what was the report about?
The dangers of... COUGH!! second-hand barbecue smoke.
Thanks for the warning.
© Phil (THE MISSING HOT LINK) Frank
Last hot link?
Nah. Leave it for him.
SHOO!! SHOO!!

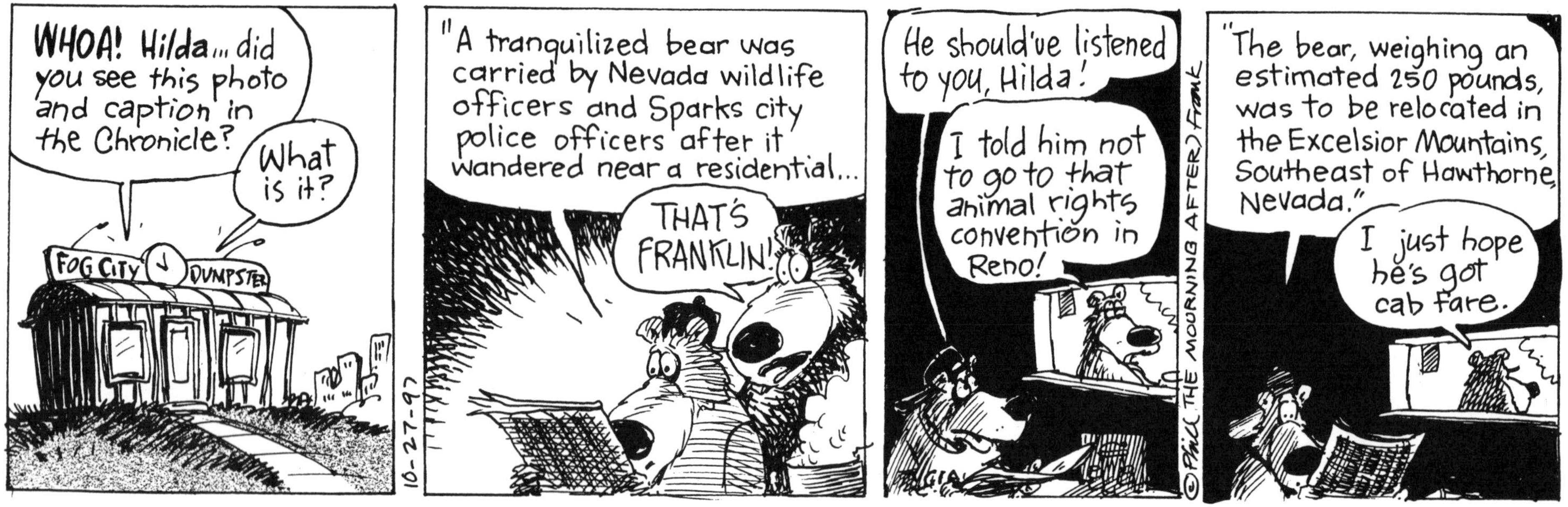
WHOA! Hilda... did you see this photo and caption in the Chronicle?
What is it?
FOG CITY DUMPSTER
10-27-97
"A tranquilized bear was carried by Nevada wildlife officers and Sparks city police officers after it wandered near a residential...
THAT'S FRANKLIN!
He should've listened to you, Hilda!
I told him not to go to that animal rights convention in Reno!
© Phil (THE MOURNING AFTER) Frank
"The bear, weighing an estimated 250 pounds, was to be relocated in the Excelsior Mountains, Southeast of Hawthorne, Nevada."
I just hope he's got cab fare.

TRANQUILIZED BEAR SEEN RECENTLY IN A CHRONICLE PHOTO, HAS TURNED OUT TO BE ONE OF THE BEARS FROM THE FOG CITY DUMPSTER. FRANKLIN WAS ON HIS WAY TO AN ANIMAL RIGHTS CONVENTION IN RENO.
10-28-97
HE HAS BEEN RELOCATED TO THE EXCELSIOR MOUNTAINS NEAR HAWTHORNE, NEVADA..
INDIAN RES.
Walker Lake
WASSUK
GILLS RANGE
GABBS VALLEY
El. 4320 ft.
Hawthorne
Babbitt
Cory Pk. 10520 ft.
Luning
Mina
Gabbs
EXCELSIOR MTS.
RIGHT ABOUT HERE!
..WHERE HE SHOULD BE WAKING UP JUST ABOUT... NOW.
Ohhh... my head... wha' happened?
Some dudes dumped you.
WHERE'S MY SOMBRERO? MY "SUPPORT YOUR RIGHT TO ARM BEARS" T-SHIRT? MY WALLET? I'VE BEEN MUGGED!!
IT WILL BE A WHILE BEFORE THE DRUGS WEAR OFF AND THE REALITY OF HIS SITUATION SETS IN:
TAXI!
TAXI!!
© Phil (FOREST GRUMP) Frank

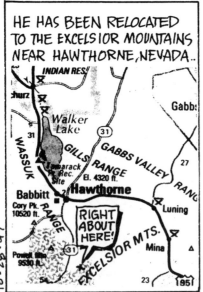

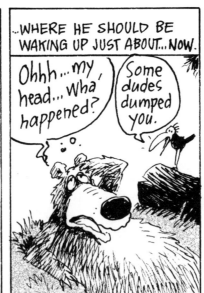

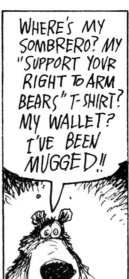

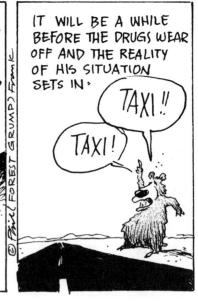

Plan to Cut Car Use in Yosemite

New Park Service proposal for buses, bikes, foot power

The Park Service proposal to eliminate summer-induced traffic gridlock was in the news again. The goal was a noble one – to minimize the number of motorized vehicles in the Valley, and get people out of their cars and closer to nature. In devising a transportation plan, the National Park Service delegated the responsibility for developing a regional mass transit solution to an organization composed of local and regional governments called YARTS. One proposal called for busing visitors to the Valley from the park's gateway communities. Resistance to busing has been strong. It seems that getting people – especially convenience-loving visitors – out of their cars is going to be harder than was expected. I couldn't ignore the subject since I love the idea of urbanites in the woods.

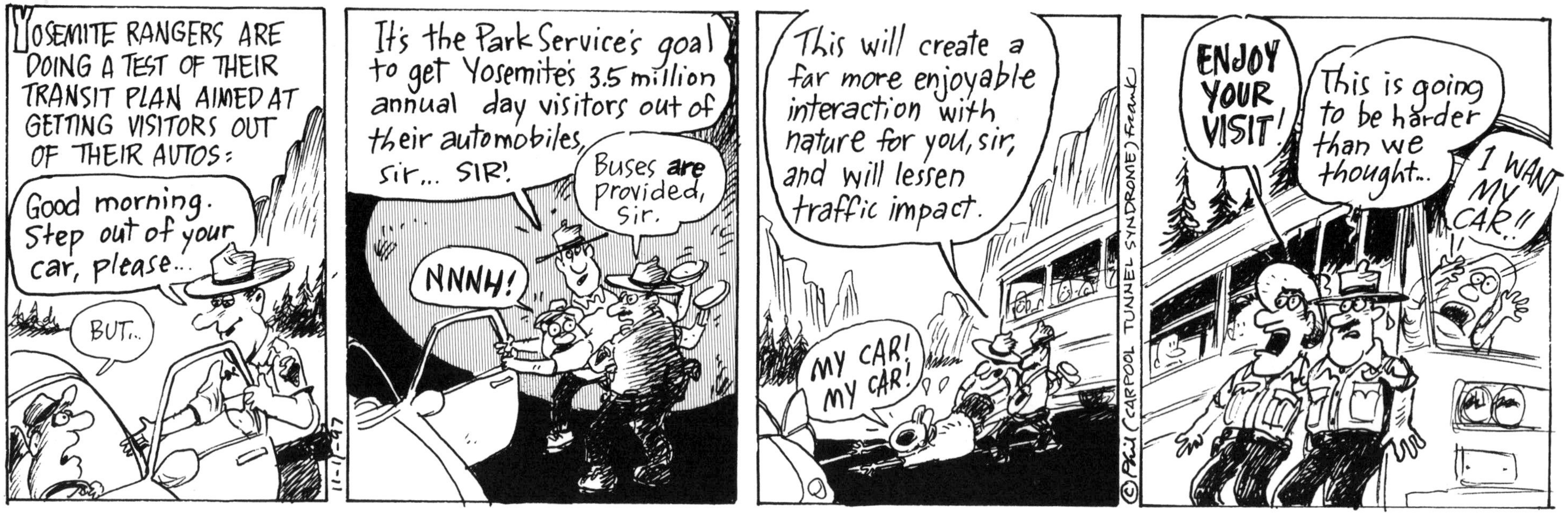
YOSEMITE RANGERS ARE DOING A TEST OF THEIR TRANSIT PLAN AIMED AT GETTING VISITORS OUT OF THEIR AUTOS:
Good morning. Step out of your car, please...
BUT...
11-1-97
It's the Park Service's goal to get Yosemite's 3.5 million annual day visitors out of their automobiles, sir... SIR!
Buses are provided, sir.
NNNH!
This will create a far more enjoyable interaction with nature for you, sir, and will lessen traffic impact.
MY CAR! MY CAR!
© Phil (CARPOOL TUNNEL SYNDROME) Frank
ENJOY YOUR VISIT!
This is going to be harder than we thought...
I WANT MY CAR!!

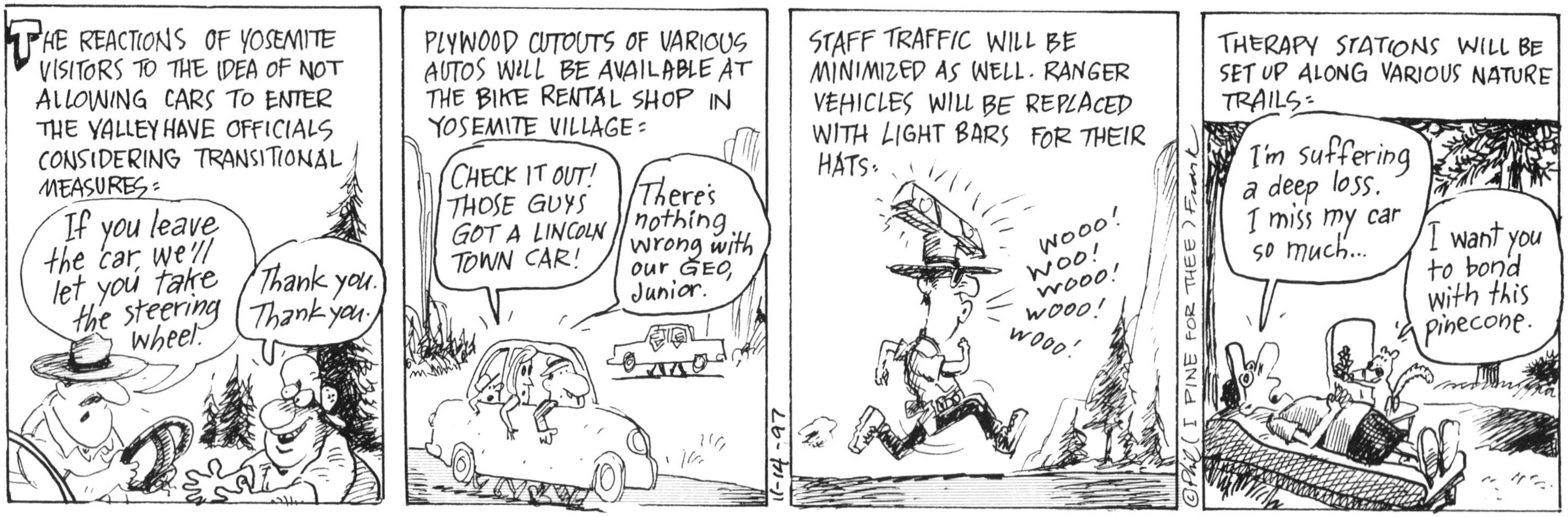
THE REACTIONS OF YOSEMITE VISITORS TO THE IDEA OF NOT ALLOWING CARS TO ENTER THE VALLEY HAVE OFFICIALS CONSIDERING TRANSITIONAL MEASURES:
If you leave the car, we'll let you take the steering wheel.
Thank you. Thank you.
PLYWOOD CUTOUTS OF VARIOUS AUTOS WILL BE AVAILABLE AT THE BIKE RENTAL SHOP IN YOSEMITE VILLAGE:
CHECK IT OUT! THOSE GUYS GOT A LINCOLN TOWN CAR!
There's nothing wrong with our GEO, Junior.
11-14-97
STAFF TRAFFIC WILL BE MINIMIZED AS WELL. RANGER VEHICLES WILL BE REPLACED WITH LIGHT BARS FOR THEIR HATS:
WOOO! WOO! WOOO! WOOO! WOOO!
© Phil (I PINE FOR THEE) Frank
THERAPY STATIONS WILL BE SET UP ALONG VARIOUS NATURE TRAILS:
I'm suffering a deep loss. I miss my car so much...
I want you to bond with this pinecone.

Park service kills 4 bears in Yosemite

By Mark Grossi
The Fresno Bee

A mother bear and her two cubs were killed in Yosemite National Park this week by wildlif managers grappling with th

Every time I hear about bears having to be destroyed because they had become threats to park visitors I feel sad. Invariably, they were bears that were habituated to humans. The carelessness of many Yosemite visitors in leaving their food unprotected or in their automobiles allowed the bears to become dependent on human foodstuffs. Killing bears is a last resort. Problem bears, when first identified, are darted, tranquilized, tagged, and relocated. Their actions are monitored with the prospect that behavior will change. If there is no hope for reform, the rangers are forced to eliminate the animals. By late November of 1997, there had been $560,000 worth of reported vehicle damage done by black bears.

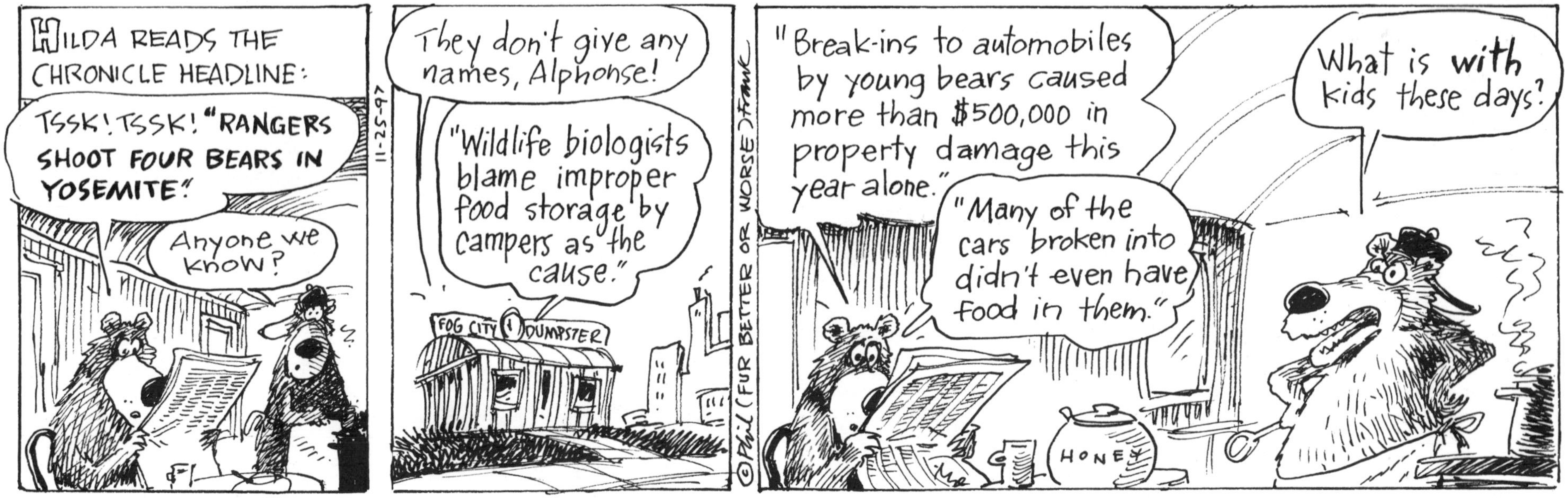
HILDA READS THE CHRONICLE HEADLINE:
TSSK! TSSK! "RANGERS SHOOT FOUR BEARS IN YOSEMITE!"
Anyone we know?
They don't give any names, Alphonse!
"Wildlife biologists blame improper food storage by campers as the cause."
FOG CITY DUMPSTER
11-25-97
© Phil (FUR BETTER OR WORSE) Frank
"Break-ins to automobiles by young bears caused more than $500,000 in property damage this year alone."
"Many of the cars broken into didn't even have food in them."
What is with kids these days?
HONEY

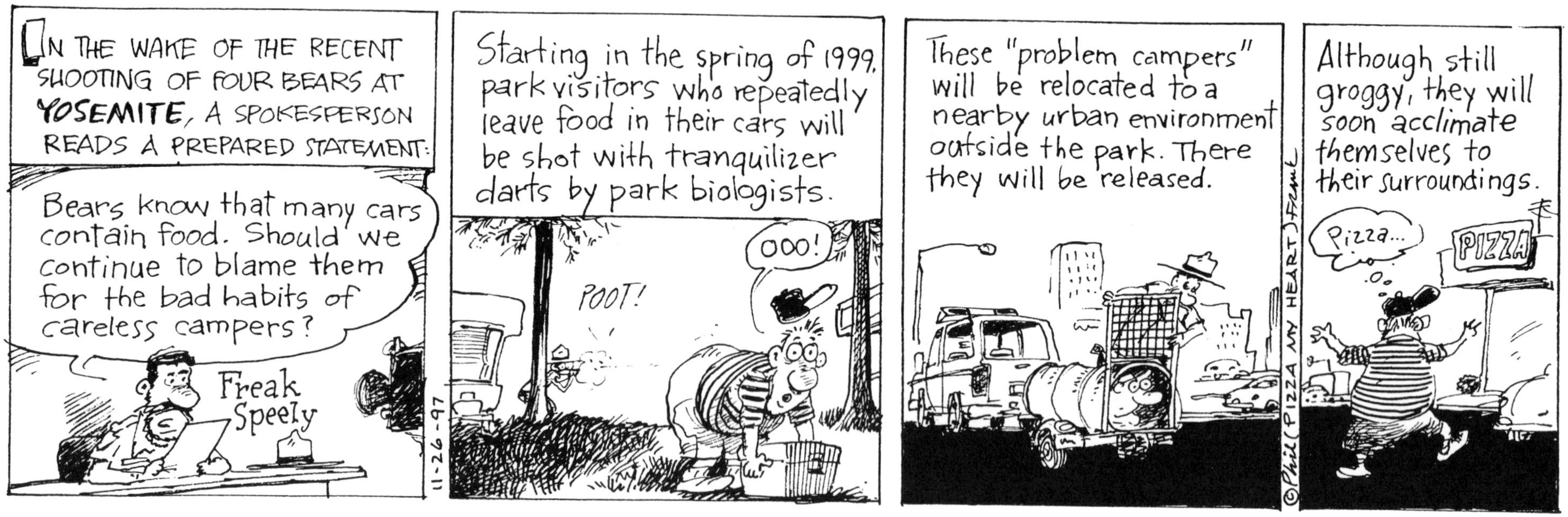
IN THE WAKE OF THE RECENT SHOOTING OF FOUR BEARS AT YOSEMITE, A SPOKESPERSON READS A PREPARED STATEMENT:
Bears know that many cars contain food. Should we continue to blame them for the bad habits of careless campers?
Freak Speely
11-26-97
Starting in the spring of 1999, park visitors who repeatedly leave food in their cars will be shot with tranquilizer darts by park biologists.
POOT!
OOO!
These "problem campers" will be relocated to a nearby urban environment outside the park. There they will be released.
©Phil (PIZZA MY HEART) Frank
Although still groggy, they will soon acclimate themselves to their surroundings.
Pizza...
PIZZA

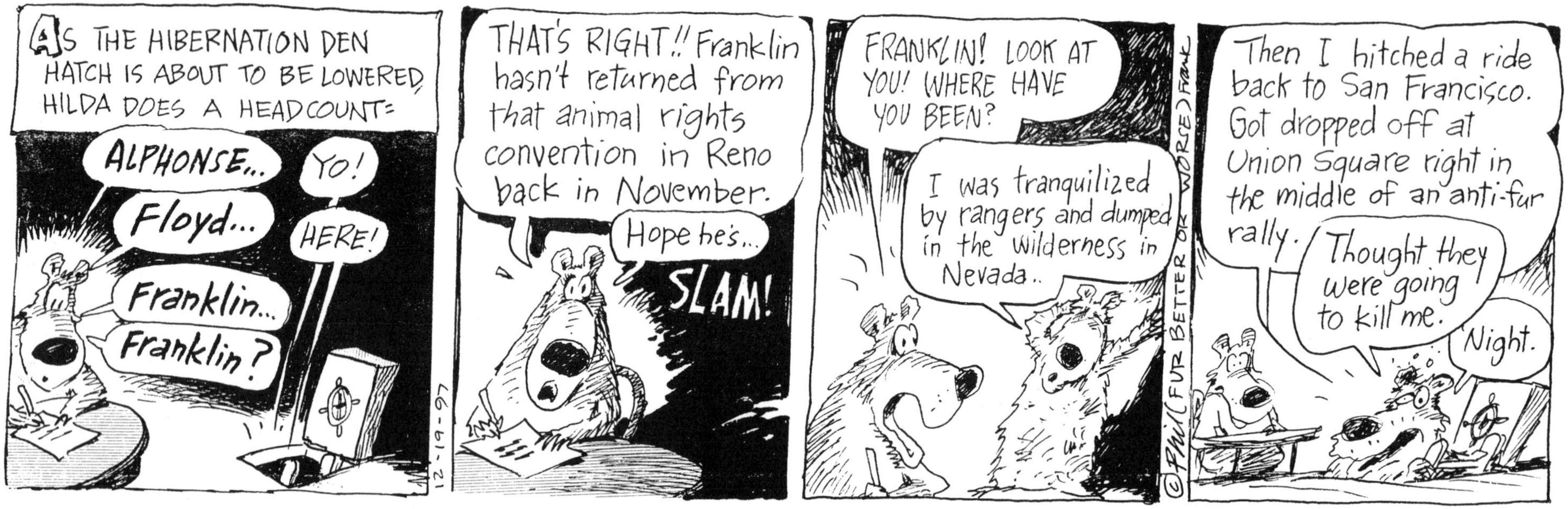
AS THE HIBERNATION DEN HATCH IS ABOUT TO BE LOWERED, HILDA DOES A HEADCOUNT:
ALPHONSE...
YO!
Floyd...
HERE!
Franklin...
Franklin?
12-19-97
THAT'S RIGHT!! Franklin hasn't returned from that animal rights convention in Reno back in November.
Hope he's...
SLAM!
FRANKLIN! LOOK AT YOU! WHERE HAVE YOU BEEN?
I was tranquilized by rangers and dumped in the wilderness in Nevada..
©Phil (FUR BETTER OR WORSE) Frank
Then I hitched a ride back to San Francisco. Got dropped off at Union Square right in the middle of an anti-fur rally.
Thought they were going to kill me.
Night.

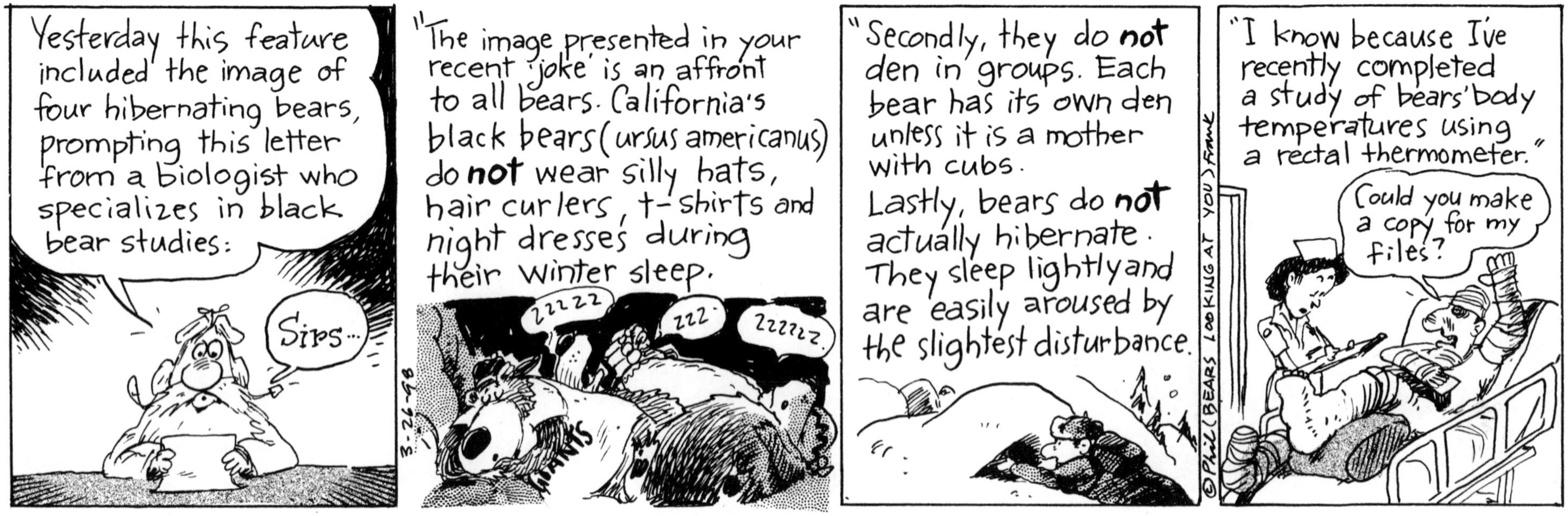
Yesterday this feature included the image of four hibernating bears, prompting this letter from a biologist who specializes in black bear studies:
Sirs...
3-26-98
"The image presented in your recent 'joke' is an affront to all bears. California's black bears (ursus americanus) do **not** wear silly hats, hair curlers, t-shirts and night dresses during their winter sleep.
zzzzz
zzz
zzzzzz
"Secondly, they do **not** den in groups. Each bear has its own den unless it is a mother with cubs.
Lastly, bears do **not** actually hibernate. They sleep lightly and are easily aroused by the slightest disturbance.
"I know because I've recently completed a study of bears' body temperatures using a rectal thermometer."
Could you make a copy for my files?
©Phil (BEARS LOOKING AT YOU) Frank

The bears are tearing up Yosemite visitors' cars. Hilda to the rescue.

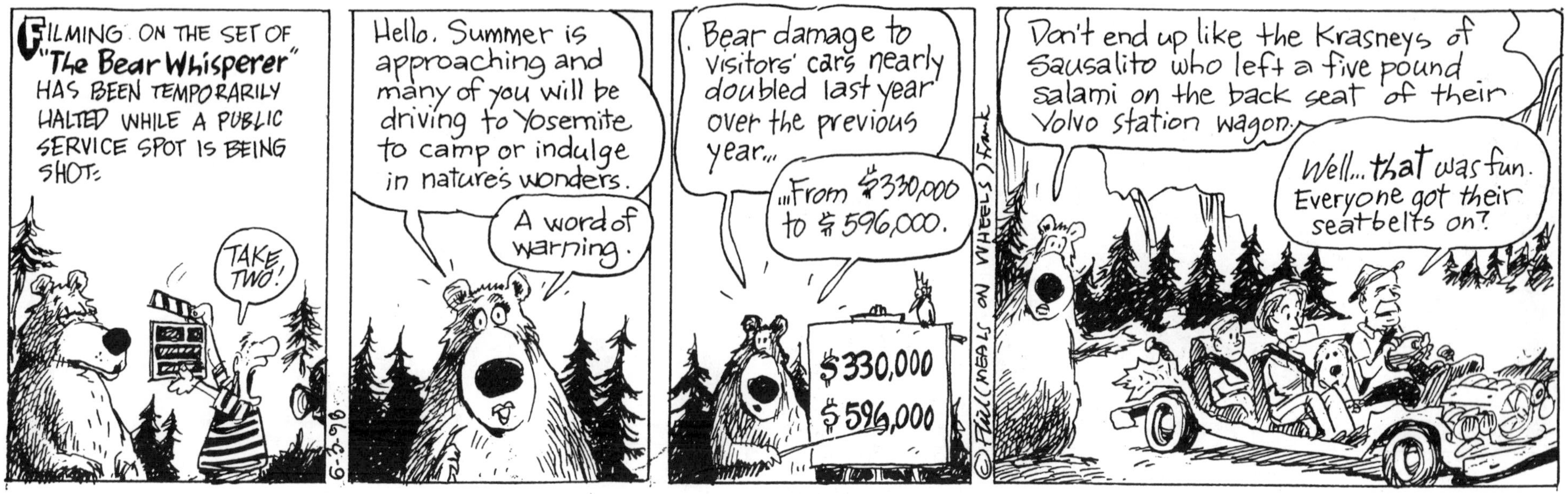
FILMING ON THE SET OF "**The Bear Whisperer**" HAS BEEN TEMPORARILY HALTED WHILE A PUBLIC SERVICE SPOT IS BEING SHOT:
TAKE TWO!
6-3-98
Hello. Summer is approaching and many of you will be driving to Yosemite to camp or indulge in nature's wonders.
A word of warning.
Bear damage to visitors' cars nearly doubled last year over the previous year...
...From $330,000 to $596,000.
$330,000
$596,000
©Phil (MEALS ON WHEELS) Frank
Don't end up like the Krasneys of Sausalito who left a five pound salami on the back seat of their Volvo station wagon.
Well... **that** was fun. Everyone got their seatbelts on?

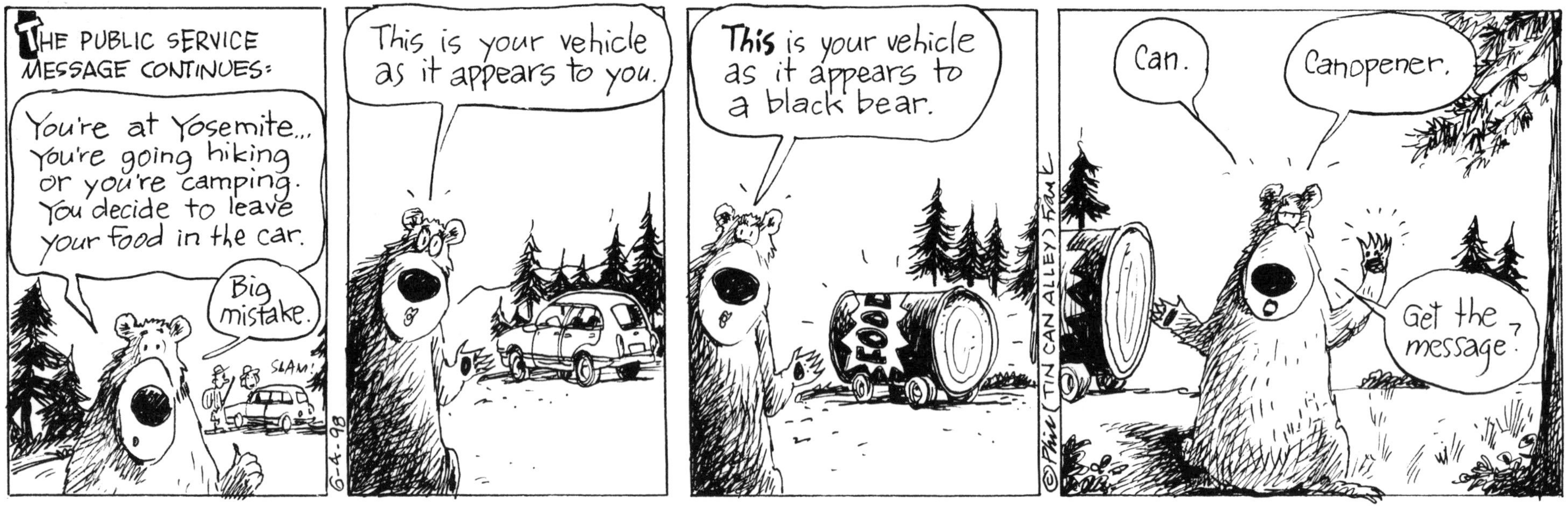
THE PUBLIC SERVICE MESSAGE CONTINUES:
You're at Yosemite... You're going hiking or you're camping. You decide to leave your food in the car.
Big mistake.
SLAM!
6-4-98
This is your vehicle as it appears to you.
This is your vehicle as it appears to a black bear.
FOOD
© Phil (TIN CAN ALLEY) Frank
Can.
Canopener.
Get the message?

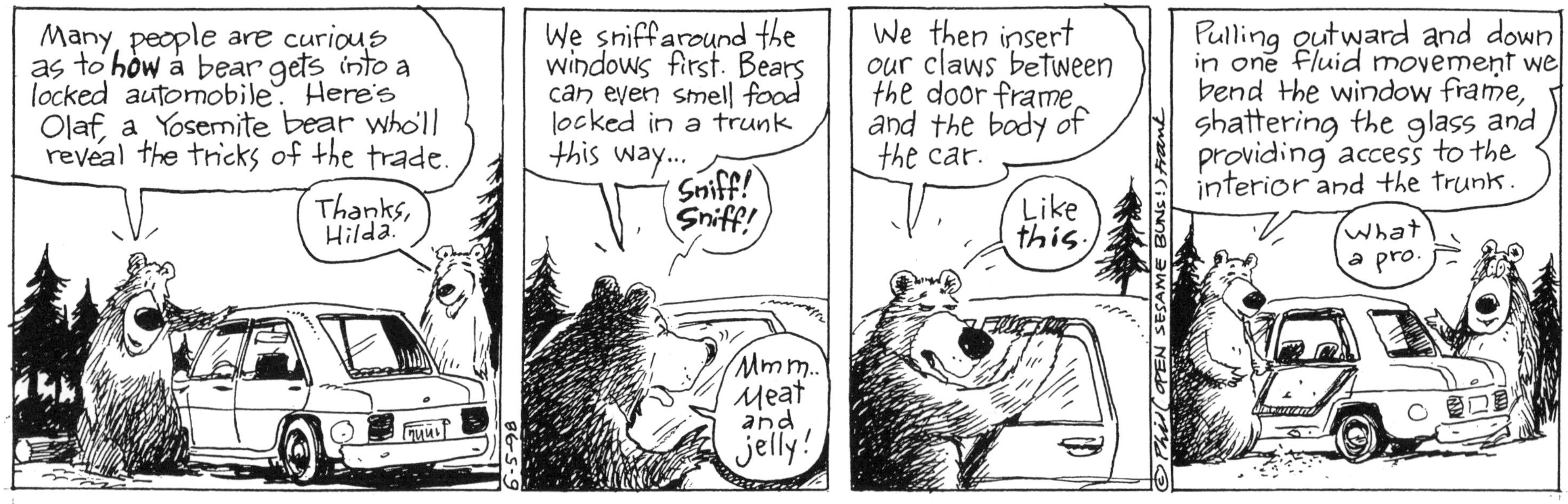
Many people are curious as to how a bear gets into a locked automobile. Here's Olaf, a Yosemite bear who'll reveal the tricks of the trade.
Thanks, Hilda.
6-5-98
We sniff around the windows first. Bears can even smell food locked in a trunk this way...
Sniff! Sniff!
Mmm.. Meat and jelly!
We then insert our claws between the door frame and the body of the car.
Like this.
© Phil (OPEN SESAME BUNS!) Frank
Pulling outward and down in one fluid movement we bend the window frame, shattering the glass and providing access to the interior and the trunk.
What a pro.

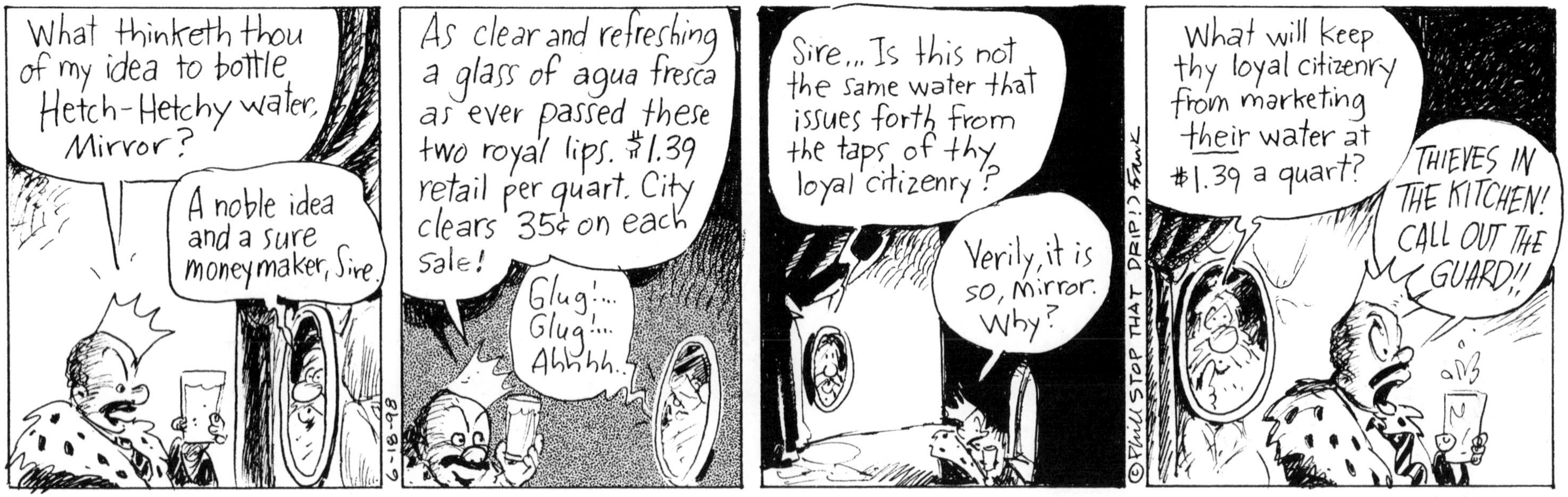

What thinketh thou of my idea to bottle Hetch-Hetchy water, Mirror?
A noble idea and a sure moneymaker, Sire.
6-18-98
As clear and refreshing a glass of agua fresca as ever passed these two royal lips. $1.39 retail per quart. City clears 35¢ on each sale!
Glug!... Glug!... Ahhhh..
Sire,... Is this not the same water that issues forth from the taps of thy loyal citizenry?
Verily, it is so, mirror. Why?
©Phil (STOP THAT DRIP!) Frank
What will keep thy loyal citizenry from marketing their water at $1.39 a quart?
THIEVES IN THE KITCHEN! CALL OUT THE GUARD!!

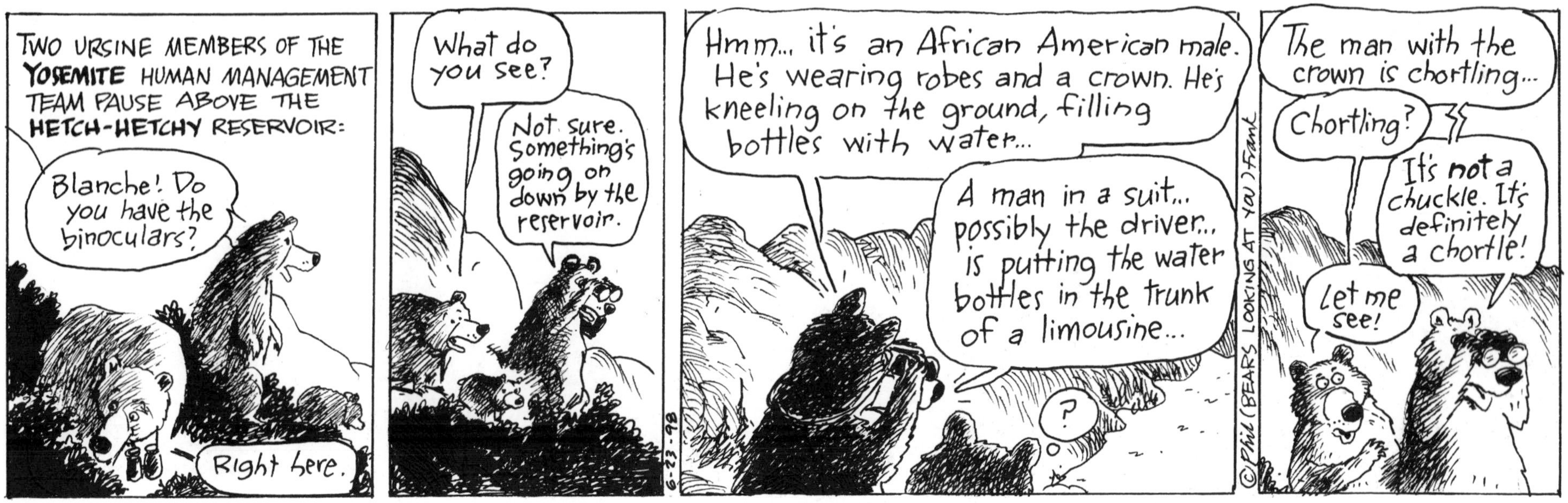

TWO URSINE MEMBERS OF THE YOSEMITE HUMAN MANAGEMENT TEAM PAUSE ABOVE THE HETCH-HETCHY RESERVOIR:
Blanche! Do you have the binoculars?
Right here.
What do you see?
Not sure. Something's going on down by the reservoir.
6-23-98
Hmm... it's an African American male. He's wearing robes and a crown. He's kneeling on the ground, filling bottles with water...
A man in a suit... possibly the driver... is putting the water bottles in the trunk of a limousine...
?
©Phil (BEARS LOOKING AT YOU) Frank
The man with the crown is chortling...
Chortling?
It's not a chuckle. It's definitely a chortle!
Let me see!

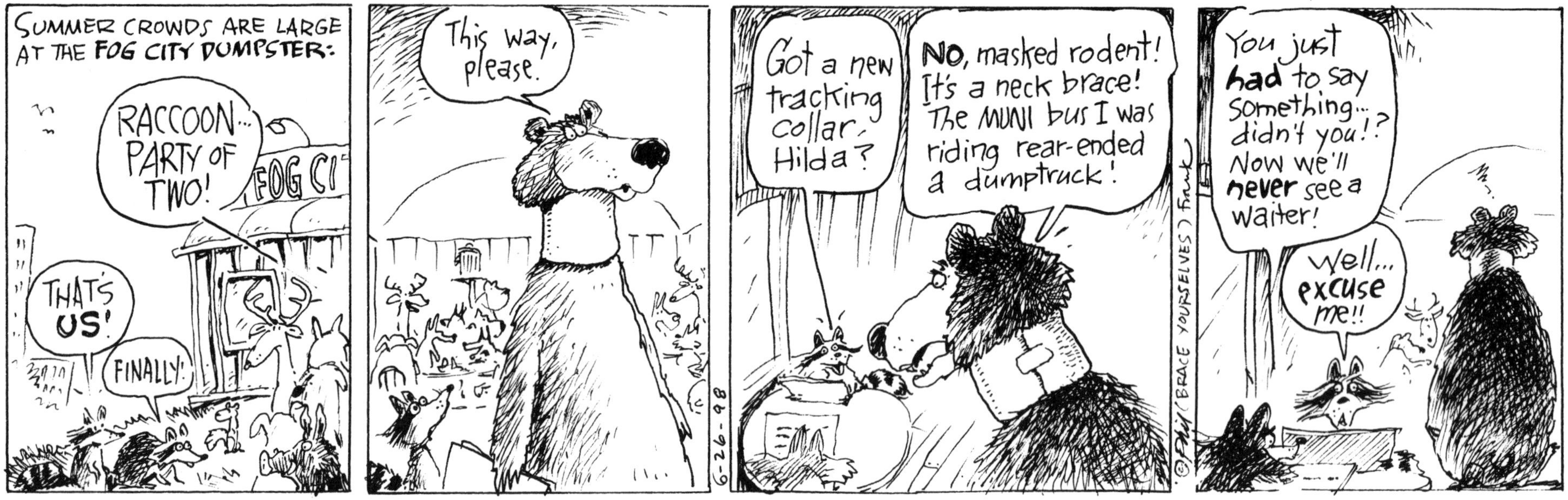
SUMMER CROWDS ARE LARGE AT THE FOG CITY DUMPSTER:
RACCOON... PARTY OF TWO!
FOG CI
THAT'S US!
FINALLY!
This way, please.
Got a new tracking collar, Hilda?
NO, masked rodent! It's a neck brace! The MUNI bus I was riding rear-ended a dumptruck!
You just had to say something... didn't you!? Now we'll never see a waiter!
Well... excuse me!!
6-26-98
©Phil (BRACE YOURSELVES) Frank

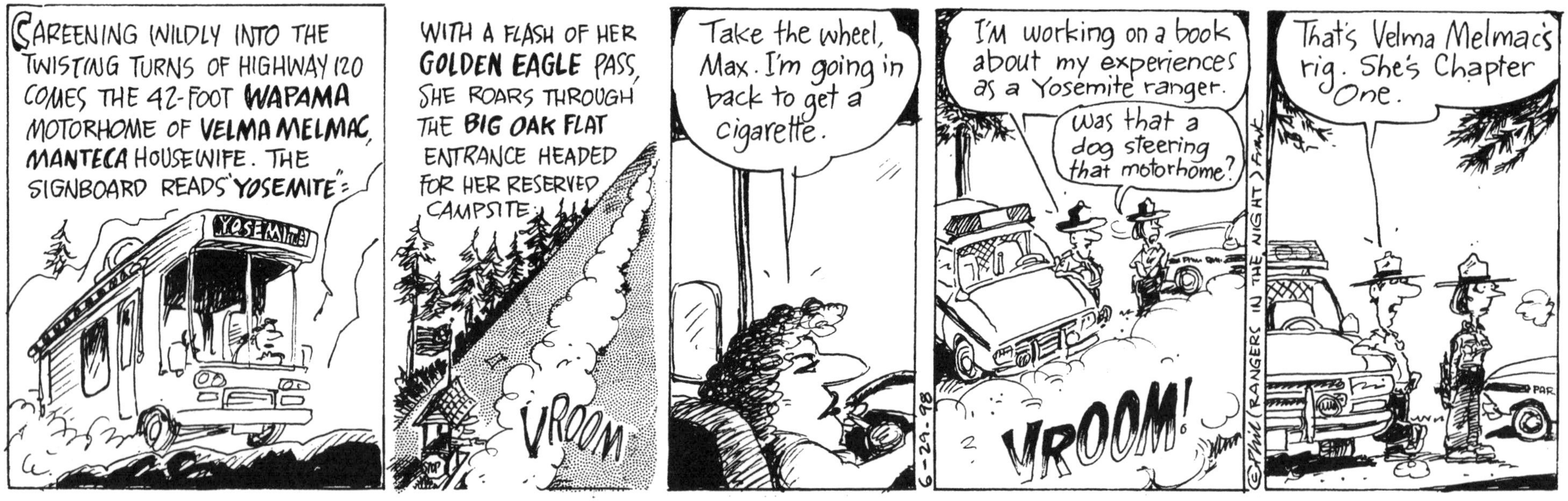
CAREENING WILDLY INTO THE TWISTING TURNS OF HIGHWAY 120 COMES THE 42-FOOT WAPAMA MOTORHOME OF VELMA MELMAC, MANTECA HOUSEWIFE. THE SIGNBOARD READS "YOSEMITE":
YOSEMITE
WITH A FLASH OF HER GOLDEN EAGLE PASS, SHE ROARS THROUGH THE BIG OAK FLAT ENTRANCE HEADED FOR HER RESERVED CAMPSITE.
VROOM
Take the wheel, Max. I'm going in back to get a cigarette.
6-29-98
I'M working on a book about my experiences as a Yosemite ranger.
Was that a dog steering that motorhome?
VROOM!
That's Velma Melmac's rig. She's Chapter One.
©Phil (RANGERS IN THE NIGHT) Frank

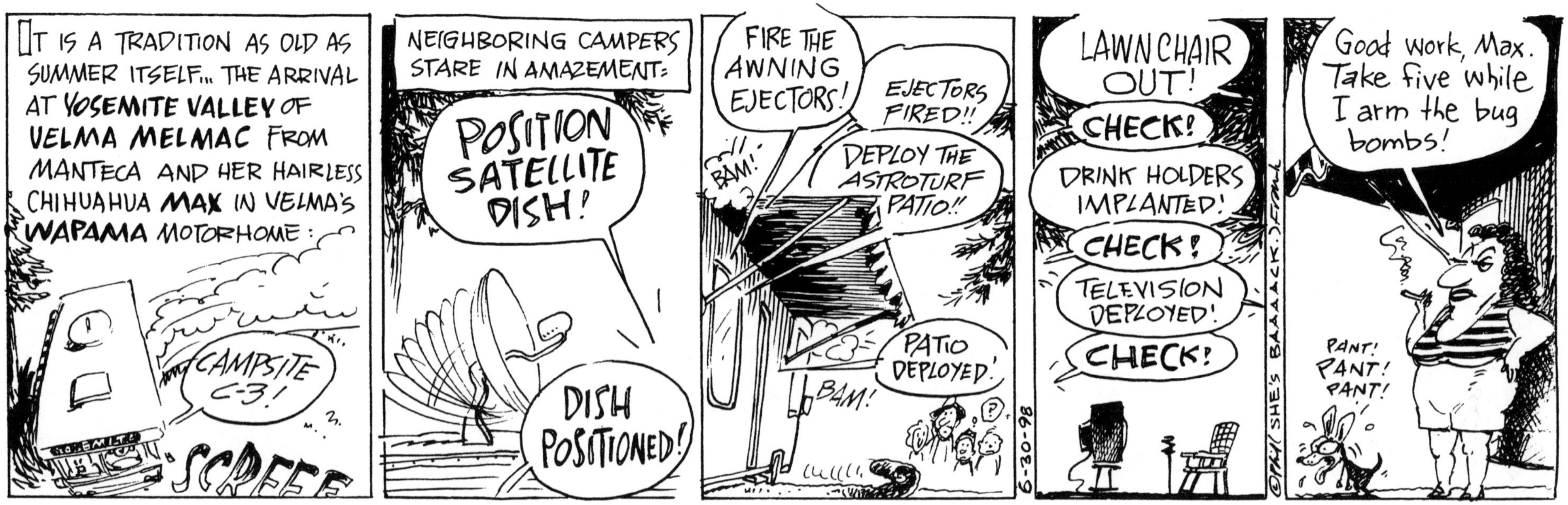
IT IS A TRADITION AS OLD AS SUMMER ITSELF... THE ARRIVAL AT YOSEMITE VALLEY OF VELMA MELMAC FROM MANTECA AND HER HAIRLESS CHIHUAHUA MAX IN VELMA'S WAPAMA MOTORHOME:
CAMPSITE C-3!
SCREEE
NEIGHBORING CAMPERS STARE IN AMAZEMENT:
POSITION SATELLITE DISH!
DISH POSITIONED!
FIRE THE AWNING EJECTORS!
EJECTORS FIRED!!
BAM!
DEPLOY THE ASTROTURF PATIO!!
PATIO DEPLOYED!
BAM!
6-30-98
LAWN CHAIR OUT!
CHECK!
DRINK HOLDERS IMPLANTED!
CHECK!
TELEVISION DEPLOYED!
CHECK!
©Phil (SHE'S BAAAACK!) Frank
Good work, Max. Take five while I arm the bug bombs!
PANT! PANT! PANT!

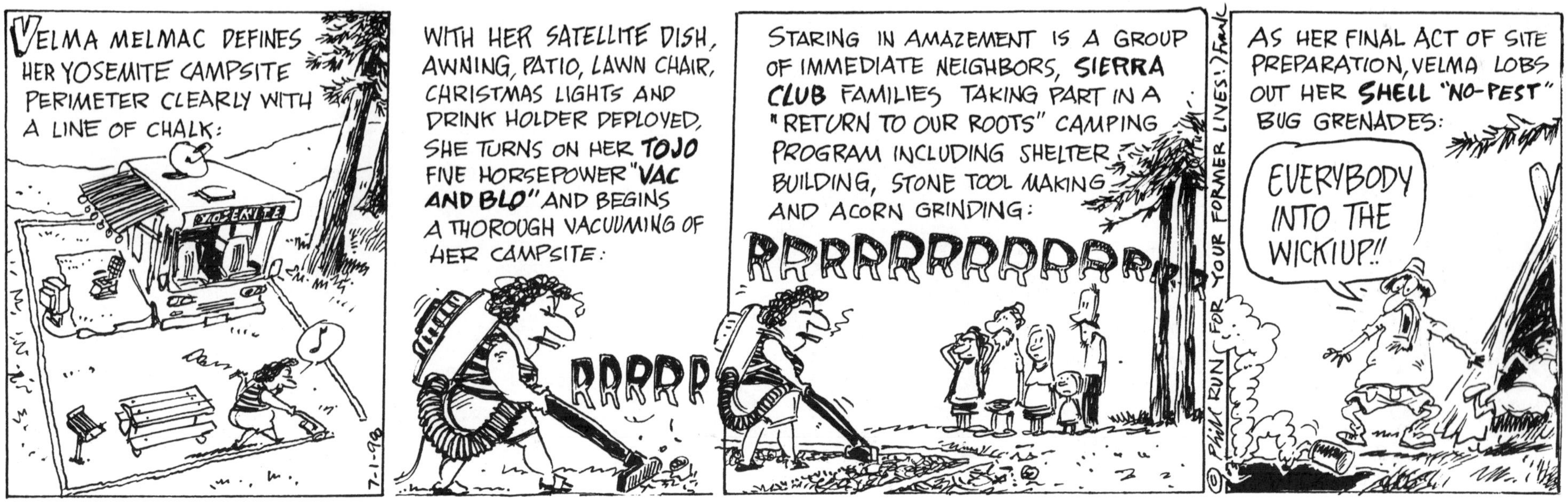
VELMA MELMAC DEFINES HER YOSEMITE CAMPSITE PERIMETER CLEARLY WITH A LINE OF CHALK:
YOSEMITE
7-1-98
WITH HER SATELLITE DISH, AWNING, PATIO, LAWN CHAIR, CHRISTMAS LIGHTS AND DRINK HOLDER DEPLOYED, SHE TURNS ON HER TOJO FIVE HORSEPOWER "VAC AND BLO" AND BEGINS A THOROUGH VACUUMING OF HER CAMPSITE:
RRRRR
STARING IN AMAZEMENT IS A GROUP OF IMMEDIATE NEIGHBORS, SIERRA CLUB FAMILIES TAKING PART IN A "RETURN TO OUR ROOTS" CAMPING PROGRAM INCLUDING SHELTER BUILDING, STONE TOOL MAKING AND ACORN GRINDING:
RRRRRRRRRRRRRRR
©Phil (RUN FOR YOUR FORMER LIVES!) Frank
AS HER FINAL ACT OF SITE PREPARATION, VELMA LOBS OUT HER SHELL "NO-PEST" BUG GRENADES:
EVERYBODY INTO THE WICKIUP!!

Mrs. Melmac: Scourge of Dirt

MRS. MELMAC WAS INTRODUCED INTO THE COMIC STRIP TO LAMPOON THOSE PARK VISITORS WHO BRING THEIR ENTIRE URBAN LIFESTYLE WITH THEM TO THE WILDERNESS. I ASSUMED THAT THIS CHAIN-SMOKING, TV-WATCHING, HAIRCURLERED MATRON HANGING **SHELL "NO-PEST"** STRIPS FROM THE TREES AND VACUUMING HER CAMPSITE WOULD BE DISLIKED BY READERS FOR HER FLOUTING OF PARK RULES AND HER ATTITUDES ABOUT MOTHER NATURE. FUNNY...READERS **LOVE** HER AND HER CHIHUAHUA, **MAX**!

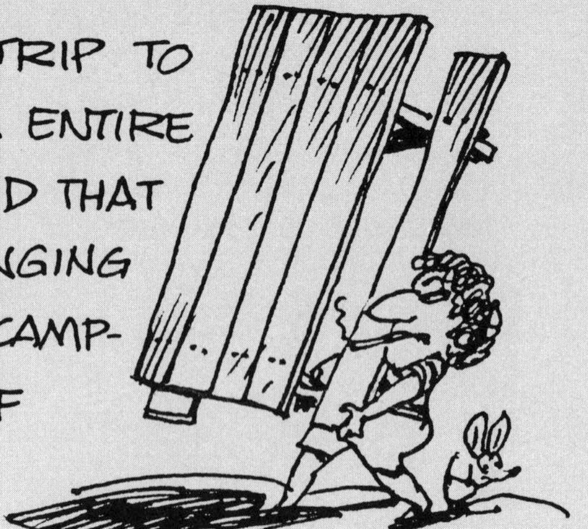

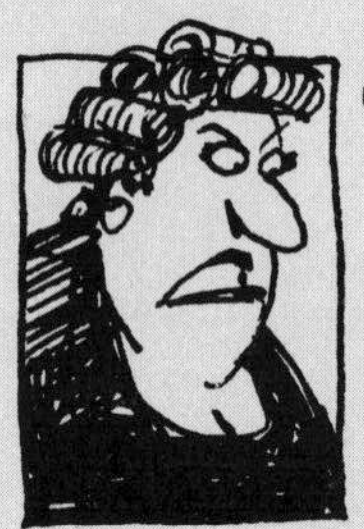

Over the years, many readers have requested more "ink time" for Mrs. Melmac. As a result we've learned more about her...that her first name is Velma... that she lives in the town of Manteca, California... that her cigarette choice is Pall Mall... that she's been married twice... that both husbands (Marvin and Melvin) died of wild mushroom poisoning and that she is currently working on a camper's cookbook titled: **"What Not to Eat in The Woods"**.

Velma owns a 42-foot **Wapama** motorhome with every earthly convenience. She plays poker with the bears, uses a **TOJO** 5-horsepower **"Vac-n-Blo"** vacuum to clean up all Yosemite nature trails and offers mixed drinks to all rangers calling at her campsite due to her neighbors' complaints.

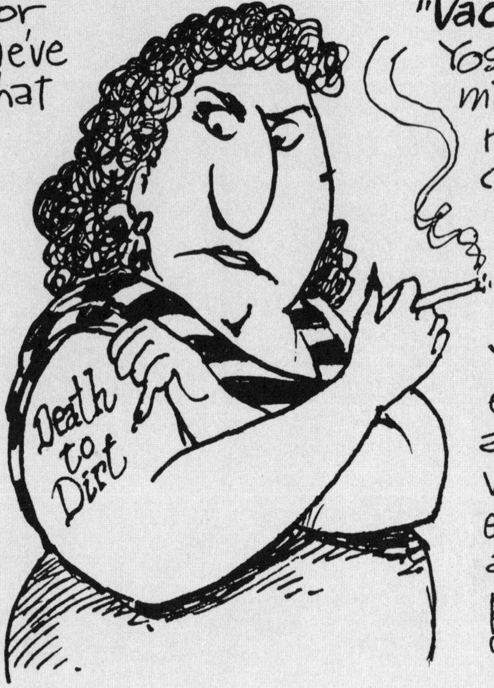
Death to Dirt

Over the years we have watched Velma's personality emerge. Through it all we have seen one wilderness experience elude her... to own a bug bomb that possesses nuclear capability!

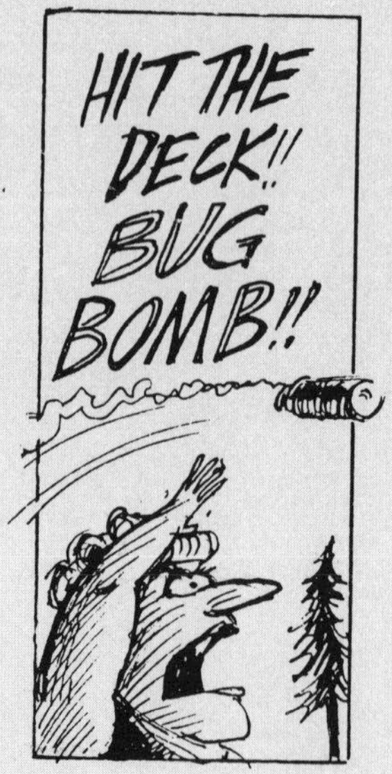
HIT THE DECK!! BUG BOMB!!

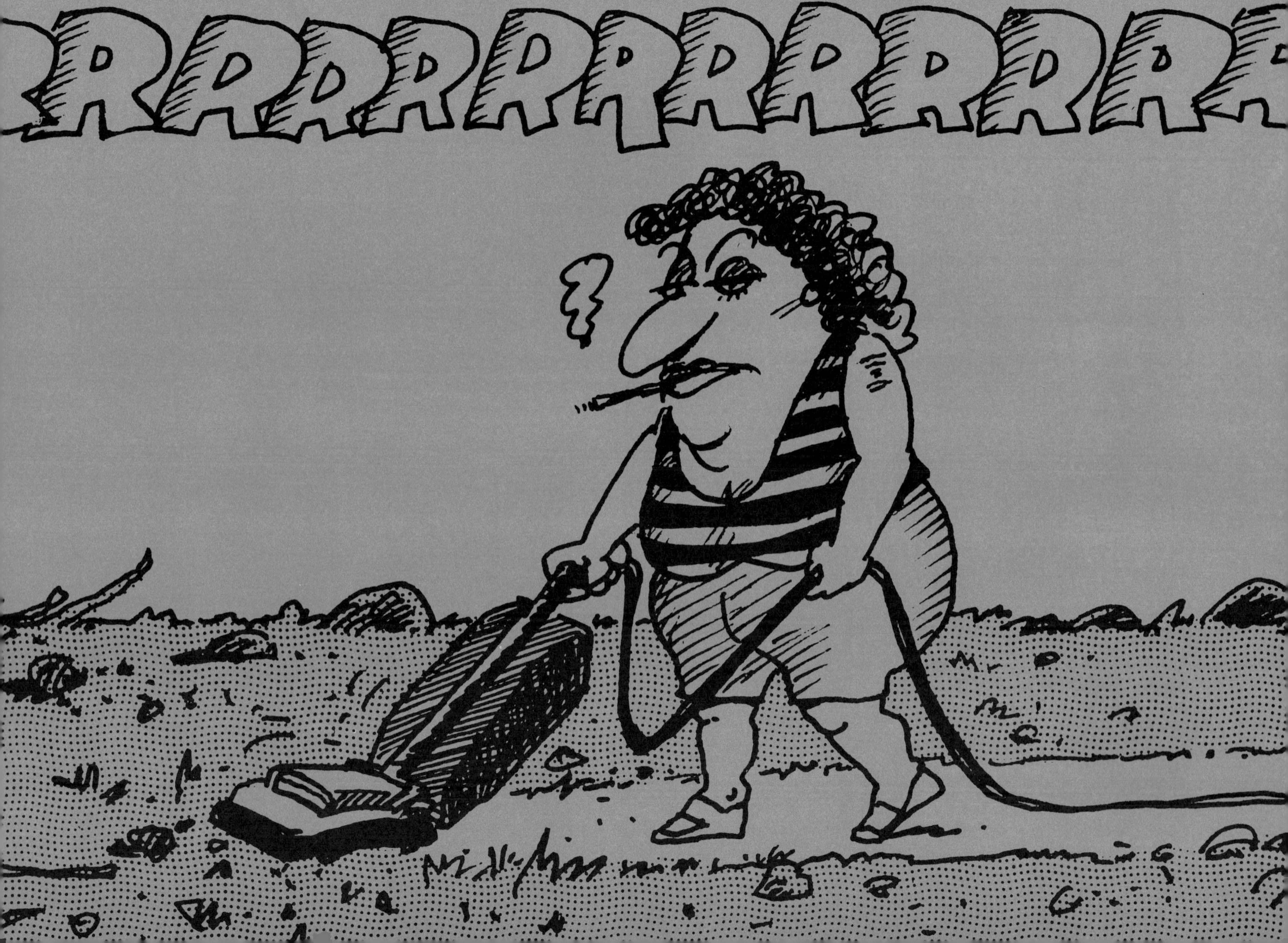
RRRRRRRRRRRRR

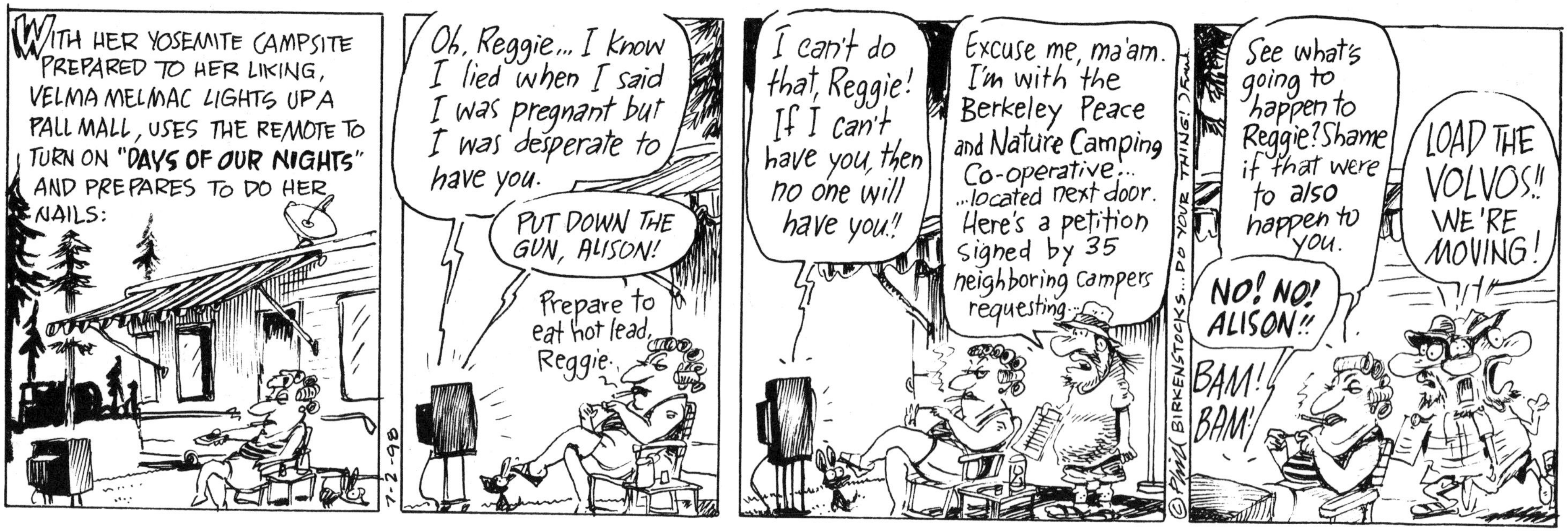
WITH HER YOSEMITE CAMPSITE PREPARED TO HER LIKING, VELMA MELMAC LIGHTS UP A PALL MALL, USES THE REMOTE TO TURN ON "DAYS OF OUR NIGHTS" AND PREPARES TO DO HER NAILS:
7-2-98
Oh, Reggie... I know I lied when I said I was pregnant but I was desperate to have you.
PUT DOWN THE GUN, ALISON!
Prepare to eat hot lead, Reggie.
I can't do that, Reggie! If I can't have you, then no one will have you!!
Excuse me, ma'am. I'm with the Berkeley Peace and Nature Camping Co-operative... ...located next door. Here's a petition signed by 35 neighboring campers requesting...
BIRKENSTOCKS... DO YOUR THING!
See what's going to happen to Reggie? Shame if that were to also happen to you.
NO! NO! ALISON!!
BAM! BAM!
LOAD THE VOLVOS!! WE'RE MOVING!

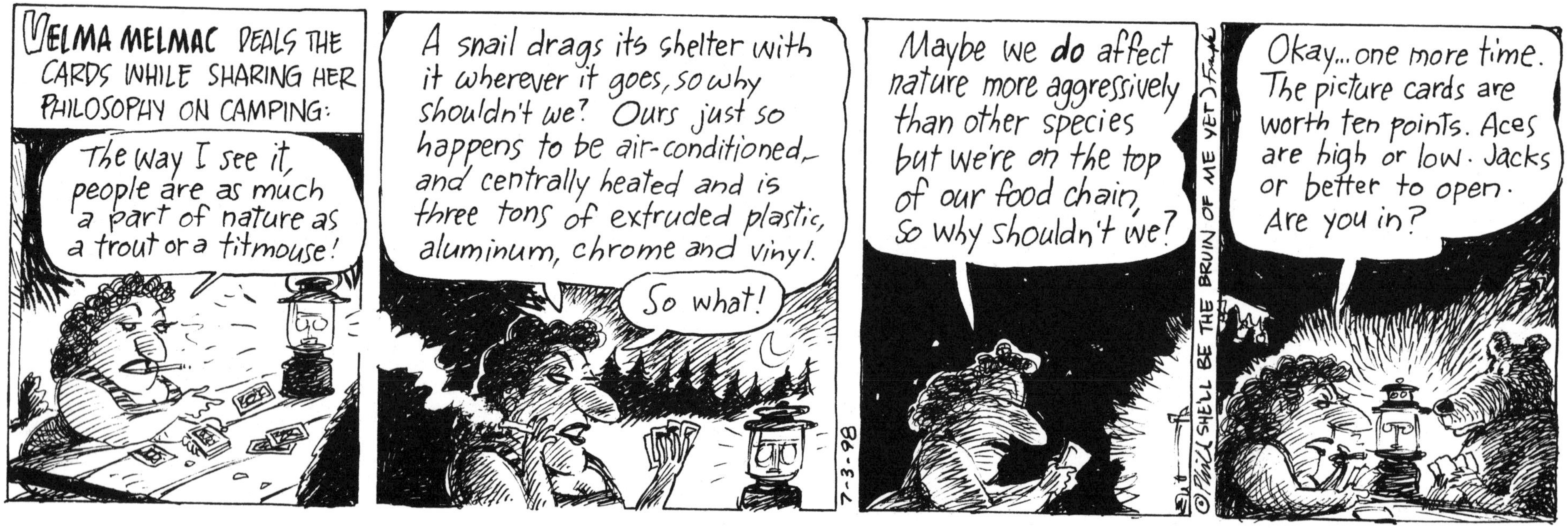
VELMA MELMAC DEALS THE CARDS WHILE SHARING HER PHILOSOPHY ON CAMPING:
The way I see it, people are as much a part of nature as a trout or a titmouse!
A snail drags its shelter with it wherever it goes, so why shouldn't we? Ours just so happens to be air-conditioned, and centrally heated and is three tons of extruded plastic, aluminum, chrome and vinyl.
So what!
7-3-98
Maybe we do affect nature more aggressively than other species but we're on the top of our food chain, so why shouldn't we?
SHE'LL BE THE BRUIN OF ME YET
Okay... one more time. The picture cards are worth ten points. Aces are high or low. Jacks or better to open. Are you in?

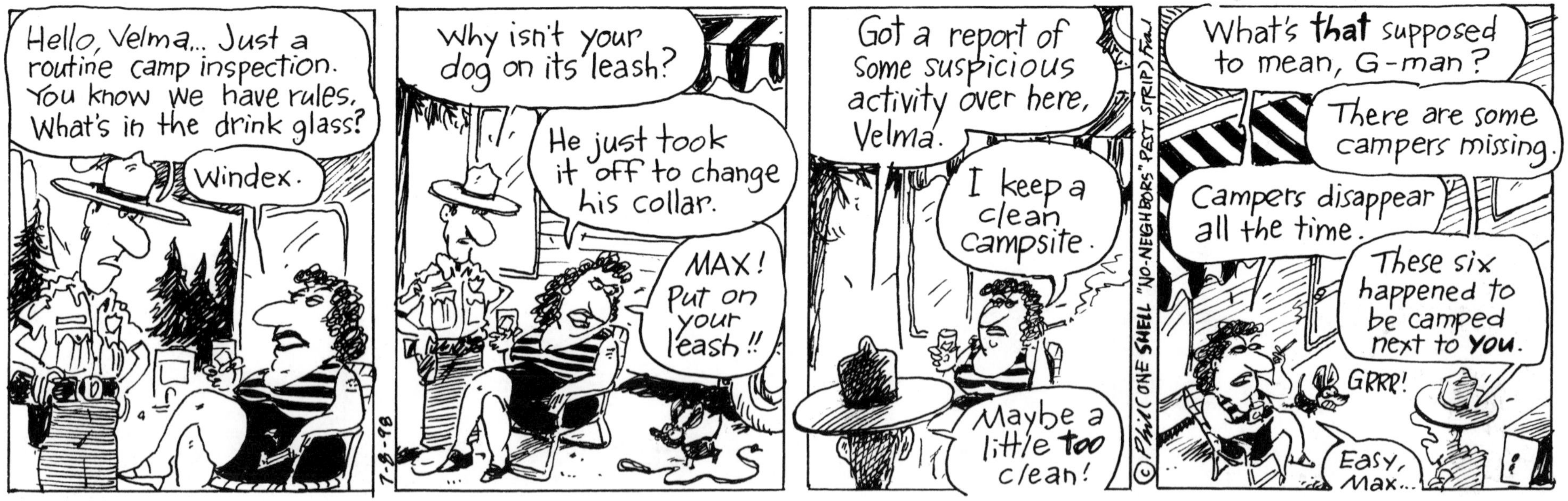
Hello, Velma... Just a routine camp inspection. You know we have rules. What's in the drink glass?
Windex.
7-8-98
Why isn't your dog on its leash?
He just took it off to change his collar.
MAX! Put on your leash!!
Got a report of some suspicious activity over here, Velma.
I keep a clean campsite.
Maybe a little too clean!
© (ONE SHELL "NO-NEIGHBORS" PEST STRIP)
What's that supposed to mean, G-man?
There are some campers missing.
Campers disappear all the time.
These six happened to be camped next to YOU.
GRRR!
Easy, Max...

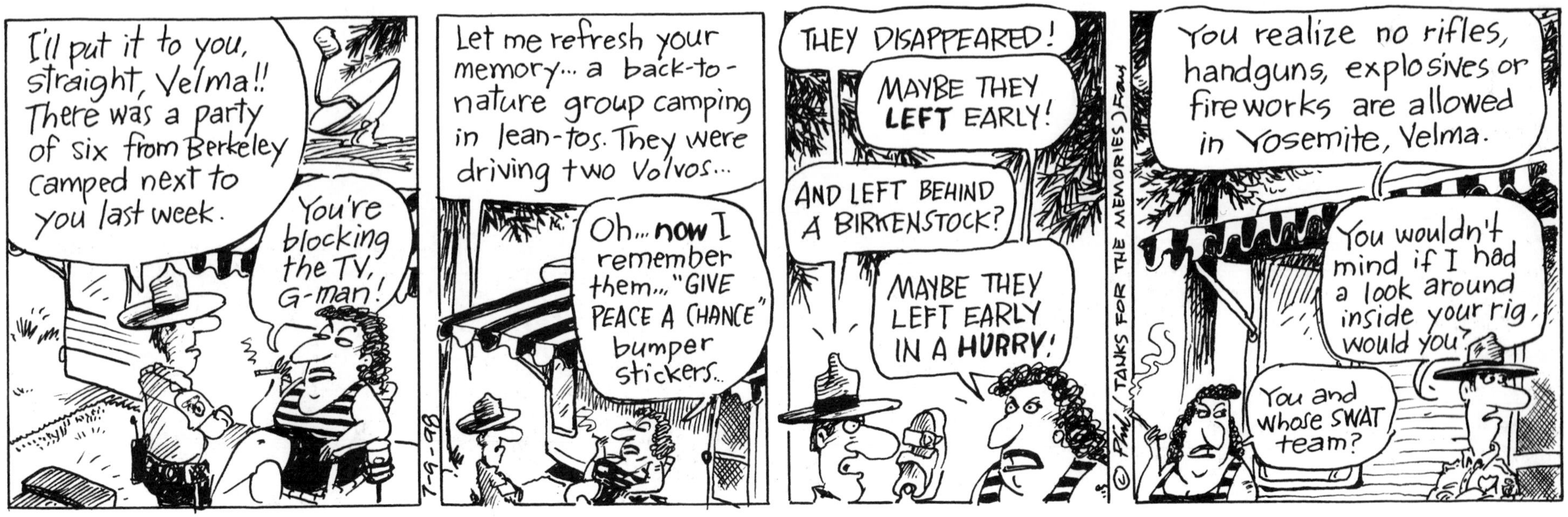
I'll put it to you, straight, Velma!! There was a party of six from Berkeley camped next to you last week.
You're blocking the TV, G-man!
7-9-98
Let me refresh your memory... a back-to-nature group camping in lean-tos. They were driving two Volvos...
Oh... now I remember them... "GIVE PEACE A CHANCE" bumper stickers...
THEY DISAPPEARED!
MAYBE THEY LEFT EARLY!
AND LEFT BEHIND A BIRKENSTOCK?
MAYBE THEY LEFT EARLY IN A HURRY!
© TANKS FOR THE MEMORIES)
You realize no rifles, handguns, explosives or fireworks are allowed in Yosemite, Velma.
You wouldn't mind if I had a look around inside your rig, would you?
You and whose SWAT team?

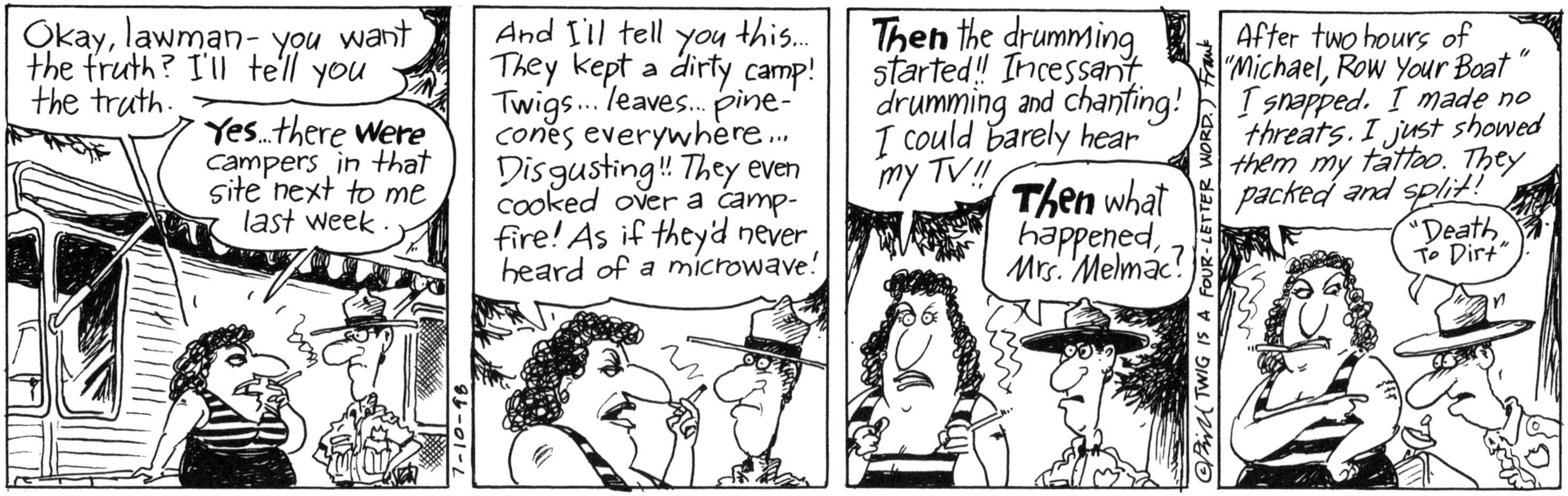
Okay, lawman- you want the truth? I'll tell you the truth.
Yes...there were campers in that site next to me last week.
7-10-98
And I'll tell you this... They kept a dirty camp! Twigs... leaves... pine-cones everywhere... Disgusting!! They even cooked over a camp-fire! As if they'd never heard of a microwave!
Then the drumming started!! Incessant drumming and chanting! I could barely hear my TV!!
Then what happened, Mrs. Melmac?
© Phil (TWIG IS A FOUR-LETTER WORD.) Frank
After two hours of "Michael, Row Your Boat" I snapped. I made no threats. I just showed them my tattoo. They packed and split!
"Death To Dirt"

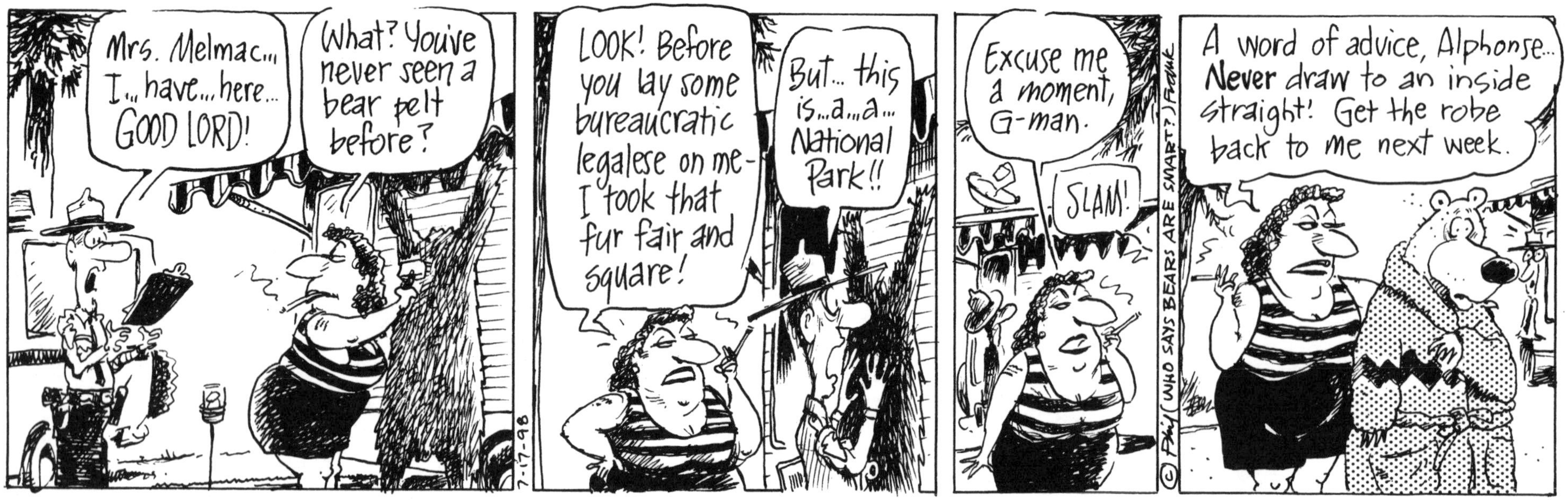
Mrs. Melmac... I... have... here... GOOD LORD!
What? You've never seen a bear pelt before?
7-17-98
LOOK! Before you lay some bureaucratic legalese on me- I took that fur fair and square!
But... this is...a...a... National Park!!
Excuse me a moment, G-man.
SLAM!
© Phil (WHO SAYS BEARS ARE SMART?) Frank
A word of advice, Alphonse... Never draw to an inside straight! Get the robe back to me next week.

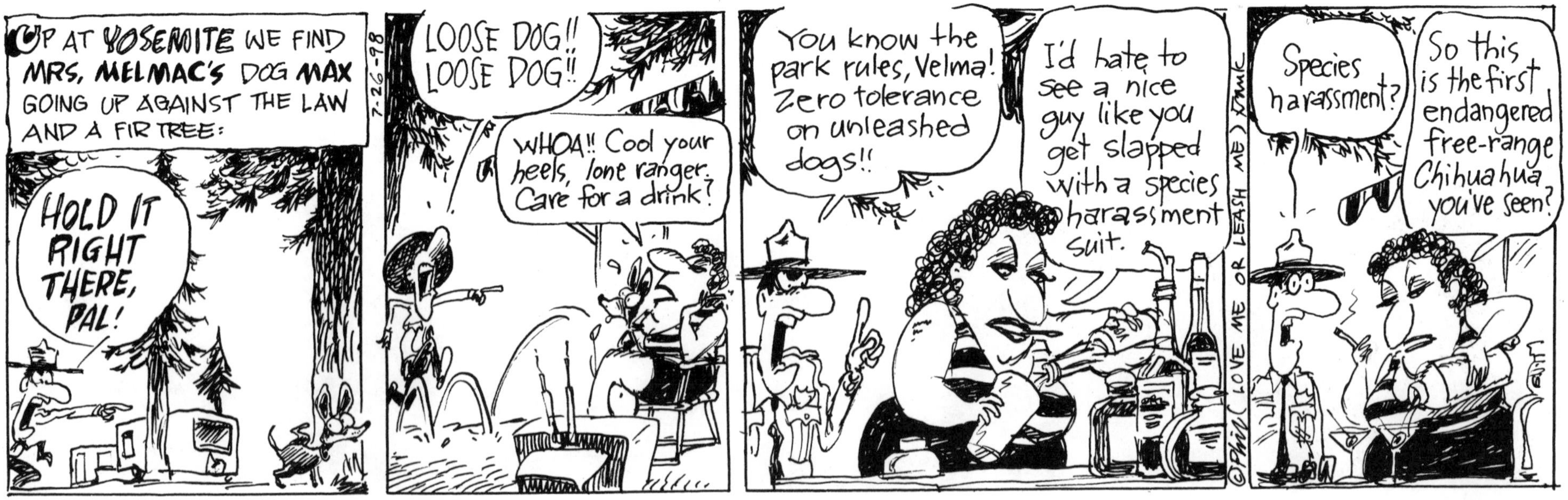
UP AT YOSEMITE WE FIND MRS. MELMAC'S DOG MAX GOING UP AGAINST THE LAW AND A FIR TREE:
HOLD IT RIGHT THERE, PAL!
7-26-98
LOOSE DOG!! LOOSE DOG!!
WHOA!! Cool your heels, lone ranger. Care for a drink?
You know the park rules, Velma! Zero tolerance on unleashed dogs!!
I'd hate to see a nice guy like you get slapped with a species harassment suit.
©Phil (LOVE ME OR LEASH ME) Frank
Species harassment?
So this is the first endangered free-range Chihuahua you've seen?

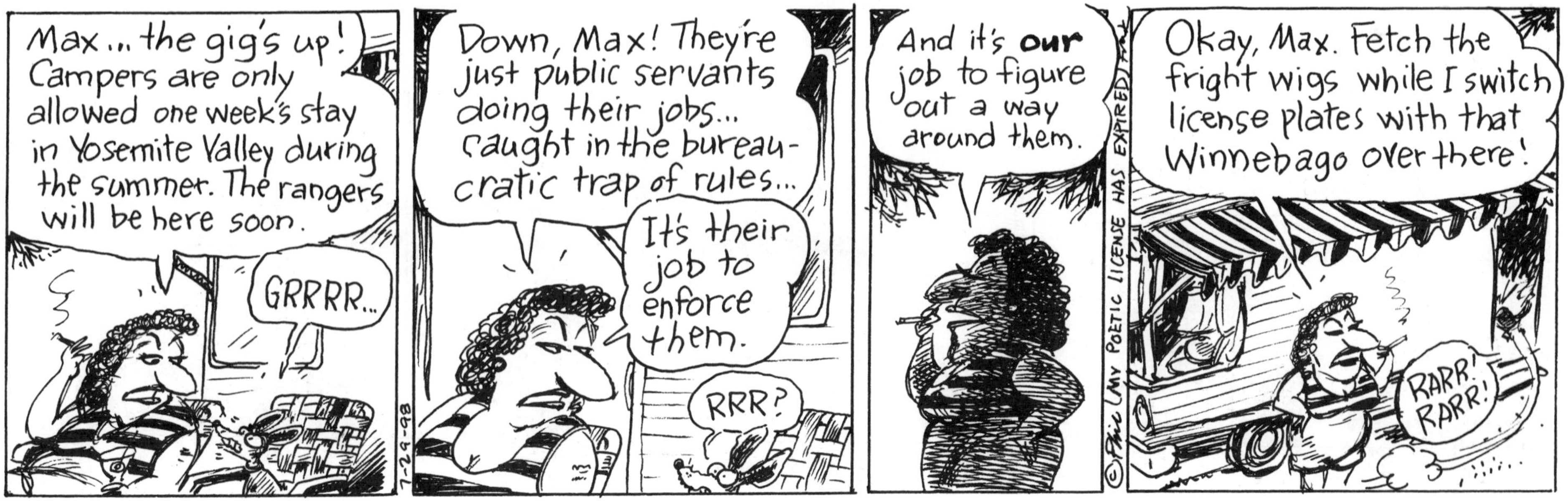
Max... the gig's up! Campers are only allowed one week's stay in Yosemite Valley during the summer. The rangers will be here soon.
GRRRR...
7-29-98
Down, Max! They're just public servants doing their jobs... caught in the bureaucratic trap of rules...
It's their job to enforce them.
RRR?
And it's our job to figure out a way around them.
©Phil (MY POETIC LICENSE HAS EXPIRED) Frank
Okay, Max. Fetch the fright wigs while I switch license plates with that Winnebago over there!
RARR! RARR!

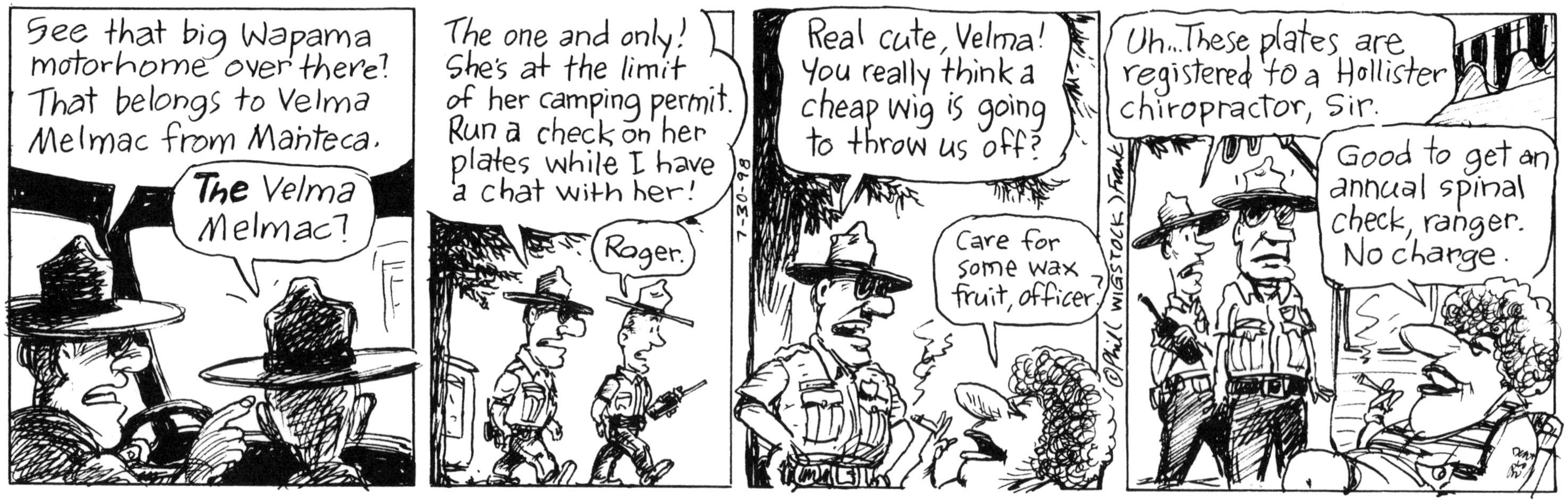
See that big Wapama motorhome over there? That belongs to Velma Melmac from Manteca.
The Velma Melmac?
The one and only! She's at the limit of her camping permit. Run a check on her plates while I have a chat with her!
Roger.
7-30-98
Real cute, Velma! You really think a cheap wig is going to throw us off?
Care for some wax fruit, officer?
©Phil (WIGSTOCK) Frank
Uh...These plates are registered to a Hollister chiropractor, Sir.
Good to get an annual spinal check, ranger. No charge.

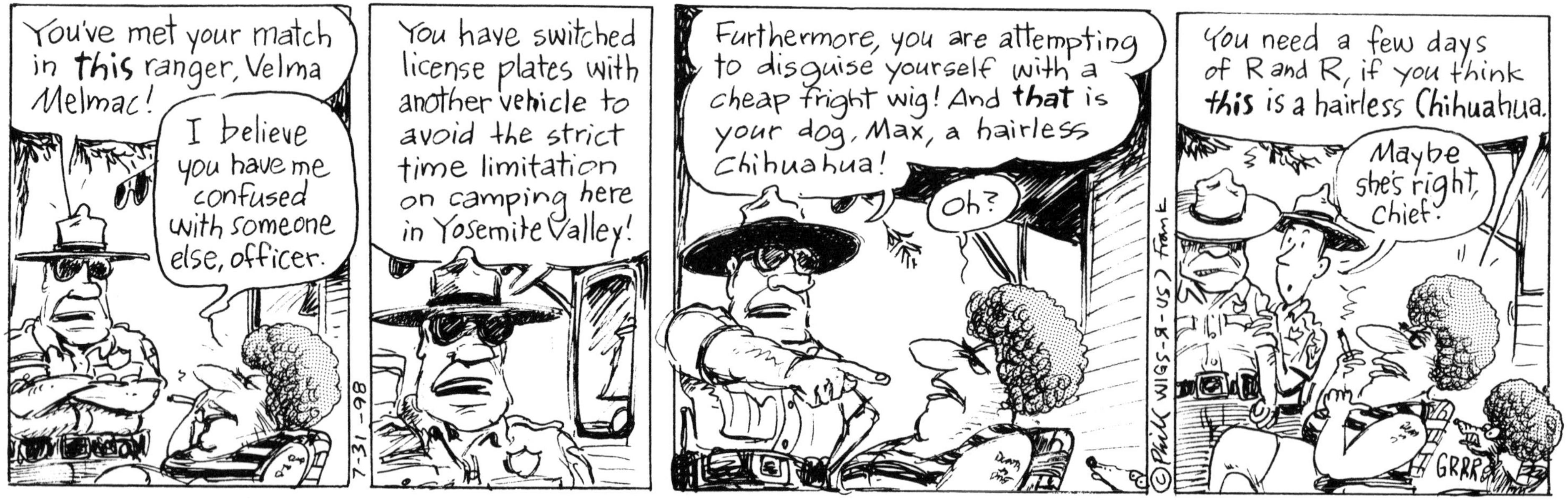
You've met your match in **this** ranger, Velma Melmac!
I believe you have me confused with someone else, officer.
7-31-98
You have switched license plates with another vehicle to avoid the strict time limitation on camping here in Yosemite Valley!
Furthermore, you are attempting to disguise yourself with a cheap fright wig! And **that** is your dog, Max, a hairless Chihuahua!
Oh?
© Phil (WIGS-R-US) Frank
You need a few days of R and R, if you think **this** is a hairless Chihuahua.
Maybe she's right, chief.
GRRR

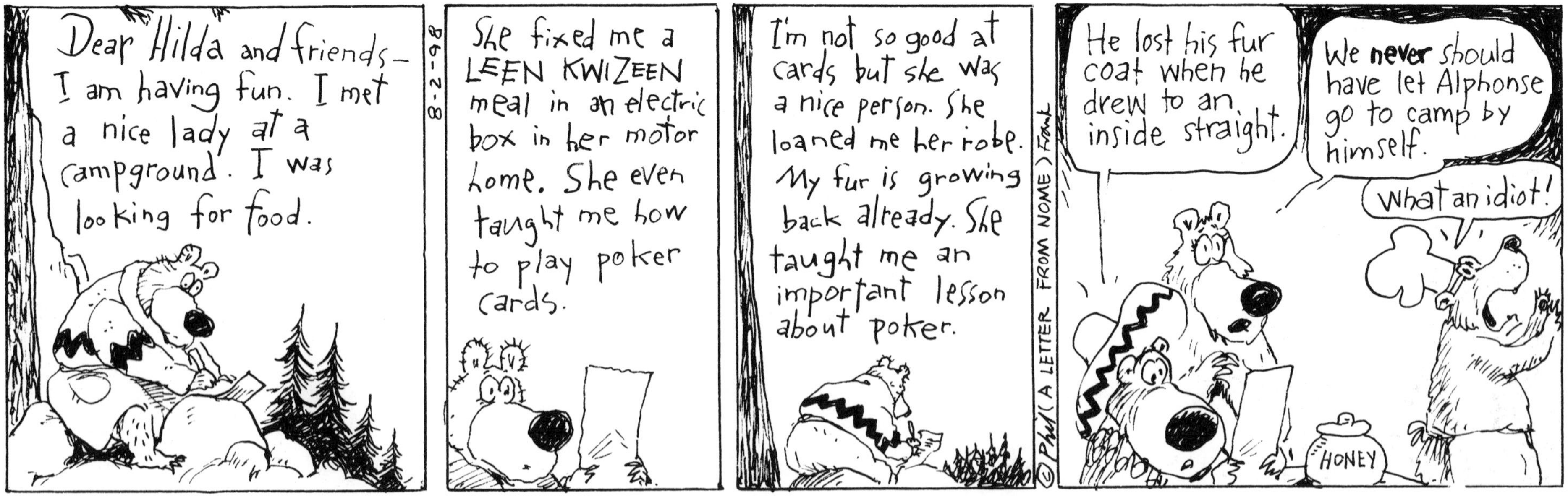

Dear Hilda and friends— I am having fun. I met a nice lady at a campground. I was looking for food.
8-2-98
She fixed me a LEEN KWIZEEN meal in an electric box in her motor home. She even taught me how to play poker cards.
I'm not so good at cards but she was a nice person. She loaned me her robe. My fur is growing back already. She taught me an important lesson about poker.
©Phil (A LETTER FROM NOME) Frank
He lost his fur coat when he drew to an inside straight.
We **never** should have let Alphonse go to camp by himself.
What an idiot!
HONEY

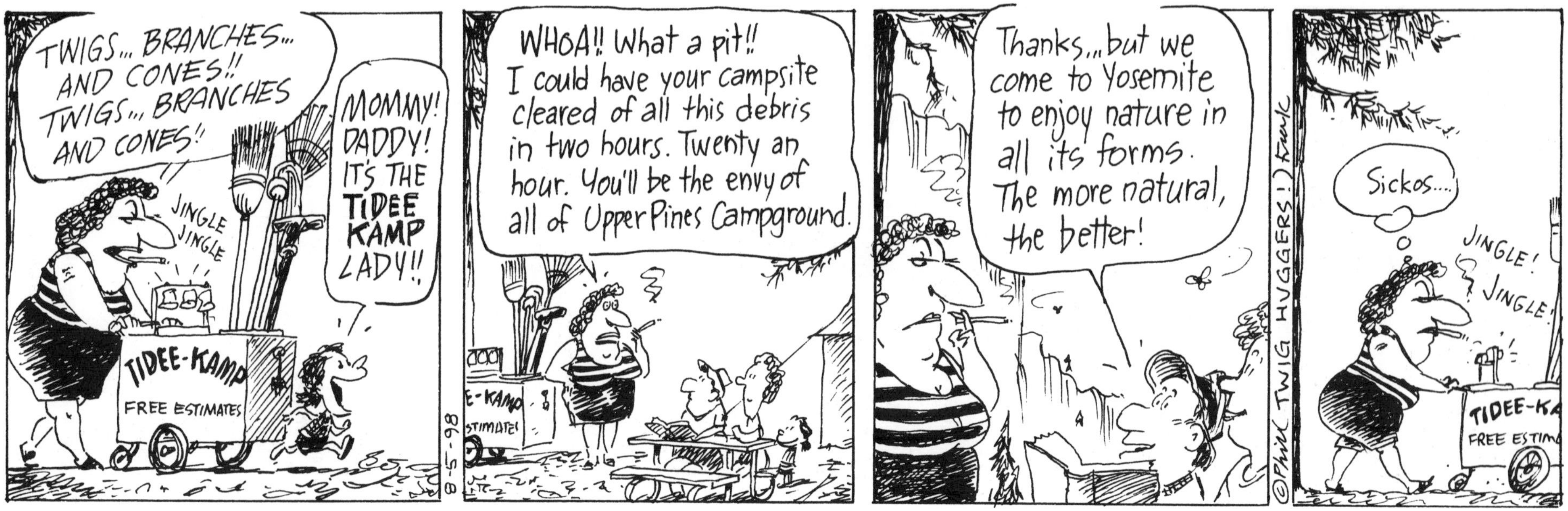

TWIGS... BRANCHES... AND CONES!! TWIGS... BRANCHES AND CONES!!
JINGLE JINGLE
MOMMY! DADDY! IT'S THE TIDEE KAMP LADY!!
TIDEE-KAMP
FREE ESTIMATES
8-5-98
WHOA!! What a pit!! I could have your campsite cleared of all this debris in two hours. Twenty an hour. You'll be the envy of all of Upper Pines Campground.
Thanks... but we come to Yosemite to enjoy nature in all its forms. The more natural, the better!
©Phil (TWIG HUGGERS!) Frank
Sickos....
JINGLE! JINGLE!

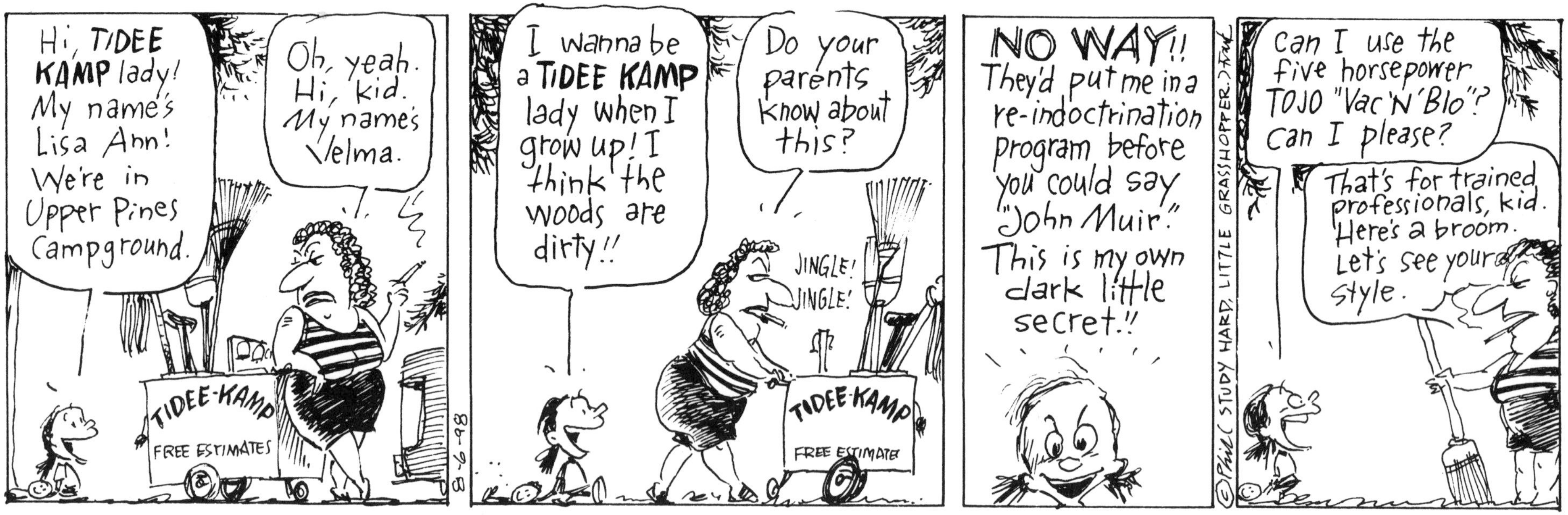

Hi, TIDEE KAMP lady! My name's Lisa Ann! We're in Upper Pines Campground.
Oh, yeah. Hi, kid. My name's Velma.
TIDEE-KAMP
FREE ESTIMATES
8-6-98
I wanna be a TIDEE KAMP lady when I grow up! I think the woods are dirty!!
Do your parents know about this?
JINGLE! JINGLE!
TIDEE-KAMP
FREE ESTIMATES
NO WAY!! They'd put me in a re-indoctrination program before you could say "John Muir." This is my own dark little secret!!
©Phil (STUDY HARD, LITTLE GRASSHOPPER.) Frank
Can I use the five horsepower TOJO "Vac 'N' Blo"? Can I please?
That's for trained professionals, kid. Here's a broom. Let's see your style.

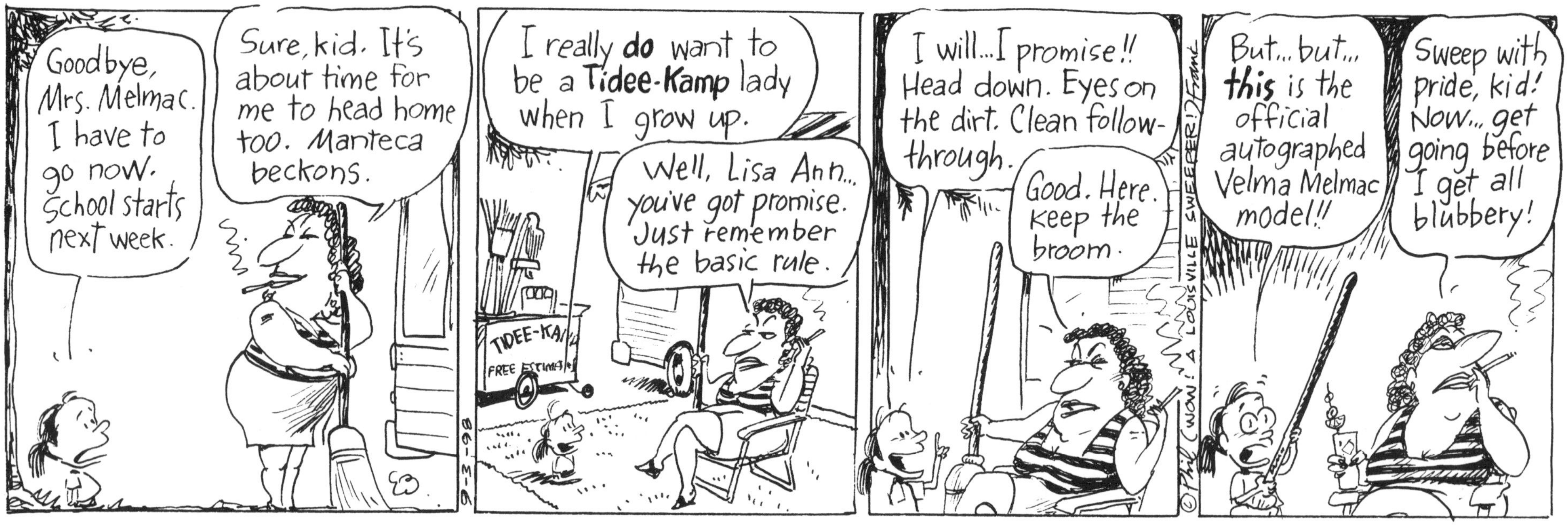

Goodbye, Mrs. Melmac. I have to go now. School starts next week.
Sure, kid. It's about time for me to head home too. Manteca beckons.
9-3-98
I really do want to be a Tidee-Kamp lady when I grow up.
Well, Lisa Ann... you've got promise. Just remember the basic rule.
TIDEE-KA
FREE ESTIMATES
I will... I promise!! Head down. Eyes on the dirt. Clean follow-through.
Good. Here. Keep the broom.
©Phil (WOW! A LOUISVILLE SWEEPER!) Frank
But... but... this is the official autographed Velma Melmac model!!
Sweep with pride, kid! Now... get going before I get all blubbery!

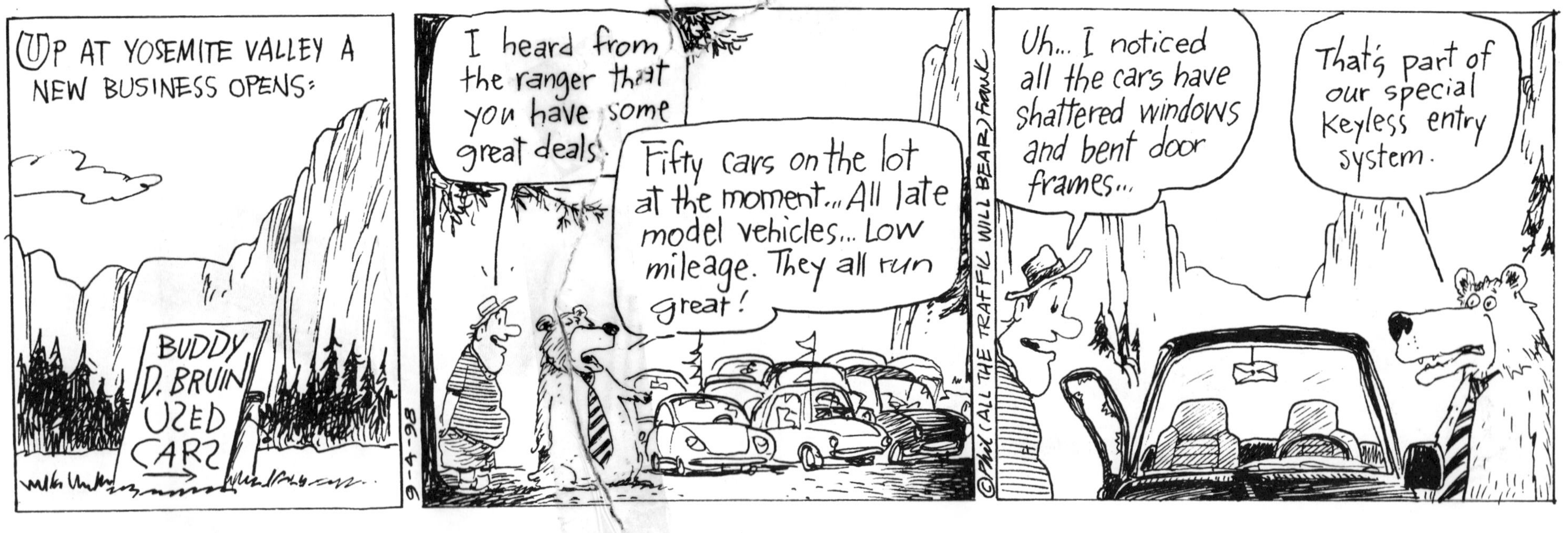
UP AT YOSEMITE VALLEY A NEW BUSINESS OPENS:
BUDDY D. BRUIN UZED CARZ
9-4-98
I heard from the ranger that you have some great deals.
Fifty cars on the lot at the moment... All late model vehicles... Low mileage. They all run great!
©Phil (ALL THE TRAFFIC WILL BEAR) Frank
Uh... I noticed all the cars have shattered windows and bent door frames...
That's part of our special Keyless entry system.

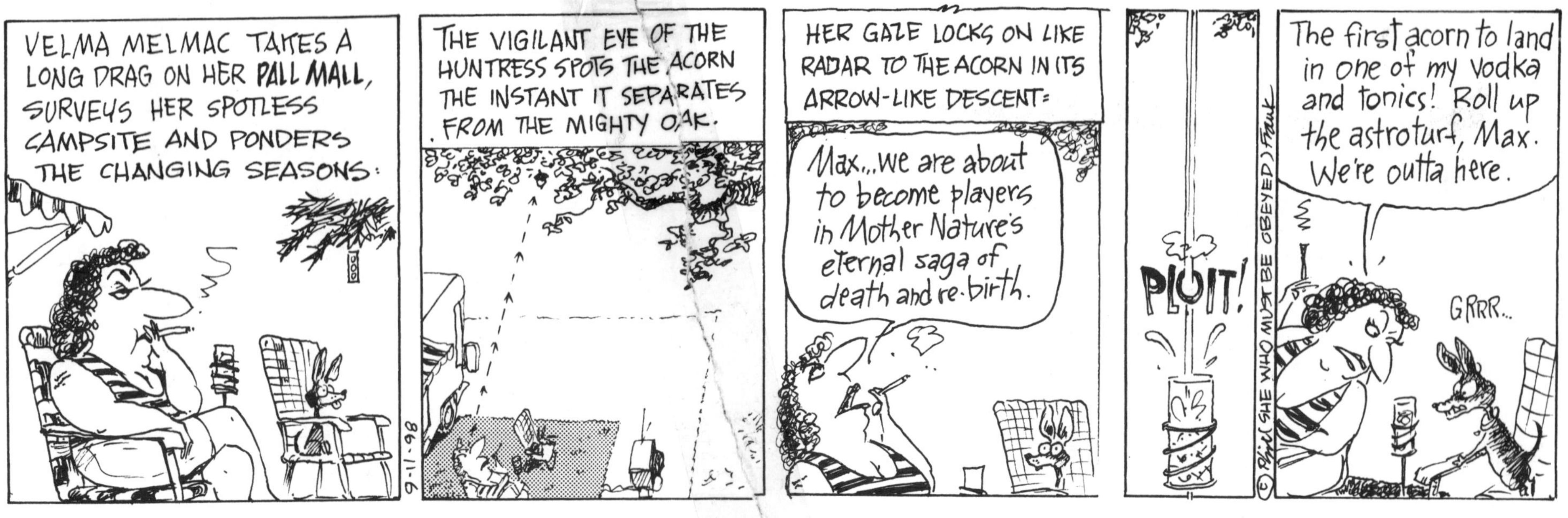
VELMA MELMAC TAKES A LONG DRAG ON HER PALL MALL, SURVEYS HER SPOTLESS CAMPSITE AND PONDERS THE CHANGING SEASONS:
9-11-98
THE VIGILANT EYE OF THE HUNTRESS SPOTS THE ACORN THE INSTANT IT SEPARATES FROM THE MIGHTY OAK.
HER GAZE LOCKS ON LIKE RADAR TO THE ACORN IN ITS ARROW-LIKE DESCENT:
Max... we are about to become players in Mother Nature's eternal saga of death and re-birth.
PLOIT!
© Phil (SHE WHO MUST BE OBEYED) Frank
The first acorn to land in one of my vodka and tonics! Roll up the astroturf, Max. We're outta here.
GRRR...

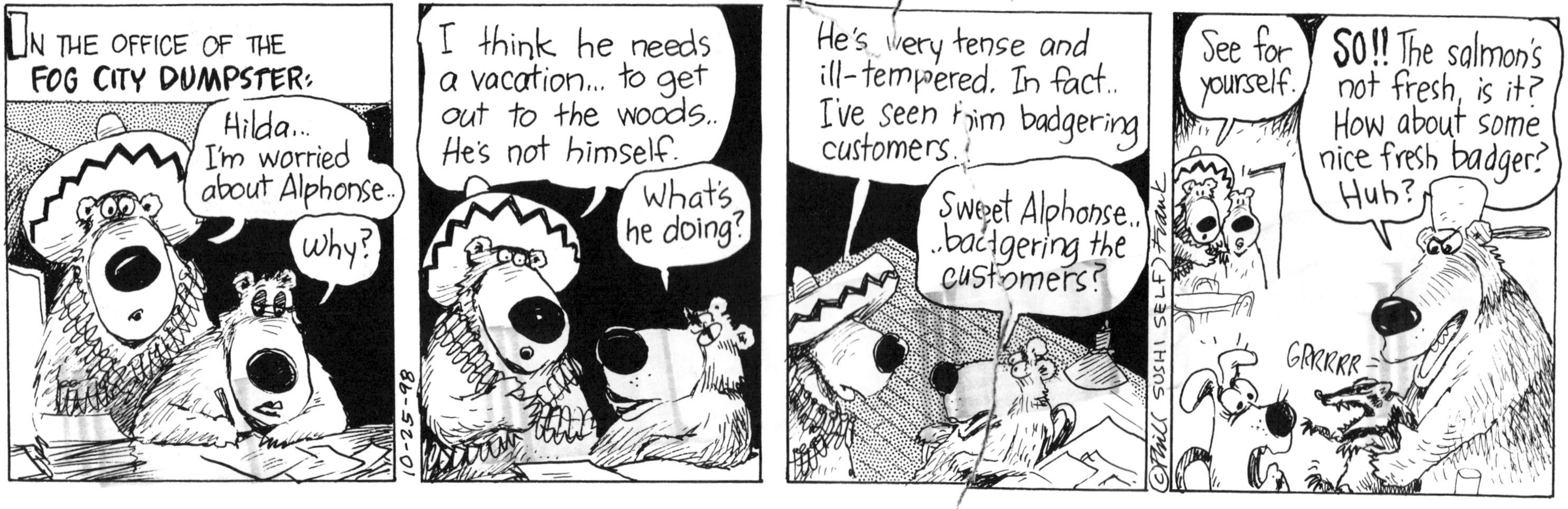
IN THE OFFICE OF THE FOG CITY DUMPSTER:
Hilda... I'm worried about Alphonse..
Why?
I think he needs a vacation... to get out to the woods.. He's not himself.
What's he doing?
He's very tense and ill-tempered. In fact.. I've seen him badgering customers.
Sweet Alphonse.. ..badgering the customers?
See for yourself.
SO!! The salmon's not fresh, is it? How about some nice fresh badger? Huh?
GRRRRR
10-25-98
©Phil (SUSHI SELF) Frank

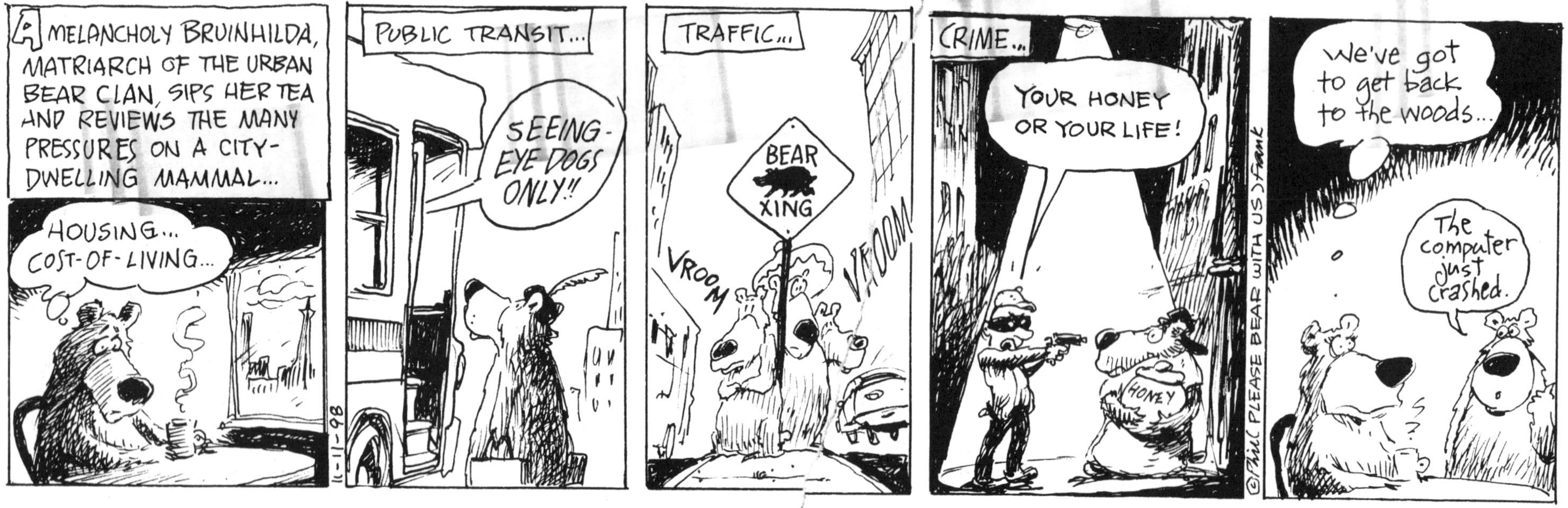
A MELANCHOLY BRUINHILDA, MATRIARCH OF THE URBAN BEAR CLAN, SIPS HER TEA AND REVIEWS THE MANY PRESSURES ON A CITY-DWELLING MAMMAL...
HOUSING... COST-OF-LIVING...
PUBLIC TRANSIT...
SEEING-EYE DOGS ONLY!!
TRAFFIC...
BEAR XING
VROOM
VROOM
CRIME...
YOUR HONEY OR YOUR LIFE!
HONEY
We've got to get back to the woods...
The computer just crashed.
11-11-98
©Phil (PLEASE BEAR WITH US) Frank

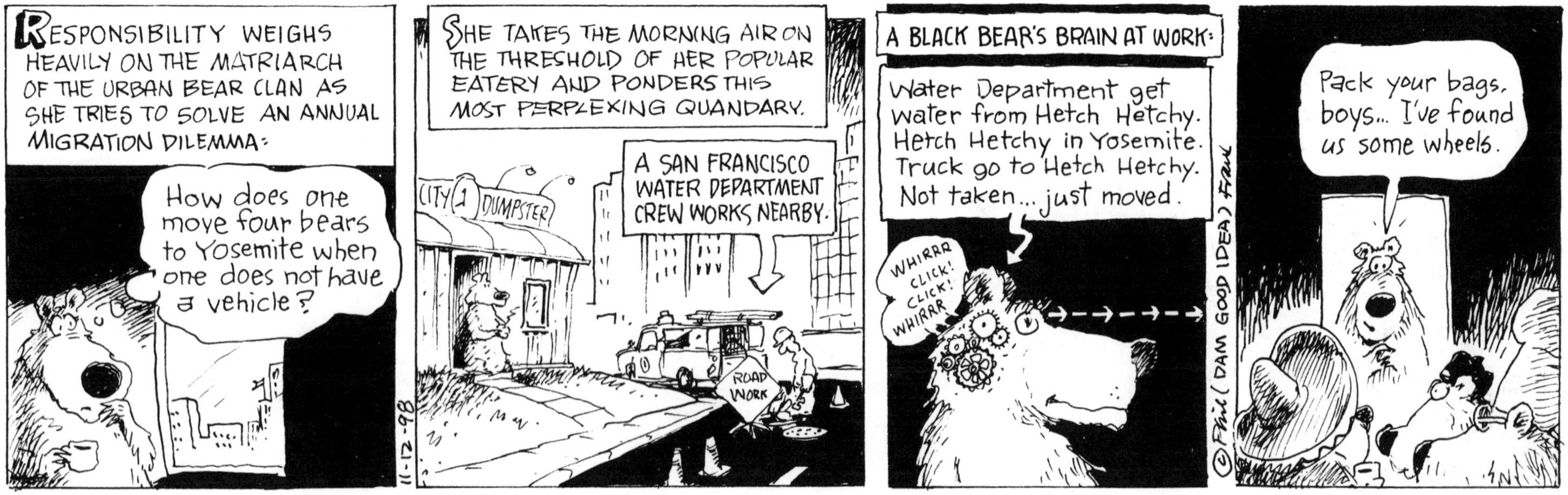
RESPONSIBILITY WEIGHS HEAVILY ON THE MATRIARCH OF THE URBAN BEAR CLAN AS SHE TRIES TO SOLVE AN ANNUAL MIGRATION DILEMMA:
How does one move four bears to Yosemite when one does not have a vehicle?
SHE TAKES THE MORNING AIR ON THE THRESHOLD OF HER POPULAR EATERY AND PONDERS THIS MOST PERPLEXING QUANDARY.
CITY 1 DUMPSTER
A SAN FRANCISCO WATER DEPARTMENT CREW WORKS NEARBY.
ROAD WORK
11-12-98
A BLACK BEAR'S BRAIN AT WORK:
Water Department get water from Hetch Hetchy. Hetch Hetchy in Yosemite. Truck go to Hetch Hetchy. Not taken... just moved.
WHIRRR CLICK! CLICK! WHIRRR
© Phil (DAM GOOD IDEA) Frank
Pack your bags, boys... I've found us some wheels.

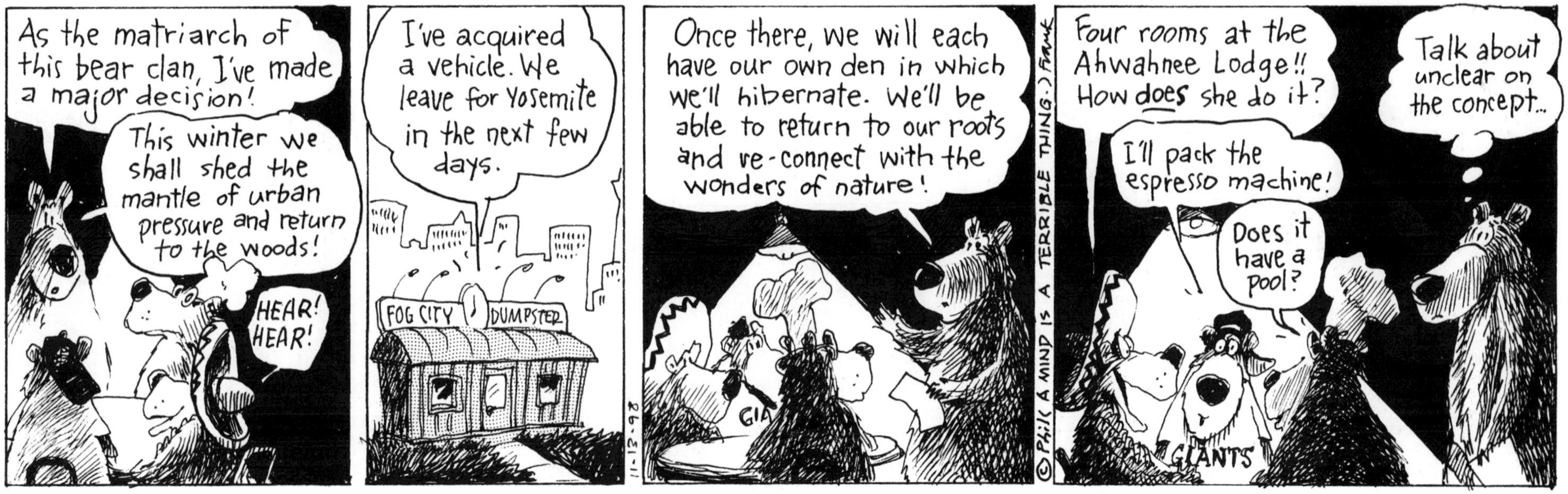
As the matriarch of this bear clan, I've made a major decision!
This winter we shall shed the mantle of urban pressure and return to the woods!
HEAR! HEAR!
I've acquired a vehicle. We leave for Yosemite in the next few days.
FOG CITY DUMPSTER
11-13-98
Once there, we will each have our own den in which we'll hibernate. We'll be able to return to our roots and re-connect with the wonders of nature!
© Phil (A MIND IS A TERRIBLE THING.) Frank
Four rooms at the Ahwahnee Lodge!! How does she do it?
I'll pack the espresso machine!
Does it have a pool?
Talk about unclear on the concept...
GIANTS

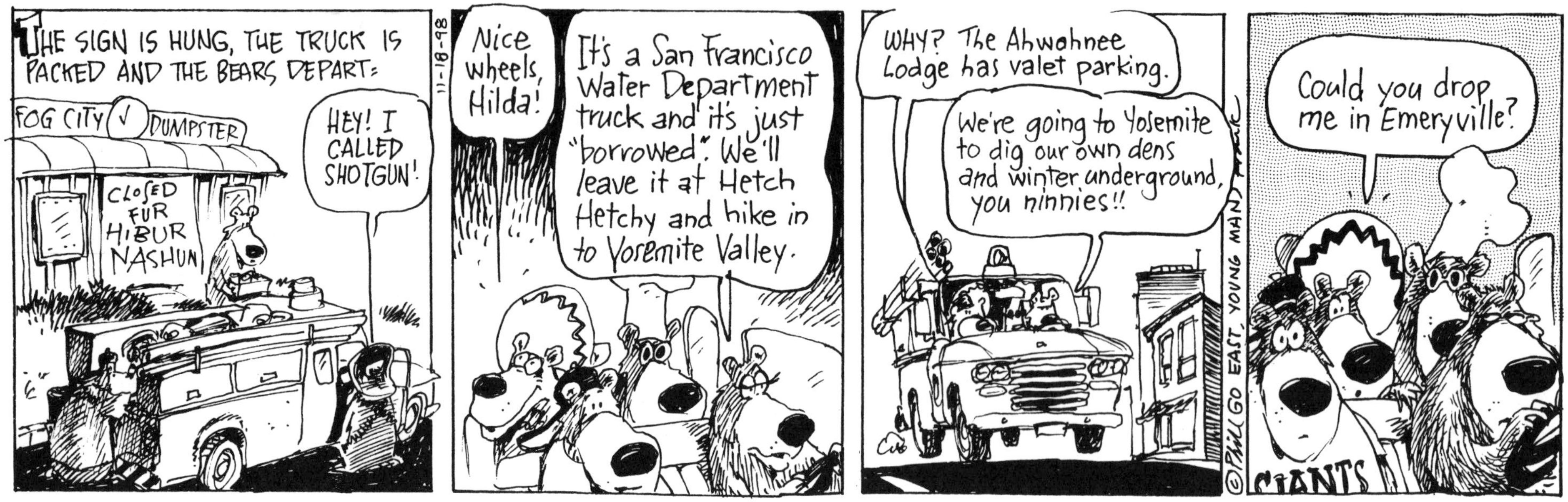
THE SIGN IS HUNG, THE TRUCK IS PACKED AND THE BEARS DEPART:
11-18-98
FOG CITY ✓ DUMPSTER
CLOSED FUR HIBUR NASHUN
HEY! I CALLED SHOTGUN!
Nice wheels, Hilda!
It's a San Francisco Water Department truck and it's just "borrowed". We'll leave it at Hetch Hetchy and hike in to Yosemite Valley.
WHY? The Ahwahnee Lodge has valet parking.
We're going to Yosemite to dig our own dens and winter underground, you ninnies!!
(GO EAST, YOUNG MAN)
Could you drop me in Emeryville?
GIANTS

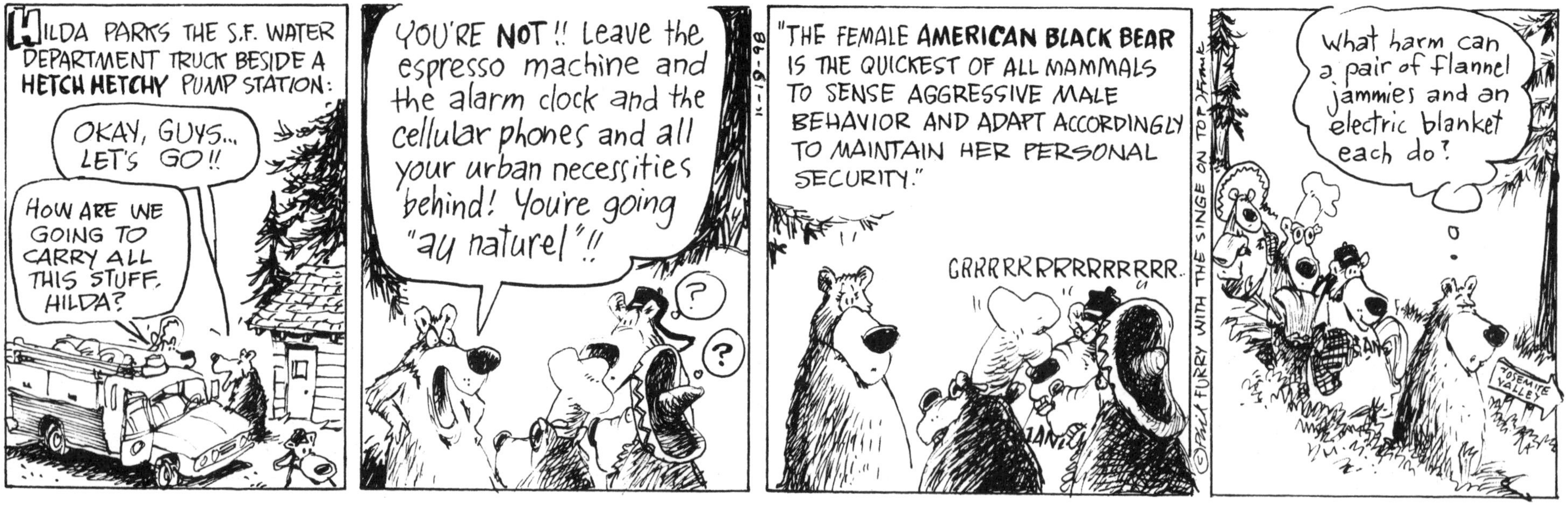
HILDA PARKS THE S.F. WATER DEPARTMENT TRUCK BESIDE A HETCH HETCHY PUMP STATION:
OKAY, GUYS... LET'S GO!!
HOW ARE WE GOING TO CARRY ALL THIS STUFF, HILDA?
YOU'RE NOT!! Leave the espresso machine and the alarm clock and the cellular phones and all your urban necessities behind! You're going "au naturel"!!
?
?
11-19-98
"THE FEMALE AMERICAN BLACK BEAR IS THE QUICKEST OF ALL MAMMALS TO SENSE AGGRESSIVE MALE BEHAVIOR AND ADAPT ACCORDINGLY TO MAINTAIN HER PERSONAL SECURITY."
GRRRRRRRRRRRRRR..
FURRY WITH THE SINGE ON TOP
What harm can a pair of flannel jammies and an electric blanket each do?
YOSEMITE VALLEY

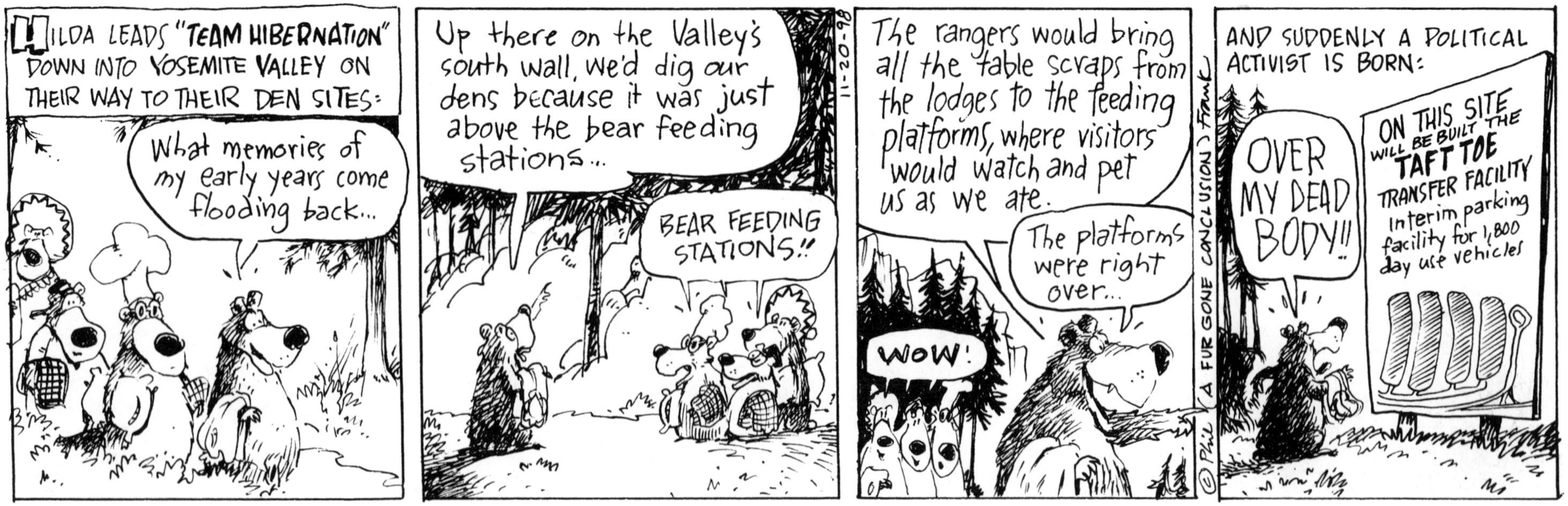
HILDA LEADS "TEAM HIBERNATION" DOWN INTO YOSEMITE VALLEY ON THEIR WAY TO THEIR DEN SITES:
What memories of my early years come flooding back...
Up there on the Valley's south wall, we'd dig our dens because it was just above the bear feeding stations...
BEAR FEEDING STATIONS!!
11-20-98
The rangers would bring all the table scraps from the lodges to the feeding platforms, where visitors would watch and pet us as we ate.
WOW!
The platforms were right over...
© Phil (A FUR GONE CONCLUSION) Frank
AND SUDDENLY A POLITICAL ACTIVIST IS BORN:
OVER MY DEAD BODY!!
ON THIS SITE WILL BE BUILT THE TAFT TOE TRANSFER FACILITY
Interim parking facility for 1,800 day use vehicles

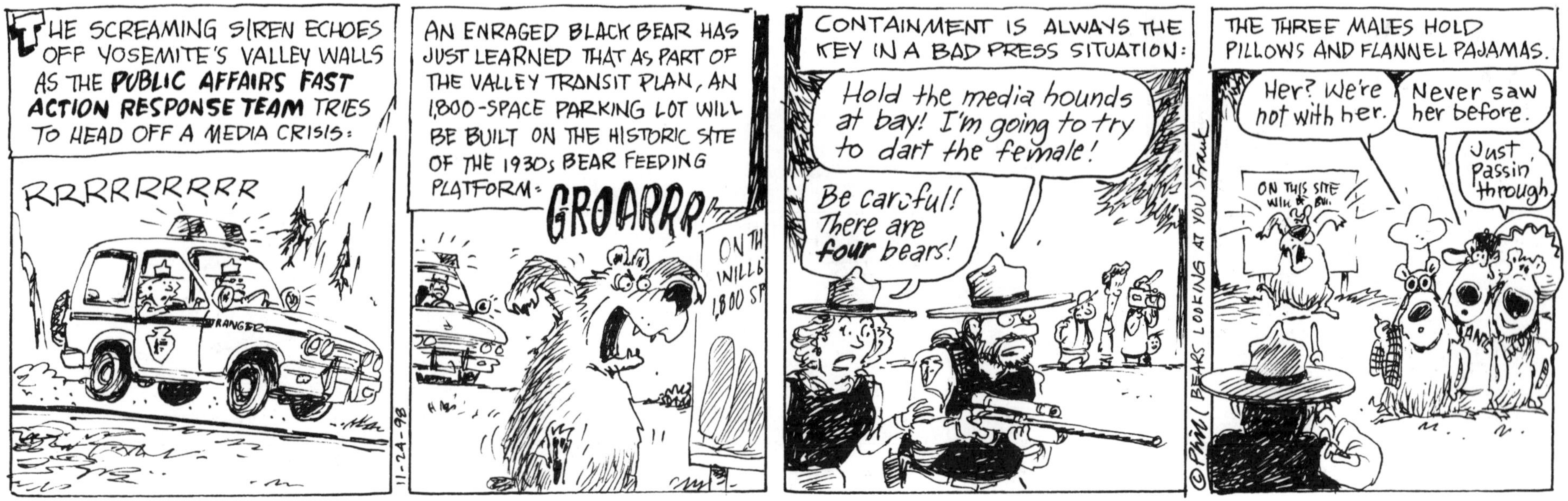
THE SCREAMING SIREN ECHOES OFF YOSEMITE'S VALLEY WALLS AS THE PUBLIC AFFAIRS FAST ACTION RESPONSE TEAM TRIES TO HEAD OFF A MEDIA CRISIS:
RRRRRRRRR
RANGER
11-24-98
AN ENRAGED BLACK BEAR HAS JUST LEARNED THAT AS PART OF THE VALLEY TRANSIT PLAN, AN 1,800-SPACE PARKING LOT WILL BE BUILT ON THE HISTORIC SITE OF THE 1930s BEAR FEEDING PLATFORM:
GROARRR
CONTAINMENT IS ALWAYS THE KEY IN A BAD PRESS SITUATION:
Hold the media hounds at bay! I'm going to try to dart the female!
Be careful! There are four bears!
© Phil (BEARS LOOKING AT YOU) Frank
THE THREE MALES HOLD PILLOWS AND FLANNEL PAJAMAS.
Her? We're not with her.
Never saw her before.
Just passin' through.

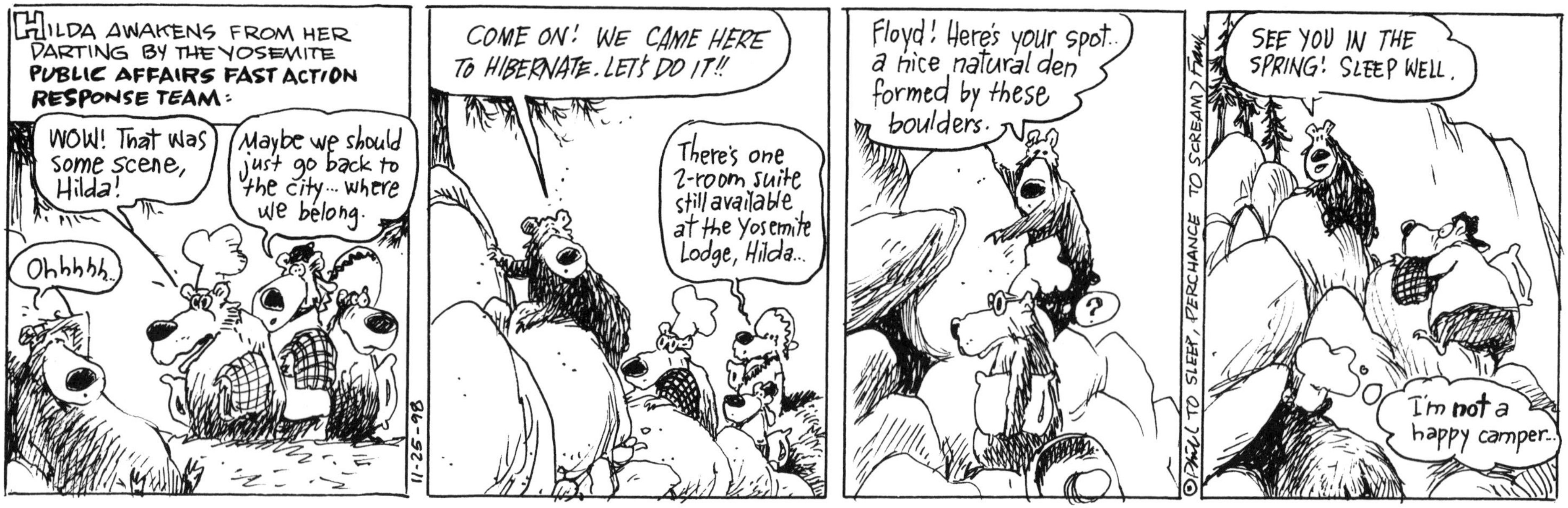
HILDA AWAKENS FROM HER DARTING BY THE YOSEMITE PUBLIC AFFAIRS FAST ACTION RESPONSE TEAM:
WOW! That was some scene, Hilda!
Maybe we should just go back to the city... where we belong.
Ohhhhh..
11-25-98
COME ON! WE CAME HERE TO HIBERNATE. LET'S DO IT!!
There's one 2-room suite still available at the Yosemite Lodge, Hilda..
Floyd! Here's your spot.. a nice natural den formed by these boulders.
?
SEE YOU IN THE SPRING! SLEEP WELL.
I'm not a happy camper..
©PAUL TO SLEEP, PERCHANCE TO SCREAM) FRANK

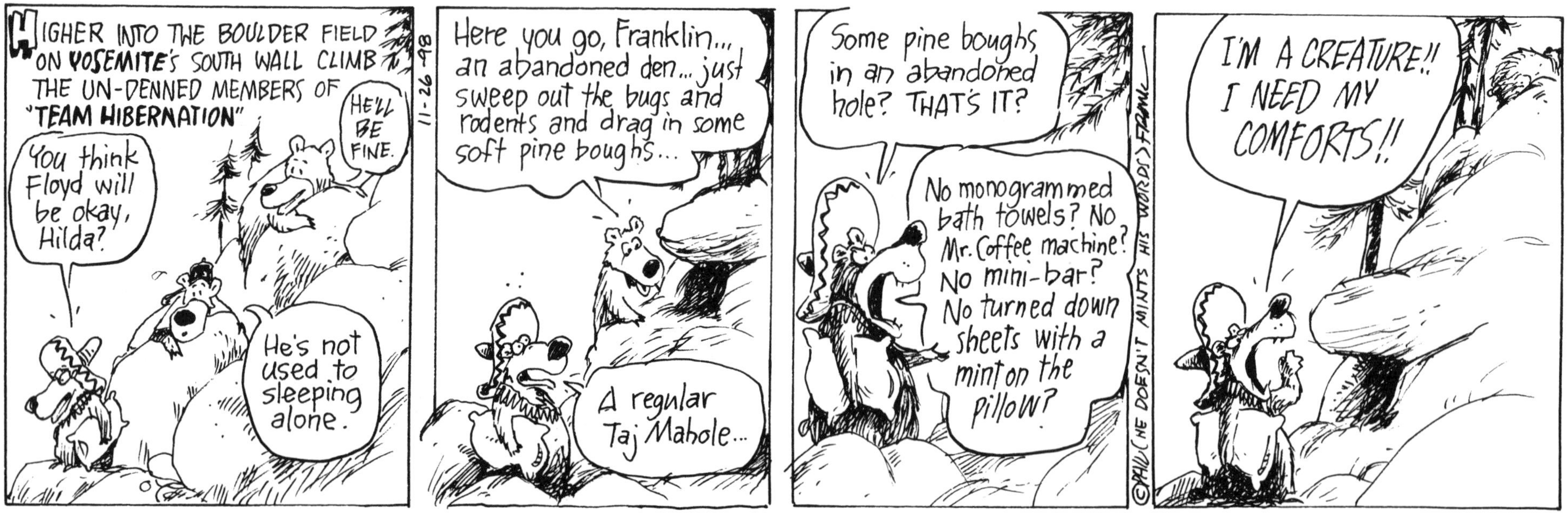
HIGHER INTO THE BOULDER FIELD ON YOSEMITE'S SOUTH WALL CLIMB THE UN-DENNED MEMBERS OF "TEAM HIBERNATION"
You think Floyd will be okay, Hilda?
HE'LL BE FINE.
He's not used to sleeping alone.
11-26-98
Here you go, Franklin... an abandoned den... just sweep out the bugs and rodents and drag in some soft pine boughs...
A regular Taj Mahole...
Some pine boughs in an abandoned hole? THAT'S IT?
No monogrammed bath towels? No Mr. Coffee machine? No mini-bar? No turned down sheets with a mint on the pillow?
©PAUL (HE DOESN'T MINTS HIS WORDS) FRANK
I'M A CREATURE!! I NEED MY COMFORTS!!

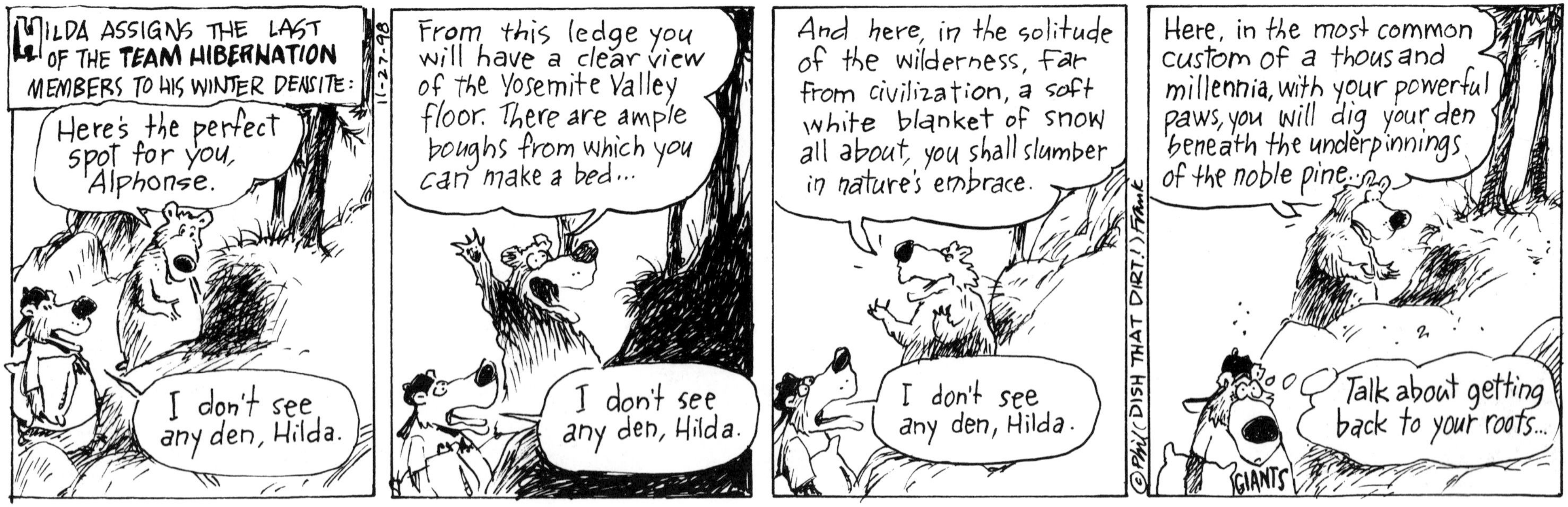
HILDA ASSIGNS THE LAST OF THE TEAM HIBERNATION MEMBERS TO HIS WINTER DENSITE:
Here's the perfect spot for you, Alphonse.
I don't see any den, Hilda.
11-27-98
From this ledge you will have a clear view of the Yosemite Valley floor. There are ample boughs from which you can make a bed...
I don't see any den, Hilda.
And here, in the solitude of the wilderness, far from civilization, a soft white blanket of snow all about, you shall slumber in nature's embrace.
I don't see any den, Hilda.
©Phil (DISH THAT DIRT!) Frank
Here, in the most common custom of a thousand millennia, with your powerful paws, you will dig your den beneath the underpinnings of the noble pine...
Talk about getting back to your roots...
GIANTS

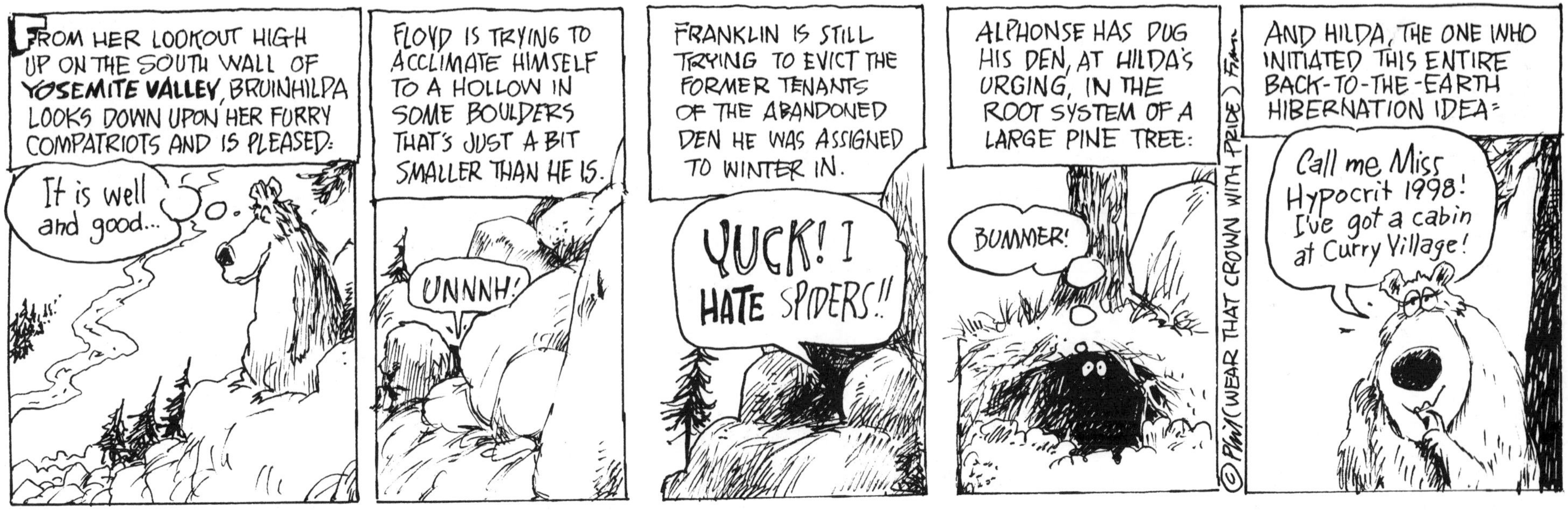
FROM HER LOOKOUT HIGH UP ON THE SOUTH WALL OF YOSEMITE VALLEY, BRUINHILDA LOOKS DOWN UPON HER FURRY COMPATRIOTS AND IS PLEASED:
It is well and good...
FLOYD IS TRYING TO ACCLIMATE HIMSELF TO A HOLLOW IN SOME BOULDERS THAT'S JUST A BIT SMALLER THAN HE IS.
UNNNH!
FRANKLIN IS STILL TRYING TO EVICT THE FORMER TENANTS OF THE ABANDONED DEN HE WAS ASSIGNED TO WINTER IN.
YUCK! I HATE SPIDERS!!
ALPHONSE HAS DUG HIS DEN, AT HILDA'S URGING, IN THE ROOT SYSTEM OF A LARGE PINE TREE:
BUMMER!
©Phil (WEAR THAT CROWN WITH PRIDE) Frank
AND HILDA, THE ONE WHO INITIATED THIS ENTIRE BACK-TO-THE-EARTH HIBERNATION IDEA:
Call me Miss Hypocrit 1998! I've got a cabin at Curry Village!

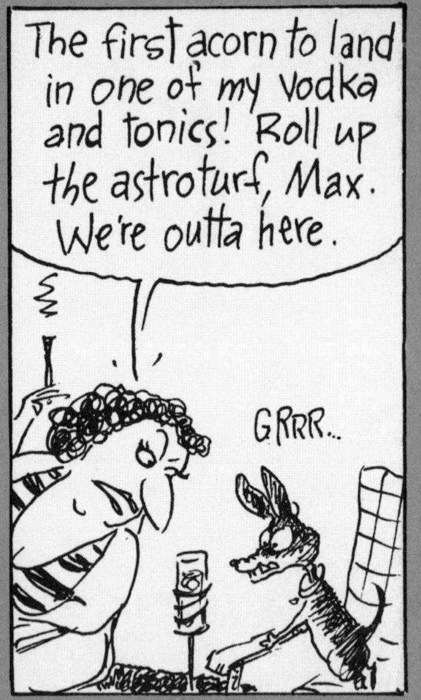
The first acorn to land in one of my vodka and tonics! Roll up the astroturf, Max. We're outta here.
GRRR..